Universities for a New World

Universities for a New World

Making a Global Network in International Higher Education, 1913–2013

Edited by

Deryck M. Schreuder

The Association of Commonwealth Universities

SAGE www.sagepublications.com
Los Angeles • London • New Delhi • Singapore • Washington DC

First published in 2013 by

SAGE Publications India Pvt Ltd
B1/I-1 Mohan Cooperative Industrial Area
Mathura Road, New Delhi 110 044, India
www.sagepub.in

SAGE Publications Inc
2455 Teller Road
Thousand Oaks, California 91320, USA

SAGE Publications Ltd
1 Oliver's Yard, 55 City Road
London EC1Y 1SP, United Kingdom

SAGE Publications Asia-Pacific Pte Ltd
33 Pekin Street
#02-01 Far East Square
Singapore 048763

Published by Vivek Mehra for SAGE Publications India Pvt Ltd, Phototypeset in 10/12 Times New Roman by RECTO Graphics, Delhi and printed at Saurabh Printers Pvt Ltd.

Library of Congress Cataloging-in-Publication Data

Universities for a new world: making a global network in international higher education, 1913–2013/edited by Deryck M. Schreuder.
pages cm
Includes bibliographical references and index.
1. Universities and colleges—Commonwealth countries—History.
2. Education and globalization—Commonwealth countries. I. Schreuder, D. M. (Deryck Marshall), editor of compilation.

LA669.5.U55 378.171'241—dc23 2013 2013034110

ISBN: 978-81-321-1339-3 (HB)

The SAGE Team: Shambhu Sahu, Punita Kaur Mann, Nand Kumar Jha, and Rajinder Kaur

Front cover photo: International students at The University of Sydney.
Photograph by Ted Healey.
Image courtesy: Sydney University World.

For our students—may higher education transform and empower your lives.

Contents

PART II: Transformations: Instruments and Symbols of Change in Higher Education

PART III: 'Impact': Regional Case Studies in Access, Equity, and Social Change

PART IV
Prospect: University Futures

PART V: Appendices of Data

List of Figures and Tables

Figures

Tables

List of Abbreviations

AAU	Association of African Universities
ACU	Association of Commonwealth Universities
AfriQAN	African Quality Assurance Network
ANU	Australian National University
ASEAN	Association of Southeast Asian Nations
AUBC	Association of Universities of the British Commonwealth
AUCC	Association of Universities and Colleges of Canada
AUQA	Australian Universities Quality Agency
AVCC	Australian Vice-Chancellors' Committee
CAAM-HP	Caribbean Accreditation Authority in Medicine and the Health Professions
CAE	College of Advanced Education (Australia)
CANQATE	Caribbean Area Network for Quality Assurance in Tertiary Education
CARICOM	Caribbean Community
CASRAI	Consortia Advancing Standards in Research Administration Information
CCEM	Conference of Commonwealth Education Ministers
CELU	Commonwealth Education Liaison Unit
CFTC	Commonwealth Fund for Technical Co-operation
CHEMS	Commonwealth Higher Education Management Service
CHESS	Commonwealth Higher Education Support Scheme
CHOGM	Commonwealth Heads of Government Meeting
CMEC	Council of Ministers of Education, Canada
CMS	Church Missionary Society (Sierra Leone)
CNAA	Council for National Academic Awards (UK)
COL	Commonwealth of Learning
CRTS	Commonwealth Reconstruction Training Scheme (Australia)
CSC	Commonwealth Scholarship Commission

CSFP	Commonwealth Scholarship and Fellowship Plan
CUSAC	Commonwealth Universities Study Abroad Consortium
CVCP	Committee of Vice-Chancellors and Principals of the Universities of the United Kingdom
DFID	Department for International Development (UK)
EPG	Eminent Persons Group
FAWE	Forum for African Women Educationalists
GATS	General Agreement on Trade in Services
GER	Gross Enrolment Ratio
HEC	Higher Education Commission (Pakistan)
HECS	Higher Education Contributions Scheme (Australia)
HEFCE	Higher Education Funding Council for England
HEQC	Higher Education Quality Committee (South Africa); Higher Education Quality Council (UK)
HERS-SA	A managed network in South Africa to improve the status of women in higher education. (It is not an acronym.)
HKCAA	Hong Kong Council for Academic Accreditation
IGNOU	Indira Gandhi National Open University
IP	Intellectual Property
IUCEA	Inter-University Council of East Africa
LAN	Lembaga Akreditasi Negara (National Accreditation Board, Malaysia)
LCME	Liaison Committee on Medical Education (USA)
MDG	Millennium Development Goal
MOOC	Massive Open Online Course
NA	National Archives (British)
NAAC	National Assessment and Accreditation Council (India)
NQF	National Qualifications Framework (New Zealand)
NUC	National Universities Commission (Nigeria)
NZUAAU	New Zealand Universities Academic Audit Unit
NZVCC	New Zealand Vice-Chancellors' Committee
OBHE	Observatory on Borderless Higher Education
OECD	Organisation for Economic Co-operation and Development
OER	Open Educational Resources
OERU	Open Education Resource University
ORCID	Open Researcher and Contributor Identification
QA	Quality Assurance

QAA	Quality Assurance Agency (Pakistan); Quality Assurance Agency for Higher Education (UK)
QAAC	Quality Assurance and Accreditation Council (Sri Lanka)
RAE	Research Assessment Exercise
SADC	Southern African Development Community
SALISES	Sir Arthur Lewis Institute of Social and Economic Studies (University of the West Indies)
SAQF	South African Qualifications Framework
SEDA	Staff and Educational Development Association (UK)
SMT	Senior Management Team
SWAAC	Senior Women Academic Administrators of Canada
TEAS	Tertiary Education Assistance Scheme (Australia)
TMRU	Tropical Metabolism Research Unit (University of the West Indies)
U21	Universitas 21
UA	Universities Australia
UCGH	University of the Cape of Good Hope (South Africa)
UGC	University Grants Commission (Bangladesh, India, Pakistan, Sri Lanka); University Grants Committee (Hong Kong, UK)
UKOU	UK Open University
UN	United Nations
UNESCO	United Nations Educational, Scientific and Cultural Organization
UNICEF	United Nations Children's Fund
USMLE	United States Medical Licensing Examination
UWI	University of the West Indies
WISE	World Innovation Summit for Education

Foreword

'Commonwealth of Learning': A Personal Perspective

The year 2013 marks the centenary of the Association of Commonwealth Universities (ACU)—the first and oldest global association of universities in higher education. There is much to celebrate in achievements, as well as an opportunity to consider the transformational changes which the diverse ACU members have experienced over recent decades, and which increasingly challenge them in this new century.

With more than 500 member institutions spread across more than 50 countries of the Commonwealth, the ACU has provided, or assisted with, a remarkable range of programmes, projects, and activities, including academic, administrative, and student exchanges; scholarships, fellowships, and bursaries; a useful flow of publications, including bulletins, newsletters, and works of academic reference; the production of well-researched reports and surveys on many subjects of critical importance to the academic community; useful benchmarking programmes, which support quality assurance, educational innovation, and relevant e-learning initiatives; guest lectures on key topics of development; conferences and seminars; university library developments as the era of the web arrives; the defence of academic freedom against the encroachment of the state; providing advice sought by governments and also, when necessary, providing advice not sought by governments; assisting with the birth of new universities and with the transformation of older university foundations; promoting and facilitating collaborative research; extending the bounds of knowledge and higher education around the world.

It is an honour to be invited to write a personal foreword for a volume dealing with the first century of an Association with such an impressive record of service and accomplishment. For some 55 years of that century, I have been a keen observer of the Association's activities and have sometimes been fortunate enough to play a role in its affairs.

Indeed, my direct involvement with the ACU began in May 1958, when I was a graduate student and a very junior part-time instructor at the University of Toronto. It came about through a conversation with Dr Sidney Smith, the distinguished and inimitable former President of the University, who had recently left that post to become Canada's Secretary of State for External Affairs. Dr Smith expressed strongly the view that in addition to all the useful ongoing activities in which the Association was engaged, there was need for a new 'mega-project', which would unite the universities of the Commonwealth in a new creative endeavour and encourage a fresh and enlarged sense of common purpose within the Commonwealth university family. He invited me to 'bend my mind to this need'.

Reflecting on major educational needs within the Commonwealth, I was struck by the lack of meaningful and feasible international learning opportunities for its students. Some weeks later I returned with the outline for a proposal for a Commonwealth scholarship plan, which would facilitate student exchange among the member institutions of the ACU. Dr Smith, with characteristic thought and enthusiasm, developed and improved the plan, presenting it in rapid succession to a Commonwealth universities congress in September 1958, then to a Commonwealth trade conference in Montreal two weeks later, and then to a Commonwealth education conference at Oxford in July 1959. Thus, the Commonwealth Scholarship and Fellowship Plan was born. Many years later, after the Plan was well up and running, I served for a spell as its Canadian Chair.

This early experience piqued my interest in the Association and, indeed, in the Commonwealth. I discovered an enthusiasm and a commitment for the Commonwealth that I have never lost—all the more so as I came to see from the inside how it could be a force for good in an unequal and conflicted world. During ensuing years, I served on the Council of the Association for a quarter of a century, as Council member and elected Chair, and then as Honorary Treasurer in difficult fiscal times and, subsequently, as Chair of the organisation's 75th Anniversary Appeal and associated events. Later, at the request of the Secretary General of the Commonwealth, I served as Chair of the

Commission on Commonwealth Studies, and then as the founding Chair of the Association for Commonwealth Studies.

In these activities I met with a great many scholars, teachers, and administrators involved in the network of Commonwealth universities, and travelled to almost every country of the Commonwealth, serving often as a guest lecturer or visiting professor en route. It was a hugely instructive and liberating experience, for which I am profoundly grateful. Over those years, I witnessed the evolution of the Commonwealth as it grew and adapted to reflect the realities, and to meet the needs, of its growing number of diverse member states and increasingly multicultural societies.

Looking back on what is now quite a long life, I cherish in particular the many friendships and associations with colleagues throughout the ACU from across the world. As I came to know more about the activities of the Association, and their significance, I came to care deeply about the organisation—though that is perhaps too strong a term to describe such an amiable and mutually supportive network. As a young founding Canadian university president, I greatly valued my institution's membership in the ACU, with access to its varied resources, both formal and informal. I know that countless others have found similarly what a quiet, steadfast, and useful contribution the Association, like the Commonwealth itself, can make in an often bleak world. May they both long continue with their good work!

The range, diversity, quality, and utility of the programmes of the ACU have been extraordinary. By any measure, it is a remarkable and valuable Association that spans most of the world's cultures and all of the world's continents to good effect, drawing together peoples from different backgrounds in many shared education-related activities, which are facilitated by a degree of shared heritage and many shared aspirations.

Much of what the ACU has initiated and accomplished over the past century is well described and assessed in this volume. But there is still more to be done, as universities, and all those engaged in higher education, adapt to the transformative changes of the present and the future. Some of these challenges, and the opportunities they bring, are also very well set forth in this volume. Among them, may I simply underline one that needs and merits more attention than it has so far received: that is, the need for universities in the ACU to pay more attention in their educational programmes to teaching and research about the Commonwealth itself. There has been a remarkable neglect of studies about the Commonwealth across the Commonwealth. There is scope and need for a great deal of cooperative research and teaching about the Commonwealth as well as about other matters of mutual interest among the universities of the Commonwealth. There is much to be gained from comparative and connectional studies that explore the dynamic and cultural dimensions of this unique international organisation, at a time when global experience is pointing to the need to think beyond the bounds of the nation state alone.

Emeritus Professor Deryck Schreuder and the other contributors have done a superb job in the planning and writing of this book. While it provides a lively and useful record of the ACU's first century and, indeed, of many aspects of higher education during that century, it also looks in a most thoughtful and useful way to many of the hurdles and opportunities that lie ahead. It constitutes a significant contribution to the thinking and literature about higher education, by raising and examining vital questions—not only for education but also for social scientists in many fields. This book is, in itself, a very substantial affirmation of the value of the interplay between the 'Commonwealth of learning' and the Commonwealth of Nations.

To close, may I express the appreciation and admiration, which I know is shared by countless people around the Commonwealth, for the extraordinary record of service given over so many years by the dedicated staff of the Association to the universities of the Commonwealth and, indeed, to higher education throughout the world. May I salute, too, the leaders and staff of the hundreds of universities across the global Commonwealth. It is they who ultimately make the ACU the dynamic success that it is.

Thomas H.B. Symons, C.C., O.Ont., FRSC
Founding President and Vanier Professor Emeritus,
Trent University, Canada
Chair, the Ontario Heritage Trust

Foreword

A Transformative Journey: The ACU Network at 100

Within the epochal international transformation of higher education, the survival and success of the Association of Commonwealth Universities (ACU) has been a singularly significant accomplishment. Globally we have perhaps witnessed changes more sweeping than all of previous human history. We have explored the outer reaches of space, plumbed the depths of the deepest oceans, deciphered the intimate chemistry of cellular life, extended life expectancy by nearly 40 years in some industrialised countries, and may well have at our disposal the technology to create life itself. Equally substantial have been the massive geopolitical shifts of the last century, encompassing two world wars that resulted in considerable changes in international power relationships between once Great Powers, and, thanks to the decolonisation movement, the creation of many new nations encompassing more than half of the world's population—a large proportion of whom live in nations comprising today's Commonwealth of Nations.

In the last few decades, the stunning expansion of technology, communication, and travel, accompanied by the collapse of the Soviet Union and the rise of deregulated market forces, has fashioned a maelstrom in which knowledge, innovation, and competition have become critical ingredients of national survival. Given the ascendancy of knowledge and the apparent 'levelling' of opportunity for individual nations to gain ascendancy in the global marketplace, nations are gambling that competitive advantage will come from the number of well-educated people in their societies. With this in mind, they have made huge investments in tertiary education, resulting in the unprecedented expansion in number and types of tertiary institutions as well as in student enrolment. The Association, which emerged as the network of connections, has today survived all this.

The ACU was spawned at a time when Britain and its people in far-flung regions of the world ruled a vast Empire. When the Universities' Bureau of the British Empire was established in 1913, its members comprised universities of Britain and those of the dominions and colonies, many constructed along the lines of the 'mother country', in particular like the University of London. These universities, dominated and populated by British people and their descendants in the distant Empire, sought to construct an organisation for the sharing of knowledge and information about each other, as well as to create a vehicle to enable exchanges of students and staff. They also sought to strengthen the intellectual ties and values of people of British origin throughout the world. Not surprisingly, reflecting the tenor of the times, there were overtones of Anglo-Saxon racial supremacy in some of the views expressed at the initial Congress of the Universities of the British Empire in 1912 that presaged the Bureau; and doubtless, these were not uncommon beliefs among members in the first two to three decades of the organisation.

In the period between the two world wars, there was a strengthening of the Bureau that enabled exchanges of information, reports, booklets, and surveys, and congresses organised at five-yearly intervals. What also drove history, in terms of the evolution of the ACU, is that the anti-colonial movement was gaining momentum in colonies of Britain. While Mahatma Gandhi's peaceful protests in India were most prominent, there was at the same time, in Africa and the Caribbean, an upsurge of trade unions and other groups of intellectuals and activists forming political parties and other groupings that sought independence from Britain. These people recognised, too, that education would be an important ingredient in ensuring the viability of any new nation, and, in this context, there was a call for formation of first-rate schools, including indigenous universities.

In 1943, in the midst of the Second World War, Britain came to recognise the inevitable with the establishment of a commission under Lord Asquith to outline plans to 'promote higher education, learning and research and the development of universities in the colonies'. There were sub-committees of the Commission that went to various parts of Africa and the Caribbean (the Committee in the Caribbean was led by Sir James Irvine), to engage the local population in discussions about formation of a university. It was out of these efforts that several university colleges were established in the colonies, including the University College of the West Indies, the University College of Ibadan, the University College of East Africa (that would become Makerere University), and so on. In framing the development of these institutions, it was decided that (like several other universities in the UK and elsewhere), they would start as Colleges of the University of London and in time become fully fledged universities. In the early years, these universities were largely staffed and managed by academics from the UK, and over the next one to two decades, local academics assumed both management and academic roles.

At the time of emergence of these 'new universities' (1948), the Universities' Bureau of the British Empire significantly changed its name to the Association of Universities of the British Commonwealth (AUBC). This move anticipated the alteration of power dynamics within the now dismantling British Empire and the emergence of independent nations with their own universities. The AUBC doubtless proved a vital resource for provision of information, enumeration of quality standards, and identification of staff for the emerging universities. The ethos of the organisation began changing from a 'British-dominated' entity to one that would become more inclusive, with broader perspectives and animated by a broad spirit of mutuality.

With the achievement of independence of the British colonies from the 1950s, the university colleges transitioned to become independent universities. In 1963 the AUBC underwent another name change consonant with the times, becoming simply the ACU. The Commonwealth of Nations had been established a few years earlier with its own Secretariat, but shrewdly the ACU Secretariat remained separate, recognising the need for 'some divide' between the academic and political.

During the decades of the 1960s through 1970s, the organisation grew in numbers and diversity, shifting from a 'Northern' to more 'Southern' configuration, as numbers of member universities from India and Africa increased. The value of the organisation—provided, for example, through programmes such as the Commonwealth Scholarship and Fellowship Plan, the annual *Yearbook*, provision of a job advertisement service, formation of professional networks, publication of policy papers and the conduct of congresses at regular intervals—served to win the support of a sizeable number of universities.

Perhaps the major challenges to the organisation have occurred in the last 20 years, a circumstance generated by a number of geopolitical, economic, and technological changes. The lessening of importance of the 'Commonwealth' is one—the result of realignment of its more industrialised members manifested by increasing linkages of the UK with Europe, of Canada with the USA and Central America, and of Australia with South East Asia, all contributing to a drift away from the organisation. A more pluralistic configuration of geopolitical power has come to international affairs. These shifts are reflected in academic institutions in these countries, where there is a diminishing presence of Commonwealth students and a broadening of ties to universities beyond the Commonwealth.

A further challenge to traditional Commonwealth universities has resulted from the stunning advance of technology, particularly information and communications technology, which itself has resulted in new forms of delivery of educational programmes; and a virtual shrinking of the Globe, with contacts between individuals now possible within nanoseconds. This has made it possible for new forms of distance education that have enabled instant interaction between student and teacher outside traditional classroom settings—and at a lower cost. The ascendancy of a deregulated, global free market in the 1980s and 1990s, where education had come to be treated as a commodity, gave rise to the creation of many private institutions (or public institutions providing education for a fee) operating widely across national borders. For example, in the English-speaking Caribbean region, it is estimated that there are as many as 100 universities ('legitimate and illegitimate') owned by extra-regional entities. The same is probably true in other parts of the world. These circumstances, for local universities, have all led to considerable competition, particularly in programmes that are likely to attract large numbers of (paying) students.

The final major challenge arises from the massive expansion of tertiary education—driven first by governments recognising the link between knowledge capital and competitive advantage in the global marketplace, and then students recognising the enhanced rewards that can be obtained with a university education. These forces have resulted in marked increases in numbers of universities, and in individual students and their families seeking access to these universities. Traditional, public-supported universities (which make up the majority of ACU membership) must meet the goal of increasing access, while preserving quality of both academic programmes and student services, without dramatic increases in public funding support. It is probably not possible for traditional universities to increase access and quality at a reduced cost. Changing any one of these factors will affect the other two variables. For example, increasing access will negatively affect quality, unless there is an increase in expenditures to support growth. The economic crisis of the last four years, even as university populations have expanded, will have serious, adverse consequences for the quality of teaching, services, and research. Circumstances favour online education, where access can be increased, with reasonable quality at relatively lower cost than that of a traditional university. But this will not universally resolve acute public higher education issues in some of the poorest states (many of which are African), which are contending with demands for increased access, yet having to cope with inadequate funding and enhanced competition from private providers. Another challenge for many of these particular institutions has been a loss of autonomy, as governments demand more direct involvement in the management and operations of public universities.

In truth, the role of government in influencing the policies and directions of universities is not limited to Commonwealth countries: both industrialised and developing nations' governments are demanding 'greater accountability' from their national universities. This has recently come to include changes in university research missions, as governments demand less abstract, individually driven investigation, with more attention being given to applied research and innovation with a view to production of commercially competitive products. Indeed, scholars (such as Michael Gibbons in this book) argue that there is increasingly a transition in process to 'postmodern universities', where research centres and institutes loosely attached to the university become more prominent. These entities will increasingly pursue research linked to specific areas of interest driven by government, private sector, and other groups. Research will be less an individual endeavour and driven more by multidisciplinary, multi-institutional teams.

No discussion concerning universities in the Commonwealth or elsewhere can ignore the crucial question of how these institutions will ensure their sustained funding. Recently in the UK, angry public demonstrations greeted a government decision substantially to increase tuition fees of university students. In developing states, the struggle to finance universities adequately, where student numbers and infrastructure costs have expanded substantially, has become a major public issue. Some governments are either unwilling to introduce fees or are prepared to settle only for token payments from students, so seriously undermining the viability of these institutions. Strategies to increase funding from sources other than government remain an essential item to be discussed by universities globally, and not least among the more than 500 members of the ACU.

The essential value of this centenary publication is that it provides an in-depth, insightful review not only of the history of the ACU, but also of the current issues that will fashion and frame the future of its diverse member institutions. It is uncertain just how the Commonwealth of Nations itself will remain relevant and viable in a world where there are massive geopolitical, technological, and economic shifts, though it is attempting to adapt its mission to meet a new world order. Despite the changing circumstances and relations of Commonwealth nations, their universities will still have much in common. The sustenance of the ACU, as an associative network of higher education providers for another century, will rely on its capacity to capitalise on this shared foundation—towards providing innovative ideas and services relevant to living in a constantly shifting global landscape.

E. Nigel Harris
Vice-Chancellor, University of the West Indies
Chair, ACU Council

Preface

Within the growing international literature on universities and higher education generally, this is a special kind of book. We have taken the opportunity of a notable educational centenary—the making and transformation of the Association of Commonwealth Universities (1913–2013) as the oldest higher education network in modern history—to reflect more generally on aspects of what has been happening to universities globally today.

The book indeed works from the evocative UNESCO proposition that we are, in fact, witnessing a veritable 'revolution' in the provision, design, and impact of higher education throughout the modern world. The social sample considered is focused on the 54 English-speaking jurisdictions of the worldwide Commonwealth of Nations—but with some connectional comparisons and connections to international developments in higher education (notably in Europe, the United States, America, and China).

Globalisation has meant that it is no longer possible to treat national or even regional developments in discrete isolation. The nearly 600 institutional members of the 'ACU' represent the entire spectrum of higher educational provision globally, and they offer a rare longitudinal study in the evolving role of universities today, and especially among the developing nations of the 'South'. Much of the fate of their societies will be determined by the missions and work of their higher education institutions. Universities will be central to the building of 'knowledge nations'; they will also be critical for the less developed countries in which skills and professionals are still in short supply.

A special concern of the volume has been a reflection on issues of human empowerment through higher education—involving both generic disciplines and professional and research programmes, as well as equity considerations (access, gender, inclusivity, and lifelong learning).

In short, this free-standing volume of critical and interrelated essays considers that protean global 'revolution' in higher education provision—the gains as well as the losses. Transformation may have been inevitable, but progress towards greater participation rates has not always been followed with quality service to students or society at large. Measuring those changes to universities since 1913 is inherently difficult, as they are also still proceeding apace.

The book accordingly also offers informed perspectives on the complex future(s) of universities in the twenty-first century—in which, paradoxically, further change is likely to be the only constant.

***

As Editor, I should immediately declare a special interest in our topic. Not only did I work with the ACU for some years, when I was an Australian vice-chancellor—serving on its Council and also on the Advisory Board to its Observatory on Borderless Higher Education—but my own life was also transformed and empowered by the very opportunities that followed from being a student at one of the 'New World Universities' of our book.

Indeed, well before that, as a child attending a very modest government school in the small and non-descript frontier town of Ndola, situated in deep central Africa (and which served as the railhead to the Copperbelt mines in the Crown Colony of Northern Rhodesia [now Zambia]), I studied a general curriculum set in England by the overseas extension studies board that was first established by London University.

My final examinations papers arrived from 'overseas' and were dramatically cut open in our school hall, before being placed before each of us. After all our scribbling, they were posted back for marking by British examiners. The results were returned in yet more sealed envelopes. I had apparently gained an 'O Level' at appropriate levels in the required subjects, and I was duly admitted to an African university, which itself owed its origins to the expansion of the 'London model' (so well described in Chapter 2 of this book). Later again, the educational door opened onto postgraduate study at major Commonwealth universities overseas, when I was lucky enough to be offered both a Commonwealth Scholarship to Canada and a Rhodes Scholarship to Oxford. So began a fortunate life in higher education, which was to span eight universities in four continents.

'Equity' and 'access' are no abstract notions to me; they mean something personal and palpable. Educational opportunity shaped my life, in providing intellectual skills and professional abilities beyond anything I had ever dreamed of as a boy growing up in the African bush. In truth, it transformed the horizons of my life—what I understood about the world and how I might live in it. That notion and possibility have fuelled my passion to see others from even less privileged backgrounds find an opportunity to make the most of their own lives and become active citizens who contribute to the well-being of their nations.

***

It would not have been possible to attempt such analytic challenges in a single volume but for the remarkable team of collegial contributors who came together to make this book. I am enormously grateful to each and every one of them for taking up the invitation (and the challenge) to address issues and themes around the broad plan of this book. Some 25 of the busiest educationalists and scholars in the world immediately agreed to devote time and offer commitment to the project, including travelling from all points of the globe to London for a symposium of all authors in late 2011. The mixture of praxis and theory was empowering. A sense of common purpose emerged, towards a volume of essays which works so well as a coherent whole. Our contributors have written beyond my best anticipations.

The initial idea for the book was greeted positively by the then Secretary General of the ACU, Professor John Tarrant, who urged us to write about the totality of higher educational changes, rather than focusing on an institutional history of the ACU alone as an organisation. His successor, Professor John Wood, offered equally strong support, together with an international outlook for our scholarly endeavours.

The resultant book accordingly differs very significantly from the fine 1963 and 1988 institutional 'histories' of the ACU at '50' (by Professor Sir Eric Ashby) and at '75' (by Sir Hugh Springer and Dr Alastair Niven); but we gladly acknowledge their pioneering scholarship.

The doyen of Canadian—and Commonwealth—educationalists, Professor T.H.B. Symons, has provided us with a personal welcome to the volume, which is both characteristically gracious and personally illuminating; while the Chair of ACU Council, Professor E. Nigel Harris (University of the West Indies), has written a Foreword that immediately anchors the book in the tough social dynamics of challenges faced by universities in the post-colonial world of today. I thank both most warmly. At various points in the project, Professor Sir Graeme Davies (University of London), Ms Svava Bjarnason (World Bank), Professors Julia Horne, and Geoffrey Sherington (Sydney), together with Dr Tamson Pietsch (Brunel and Sydney), gave this Editor more assistance than they could have realised. Dr Pawan Agarwal (Planning Commission, India) also made a special contribution to the volume. As Librarian and archivist of the ACU, Mr Nicholas Mulhern contributed so much more than key documentation. For the excellent cover image, we thank Mr Ted Healey (photographer) and Mr Richard North (Sydney), as well as Ms Natasha Lockhun (ACU) and the SAGE design team.

If the final text reads as well as it does, and is free of egregious errors, it is not least due to our outstandingly professional copy editor, Ms Yvonne Percival. I have also enjoyed the support of the Faculty of Education and Social Work at the University of Sydney throughout this project, where Ms Kimberly Hammond has been most generous in her assistance.

Attention is here drawn to the Centenary Website of the Association of Commonwealth Universities, which contains a range of valuable data—institutional and financial—developed by the ACU's archivist, which could not be included in the already large appendices to this volume.

Finally, it is my pleasure to record my debt to our publishers, SAGE, New Delhi.

The then Vice President (Commissioning) Dr Sugata Ghosh immediately welcomed the project to their distinguished 'list' on higher education publications; the commissioning editor, Mr Shambhu Sahu, has been a friend of the project; the production editor, Ms Punita Kaur Mann and team were meticulous editors at SAGE; while the Managing Director and CEO, Mr Vivek Mehra, took a personal interest in the project. The ultimate volume is a tribute to their combined professionalism and commitment.

We dedicate this book to the students of our universities—school-leavers or mature learners, undergraduates or postgraduates, general degree candidates or professional credential aspirants. They are the future of our complex twenty-first-century world and of human well-being in our communities.

May Day, 2013

Deryck Schreuder
General Editor, *Universities for a New World*
Faculty of Education and Social Work
The University of Sydney

Introduction: Why Universities? Anatomy of Global Change for Old and New Universities

Deryck M. Schreuder

> An academic revolution has taken place in higher education in the past half century marked by transformations unprecedented in scope and diversity. Comprehending this ongoing and dynamic process while being in the midst of it is not an easy task.
>
> (Altbach, Reisberg, and Rumbley, 2009)

Universities matter. That has endured over time. But, their special significance for the twenty-first century reflects a role and transformation amounting to what UNESCO has described as a veritable 'revolution' in higher educational provision within modern global history (Altbach, Reisberg, and Rumbley, 2009: i). How do we get the measure of these developments, given that they are still in motion, and when the only constant in higher education now appears to be change itself?

A little history helps. Traditionally, these most ancient survivors of the medieval world were associated with knowledge preservation, religious values, and social ethics. Later they were linked to elites, professions, and liberal humanism: the 'Idea of a University' was famously declared (by John Henry Newman's public lectures of spring 1852 in Dublin) to be about the self-realisation that came from engagement over fundamental knowledge between tutor and student (Newman, 1852). But in fact, from the Industrial Revolution forward and the making of the modern state, universities became increasingly integral to science, technology, and the production of professional experts (Anderson, 2006). During the First and Second World Wars, they were harnessed to advance national defence and geopolitical interests, something which endured into both the Cold War era and then into the Space Race (Bok, 1990).

Most recently, however, universities have been drawn into the making and advancement of 'knowledge nations', with both a strongly utilitarian and an economic rationale. Bolton and Lucas have sharply identified a new ideological discourse involving 'the primacy of direct economic benefit' in public policy regarding universities (Bolton and Lucas, 2008: 6). An Australian chief scientist could articulate that paradigm by pointing to 'the potential of universities to play a central role as dynamos of growth in the innovation process and be huge generators of wealth creation' (Batterham, 2000, quoted in Bolton and Lucas, 2008: 6). State education ministers and vice-chancellors have increasingly advanced a focus on the so-called STEM disciplines (science, technology, engineering, mathematics)—somewhat at the cost of the social sciences and the humanities. Research strategies have often shifted from undifferentiated support for broadly basic research, to 'priority areas' set by national councils, and all involving 'end-users'. Famously, a key British state paper, entitled *A Vision for Research*, conceptualised the new role for universities as acting 'more like consultancy organisations' (Thomas, 2010: 13), rather than as stand-alone entities of curiosity-driven research.

More prosaically, in terms of state social planning, other educationalists and policymakers have highlighted the role of higher education institutions as the key developers of human capital, which in turn is seen to underpin labour market planning for the modern industrial state. Universities are thought to be too important for national prosperity to be left to academics alone. Globalisation has meant freer exchange of goods and peoples; but that has only exacerbated the drive to make and keep knowledge workers in the high-skill end of production. Higher education is there not least to ensure that national workforce contains the right mix of skilled human capital—workers who can both ensure value adding in traditional production sectors, as well as driving the creative industries themselves. For some political leaders, universities have unrealistically come to represent a kind of 'magic porridge machine'—the source of almost endless innovation, employment, and revenue (Wolfe, 2002).

Others again have seen higher education more in terms of 'social capital' and the making of the good society. In their vision, universities exist as a 'light on the hill' for confronting deep divisions of social inequality, illiteracy, and endemic discrimination—towards creating more equal and humane civic cultures (Bjarnason and Coldstream, 2003). Universities are one vital aspect of this concern for a better world as vital instruments of social equity and individual empowerment, there to challenge disadvantage, inequality, and globalised marginalisation—a theme common to many social aspirations in developing nations around a conflicted world (Davis, 2010).

In short, these 'transformations' have all been a far cry from the 'Bologna moment' of the thirteenth century, when Europe spawned the first of several '*universitas*', or from the earliest Arab institutions of learning, and the scholarly traditions of ancient China. As the 2009 UNESCO report concluded: 'Arguably, the developments of the recent past are at least as dramatic as those in the 19th century when the first research university emerged in Germany and then elsewhere, and fundamentally redesigned the nature of the university worldwide.' Indeed, the changes over the last few decades are probably 'more extensive due to their global nature and the number of institutions and people they affect' (Altbach, Reisberg, and Rumbley, 2009).

A strong debate has surrounded the transformation and its consequences (ANU, 2004). The President of the British Royal Academy (Professor Sir Keith Thomas) has been led to ask critically of the outcome, 'What are universities for?' He has offered his own humanistic answer to this question: 'From medieval seminary to consultancy campus, universities have served the needs of society—but those needs go beyond economic success or technological advancement' (Thomas, 2010: 13). The great debate continues into the new century ahead (Maskell and Robinson, 2001).

This book involves that contestation, taking as its datum and intellectual reference point for analytic departure the Centenary of the ACU in 2013. The volume broadly canvasses the manifold changes and the challenges within the Commonwealth university story through specific sections that focus on 'history', 'dynamics', and 'prospect'. These all illuminate the extraordinary evolution of modern international higher education. While we do not attempt a global history of those protean movements and institutions, our social sample draws from the international network of over 500 universities which form the ACU itself, and which, in turn, reflect the post-secondary story of 54 nations across the globe, covering over 2 billion peoples residing in jurisdictions which straddle 'North/South' (94 per cent of whose citizens are, in fact, Africans or Asians). It is a multifaceted story, which this book attempts to explore through a variety of analytic, narrative, regional, and policy perspectives.

'Losses and Gains'

First, let's address the more general drivers of transformational change in higher education over the recent past.

Newman himself proposed an informal 'law' of social change—that it invariably involves a dialectic of both 'losses and gains' (Ker, 2009). In this case, the positives surely outweigh the negatives as access to higher education spreads ever more widely for the peoples across the globe; as research advances fundamental knowledge; and as universities learn to serve their societies with a deeper sense of 'engagement'. But there is also a negative cost-ledger.

Looking initially to the 'gains'—and working from a glass-half-full idiom—it is not difficult to establish that credit side of the current higher education ledger.

- Participation rates are at historic levels. 'Massification' has meant a move away from elite systems to infinitely greater social inclusion through participation targets and equity outcomes. In 2013 there are now some 160 million university students enrolled globally in all forms of 'higher education'. Graduate outcome numbers also grow every year—being strongest in the Organisation for Economic Co-operation and Development (OECD) economies, but also sharply rising across Latin America and the Caribbean, with only Africa still lagging in access and graduates, though some regions (notably South and West Africa) are defying that trend. The United States is by far the leader in the flow-on from high school to college or university participation—perhaps as much as 60 per cent—while a major review of its sector (Spellings Commission Report, 2006) has stressed the urgent need not only to avoid complacency, but also to redouble policy strategies to tap talent among lower socio-economic status classes and marginalised ethnic groups. Other developed economies (notably in Western Europe and Australasia) are also now 'aiming high' in trying to match those participation goals towards becoming 'knowledge nations' based in skilled human capital. As the *Economist* magazine editorialised, the greatest asset for the modern nation is talent (*Economist*, 2012).
- Internationalisation most directly now means more individuals across the globe engaging in forms of trans-border education as

'international students'. That figure has already reached some 3 million enrolments, and is set to rise significantly in the decades ahead (potentially doubling by 2020). The benefits of this engagement with tertiary study for their societies—and for globalisation—are palpable. International students invariably mean both fees for the institutional hosts and the transfer of skills back to the home society.

- Taking advantage of the ICT explosion, new pedagogies and new modes of delivery are transforming the student experience, as well as underpinning e-learning plus the shift to 'lifelong learning' among mature-age working citizens. New vistas of knowledge and professional skills are opening up for individuals who previously could never have contemplated a university experience or graduate training. Symbolising that potential future has been the arrival of the MOOC (Massive Open Online Course), where some major universities have opened select aspects of their course curriculum to free entry. It is only a short step from purely 'online' to 'access-plus-feedback', and even assessment and the issuing of validated credentials. The campus university is hardly doomed, but this opens new modes of learning alongside new user-friendly IT (Daniel, 2012).
- Forms of 'knowledge generation' and 'knowledge transfer' have been massively advanced. Exceptional basic research is currently being undertaken right across the spectrum of the natural and human sciences—quite often in the new accelerator of research centres—while new ways have been created to connect laboratory research with commercial production, through systems of 'innovation' (which brings together researchers and venture capital to exploit key intellectual property [IP]). Major research-intensive universities globally have maintained quality and outcomes without entirely losing their academic souls.
- New knowledge, combined with the new ICT advances, has also opened an entire new area of human endeavour and productivity. Richard Florida has evocatively pointed to the role of 'the creative classes' (Florida, 2002). Nations require not only capital but also skilled technical workers. The combination can be hugely powerful, leading to some of the most successful companies in history. It is no accident that the new giants of the age of globalisation have been Steve Jobs (Apple) and Bill Gates (Microsoft). The world of social media is but the most obvious aspect of an era in which the

'web' has become both an underpinning facilitator and the provider of instructional knowledge for societies—both 'advanced' and 'developing'.

- In societal terms, many states are also discovering the power behind Thomas Jefferson's aphorism that 'Education is the best defence of the nation'. Education and skilling can work both to underpin the prosperity of a nation and to nurture the communal values of a civil society. The alternate 'cost of ignorance' can be even more costly for a nation: endemic poverty and social divide, gender inequality and youth disengagement, poor public culture and poor public policy, international economic dependency, and global marginalisation.
- Funding this extraordinary expansion in higher education provision globally has also exemplified considerable public policy creativity, with much of it redrawing the boundaries been public and private. Even older public universities are no longer able to rely on public resourcing alone (Marginson and Considine, 2002). In turn, the cash-strapped state of the modern era—notably in the developing societies—has looked increasingly to the establishment of private providers. Their quality may be variable, but they keep alive the aspirations of massification among aspiring citizens who happen to live in low-GDP economies.
- Multiple income streams have become the lifeblood of universities globally, with only the best few (endowed with benefactions) able to claim the purity of real fiscal autonomy. Those funding streams begin with growing student fees and then add competitive national and international research grants, industry contracts, professional services IP and patents through 'commercial arms', and finally the pursuit of endowment funds from foundations and trusts. The quantum of resources has risen remarkably, along with dependency and changes in 'mission'. The age of the 'Faustian bargains' had arrived (Washburn, 2005).
- While there has been much negative commentary on universities becoming 'corporatised', in fact a season of professionalisation had at last arrived to move institutions towards more business-like practices, even if they had not actually become businesses per se. At the best of the administratively 'reformed' campuses, strong and creative leaders give a sense of enlarged mission to their institutions; and some adopt positive roles in national policy

formulations and directions. (At their worst, they can become corrosive of professional trust and academic freedom.)
- The story of the modern university is largely still a national story, with outreaches to work in overseas markets internationally. But there are already pointers to a future era in which institutions become transnational enterprises akin to multinational corporations. Campuses are being created in key market regions. Corporate universities are coming into being to serve their own industrial and financial sectors. 'Networks' of universities are also being formed to collaborate and interact at new levels. Some political jurisdictions (such as in Singapore) are establishing education 'hubs', where national and international players are concentrating to serve entire regions, let alone students from further afield. A de-centred geopolitical world is witnessing the growth of a de-centred educational configuration to meet global demands for professional skilling.

Yet, on the less positive side, the very manner of how all this creativity has been achieved is increasingly challenging the very core concept of 'the university' itself. There are certain 'losses' to be reckoned with. One notable academic assessment of the modern campus culture has been sharply entitled *The University in Ruins* (Brewer, 1996). From the distinguished 'Futures Project' (at Brown University in the USA) has also come a measured, but salutary judgement:

> Universities have held a privileged position because they have focussed on the needs of society, rather than self-gains...But in a market driven environment this special status is endangered—universities will be pressed to focus on the short term gain that competitive new forces offer, and will search for ways to maximise institutional, rather than pursue the longer term goals that have formed the backbone of higher education for centuries.
>
> (Newman, 2000)

Underpinning the university revolution has indeed been a transformation of the very concept of the institution itself. For a start, it is no longer clear what today actually constitutes a 'university' globally in the twenty-first century. The most recent international social science survey points to between roughly 10,000 and 17,000 institutions with that asserted claim of 'university' in their title—the discrepancy in numbers arising not from a census failure, but from the inability to measure against a robust and universally agreed descriptor. Claims for university status are all too easy, while the measurable educational ethos is less certain. Ivory towers were easier to define than the concrete and glass campuses of today, or even the dedicated spaces in high corporate buildings in the heart of cities.

Whether such contemporary universities fully meet the more traditional criteria of the university 'Idea' is debated strongly (Pelikan, 1992). Many new institutions have, in truth, taken over the 'idea' and given it new utilitarian meanings for a new century, where both 'massification' and 'innovation' have become the great social aspirations. Moreover, as Stefan Collini has astutely observed in *What Are Universities For?* (Collini, 2012: 95), the university of today is led and administered in ways that represent a new organisational culture. Largely abandoned—or never fully embraced—is the old precept of 'collegiality' as a basis for authority and management in the university: the essentially democratic notion of academic teachers in a social fellowship, and in which the vice-chancellor (or president) is merely the first among equals among the staff.

Universities now increasingly shadow versions of corporate structure and top-down managerial culture. Strong executive leadership is prized, and the 'steering core' of many universities is now the president/vice-chancellor, supported by an extensive range of senior portfolio managers, including those with a professional (rather than academic) background. The balance of total staff numbers has even has tilted away from academic teachers towards professional employees—perhaps as many as two-thirds of university staff in the US are actually non-academics.

Because much of the development of university education is now demand-driven, and because the state is often unable to meet the funding burden of expanding public sectors (ranging from education to health and welfare), there is now, moreover, an emerging phenomenon of 'private university' initiatives across the globe. 'Private' often used to mean elite and affluent; while the opposite can now apply in resource-poor societies. 'Private' has become the new 'public'—when the state is unable to meet the needs of its citizens and its developmental aspirations for the nation, the community looks to private providers. Looking across the globe, it can broadly be said that the public university survives best in the developed world, while the creation of private institutions has defined the developing world. Members of the BRIC group of nations (Brazil, Russia, India, China) are now, for example, relying ever more heavily on the private sector to meet educational aspirations, to which could be added such populous developing nations as Indonesia and the Philippines. Interestingly, the World Bank itself has come to see investment via private providers (not least through repayable micro-loans) as a potentially cost-efficient means of meeting educational disadvantage by matching institutional provision to social demand.

The overall consequence is that the traditional 'university' (whether public or private)—grounded in a teaching–research nexus, established on a single campus, and often serving an elite number of 18- to 21-year-old students—is now not so much a dying species as a distinct minority phenomenon, as higher education swings opens the inclusivity and aspirational doorways. The university outreach has also extended through multi-campus and multinational operations, while the student education process may now be happening through blended or distance education or e-education; and the social experience can involve a fixed-term degree or lifelong learning over many years and several interactions with a university. Articulations from college or private provider to university are also common. 'Elite' is no longer a proxy for institutional distinction or purpose or success for universities. Staff–student ratios may be worsening, but access is growing incrementally. Quality in ICT support and infrastructure is not a cheap investment in dealing with expanding numbers (and stasis in staffing numbers); but it is the beguiling dream of policymakers and funders that more students can be educated with less direct state investment.

University 'missions' have also come to reflect an increasingly more utilitarian focus. A considerable number of modern universities have grown out of colleges of advanced education or institutes of technology. Their parentage is palpably evident. Others again are new public foundations or private incorporations, with a sharply defined sense of operational goals towards professional outcomes (Schreuder, 2006). University is no longer a coming-of-age phenomenon for a mass of students: it rather represents empowerment in leaving poverty behind, or towards meeting goals in skilling and training. In the measured assessment of the OECD, 'the mission of most institutions in most countries today is to teach less of the basic disciplines and offer more in the way of professional programs to a far wider range of students than in the past' (Altbach, Reisberg, and Rumbley, 2009: viii).

Moreover, even 'public universities' now often rely heavily on fees (domestic and international), as well as income generated from consultancies, commercial activities, IP, and contract research—prompting leading scholars to describe modern universities as fundamentally 'enterprise institutions' (Marginson and Considine, 2002). Higher education itself is a competitive 'industry', with brand and ranking being critical in establishing a successful presence in the student marketplace. That market is also price-sensitive, and influenced by currency fluctuations, making it a treacherous zone in which to engage in long-term planning strategies for recruitment.

There is also a competitive market for 'knowledge workers', as universities search globally for teaching and research talent. Globalisation here means the free movement not only of goods and ideas but also of skilled professionals themselves (Ennew and Greenaway, 2012). Sometimes overdramatically called a 'brain drain', there is still indeed a general flow of such academics and researchers from 'South' to 'North'; but in China, India, and parts of Africa, there is an evolving strategy to 'bring-back-home' such skilled postdoctoral and academic staff from 'North' to 'South'.

An age of internationalisation is increasingly reflected in the dynamics of global diasporas involving academic teachers and researchers. The age of tradition and certainties on campuses is under threat, while also being the source of transformation and growth. Much of globalisation has also reflected the universalising of the English language as the mode of communication in knowledge generation—which has facilitated internationalisation in higher education, while also somewhat homogenising the creativity of former cross-cultural encounters (Douglas, Judson King, and Feller, 2009).

That kind of dialectic tension is indeed evident across the whole spectrum of the contemporary university experience and operation.

- High quality is expected of universities by all the stakeholders—yet the pressure is for ever-expanding mass systems of broad educational provision, with an emphasis on equity, inclusivity, and enhancement.
- Academic autonomy is lauded as a core value for universities—while pressures for deep social engagement often mean governance and mission determined by external forces (including the populist state).
- Diversity of academic institutional missions is lauded to meet ever more complex societal needs—yet the force towards uniformity of performance and provision often pushes downwards, towards lowest common denominators in funding and role.

- Political leaders extol the virtues of knowledge nations—but are rarely ready to meet the educational costs involved, and are inclined to look for cost-efficiencies in austere funding and ever heavier staff loads.
- Pure research is almost universally praised in the abstract—while national and industrial research policy imperatives point towards short-term outcomes that are intended to underpin 'innovation'.
- Global rankings rely heavily on research citations—yet national jurisdictions are often focused on the necessity of underpinning labour market planning or on confronting social disadvantage.

Perhaps most emblematically, pride in ancient traditions and heritage campuses is often esteemed in an iconic public myth (being much used in recruitment branding), when in fact the traditional 'uni-versity' has often become the transformational 'multi-versity' involving multi-campuses; multiple high-rise concrete structures; multitudinous faculties, centres, professional schools, and 'commercial arms' involving thousands of staff (academic and general) and students (undergraduate, postgraduate, and international); supported formidable budgets; and all managed by corporate-style executive leadership (Kerr, [1963] 2001). It has increasingly become a case of: 'The university is dead; long live the university.'

'Commonwealth': Case Study in Global Educational Transformation

That complex international story finds an evocative sampler in the history of higher education within the diverse and populous Commonwealth of Nations.

Once coterminous with the British Empire itself, the 'Commonwealth' is now a global network of voluntary association and interactions. 'Greater Britain' has become Greater World. If it remains 'British' at all, it is in terms of the English language and certain cultural atavisms—ranging from government and law, class and family, to religion and sport. Many of those elements, however, are transformed by local indigenisation—there are now multiple 'Englishes' spoken around the world, just as there are variants in the civic and cultural legacy of empire. The Empire itself has also 'struck back', with the United Kingdom itself being a study in multiculturalism through inward migration from Asia, Africa, and the Caribbean. The British have ultimately come to inhabit one of their post-colonial successor states of the decolonisation era (Darwin, 2012).

The meaning of all this for universities is palpable and simply stated. With the expansion of Empire power, and with a British diaspora of settlers, went institutions of education and professional cultures. London University, particularly, played a crucial role in exporting secular institutional forms of university education: the first and dramatic form of 'distance education'. A certain coherence and commonality came to exist across these new universities in the new societies of settlement, as well as the tertiary institutions of the dependent empire (such as in Africa, Asia, and the Caribbean). That lasted broadly until decolonisation, when it began to fracture through the emergence of 'post-colonial' societies. Globalisation was then to sweep away the remnants of an old order, and see the emergence of new-style institutions and associations. Just as power was devolved, so the world became a series of de-centred regions.

Just how this actually happened is not always easy to discern. But using our case-example of the Commonwealth universities and their Association's peak body (the ACU), we have a rare sampler, which exemplifies a global story. Indeed, the radically changing character of the initial Universities Bureau of the British Empire (formed 1913), which later morphed into the Association of Commonwealth Universities, encapsulates these developments. This can be mapped through the transformations that took place in the national jurisdictions that made up the Commonwealth societies through the period of decolonisation and the Cold War—notably, massive expansion of provision in post-independence nations, coupled with a spread that was wider than the old Empire–Commonwealth culture, even of the English-speaking peoples which embraced the transatlantic communities.

Commonwealth Biography: Eric Ashby's 'History' of the ACU at Its 50th Anniversary (1963)

Capturing the measure of that social and institutional 'transformation' can well begin from the benchmark of the excellent golden anniversary History of the ACU, published in 1963 by the Association, and written by one of its most distinguished scholars and academic leaders, Professor Sir Eric Ashby (1904–92)—scientist, ACU Council Member and Cambridge College Master. The book (Ashby, 1963) is also indirectly a portrait of its redoubtable author, his attachment to liberal–humanistic educational goals, and his identity in a cultural and special entity called 'Commonwealth'.

In an extended academic career, Ashby moved from science researcher to lecturer, professor to vice-chancellor (and Cambridge Master). Even more significantly, he served no less than six different British and Commonwealth universities—ranging from Imperial College, London (where he was educated and did his graduate work in botany), to English and Northern Irish universities (Bristol and Manchester, Belfast and Cambridge), and also externally overseas in the old Dominions state of Australia (at the University of Sydney from 1938 to 1945, where he declined the vice-chancellorship). His war service, significantly, saw him acting as scientific adviser and chargé d'affaires in Moscow. The apogee of his academic career came at Cambridge, where he was Fellow (and later Master) of Clare College, while also founding agent in creating Clare Hall (dedicated to postgraduates and research fellows, not least from Commonwealth nations). During 1968–69 he was elected and served as the Cambridge Vice-Chancellor.

Alongside his 'home' duties in university education, Ashby also made considerable contributions overseas to British 'colonial' educational developments. His focus was almost as much on the 'Empire–Commonwealth' as on the United Kingdom, in offering increasingly important initiatives towards new university foundations and development policy in Africa (there were 10 periods of duty in 12 nations, including chairing the noted 'Carnegie Commission' to Nigeria); researching and writing on higher education in independent India; involvement in the divided South African higher education system; chairing the Commonwealth Scholarship and Fellowship Plan for the entire 1960s; as well as serving on the planning council that led to the founding of the Australian National University. In all these Empire–Commonwealth contexts, Ashby held strongly to the notion of education as nation-builder. The university was there to play a special role as generator of new knowledge drawn from the creativity of free-standing research. The university itself was to be the proponent of a particular kind of technological innovation—one that combined pure science and social application in the name of public good.

Rarely has an Imperial life peerage—he was 'Baron Ashby' from 1973—been so well based in the higher education of the Commonwealth at large. Not so surprisingly, he was a natural choice to write the benchmark study of the ACU in 1963. Few studies in institutional history have quite so closely reflected the first-hand experience and ethos of a single life trajectory and particular historic era.

Through his study, Ashby provides a unique view of the British university environment from the inside at a particular time—a 'tilt-moment', as it might be called today. Here is the Anglo-Imperial campus before geopolitical and educational changes transformed a traditional 'British world', including higher education institutions then modelled on aspects of the older metropolitan system of Great Britain. It is therefore fascinating to compare the world that Ashby evokes—through skill and empathy—with the character and form of universities that were to follow. It is as if we are viewing an historic environment before a veritable tsunami of social change comes to sweep across the Commonwealth campuses of the globe, leaving a transformed educational landscape.

The very title of Ashby's history—*Community of Universities* (1963)—exactly represented his idealistic theme: 'the idea of cohesion among the universities of the Commonwealth', as he expressed it himself. The ACU itself he saw as 'a federation founded on sentiment', with the aim of the organisation, since its foundation (in 1913), 'to be a society and not a bureaucracy'. With affection, Ashby describes the vivid story of how when the initial delegates from British and colonial institutions first met (on 5 July 1912) to explore and the idea of a 'bureau for universities' based in the Imperial capital, it was recorded by a participant that they appeared 'like children gathering round the family hearth' (Ashby, 1963: 9).

This Anglo-Imperial community of fealty and common culture had surely, over time, become more complex and diverse. But, for Ashby, its educational institutions continued to embrace the same core missions and values:

> Transplanted universities do not indefinitely remain replicas of the stock from which they come.... The universities of India and Australia have long departed a long way from the University of London. Yet they are unmistakably universities; notwithstanding local differences in emphasis they pursue similar curricula; they aspire to remain on the 'gold standard' of scholarship; none of them could stand alone, and their strength lies in the fact that they share a common tradition and they freely draw on one another's resources.... It is no wonder that the universities of the Commonwealth—indeed the whole Western world—are held together in an undefined but indivisible society.
>
> (Ashby, 1963: 92)

More politically, Ashby broadly saw a 'Commonwealth education' as working to knit together the successor states of a decolonised empire informed by 'a common tradition' of learning. 'The Commonwealth family will continually diversify', as he wrote with typical optimism in his history. 'It therefore becomes of prime importance to promote the free trade in ideas, and of men who specialise in ideas, between Commonwealth countries. This is most easily done through the universities.'

It is all too easy to mock such high idealism in the twenty-first century when, in truth, an earlier generation of academic leaders espoused such perceptions and language. But if the Ashby view was ever true in its time, history has not been kind to its legacy. The Commonwealth itself changed significantly in an age of geopolitical transformation after the Cold War. Some saw it as simply a shadowed version of the old Empire with little substance after the smile of power receded from Great Britain. But as Stephen Howe has perceptively argued, the Commonwealth has now re-emerged from global changes to become a useful middle-range international organisation, with special significance for capacity-building in the developing world (Howe, 2002: 113).

The same could be said of the ACU itself. It could no longer claim to be the totality of universities within the Commonwealth; nor to mirror a uniform set of university missions and values; nor to be overtly an agency of 'Commonwealth' itself. A complex world order had produced complex local societies and institutions. Ashby's unity had gone. But, in fact, a new and diverse vitality was soon to be found across higher education in the Commonwealth. The universities, most of whom axiomatically were members of the ACU, were emblematic of Commonwealth. And if the universities symbolised the very nature of a Commonwealth Ideal, they were also taken to be enhancers of the global organisation as it evolved in a changing world. Partly this was to meet obvious needs in education and professional training; but partly it also extended to building a Commonwealth culture of shared values and allegiances.

Commonwealth Higher Education after Ashby: The Currents of Change

Ashby's essentially liberal humanistic beliefs about the meaning and efficacy of higher education had, in fact, already faced certain utilitarian challenges before the transformational challenges and changes of the later decades of the twentieth century. While working in Australia in the 1930s, for example, Ashby had already clashed educational swords with John Philip Baxter, an early and creative proponent of professional vocational learning embedded in an industrial nexus (Forsyth, 2010). Baxter was notably instrumental in the founding and shaping of the Sydney Technical College at Kensington, which duly became the University of Technology (from 1949), and later the University of New South Wales (UNSW), but which was long known affectionately by staff and students alike as 'Kenso Tech' (O'Farrell, 1999: 84–135).

In modern language, Ashby and Baxter held fascinatingly contrasting views over what constituted appropriate 'graduateness'. Eric Ashby essentially stood in the tradition of J.H. Newman—universities educated the whole person as citizen, through individual learning and free-standing scholarship—while J.P. Baxter had a distinctly more utilitarian view of higher education as shaping a wide range of professional outcomes through the acquisition of key skills drawn from an interface with industry. Ashby deeply valued 'technology' as a broad tool for social advancement, which grew out of the unified research culture of universities. Baxter imbued technology without its own instrumental power and saw its origins in the nexus of state, industry, and education (Forsyth, 2010; Forsyth, forthcoming).

If Ashby can be said to have worked from within the academy, Baxter exemplified a new breed of educators who were to come from outside the Ivory Tower. Prior to migrating to Australia, he had indeed worked in the British and American nuclear industries. After his seminal period as Vice-Chancellor of UNSW, he was to return to the industry as head of ANSTO (the Australian nuclear energy organisation). Today we might say that differentiated university missions are deeply valuable to a national society. But, in their time, there appeared to be fundamentally rival scenarios for educational development, with Ashby remaining deeply committed to a traditional view of universities, their autonomy, educational missions, and research culture.

That settled view was to be fractured by major social and political change, which surged through global campuses after about 1960, the very time when Ashby was writing his History of the ACU. A new era of university education was in truth about to 'happen'. Indeed, now began the widening of a previously select—even elite—environment to become one of mass higher education across the former 'Anglo-world'. This started in the United Kingdom itself, before increasingly drawing in the former Dominion societies and finally involving the decolonised independent nations of the nascent Third World.

The ACU continues to be a highly successful networked association of over 500 universities globally. But in its own transformation there lies a fascinating perspective on 'the world we have lost'. The past is here not so much a foreign country that we cannot recognise—aspects of the old university systems persist—but the totality of change is striking.

- Where Ashby simply presumed that membership of the ACU would be coterminous with the university foundations throughout the Commonwealth—starting with the institutions in the Mother Country—that is simply no longer true. For example, at 2012 only just over, half of the UK's much expanded higher education system are ACU members (78), while in the loyal 'old dominions' the situation is not hugely different (30 of 41 in Australia, and 28 in Canada's even bigger system). The great balance of the ACU membership (over 550 universities in 37 of the Commonwealth's 54 countries) has tipped towards members from developing nations, with their large populations and huge social challenges. The Associate Membership' category has also allowed for the presence of non-Commonwealth states, a trend that is likely to increase.
- Those issues in economic development and state governance have pressed strongly on the agenda of universities within the emerging nations of the Commonwealth and of the agenda of the ACU. The human challenges are immense in social well-being and citizenship. India alone has 1.2 billion people, and there are 176 million in Pakistan, 156 million in Bangladesh, and 154 million in Nigeria. Here the 'Association' particularly offers deeply valuable networking, capacity-building, and positioning possibilities for their extensive and protean institutions of higher education, research, and training.
- A globalised world has also meant that universities have diversified their international connections and institutions. For some this has meant a focus on linkages with American organisations or research consortia; for others it has led to a focus of active participation in more regional groupings, such as those of the European or Asian or 'Pacific Rim' universities. They may, or may not, see these memberships as coterminous with measurable outcomes from the ACU membership network. University missions, and the

value of membership fees, are also involved within the defining of international strategies (ANU, 2004).

- Most powerfully of all, several formal 'networks' of elite universities now exist, which pursue collaborative and connectional projects, ranging from research to staff and student exchange. The pioneer (and perhaps best known) of these is 'Universitas 21', which still reflects its origins in institutions that exist within the Commonwealth, but then reaches out to involve university 'foundations' based in diverse regions of the world, from America to Asia. The 'World Universities Alliance' is now also developing strongly in a similar manner, anchored in its own secretariat and involving international members who happen to straddle the globe. Finally, we are seeing the beginnings of global distance e-learning institutions, which pay no respect to national boundaries, nor to historic origins in entities such as the Commonwealth. For them, the world is their educational oyster in expanding private university provision globally.
- The changing criteria for ACU membership, moreover, tell their own revealing story. The presumption behind Ashby's 'golden standard' of scholarship now seems fanciful in an essentially fragmented global environment of diverse institutions claiming the title of 'university'. A pluralist set of missions and outcomes, standards and quality, size and character has only highlighted the impossibility of working to fixed, globally normative criteria for 'universities'. The ACU has pragmatically, and shrewdly, recognised this diversity of higher education—by state and performance—through setting in place a protocol of membership criteria that work from principles of inclusivity and rely on the criteria of national jurisdictions. A de-centred Commonwealth and international order results in de-centred criteria. Accordingly, all full ACU members must be both 'legally incorporated and situated in the Commonwealth', and 'must be approved by the appropriate government authority to provide higher education' from whom they also gain their authority 'to award their own degrees'. The ACU's own eligibility test criteria are set broadly, not austerely: aspirant members 'must have at least 250 full-time students (50 per cent of whom must be studying at first or higher degree level)', and 'they must have graduated at least one cohort of students' (ACU, 2012: 1).

- Moving ever further from the Ashby view of the university systems, all this points to a social reality that is often masked by a certain political correctness in educational environments, where policymakers and political actors simply accept that 'same-by-name' equals 'same-by-performance' and 'same-by-standards'. And in the globalised environment, of geopolitics and cross-cultural sensitivities, the spirit of internationalism often glosses over the inequalities and variations between universities, their standing and outcomes. National ministers of education all too easily yield to boosting of their own diverse university sectors—by labelling all their higher education institutions as 'world class'—when in fact there are considerable disparities in what are constituted as 'universities' globally. A great challenge lies not only in expanding provision, but also in assuring quality in all institutions.

Our Book: Structure and Strategy

There is no simple or single way of analysing this story of transformation in higher education. Each study has to establish its own approach and strategy. This book works around a transcending theme—the ways in which the Commonwealth university story provides a vantage point for viewing the wider global changes to universities, and it does so through a practical division of its analytic chapters.

- After the *Preface* and *Foreword*, which contextualise the origins of this book within the Centenary of the ACU (1913–2013), this succinct *Introduction* aims to locate our volume within the international literature debating the fate and future of universities today. The ACU centenary is taken as the base for a critical examination of the higher education revolution of recent decades.
- *Part I* is concerned with 'History': the dynamics of university expansion in the Commonwealth (not least through the export of the 'London model' of secular public institutions of learning), by taking 1913 (and the formation of the ACU) as its point of departure. It also explores the ways in which 'capacity-building' became a key feature of the role of the ACU as the world's oldest

university network, and of the consequent development of 'knowledge nation' state strategies.

- *Part II* highlights certain key themes in the revolutionary processes of change in higher education and training, research, and community engagement: the ongoing impact of e-learning, the power of innovation, gender and university leadership, the assurance of quality in mass education systems, and the empowering role of student mobility—not least through the remarkable Commonwealth Scholarship and Fellowship Plan, which has had a close organisational relationship with the ACU.
- *Part III* grounds that transformational phenomenon in the social experience of the great global regions of Commonwealth: sub-Saharan Africa, South Asia (especially involving India and Pakistan), Australia and the Caribbean. Select national types of Commonwealth jurisdictions are taken as samplers of our story—notably post-Dominion members, developing countries and 'small states'—towards a fuller understanding of the varying roles, and of the challenges faced by universities, within their diverse home societies.
- *Part IV* moves to 'Prospect': by canvassing both the educational agenda for change in the near future, as well as 'looking over the horizon' at the potential 'futures' awaiting universities in the twenty-first century. The past is no guarantee towards assuring success, nor in predicting change. But to ignore recent global dynamics and lessons in higher education is to fail the test of responsible social science—its capacity for informing policy and practice across the university jurisdictions of the world, and not least among the many institutions of the Commonwealth of Nations.

Looked at over the *longue durée* of history, and especially of the quickening tempo of radical change which constitutes the decades of the later twentieth century, one sobering lesson stands out from this volume for the institutional providers of higher education, both public and private. This concerns the resolute commitment to change and constant development. As Harold Shapiro, a former Princeton President, once wisely remarked (Shapiro, 2001), the test of a university is not what it is, but what it is becoming.

Bibliography

ACU (2012) 'Membership Criteria'. Available online at www.acu ac.uk/membership/join-us/membership-criteria (downloaded on 10 November 2012).

Altbach, P.G., Reisberg Liz, and Rumbley, L.E. (eds) (2009) *Trends in Global Higher Education: Tracking an Academic Revolution.* A Report Prepared for the UNESCO 2009 World Conference on Higher Education. Paris: UNESCO.

Anderson, R. (2006) *British Universities—Past and Present.* London: Hambledon.

ANU (2004) '*ANU—University with a Difference*'. *The Report of the Committee established by the Council of the Australian National University to Evaluate the Quality of the University's Performance,* chaired by Professor D.M. Schreuder, Canberra, September 2004.

Ashby, E. ([1963] 1988) *Community of Universities: An Informal Portrait of the Association of Universities of the British Commonwealth 1913–1963.* Cambridge: University Press. See also Springer, H. (with Niven, A.) (1988) *The Commonwealth of Universities: The Story of the Association of Commonwealth Universities, 1963–1988.* London: ACU.

Bjarnason, S. and Coldstream, P. (2003) *The Idea of Engagement—Universities in Society.* London: ACU.

Bok, D. (1990) *Universities and the Future of America.* Durham, NC: Duke University Press.

Bolton, G. and Lucas, C. (2008) *What Are Universities For?* Brussels: League of European Research Universities.

Brewer, Bill (1996) *The University in Ruins.* Cambridge, Mass.: Harvard University Press.

Collini, S. (2012) *What Are Universities For?* London: Penguin.

Daniel, J.S. (2012) Making sense of MOOCS: Musings in a Maze of Myth, Paradox and Possibility. *Journal of International Multimedia Education.* http://jime.open.ac.uk/article/2012-18/html (last accessed 7 July 2013).

Darwin, J. (2012) *The Unfinished Empire—The Global Expansion of Britain.* London: Allen Lane.

Davis, G. (2010) *The Republic of Learning. Higher Education Transforms Australia.* The Boyer Lecture Series, 2010. Sydney: ABC Books.

Douglas, J.A., Judson King, C., and Feller, I. (eds) (2009) *Globalisation's Muse. Universities and Higher Education Systems in a Changing World.* California: Berkeley Public Policy Press.

Economist (2012) For richer, for poorer. Special Report, *Economist*, 13 October.

Ennew, C. and Greenaway, D. (eds) (2012) *The Globalisation of Higher Education*, 34–39. London: Palgrave Macmillan.

Florida, R. (2002) *The Rise of the Creative Class. And How It Is Transforming Work, Leisure and Everyday Life*. New York: Basic Books.

Forsyth, H. (2010) Academic work in Australian universities in the 1940s and 1950s. *History of Education Review*, 39(1): 38–50.

Forsyth, H. (forthcoming) Negotiating the benefits of knowledge: International networks and technology in Australian post-war universities. *History of Education Review*.

Howe, S. (2002) *Empire: A Very Short Introduction*. Oxford: Oxford University Press.

Ker, I. (2009) *John Henry Newman. A Biography*, especially 376–417. Oxford: Oxford University Press.

Kerr, C. ([1963] 2001) *The Uses of the University*. 5th ed. with a new Preface. Mass.: Harvard University Press.

Marginson, S. and Considine, M. (2002) *The Enterprise University: Governance and Re-invention in Australia*. Melbourne: Cambridge University Press.

Maskell, D. and Robinson, I. (2001) *The New Idea of a University*. London: Haven Books.

Newman, F. (2000) *Saving Higher Education's Soul*. The Futures Project. Providence, RI: Brown University.

Newman, J.H. ([1852] 1873) *The Idea of a University Defined and Illustrated*. Expanded 3rd ed. London: Longmans, Green and Co. See also Turner, F. (ed.) (1996) *J H Newman's Idea of a University*. New Haven, Conn.: Yale University Press.

O'Farrell, F. (1999) *UNSW—A Portrait. The University of New South Wales, 1949–1999*. Sydney: UNSW Press.

Pelikan, J. (1992) *The Idea of a University. A Re-examination*. New Haven, Conn.: Yale.

Readings, Bill (1996) *The University in Ruins*. Mass: Harvard University Press.

Schreuder, D.M. (2006) *'Who Killed Newman'? The Ideal of a University and Its Enemies*. The Cable Lecture, 1996. Sydney: St James Institute.

Shapiro, H.T. (2001) *Professional Education and the Soul of the American Research University*. Ann Arbor: Michigan University Press.

Spellings Commission Report (2006) *A Test of Leadership: Charting the Future of US Higher Education*. Washington, DC.

Thomas, K. (2010) What are universities for? *Times Literary Supplement*, May, 13–15.

Washburn, J. (2005) *University Inc—The Corporate Corruption of Higher Education*. New York: Basic Books.

Wolfe, A. (2002) *Does Education Matter? Myths about Education and Economic Growth*. London: Penguin.

PART I

History: Network and 'New World'

Prelude

Part I establishes our theme of 'Network and New World'—the interconnected history of expanding universities old and new, and of the utility they found in mutual collaboration. It also, of course, provides a deeply valuable way of exploring the twentieth-century academic revolution that transformed higher education from the inside of the participating network members. The apparently domestic history of the ACU as an institution—detailed here in two highly professional chapters—soon opens out onto the vista of a global higher education story.

Several overarching themes and issues of significance stand out.

Network and Internationalisation

The century-old ACU network anticipated the internationalisation of higher educational institutions as they came to respond to new modes of operation and to engage in international student movements. Distance learning was pioneered and new modes of social access and equity were progressively embraced. In its congresses and publications and professional services, the evolving ACU reflected transforming modes of governance, funding, pedagogy, and outreach within the university members and their societies.

From Distance Education and External Degrees to 'Massification'

Through its intimate connections to London University, with its remarkably innovative 'External Degree' capacity, the network ultimately reflected the birth of new world universities, in a project that, over time, transformed lives and societies. Elite institutions only very gradually dissolved into more open educational providers; but the path towards 'massification' was being laid.

As late as the 1960s, Britain itself had only 4 per cent of its senior school leavers at university, while the figure in the Dominions was no better, and in the Crown Colonies (in Africa especially) was even worse. India already had large student numbers, but they were a tiny proportion of the whole population. Yet, as the incisive chapter on the expansive 'London model' (Chapter 2) quietly signals, these modest beginnings produced some stellar individual graduates, whose leadership changed the world—such as Mahatma Gandhi and Nelson Mandela—coupled with writers who made us see the whole differently—such as Wole Soyinka from West Africa and Derek Walcott from the Caribbean.

Those first generations ultimately became the harbinger of a veritable spring in access and equity within new world educational environments. By 1990 there were some 70 million students in higher education across the globe. That journey is the theme of Parts II and III.

Inventing Knowledge Nations

Changes in the nature of universities rarely came from within academe. Campus and college focus was traditionally associated with teaching and learning. Modern issues of governance and academic freedom, access and fees, research performance and professional studies, quality assurance and the key performance indicators of outcomes—all these were absent. Universities belonged to the dons. That relatively comfortable view and environment was dissolved quite quickly—indeed even shattered—by the apparently sudden arrival of state policies and stakeholders, who now saw higher education as too important to be left to academics.

In short: the massive changes that underpinned the 'academic revolution' (so well described in Chapter 3) was a purposeful choice by governments, whose range now intruded not merely into funding but also into mission and performance.

The Missing Link: Southern Perspectives in Higher Education Histories

The narrative and analysis of this volume also reveals real lacunae in the history of universities—where the focus has so often been strongly on Europe and the trans-Atlantic societies (Anderson, 2006; Collini, 2012; Kerr, 2001; Pelikan, 1992; Ruegg, 2004). Moreover, major revisionist studies of Empire, and of 'the British World', have also hitherto shown little interest in higher education as such (Belich, 2009; Bridge and Federowich, 2003; Darwin, 2012; Levine, 2007; Louis, 1998–99; Magee and Thompson, 2010).

This book opens the door on scholarly possibilities of 'righting and writing' that balance. Perhaps John Pocock's famed call for a new history, which integrates the 'periphery' and 'metropolis', will find its moment (Pocock, 1975). It is appropriate that a more 'Southern' perspective be brought to the globalised transformation in higher education.

Network and Capacity-building

The network is seen to come into its own as 'capacity-building' became a leitmotif of its operation, notably after the Second World War. Partly this reflected a growing strength as a professional service-provider in policy and training, scholarship administration and information supply, personnel appointments and professional staff development. But, more still, the genius of the small organisation lay in its capacity for recognising a mutuality of institutional enhancement—through formal congresses (often on key contemporary themes of development), but also through a web of connections, as institutions found utility in their external associations of knowledge-sharing and co-operation.

The world's first global network was born as it subsumed the 'bureau', and its metropolitan origins, in becoming a member-based system of association. In that way, the network foreshadowed the arrival of the decentred, post-colonial world of states, which followed the fall of empires and even the ending of Cold War geo-politics. Along with it came an era of enrolment gains, which featured its own members; and which soon acquired the cumbersome (but evocative) term 'massification', reaching an astounding 160 million by 2012, with the greatest growth yet to come through new modes of e-learning assisting developing societies. Gender barriers were also to fall, so that the majority of undergraduates across global higher education are now women. It is one of the great stories of modern history.

A 'Domesday Book' for Higher Education Globally?

Finally, in the very public record of the ACU there can be found a rich insight into this history of new world universities. For example, there is the extraordinary set of annual ACU Yearbooks—published from a slender 1914 'catalogue' to the multi-volume boxed sets of 1988—and which chronicle the basic anatomy of the thousands of institutions that have, at some stage or another, been participants in the network. Here are the details of staff, disciplines, student numbers, research profiles and overall budgets. The information, of course, was submitted by the institutions themselves, and it is surely open to individual errors, biases, and omissions in reporting. But, at a macro level, that margin is (as the pollsters would say) within acceptable bounds in establishing the evolving nature of those institutions 'en masse'. It might even be suggested that here is a vast global 'Domesday Book' in higher education, reflecting the complex (and largely unwritten) history of new world universities.

Bibliography

General Surveys

Altbach, P.G., Reisberg, L., and Rumbley, L.E (eds). (2009) *Trends in Global Higher Education: Tracking an Academic Revolution*. A report prepared for the UNESCO 2009 World Conference on Higher Education. Paris: UNESCO.

Bjarnason, S. (2009) A New Dynamic: Private Higher Education. *Proceedings of the World Conference on Higher Education*. Paris: UNESCO.

Maxey, K. (2009) *Student Mobility on the Map: Tertiary Education in the Commonwealth on the Threshold of the 21st Century*. London: UKCOSA.

Scheller, C., Lungu, I., and Wachter, B. (2009) *Handbook of International Associations in Higher Education: A Practical Guide to 100 Academic*

Networks World-wide. Brussels: Academic Cooperation Association (supported by Asia Europe Foundation and Asia-Europe Meeting Education Hub).

UNESCO Institute of Statistics (2011) *Global Education Digest 2011: Comparing Education Statistics across the World*. Canada: UNESCO.

Works Cited

Anderson, Robert (2006) *British Universities, Past and Present*. London: Hambledon Continuum.

Belich, J. (2009) *Replenishing the Earth: The Settler Revolution and the Rise of the Anglo-World, 1783–1939*. Oxford: Oxford University Press.

Bridge, C. and Federowich, K. (eds) (2003) *The British World: Culture, Diaspora and Identity*. London: Taylor and Francis.

Collini, S. (2012) *What Are Universities For?* London: Allen Lane/Penguin Press.

Darwin, J. (2012) *Unfinished Empire: The Global Expansion of Britain*. London: Allen Lane.

Kerr, C. (2001) *The Uses of the University*. 5th ed. Cambridge, Mass.: Harvard University Press.

Levine, P. (2007) *The British Empire: Sunrise to Sunset*. London: Pearson Longman.

Louis, W.M.R. (Series editor) (1998–99) *The Oxford History of the British Empire Series*. 5 vols. Oxford: Oxford University Press.

Magee, G.B. and Thompson, A.S. (2010) *Empire and Globalisation: Networks of People, Goods and Capital in the British World, c 1850–1914*. Cambridge: Cambridge University Press.

Pelikan, J. (1992) *The Idea of a University: A Re-examination*. New Haven, Conn.: Yale.

Pocock, J.G.A. (1975) British history: A plea for a new subject. *Journal of Modern History*, 47.

Ruegg, W. (ed.) (2004), *Vol. III: Universities in the Nineteenth and Early Twentieth Century*. A History of the University in Europe. Cambridge: Cambridge University Press.

Select ACU Publications and Websites

Universities' Bureau of the British Empire/Association of Universities of the British Commonwealth/ACU (1914–2008) *Commonwealth Universities Yearbook*. London: Universities' Bureau of the British Empire/AUBC/

ACU. (Originally *The Yearbook of the Universities of the Empire*; later *The Yearbook of the Universities of the Commonwealth [1948–57]*; then *The Commonwealth Universities Yearbook* [1958 onwards]).

ACU Bulletin of Current Documentation (ABCD), 1–139 (June 1971–June 1999); Bulletin, 140–60 (October 1999–August 2004), 161 (August 2007 to date).

ACU (1974) *Commonwealth Universities and Society: The Report of Proceedings of the Eleventh Congress of the Universities of the Commonwealth*, Edinburgh, August 1973. London: ACU.

——— (1976) *Research Strengths of Universities in the Developing Countries of the Commonwealth*. London: ACU.

——— (1984) *Research Opportunities in Commonwealth Developing Countries*. London: ACU.

——— (1988) *What Can We Do for Our Countries? The Contribution of Universities to National Development: The Report of Proceedings of the Fourteenth Congress of the Universities of the Commonwealth*, Perth, February 1988. London: ACU.

——— (1994) *People and the Environment: Preserving the Balance: The Report of Proceedings of the Fifteenth Congress of the Universities of the Commonwealth*, Swansea, August 1993. London: ACU.

——— (2012) Benchmarking Programme. Available cnline at www.acu.ac.uk/member_services/benchmarking_programme/benchmarking_programme (last accessed on 23 May 2012).

Bjarnason, S. and Coldstream, P. (eds) (2003) *The Idea of Engagement: Universities in Society*. London: ACU.

Bourne, R. (ed.) (2000) Universities and Development: *A Report on the Socio-economic Role of Universities in the Developing Countries of the Commonwealth*. London: ACU.

Kubler, J. and Tarrant, J. (2008) *Shifting Horizons: Issues Facing Universities in the Commonwealth: An ACU Consultation*. London: ACU.

Kubler, J. and Tarrant, J. (2009) *Working in Tandem: Identifying and Responding to the Issues Facing our Members*. London: ACU.

Histories and Monographs

Ashby, E. (1963) *Community of Universities: An Informal Portrait of the Association of Universities of the British Commonwealth, 1913–1963*. Cambridge: University Press.

Carr-Saunders, A.M. (1961) *New Universities Overseas*. London: George Allen and Unwin Ltd.

Harte, N. (1986) *The University of London, 1836–1986: An Illustrated History*. London: Athlone Press Ltd.

Kenyon Jones, C. (2008) *The People's University, 1858–2008*. London: University of London.

Pattison, B. (1984) *Special Relations—The University of London and New Overseas Universities, 1947–1970*. London: University of London.

Springer, H. (with Niven, A.) (1988) *The Commonwealth of Universities: The Story of the Association of Commonwealth Universities, 1963–1988*. London: ACU.

1

Out of Empire: The Universities' Bureau and the Congresses of the Universities of the British Empire, 1913–36

Tamson Pietsch

On 28 January 1913 the first meeting of the Organising Committee of the Universities' Bureau of the British Empire took place in the Bloomsbury buildings of the University of London.

Appointed the previous year by the inaugural Congress of the Universities of the British Empire, seven of its members had been nominated by the overseas universities (two from Canada, and one each from Australia, New Zealand, the Cape, India and one from the rest of the Empire) and seven represented the universities in the United Kingdom. The committee's task was to establish a 'Central Bureau' that might act as a 'clearing house': 'an organ for the purpose of continuing [the] communication of knowledge and comparison of varied experience', begun at the Congress. It set about doing so by attending to practical arrangements (Ashby, 1963: 10).

The members of the committee appointed a chairman (the representative of the Scottish universities, Sir Donald MacAlister), decided on a name for the new organisation—the Universities' Bureau of the British Empire—and discussed where its headquarters might be. They also discussed finance and the appointment of staff, and began the task of collating information about universities from across the Empire. In doing so, the members of the committee in Bloomsbury brought into being the first-ever association of British universities, either at home or abroad—an organisation that would eventually grow into the Association of Commonwealth Universities (UMA: UM312/1913/61a).

However, if the Universities' Bureau was born in 1913, its gestation began 10 years earlier in the Edwardian movement for closer imperial union. During this period two attempts were made to establish a central universities' council or bureau. The hopes that fostered these Edwardian efforts, together with the concerns that led to their failure, would also influence the Bureau's development. Indeed, a focus on the settler colonies, a concern with fostering informal connections, and a reluctance on the part of universities to sacrifice their autonomy, would condition the Bureau's activities and its sense of self up until the Second World War.

Pre-history

In 1911, R.D. Roberts, the Organising Secretary of the approaching inaugural Congress of the Universities of the British Empire, prepared a document in which he traced the event's origins back to the 'Conference of Allied Colonial Universities', held in London in 1903 (UMA: UM312/1912/25). Informed by the contemporary desire to foster imperial connections, this gathering had been organised by the Canadian novelist and Conservative Member of Parliament for Gravesend, Sir Gilbert Parker. Parker had initially envisaged the event as a dinner for colonial graduates, but in the context of the heated contemporary discussion about Tariff Reform, it soon grew in scope and scale (Thompson, 2000: 26; Bell, 2007).

Eventually attended by many of Britain's leading public figures—including the Liberal Member of Parliament R.B. Haldane, the Colonial Secretary Joseph Chamberlain, and the British Prime Minister A.J. Balfour, as well as numerous representatives from universities in Britain—the conference was accompanied by the round of parties and 'inevitable dinner[s]' typical of Edwardian imperial conventions and billed by Parker as a gathering at which people representing 'educational interests from all parts of the Empire' would be present (*Empire Review*, 1903: 120). Yet for all this pomp, the conference was not quite as representative as Parker made out. The universities from India were not invited, and the Australasian universities were forced to appoint individuals in Britain to attend on their behalf due to the last-minute nature of their invitations (USA: G1/1/11).

But Parker's 1903 conference did constitute the first attempt to bring together universities from across the British Empire. At the conference, attendees affirmed what they saw as the racial and cultural bonds linking the settler colonies and Britain, and attested to the common cause of their universities (*Empire Review*, 1903: 73, 76–77, 109, 118, 120). As the liberal politician and historian James Bryce announced at the meeting:

> We have two aims, and those two aims are closely bound together. One aim is to develop the intellectual and moral forces of all the branches of our race wherever they dwell, and therewith also to promote learning, science and the arts by and through which science is applied to the purposes of life. The other aim is to strengthen the unity of the British people dispersed throughout the world.
>
> (*Empire Review*, 1903: 177)

With statements like these, the representatives at the 1903 conference gave voice to an expansive conception of the British nation—what R.B. Haldane called 'the great British nation in its different parts'—that would underpin the Bureau's later history. This conception was premised upon what were perceived to be the already existing connections between universities in Britain and the settler colonies. As the Vice-Chancellor of the University of Cambridge, F.H. Chase, argued: '[w]e have not to create an affinity between [these universities]', rather it 'is the business of this Conference to recognize their affinity and to make it effective for practical purposes' (*Empire Review*, 1903: 118, 178).

This urge to give practical form to existing connections led the 1903 conference to resolve to establish a 'representative Council' in order to promote relations 'between the principal teaching universities of the empire' (*Congress*, 1912: 310–11; *Empire Review*, 1903: 69). Borrowing the language of imperial federation, speakers argued that the interests of the whole nation would be served by better incorporating the resources of its various parts. As Roberts wrote in his 1911 historical summary, '[T]he key-note of all the speeches was the need for co-operation and even for federation' (*Empire Review*, 1903: 115).

These early intimations of a federalised university organisation fell into abeyance in the heat of the Tariff Reform election of 1906 and nothing came of the Council. But these ideas were taken up again by the League of Empire at the Imperial Conference on Education in 1907 (UAA: S200/1905/22).

Drafting an agenda in which the first item was a proposal for the federation of the British Empire through education and the second was a plan for a permanent central bureau, the League eagerly sent copies to the various boards of education in the various colonies. But their replies gave voice to another sentiment that would dog the subsequent history of the Bureau. Many colonial boards dismissed federation entirely, while others were extremely unenthusiastic about the plans for a central bureau (Greenlee, 1979: 58). At the meeting itself, every attempt to introduce into discussion schemes designed to centralise the curriculum were met with the delegates' 'grave misgivings' or outright rejection. Although they freely acknowledged their shared connections and common aims, as James Greenlee pointed out, 'neither the British nor the Dominion boards [of education] proved willing to submerge their autonomy in a certralized [*sic*] imperial system' (Greenlee, 1979: 59, 60).

In 1907 it was clear that although they attested to their membership of a common community, universities were unwilling to consent to anything that they thought would compromise their autonomy.

The 1912 Congress and the Birth of the Bureau

These were mistakes that, a few years later, R.D. Roberts was careful not to make. In late 1909, the English civic universities and colleges had approached the University of London and asked it to host a 'Modern Universities Congress', which they hoped would 'convey to the public mind, particularly at the seat of Government…[the universities'] claims to public support' (ULA: ST2/1/11/17 Nov 1909).

However, with their own external degree programme perhaps in view, the Academic Council of the University of London had seen these aims as part of an imperial, rather than a national, discussion and suggested they instead be raised within the context of an Empire-wide universities' congress. The Senate duly adopted their resolution, and elected a 'preliminary' committee which, by June the following year, had appointed Roberts as its Organising Secretary (ULA: ST2/1/11: 15 Dec 1909; 23 Feb 1910; 15 June 1910).

Not only did Roberts make sure that this time the Indian universities were invited, but from the beginning he also included both the

Indian universities and the settler institutions in the planning process. At his suggestion, regional planning conferences were held, bringing the universities in the various colonies together, often for the first time. Although these meetings laid the foundations for what would later become national conferences, in 1912 they remained essentially subcommittees that met as constituent parts of a wider imperial enterprise. They helped to feed information about the colonial universities' wishes and concerns back to Roberts in London. As he made clear in a statement intended for distribution to the press, unlike the 1903 and 1907 meetings, the 1912 Congress was to be truly representative and consultative. In contrast to the earlier events, it would not seek formal federation (*Congress*, 1912: 4).

But, like Parker's 1903 conference, the 1912 Congress was much more than an academic meeting. When the delegates arrived in London, they were greeted with a full programme of events, with tours to various universities across the United Kingdom running both before and after the event. At Aberdeen, delegates were entertained at luncheon in the Palace Hotel by the Principal, G. Adam Smith; at Edinburgh, they attended a concert arranged by the Union Musical Society; at Durham, they went round the castle; and at Oxford and Cambridge, they were guests at the various colleges. All these visits were accompanied by dinners and toasts and honorary degree ceremonies, and were attended by wives and daughters as well. But by Monday, 1 July, they were all back in London to attend the theatre, to lunch the next day with the Prime Minister and Prince Arthur of Connaught at the Savoy Hotel and to go to the formal reception at the University of London that was attended by more than 2,500 guests (*Congress*, 1912: xiv–xxvi).

In and around these London events, the Congress itself took place. Thanks to Roberts' consultative approach, its agenda was much more extensive and practical than that tabled in either 1903 or 1907. Some of the questions that featured in 1903, such as the specialisation of studies, reciprocal recognition, and teacher and student interchange were again on the programme, but issues such as residential facilities, entrance requirements, remuneration, university extension and the position of technical and professional education were also subjects of individual sessions.

However, through all these discussions continued to run the themes that had attended the earlier meetings. Delegates once again emphasised the existing connections linking universities, invoking—despite the presence of the Indian delegates—an expansive conception of the

British nation that extended to the settler colonies. Lord Strathcona spoke of the great 'Anglo-Saxon Community', George Parkin alluded to 'our British people', while James Barrett spoke of welcoming to Australia's shores 'people of our own race' (Ashby, 1963: 6; *Congress*, 1912: xxii, 217, 307, 310). Similarly, delegates expressed their wish that these connections should be fostered and given what Oxford's P.E. Matheson called 'practical recognition'. But at the same time, there were also repeated assertions of the independence of British universities. As Matheson continued:

> [I]f unity is a vital principle of our commonwealth of learning, that does not mean uniformity. Variety is one of the 'notes' of our political arrangements, and it is no less vital in our educational structure.
>
> (*Congress*, 1912: 198)

Indeed, this was a point that those proposing the establishment of a body that would act as 'a connecting link between all our world-wide experiences' were especially keen to emphasise. 'Individuality and independence rather than uniformity constitute the characteristic note of British Universities,' George Parkin reassured the delegates, 'and anything that tends to unnecessary uniformity would be open to strong objection' (*Congress*, 1912: 323).

Charged with the task of fostering ties between universities, but restricted by its need to respect their autonomy, the Bureau was initially conceived as a body that would focus on building informal connections, and this was the chief role laid out for it in 1912 by Parkin. He suggested that the Bureau might produce a 'University Year Book' that provided, in one volume, information about the specialisms, entrance requirements and staff of all the universities of the British Empire and serving as 'the missing link' between them (*Congress*, 1912: 323). It might also collect information about approaching appointments and distribute them throughout the university world; it might arrange the temporary exchange of professors and circulate information about courses that would enable the 'interchange' of students; and it might organise another Congress. More hesitantly, Parkin proposed some practical measures he thought might also be helpful—a common matriculation standard and a degree of specialisation between institutions—but his emphasis remained on ways that 'intimate co-operation' might be 'obtained by frequent and friendly consultation' (*Congress*, 1912: 315).

These were the suggestions that the organisation that was brought into being in January 1913 set about enacting. It rented a room in the Imperial Institute in South Kensington in London, appointed a part-time assistant secretary, advertised itself as an appointments agency, and began planning a second Congress. In 1914 it also published the first edition of the *Yearbook*, which provided, in one volume, information about the courses, entrance requirements and staff of all the universities of the British Empire.

For its first six years the Bureau was funded entirely by the voluntary subscriptions of its members. The suggested contribution from the bigger institutions was £50 a year, and £25 from the smaller ones, but some universities were more reluctant than others. As Ashby noted in his memoir, Cambridge initially declined to subscribe and Sheffield never made a payment. By contrast, many of the colonial universities were more enthusiastic. For four years Adelaide paid £20 per annum, the University of New Zealand £25 per annum, and Melbourne made an annual contribution of £60 (UAA: Series 200/1914/208; UNZ: W3119/Vol. 7/Jan. 1917; UMA: UM312/1920/444).

But despite this varied commitment, the Bureau's early life was promising. Working within the bounds established at the 1912 Congress, the Bureau squared the circle of imperial co-operation and university independence, by focusing on ways it could foster the already existing ties that university delegates had been pointing to since Gilbert Parker's conference in 1903.

The Bureau between the Wars, 1918–39

The outbreak of war in 1914 seriously curtailed the Bureau's growth, but it limped through, sustained largely by the efforts of its Honorary Secretary, Alex Hill, also Principal of the University College of Southampton.

When the conflict ended, the Bureau was the only formal association of universities in Britain. Under its auspices, the first Conference of British Universities was held in May 1917, to consider the establishment of a PhD in Britain. The conference adjourned for a year so that representatives could ascertain the views of their respective governing bodies. On the day before the conference reconvened, the Foreign Secretary, A.J. Balfour, summoned the delegates to the Foreign Office. Having recently returned from a trip to the United States, he pressed upon the universities the need to establish a doctorate in order 'to divert to Britain the traffic in scholars and scientists which before the war had gone to Germany'. But in addition to the PhD, Balfour—a prominent member of the 1903 conference—also made clear his desire to see extended 'the tentative efforts at common expression, which began in 1912 with the foundation of the Bureau', seeing it as an organisation that would help to 'facilitate the interchange of students' (Ashby, 1963: 21–22).

At the meeting in 1918—attended not only by representatives from all the British universities, but also by those from Australia, Canada, and New Zealand—both proposals were enacted: the PhD was inaugurated; and a 'Standing Committee' consisting of the executive committee of the Bureau and the vice-chancellor or principal of each university in the UK was established. It was, therefore, under the Bureau's auspices that the British universities first came together.

In this new climate of government interest, the Bureau's Committee lobbied for some much-needed financial support. In early 1919, the Board of Education made it a one-off grant of £5,000, subject to two conditions: that it become a corporation capable of holding property, and that it pay for its maintenance out of its own funds. These stipulations forced the Bureau to institutionalise, but they did not significantly change its essential character. For although in 1919 the organisation incorporated under the Companies Act, attempts to consider its wider role immediately became mired in conflict.

In July 1919, Ramsay Muir (a member of Sadler's Commission on Calcutta University) and Gregory Foster (the Provost of University College London) were appointed to a sub-committee and asked to produce a paper on the aims and objectives of the organisation. In their subsequent report they noted that the 'present machinery for managing the Bureau would be inadequate for the functions it would be called upon to perform', and recommended the establishment of a formally elected representative council to oversee its work and annually to appoint its officers. But Alex Hill objected to these moves, accusing Muir of exceeding the terms of the sub-committee's reference. As Ashby pointed out, 'one cannot help feeling that the technical objection covered a disinclination on Hill's part to see the Bureau become more formal and professionalized' (Ashby, 1963: 28–29).

For a time in 1920 there was a suggestion that the organisation should seek a Royal Charter, but this was resoundingly rejected by the member universities, which were still concerned about their autonomy. In the end, the Articles of Association remained, though in amended form. Hill retained his ongoing role as Honorary Secretary, and the Bureau continued throughout the 1920s to be an organisation characterised by largely informal practices and procedures (USA: G3/13/723; *Congress*, 1921: 434).

However, in the immediate aftermath of the war, the financial injection from the Board of Education helped the organisation to spring into new life. It purchased a 10-year lease on a house at 50 Russell Square, and looked to its members—both in Britain and overseas—to fund its operational costs (Ashby, 1963: 10–16, 23–26). Meanwhile, the universities sought to reposition themselves as national institutions that were helping to rebuild the post-war world. On the one hand, they highlighted their role in fostering scientific knowledge and, on the other, they emphasised their role in shaping the character of Britain's new economic and social elites.

The Bureau became the representative body for the emerging university sector. By 1919 Alex Hill could write: '[I]n a very much larger sense than heretofore the Bureau is now recognized by the Board of Education, the Treasury, the Foreign Office, and the other Government Departments as their medium of communication with the Universities' (UMA: UM312/1920/444).

Yet despite its new contribution to home, the Bureau's horizon continued to stretch abroad. For, as far as the Bureau was concerned, its new domestic activities were part of its broader imperial mission and the ways it found to deal with the new challenges of the period reflected its own expansive definition of the British nation. Fundamentally, it was by improving access horizontally across the Empire, rather than vertically among the people at home, that the Bureau believed its contribution to nation-building lay.

But in pursuing this agenda, the Bureau was constrained by its inability to act on behalf of its member institutions. For, despite the wishes of the government, the universities remained highly sceptical of anything that seemed to threaten their independence. Therefore, the Bureau set about resuming its pre-war task of incorporating the resources of the British 'overseas universities' through a more efficient distribution of information, producing a steady flow of reports, booklets, surveys, programmes and circulars designed to facilitate unofficial, rather than official, coordination. These included 'lists of Students from abroad studying in the Home Universities', statements of the Bureau's accounts and minutes of its meetings, titles of theses approved for research degrees, proposals for graduate-tours, and various agitations about ways to foster student exchange. A large amount of information was procured for the annual editions of the *Yearbook* and a flurry of consultative correspondence took place in the lead-up to the Congresses, which the Bureau continued to organise every five years. By informing universities about each other, the Bureau sought to build the links between them (UMA: UM312/1921/482; UM312/1927/557).

It also strove to foster the informal ties between individual scholars: first, through its focus on 'interchange' or mobility; and second, through the Congresses themselves. Indeed, the subject of 'interchange' was one that had been a feature of Congress meetings since the 1903 conference. While the Rhodes and 1851 Exhibition Scholarship programmes were repeatedly cited as exemplary ways of enabling student mobility, when it came to staff, various schemes were proposed. In 1921 the institution of a system of sabbatical leave was suggested; in 1926 energy focused on establishing an Empire-wide Federated Superannuation Scheme; and in 1936 a special committee was established 'to inquire into the possibility of effecting the exchange of members of University Teaching Staffs' (*Second Congress*, 1921: 388–92; *Third Congress*, 1926: 244; *Fifth Quinquennial Congress*, 1936: 230).

Nor was the Bureau inactive between the Congresses: in 1922 it appointed 'interchange correspondents' in each university, and by 1927 it could report that it had 'arranged for the temporary exchange of junior posts between teachers in Great Britain and teachers in the Dominions' (UMA: UM312/1927/558).

Indeed, the quinquennial Congresses themselves were designed as much as occasions at which academics from across the Empire could come together, as they were opportunities for the formal exchange of ideas. As A.C. Seward, Vice-Chancellor of the University of Cambridge, noted in the closing session of the 1926 meeting, 'the great advantage of a congress is not so much what one gets from listening to discussions but from the personal contact between the members' (*Third Congress*, 1926: 261). Repeating the pattern set by Parker's 1903 conference, each meeting was accompanied by a dizzying array of social events, official dinners, honorary degree ceremonies, train journeys, and university tours that afforded every opportunity for delegates to forge and foster relations with each other. At the same time, as they sought to formalise and describe the personal connections that wrapped up the British academic world, the Congresses also worked to re-inscribe and extend them.

However, despite its best efforts, in the 1920s the Bureau continued to struggle to win the confidence of many of its members. In part this was because, for the older settler universities in particular, it did not seem to offer anything particularly new. Replying in 1925 to a letter from the Bureau advertising its services as an employment and introduction agency, information centre and a 'firstrate club', the registrar of the University of Melbourne was clear about this (UMA: UM312/1924/503). After acknowledging that some of the members of his University 'from time to time call upon [the Bureau]', and expressing his hope that they might do so more in the future, the registrar explained that

> [t]his country [Australia] and this University in particular is not yet (and I hope never will be) very rigidly cut off from the Old country. Most of our Professors come from British Universities and have Home connections so that when they go to England they do not go as strangers in a strange country.
>
> (UMA: UM312/1925/503)

Indeed, in 1926, following a request from the Bureau for the University of Melbourne to increase its annual grant, the registrar responded by reducing it to only £20 per year (UMA: UM312/1926/535)! Oxford and Cambridge, too, continued to remain sceptical of the Bureau's value. For example, despite its efforts to collate and disseminate information about admission, in 1928 Oxford still insisted on communicating directly with Dominion universities regarding entrance requirements (UMA: UM312/1928/176). As far as the more established universities were concerned, the Bureau had been grafted onto an already existing system of personal connection that was largely independent of its efforts and offices (Pietsch, 2013).

But distrust in the organisation also sprang from its lack of professionalism. Administered by the proprietorial Alex Hill, throughout the 1920s it laboured with too few employees in a dilapidated building at the Imperial Institute and struggled to manage the one task that was clearly its own: the dissemination of information (Ashby, 1963: 32).

Between 1921 and 1925 the Bureau only just broke even, and in 1926 it lost £400 on the distribution of the *Yearbook* alone. Universities began to withdraw their support, with subscriptions from them declining from £2,776 in 1924–25, to between £2,169 and £2,483 in the years before 1929. As the report for 1931 outlined: 'These defects caused congestion and delays, discouraged initiative and rendered impossible the development of a coherent and purposeful policy' (Ashby, 1963: 103; *Fourth Congress*, 1931: 261, 251; UMA: UM312/1926/535).

The death of Alex Hill in 1929 created an opportunity for reform. Frank Heath, formerly Secretary of the (British) Department of Scientific and Industrial Research, was appointed to review the Bureau's workings. Increasing the staff, and doubling the annual expenditure, Heath also proposed constitutional changes that substituted the old Articles of Association under which the Bureau operated as an association of persons, with new ones that defined it as a 'world-wide association of corporate bodies—of Universities' (*Fourth Congress*, 1931: 213). Heath also suggested a minimum subscription rate and proposed converting the Executive Committee (which was formerly required to have between 10 and 20 members) with an Executive Council (which would consist of 21 members from various parts of the Empire).

Given the difficulties faced by previous efforts at organisational reform, it is perhaps not surprising that the passage of these constitutional changes was anything but smooth. Once again, fears that universities' autonomy would be compromised drove the disquiet. As Ashby records, in the end it was Michael Sadler's suggestion that a sentence stipulating that 'the powers of the Association shall not be exercised in any such way as to restrict the powers and duties exercised by the constituent members under the several charters, statutes, regulations and other instruments of their self-government' that saved the day (Ashby, 1963: 36–37).

Heath's reforms revived the Bureau, and from the early 1930s universities and colleges from various parts of the Commonwealth began increasingly to use its services. One of these was the appointments service that had been so scorned by the Melbourne registrar in 1925. Initially, it was the newer and smaller universities—some in the settler colonies but mostly those in India and the new university colleges growing up in East Asia—that were the keenest. But increasingly the older settler institutions were also persuaded. Although in 1932 Melbourne was still sceptical—'I am afraid that we do not look upon our membership of the Bureau as being of very much practical use', wrote the registrar—by 1933 both it and Sydney were employing Heath on a trial basis to chair their selection committees. Indeed, from the mid-1930s the Bureau offered a more professional—and cheaper—appointments service than could committees of selection constituted through individual university networks. By 1933 the Bureau could report that '[u]niversities overseas are enlisting the services of the Bureau more and more in filling vacant appointments' (UMA: UM312/1933/403).

The Bureau's standing with its member universities was also enhanced by its management of the grant made to it by the Carnegie Corporation of New York in 1930, the terms of which stipulated only that the sum of US$40,000 should 'be expended for the benefit of Empire Universities Overseas' (*Times*, 1932). After spending some of this money to enable settler and Indian delegates to attend the 1931 Congress, the Bureau determined that the balance should be used to permit 'selected members of the teaching and administrative staffs of oversea [*sic*] universities' to visit the United Kingdom for the purpose of advanced study or research work. Bringing such individuals 'into personal contact with each other' would, the Bureau felt, 'promote closer cooperation between the oversea [*sic*] and the home universities' (*Times*, 1932).

Together with Heath's reforms, the management of the Carnegie Grants helped to raise the Bureau's profile in the eyes of its member institutions. In offering the possibility of tangible benefits, it provided an incentive for universities abroad to begin to utilise the Bureau's other services as well. Thus, it was not until the 1930s that the Bureau began to assume the functions that had been imputed to it at its inception.

Yet the Bureau's commitment to an expansive conception of the British nation also masked tensions within it. The differences between Oxford and Cambridge and the newer colonial and civic universities became particularly evident in discussions about the 'specialisation of studies'. This was the idea that, in order to maximise their 'efficiency', each university should be specialising in a particular set of subjects, which built upon what Lord Crewe called 'its local advantages'—the natural, industrial or professional character of the region in which it was located (*Second Congress*, 1921: 292). As far as the Bureau was concerned, the 'nation, as a whole' included the British settler colonies, and therefore the 'distribution of studies' should encompass colonial universities as well (USA: G3/13/723). But such specialisation was initially thought to be contingent upon universities accepting each other's matriculation examinations. This was a move that both the colonial and the newer civic universities welcomed, but it met with resistance from the ancient English universities.

Professor J.W. Gregory, who represented the University of Melbourne at the 1921 Congress, summarised their objection succinctly when, in his report of the event for the Melbourne Council, he described 'the impossibility of securing uniformity of treatment throughout the Universities of the Empire'. In Britain, he pointed out, university 'officials at once consider the application of any proposal to the smaller theological Universities of Canada or perhaps of some of the less efficient departments in the increasing universities of India'. He suggested that it was this that made them unlikely to adopt a universal standard (UMA: UM312/1921/113).

In fact, as Gregory's comment suggests, the place of the Indian delegates at the Bureau remained a fraught one. The official rhetoric of the inter-war Congresses was one that, nominally at least, extended to all the universities of the British Empire. Indeed, as Sir Deva Prasad Sarvadhikari from Benares noted, the 1921 Congress 'differ[ed] from the last', because at it the Indian universities for the first time enjoyed 'all the advantage of corporate life' (*Second Congress*, 1921: 420).

Hong Kong, Malta and Rangoon sent official delegates to the Congresses from 1912, 1921, and 1926, respectively (with Shantung in China also doing so in 1926), and by 1931 Raffles College and the King Edward VII College of Medicine in Singapore together with the Imperial College of Agriculture in Trinidad were also able to send non-voting representatives. Congress discussions after 1926 were characterised by less overt references to 'racial unity' and by more coded celebrations of apparently 'shared' cultural norms, such as law and literature, history, 'common ideals', and mutual loyalty.

But despite these representative and discursive shifts, little actually changed. The Indian and South East Asian delegates were merely grafted onto an older imagining of the socially and racially circumscribed British academic world that had been articulated since 1903. This marginalisation was reinforced by Congress programmes that did little to address the place of India. As Professor J. Mitter from Allahabad noted in 1936, 'it was the Dominions which were chiefly referred to and…India unfortunately seemed to take a very back place' (*Fifth Congress*, 1936: 64). The 1931 plea of Aligarh's representative, Fakhruddin Ahmad, that the Bureau should give 'greater attention to the discussion of the Indian University problems and their solution, so that the much desired end of closer co-operation and understanding with Indians may be more rapidly and surely attained', went unheeded (*Fourth Congress*, 1931: 212).

The inter-war Congresses, therefore, exhibited the same contradictory language and the same 'durability of British ideas of "racial" hierarchy' evident in other aspects of British imperial culture in this period (Furedi, 1998; Stephen, 2011: 167; Tabili, 1994). Although the professional activities of the Bureau were officially extended to Indian and

South East Asian institutions, in this period the essential 'British' and unofficial character of the community that the Bureau had originally been designed to foster was not fundamentally re-imagined.

Conclusion

Despite the appearance of alternate political currents that were beginning to frame new national and international alliances, an older, affective and expansive vision of the British nation remained central to the Bureau's sense of its role between the wars.

The Second World War would bring much broader changes to its self-conception and design. But for its first 25 years, the Bureau remained an organisation that—characterised by largely informal modes of operation and focused on fostering unofficial forms of connection—still bore the marks of its early growth and development.

Bibliography

Works Cited

Ashby, E. (1963) *Community of Universities: An Informal Portrait of the Association of Universities of the British Commonwealth, 1913–1963.* Cambridge: University Press.

Bell, D. (2007) *The Idea of Greater Britain: Empire and the Future of World Order, 1860–1900*. Princeton, N.J.: Princeton University Press.

Congress of the Universities of the Empire, 1912: Report of Proceedings (1912). London: Hodder & Stoughton.

Empire Review (1903) Official Report of the Allied Colonial Universities Conference. *Empire Review*, 6: 71–128.

Fifth Quinquennial Congress of the Universities of the British Empire, 1936: Report of Proceedings (1936). London: G. Bell & Sons.

Fourth Congress of the Universities of the Empire, 1931: Report of Proceedings (1931). London: G. Bell & Sons.

Furedi, F. (1998) *The Silent War: Imperialism and the Changing Perception of Race*. London: Pluto.

Greenlee, J. (1979) The ABC's of imperial unity, *Canadian Journal of History* 14: 49–64.

Greenlee, J. (1987) *Education and Imperial Unity, 1901–1926*. New York: Garland.

Pietsch, T. (2013) *Empire of Scholars: Universities, Networks and the British Academic World, 1850–1939*. Manchester: Manchester University Press.

Second Congress of the Universities of the Empire, 1921: Report of Proceedings (1921). London: G. Bell & Sons.

Stephen, D.M. (2011) 'Brothers of the Empire?': India and the British Empire Exhibition of 1924–25, *Twentieth Century British History*, 22: 164–88.

Tabili, L. (1994) *We Ask for British Justice: Workers and Racial Difference in Late Imperial Britain*. Ithaca: Cornell University Press.

Times (1932) Empire Universities Carnegie Research Grants. *Times*, 6 June 1932, London.

Third Congress of the Universities of the Empire, 1926: Report of Proceedings (1926). London: G. Bell & Sons.

Thompson, A.S. (2000) *Imperial Britain: The Empire in British Politics, c.1880–1932*. Harlow: Longman.

UAA. S200. University of Adelaide Archives. Registrar's Correspondence.

ULA. ST2. University of London Archives. Minutes of Senate and Appendices 1909–10.

UMA. UM312. University of Melbourne Archives. Registrar's Correspondence.

UNZ. W3119. University of New Zealand Archives. Minutes of Proceedings of the Senate of the University of New Zealand.

USA. G3. University of Sydney Archives. Registrar's General Subject Files.

Yearbook of the Universities of the British Empire, 1918–19 (1918). London: G. Bell & Sons.

2

After Empire: The 'London Model' Transformed since the Second World War

Graeme Davies and Svava Bjarnason

Introduction: Unity in Diversity

From the first concept of a bringing together of the universities of the then British Empire, through the formal creation of the 'Universities' Bureau' in 1913, and the quinquennial Congresses in the inter-war years to 1939, there emerged a remarkable co-operative network of professional higher education association and provision.

Over that period, there was indeed a steady build-up in trust as the original concerns and suspicions of the colonial universities were overtaken by positive outcomes engendered by interchange, frequent meetings, commitments to networking collaboration and to the recognition that, even in the higher education domain, 'the whole can be greater than the sum of its parts'. A continuous and critical thread that ran through the whole of this period up to 1939 was the unfaltering commitment of the member universities, both in the UK and abroad, to the belief that any formalised Association must not impinge on the autonomy of individual institutions.

One important aspect of this autonomy was the belief that schemes designed in any way to centralise the curriculum were quite unacceptable.

To some extent this could be seen as paradoxical, since a great many of the staff of the universities across the Empire had common academic experiences, including exposure to curricula that had much in common. It can be argued that this commonality of experience was reinforced by the central role that the Bureau increasingly played in facilitating the appointment of UK academics to posts in the colonial universities. Nevertheless, it was the belief that continued to be seen as important, as events unfolded in the post-war period.

Not surprisingly, little development occurred in the war years of 1939–45. If anything, there was a weakening of cohesion, which led to a 'moment of danger' in 1946, identified by Ashby (Ashby, 1963: 37), 'when the fatigue of war and preoccupation with their domestic post-war problems left universities very little energy to think about inter-University affairs'. The situation was positively advanced by a combination of individual enthusiasm and careful negotiation, which led to the Congress in Oxford in 1948, when the Bureau 'almost silently and with evident relief' (Ashby, 1963) evolved into the Association of Universities of the British Commonwealth (AUBC).

In parallel with the growth of the Commonwealth interest across the globe, there was a particular growth of interaction between the British universities and universities in Canada and the United States. In each of these jurisdictions there was a clear recognition that there would be both societal and economic benefits in growing the numbers of graduates emerging from higher education institutions. This was, of course, equally the case across the Commonwealth, which in turn led to expansion of the various university systems.

This chapter sets out the crucial role that the University of London has played over the course of the last 150 years in extending the reach of the UK's model of education, and also in supporting the establishment and growth of universities in the UK and throughout the Commonwealth. Here was a veritable making of new universities in the New World.

The London Model and Distance Learning

The University of London was established by Royal Charter in 1836; and in England, only the Universities of Oxford and Cambridge predate it. It grew out of University College London, founded in 1826, and King's College, London, founded in 1829.

The University of London was initially established as a federal body, to act as an examining body for its colleges and other 'approved institutions' within its powers to award degrees embodied in the original Charter. It acted solely in this capacity until 1858. It awarded its first degrees (29) in the Arts in 1839. In 1858, the University opened its degrees to any (male) students, regardless of their geographical location; the first women students graduated in 1880.

This led to the University assuming a very seminal role in the dissemination of educational opportunities both in the UK and across the wider Commonwealth. In essence, it was the birth of what is now widely known as 'distance learning'.

In so far as the Bureau, the AUBC and its successor—the Association of Commonwealth Universities (ACU)—are concerned, the connection with the University of London is strong historically. The University hosted the first Congress in 1912 and subsequent Congresses in 1931 and 1963. But it played a much more important role in the university world through making available its External Degree from 1858.

The External Degree concept was based upon very simple premises.

First, as pointed out by Kenyon Jones in her comprehensive history of the External Degree programme and system (Kenyon Jones, 2008), it is the key clause 36 of the 1858 Charter of the University of London that is a statement 'of one of the most enduringly significant changes and developments ever in British (and, later, worldwide) higher education':

> We [Queen Victoria] do further will and ordain, That persons not educated in any of the said Institutions connected with the said University shall be admitted as Candidates for Matriculation, and for any of the Degrees here by authorised to be conferred by the said University of London other than Medical Degrees, on such conditions as the said Chancellor, Vice-Chancellor and Fellows, by regulations in that behalf shall from time to time determine, such Regulations being subject to the Provisoes [*sic*] and Restrictions herein contained.
>
> (Kenyon Jones, 2008)

The significance lies in the words 'not educated', as this opened the London degree to all potential students who could fulfil the entry requirements and pay the fees. The change was unexpectedly far-reaching. As such, it provided access to students across the world and, over the years, a great many persons of distinction gained their academic qualifications through making use of what became known as the 'London external system'. These include the Nobel prize winners Ronald Coase

(Economics), Frederick Gowland Hopkins (Medicine), Wole Soyinka (Literature), Derek Walcott (Literature), and Nelson Mandela (Peace); and distinguished politicians and writers, such as H.G. Wells, Mahatma Gandhi, Wilfred Owen, D.H. Lawrence, and Dr Luisa Diogo (Prime Minister of Mozambique).

But the benefits of this system were very wide-reaching in international educational terms. Later in the century, it enabled a new wave of regional universities around the UK, funded by local benefactors, to award London degrees while they waited for their own Royal Charters—which then endowed them with their own degree-granting powers. It also allowed the extension of this permission to cover the whole of the then British Empire. Mauritius, in 1865, was the first colonial government to take advantage of this enabling permission, by then establishing its first university.

The second premise—one that has played a critically important role even to the present day in maintaining the quality and integrity of the degree—was the procedure wherein examination papers were sent to authorised institutions at home and abroad; and where students were made to sit under rigorous supervision, with the scripts being returned to London scholars for marking and grading. This procedure also made it possible for students, including those committed to earning their living while studying, to proceed to a degree without going to college at all. Thus, within a scrupulous and thorough assessment system, the open and flexible distance education procedures so currently prevalent were anticipated by more than 100 years.

Not surprisingly, this led to a very rapid and extensive expansion of higher education provision across what is now the Commonwealth, as governments sought to meet the burgeoning demand. The example of Mauritius was followed in South Africa and the West Indies in 1871, when examination centres were set up in those regions. In the 1880s and 1890s, centres were established in Canada, New Zealand, Sri Lanka (Ceylon), Hong Kong, Australia, the Bahamas, Bermuda, Singapore, and Nigeria. By 1943 there were more than 50 centres overseas (Kenyon Jones, 2008). There were also centres in countries outside the Commonwealth—for example, China, Iraq, Turkey, Egypt, Thailand (Siam), Argentina, Saudi Arabia, and the United States.

However, in the present context, it is the extensive network in the UK and across the now Commonwealth that is the most significant.

Early Foundations and Transformations

While it is clear that the University of London, through its External Degree, played a very important role in the expansion of higher education across the Commonwealth, the story does not end there.

Many colleges had been established by governments for the delivery of the learning necessary to bring students to an educational level that made it likely that they would be successful in the London examinations. While it must be acknowledged that those examinations per se were closely related to, and dependent upon, curriculum content largely determined in London by the colleges of the University, there was encouragement, whenever possible, to bring into courses subject matter that related to local circumstances and events. Quite naturally this led to a growing desire in the various jurisdictions for the local colleges to become universities in their own right.

It is not surprising that, in the first instance, the University of London played a significant role in the development of the university system in the UK. All the English and Welsh universities founded between 1849 and 1949, and many other colleges that subsequently became universities, served what was a form of 'apprenticeship' through offering London degrees by external study for comparatively short periods, before they received the Royal Charters that authorised them to award their own degrees (Kenyon Jones, 2008).

However, there was a small group of universities in the UK—Nottingham, Southampton, Leicester, Hull, and Exeter—that had more long-standing dependence upon the University of London. These had been established as University Colleges in 1881, 1902, 1918, 1922, and 1927, respectively, but they did not gain the Royal Charters which gave them full University status until well into the twentieth century.

The formal histories of each of these institutions make clear that there was an increasing sense of frustration with their state of dependence, since there was a manifest need to meet the curricula and operational requirements of the University of London. Each institution had extensive dialogue with the appropriate authorities as they pursued independence, and progressively they gained their individual Royal Charters—Nottingham in 1948, Southampton in 1952, Hull in 1954, Exeter in 1955, and Leicester in 1957. (In this context, it is of interest to note that a Royal Charter is a formal document issued by the reigning monarch as 'Letters Patent' which, in the case of a university, grants inter alia degree-awarding powers.)

For the overseas institutions, however, the situation was much more complex. First, there was a significant educational divide between the major countries of what is now the Commonwealth and the smaller colonial jurisdictions. The major members—Australia, Canada, India, New Zealand, and South Africa—were granted the right to have universities as part of the instruments agreed either before, or when, they were granted their special status as Dominions. Thus, by the end of the nineteenth century there were well-established universities and/or university colleges in each of these colonial regions.

This privileged position was also accorded to some other jurisdictions within the then British Empire, notably Hong Kong, Singapore, and Ceylon (Sri Lanka). However, developments in all these countries were influenced by the University of London—not through affiliation, but through adopting the affiliated structure of the University of London. For example, although the universities in New Zealand never had a formal link with the University of London, it is interesting to note that when the University of New Zealand was constituted in 1874, it was effectively a federal university modelled on the University of London functioning principally as an examining body. This was also the case for the University of the Cape of Good Hope, when it was constituted in 1875 and authorised to be responsible for examinations throughout South Africa. In Canada, similar structures were adopted, but on a regional basis. For instance, the University of Toronto acted as an examining and degree-awarding body for the Province of Ontario from 1853 to 1887, by utilising an operating model based on that of the University of London.

In this context, the position in Ceylon (Sri Lanka) was particularly unusual, since the evolution that led to the creation of the University of Ceylon in 1942 involved academic relationships with both the Universities of Oxford and London (Carr-Saunders, 1961: 240–41). That with Oxford was more advisory in nature, whereas the relationship with London was, as it became with other institutions, based on the availability of examinations of the required status.

Turning Point: The Asquith Commission 1943

In so far as the other colonial jurisdictions were concerned, undoubtedly the most significant event was the setting up of the Asquith Commission in August 1943, which reported in June 1945 (Cmd. 6647, 1945). The terms of reference for the Commission were quite clear:

> To consider the principles which should guide the promotion of higher education, learning and research and the development of universities in the Colonies; and to explore the meanings whereby universities and other appropriate bodies in the United Kingdom may be able to co-operate with institutions of higher education in the Colonies in order to give effect to these principles.
>
> (Cmd. 6647, 1945)

The work of the Commission was strongly influenced by previous deliberations in a Sub-Committee of the Colonial Office's Advisory Committee on Education in the Colonies—chaired by Professor H.J. Channon—which submitted a significant report in May 1943. The important work of the Channon and Asquith bodies has been very well documented—see, for instance, Carr-Saunders (1961), Maxwell (1980), and Pattison (1984).

The Asquith Commission came forward with 68 recommendations under key headings, including:

- the place of universities and university colleges in the development of higher education
- academic life and range of studies
- the staffing of universities
- the place of research
- an Inter-University Council for Higher Education in the Colonies
- the governing authority of Colonial universities and colleges
- the period of transition from college to full university status
- entrance qualifications
- scholarships and financial assistance
- colonial students in this country (the UK)
- finance
- the training of teachers
- the medium of instruction and linguistic training

In general educational terms, the creation of the Inter-University Council was of great significance and would have very far-reaching effects. The development of the Inter-University Council and its seminal contributions to higher education are described very fully by Maxwell (1980).

As far as the role of the University of London was concerned, there was one very important recommendation that read as follows:

> It is recommended therefore that for this interim period the Colonial colleges should enter into a special relationship with London University under which, subject to certain safeguards detailed in the report, their students may be awarded the degrees of that University. The University has agreed to consult with the colleges in order to secure that while the standard of the London degree is maintained, the syllabuses and examination requirements should be adjusted to meet local conditions.
>
> (Maxwell, 1980)

The 'safeguards' referred to a basic stipulation from the University of London that: 'the Colonial colleges which participate in the scheme must have reached a certain stage in development'. This meant that in order to participate, a college must, for example 'have an adequate staff, whose control of academic work is constitutionally established; it must be adequately equipped and must have satisfactory standards of entrance requirements' (Cmd. 6647, 1945: 41).

The Senate of the University of London had made it quite clear that it was fully committed to the scheme, by indicating that 'it had the following aims prominently in mind':

> (i) the establishment of direct and easy co-operation between the Academic Boards of the Colonial colleges and the Senate of the University,
> (ii) the institution of a regular system of consultation between the authorities of the University and the staffs of the colleges upon questions of syllabuses and examination requirements,
> (iii) the promotion of personal contact between the external examiners appointed by the University and the teachers in the colleges, in part by visits of the examiners to the colleges,
> (iv) the participation of members of the staffs of the colleges in the actual work of examining their own students.
>
> (Maxwell, 1980)

The intentions of the Asquith Commission were simple and clear (Cmd. 6647, 1945: 10–14): 'the early creation of universities so situated that, as far as is compatible with geography, the remaining areas of the Colonial Empire shall be served by one of them'. They saw the development of university systems as 'an inescapable corollary of any policy which aims at the achievement of Colonial self-government'.

Further, they saw the evolution of these systems as a process of steady progress, from the setting up of university colleges without degree-awarding powers—this is where the University of London came in—to the development of universities empowered to grant degrees. The Commission emphasised the importance of this evolution being pursued with vigour, simply stating: 'We believe that there should be no undue delay in converting these colleges into universities.'

Matters then proceeded apace. The flexibility of the London 'external' system was based upon a commendable belief that there should be an open approach to the way in which external students prepared themselves for examination. This was seen to be very helpful. For example, no difference was seen between students who had pursued their studies by working independently and those who may have attended college or had access to other forms of outside advice such as, in those days, a correspondence course. This flexibility is still central to the London 'external' programme, except, of course, that now the outside advice is most likely to come through the Internet.

Growth and Consolidation: 1948 and Beyond

Three bodies played critical roles in taking matters forward in the period between 1948 and the early 1960s:

- the Inter-University Council for Higher Education in the Colonies ('in the Colonies' was replaced by 'Overseas' in 1955),
- the Colonial University Grants Advisory Committee, and
- the University of London Senate Committee on Higher Education in the Colonies.

Where possible, they sought to build on existing educational resources in the various Colonies. In some cases, there were well-established colleges more than ready for development, such as Raffles College in Singapore, Codrington College in Barbados, the Prince of Wales College at Achimota in the Gold Coast (now Ghana), Fourah Bay College in Sierra Leone, and the Technical College at Makerere in Uganda. There was also Gordon Memorial College in Khartoum in the Sudan which, while not formally in a Colony, had been part of the deliberations of the Asquith Commission.

However, as is emphasised by Brosseau (2000: 19 et seq., 110), the geographic distribution of existing colleges across the Colonies was very uneven. The most glaring inconsistency was Africa which, in 1946, had only a third of the establishment institutions, despite the population being two-thirds of the Colonies at large. Implementation of the recommendations of the Asquith Commission recognised these inconsistencies, as the existing colleges were developed and new colleges were established. Thus, the university colleges landscape developed comparatively rapidly through the formation of the following institutions:

- University College of the West Indies (1948),
- University College of the Gold Coast, Accra (1948),
- University College, Ibadan (1948), and
- University College of East Africa, Makarere (1949).

The University of London worked with these institutions through a 'special relationship' determined by its Senate Committee, and which had prepared an advisory document to that end (Pattison, 1984: 33 et seq.). This document indicated the general lines through which relationships should develop:

> The Committee has come to the conclusion that it should not advise the Senate at this stage to prescribe any rigid regulations. In recommending any particular Colonial College to the Senate, the Committee would prefer to consider the special circumstances of the institution in relation to the fundamental purpose of the scheme, namely that the University should assist the College through the various stages of its development towards autonomous university status. The Committee will therefore have regard not only to the extent to which a college has already acquired the characteristic qualities of a university, but also to the evidence of its intention to strengthen itself in this regard as rapidly as possible by appropriate stages as opportunity occurs. The Committee is confirmed in this attitude by the fact that the Senate has expressed its readiness to help and advise the Colonial Colleges, if requested to do so, in connection with diploma courses, as well as with courses leading to a degree.
>
> (Pattison, 1984: 33 et seq.)

This document also set out what were considered to be the essential characteristics of a university college seeking, in due course, university status:

It may be of assistance to colleges who may desire to seek association with the University if the Committee expresses its agreement with the general underlying assumptions as to the characteristics of a university contained in the Report of the Asquith Commission and in particular with the following points:

1) A university should encourage the pursuit of a regular and liberal course of education, promote research and the advancement of science and learning, and organise, improve and extend education of a university standard.
2) It should be ready to accept the responsibilities of intellectual leadership in the community it serves and should endeavour to promote within that community a culture rooted in scholarship and knowledge. To this end it should establish and maintain close relations with other forms of educational activity within its area.
3) It should seek to attract to its service teachers of the highest quality who are able and prepared to contribute to the advancement of their respective subjects. To this end it should offer appropriate conditions of service and remuneration; in particular it is of primary importance that the members of its staff should not be so burdened with teaching duties that they have not adequate time to devote to research.
4) It should make provision for the encouragement of corporate and social life among its students.
5) It should provide equipment and laboratories and build up a University library adequate not only for the needs of its undergraduate students but also for the research needs of its teachers and senior students.
6) The constitution of its Governing Body and its Charter, Statutes or other instruments of government should be such as are appropriate to an autonomous University capable of controlling the development of academic policy.

(Pattison, 1984: 33 et seq.)

Because this guidance was quite general in nature, it was expected that the colleges would work with the Inter-University Council and, in turn, other UK universities, in taking forward their development. Pattison (1984) describes in detail how the Senate Committee and the Inter-University Council worked together in the interests of both the existing and the new university colleges. In this context, one of the very important roles that the Inter-University Council played was in helping colleges with the recruitment of academic staff. Here the University of London again had a special role, since a member of its staff was always included in interviewing/appointing committees set up by the Inter-University Council.

But when considering the contribution that the University of London made to the development of higher education more widely, it is now instructive to consider the particular case of the University of Khartoum. Almost immediately after the publication of the Asquith report (in July 1945), the then Gordon Memorial College in Khartoum sought to establish a relationship with London, despite the fact that the Sudan was an Anglo-Egyptian condominium and not actually part of the Empire. After various exchanges and visits, this association was accepted by the University of London Senate in May 1946. The first graduates completed their University of London degrees in 1950 and, in 1951, the institution was renamed 'University College, Khartoum'. It was established as the University of Khartoum, with his own degree-awarding powers, in 1956, when the Sudan gained independence.

The University of London was not alone in sharing its experience with institutions in the Colonies. The development of Fourah Bay College, established in 1827 by the Church Missionary Society, eventually to become the University of Sierra Leone, does not feature in relation to the University of London. Unusually for one of the colleges identified by the Asquith Commission as a site for development, it had been affiliated to the University of Durham in 1876, and finally gained its own Royal Charter in 1960.

The development of the first four university colleges in Africa was not always smooth, although this was more often than not a consequence of local issues rather than any failings in the 'special relationships'. Nevertheless, they did each establish themselves as sound academic institutions over a period of time. Not surprisingly, there was pressure to set up other colleges, and there was progressive growth, with a view to building greater capacity and access on the continent. A College of Technology was established in Kumasi in Ghana in 1951. The work of the Carr-Saunders Commission led to the foundation of the University College of Rhodesia and Nyasaland in 1955. This was followed by the setting up of University College, Dar es Salaam, in 1961, University College of Cape Coast in 1962, and University College, Nairobi, in 1964. All of these institutions had 'special relationships' with the University of London.

By this time, the earlier university colleges had developed considerably, and their need of the 'special relationship' was diminishing. This, together with the gaining of independence of the countries within which they were located, then led progressively to all the university colleges becoming universities with their own degree-awarding powers. This transition often followed from the deliberations of local jurisdictional committees/commissions. The sequence was as follows:

- University of Ghana, 1961
- College of Technology, Kumasi, 1961 (as the Kwame Nkrumah University of Science and Technology)
- University of Ibadan, 1962
- University of the West Indies, 1962
- University of Cape Coast, 1971

Makarere University, the University of Nairobi and the University of Dar es Salaam—all became universities in their own right in 1970, having been brought together in 1963 as the University of East Africa.

Going Forward: The Continuing Role of London University

The role of the University of London in developing higher education opportunities at home and abroad did not stop, or even slow down, when these institutions gained their independence. As is made clear by Kenyon Jones (2008), the External system was active in many spheres, both in the UK and abroad, throughout the time from its fledgling beginnings in Mauritius in 1865 through the 1960s to the present day.

It is currently active in more than 180 countries and provides support for more than 50,000 students. In 2010, it was formally designated as the 'University of London International Academy'—a reflection of the need to recognise that international higher education is of fundamental significance in the educational arena. Its principal mode of operation is still through partnership with higher education institutions in the many jurisdictions it serves, both within and outside the Commonwealth. Indeed, even in recent years, it has played a significant role in supporting institutions that have pursued successfully the gaining of their own degree-awarding powers.

The University of London today is one of the most important federated universities in the world, comprising 18 self-governing colleges, all located in the greater London area, with outstanding national and international reputations. In total, the colleges have over 135,000 students, with more than 25 per cent of these students from overseas.

The 18 colleges collectively cover all disciplines of study, and include the original members, University College London and King's College London, along with others such as the London School of Economics and Political Science, the Institute of Education, the Royal Academy of Music, the Royal Veterinary College, the London Business School, and the Courtauld Institute of Art.

In supporting and promoting higher education in a large number of countries, the University of London has contributed much to what is now known as the 'Knowledge Society'. But this is only one of many inputs. There has been a steady, widespread, and unremitting evolution, both culturally and technologically, of the way in which educational opportunities are presented and disseminated. There have also been a very significant number of professional, cultural, and social developments, initiated and supported by a variety of bodies, including the ACU itself. Not the least of those has been the creation of a unique network of institutional associations across the Commonwealth.

Taken together, here is a special achievement and legacy within the international history of higher education in the globalised world of the twenty-first century.

Bibliography

Ashby, E. (1963) *Community of Universities: An Informal Portrait of the Association of Universities of the British Commonwealth, 1913–1963*. Cambridge: University Press.

Brosseau, C. (2000) *From Colonial Colleges to Commonwealth Universities 1946–1965*. Unpublished M. D'Anglais thesis: Université d'Angers.

Carr-Saunders, A.M. (1961) *New Universities Overseas*. London: George Allen and Unwin Ltd.

Cmd. 6647 (1945) *Report of the Commission on Higher Education in the Colonies*. London: HMSO.

Harte, N. (1986) *The University of London, 1836–1986: An Illustrated History*. London: The Athlone Press Ltd.

Kenyon Jones, C. (2008) *The People's University, 1858–2008*. London: University of London.

Maxwell, I.C.M. (1980) *Universities in Partnership*. Edinburgh: Scottish Academic Press.

Pattison, B. (1984) *Special Relations—The University of London and New Overseas Universities, 1947–1970*. London: University of London.

3

Knowledge Nations: Making the Global University 'Revolution'

Svava Bjarnason and Graeme Davies

Introduction: The Coming of an Educational Revolution

The 'landscape' for this chapter is the last quarter century, which has been a period of exceptional change for higher education across the Commonwealth and beyond. It is clearly not possible to provide a fully comprehensive review of all the issues in this chapter. Instead, what follows is a macro-perspective, which highlights the critical aspects of change that transpired at the turn of the last century and in the early years of the twenty-first century.

In 1988, the then Secretary General of the ACU, in his 'forward look' at the future for the universities of the Commonwealth and beyond, identified a number of 'new' political and economic imperatives, which were beginning to impact upon the world of higher education (Christodoulou, 1988). He foreshadowed changes that he saw as becoming realities for vice-chancellors over the course of the coming decades. These changes included:

- greater partnerships across and beyond the Commonwealth
- challenges to university autonomy, with increasing government intervention

- moves towards education that is more focused on the development of human capital in support of economic growth
- enhanced staff and student mobility

Secretary General Christodoulou's perspective was prescient. It is a perceptive framework on which to build a vision of the future.

From Elite to Mass Access

Historically, universities have existed primarily to provide the intellectual training ground for the next cadre of intellectuals and civil servants, while continuing to push back the boundaries of knowledge through the advancement of research. This research impacted significantly on teaching, and there was a clear intention to ensure that those emerging from the universities had a strong theoretical grounding. Admission to universities was traditionally restricted to the privileged elite, determined either by their background or by their academic achievements. As a result, participation rates in higher education were low.

Since the 1980s, the numbers of institutions—and the types of institution—have increased significantly. Further, they have shifted from being highly selective to being more egalitarian, driving the age participation rate from single-digit percentages in many countries to 50 per cent and beyond. Disparities remain, however (Altbach et al., 2009: 8):

- Sub-Saharan Africa has the lowest current level of participation (at around 5 per cent).
- Participation rates in East Asia and the Pacific have risen significantly (estimated now at 30 per cent).
- In North America and Western Europe, participation rates are dramatically higher (at more than 70 per cent in select jurisdictions).

In parallel, the education policies of governments in many Commonwealth countries have evolved since the 1980s, so as to change the very nature of the university system, acknowledging the need to expand and diversify.

One indication of this is the evolution of policies that sought to bring technical education closer to the university—as took place in the UK in the 1990s, with the abolition of the polytechnic sector, and again in South Africa in 2004, with the absorption of the technikons. Through these and similar reforms, the very nature of what is taught in a university has changed, with the introduction of 'transferable skills' as a critical factor leading to employability, and with the emergence of the notion of twenty-first-century skills as being critical for graduates. But, in that context it must be recognised that

> the State is faced with policy goals which are in tension. On the one hand it seeks to bring the total system of [UK] higher education into a common framework so that the entire system is adding maximum value to the general aim of regenerating the economy and on the other hand subsidiary tensions reduce the extent of commonality.
>
> (Barnett and Bjarnason, 1999: 103)

Various changes in the funding methodology in higher education have also had an impact on diversification. Pressure came from sector-wide schemes, such as common funding methodologies, that seemed to encourage convergence of mission. This was a challenge to the structure of higher education, which had moved to embrace a wide range of missions, especially following the sector mergers referred to above. To many in the jurisdictions affected, particularly in the UK, this was a retrograde step. Divergence of mission was seen as being very much in the interests of students, since it offered them the prospect of very different educational experiences and, because of differences in their educational backgrounds and attainments, a higher likelihood that they could find programmes that were more closely aligned with their particular personal interests and ability. Fortunately, this 'mission drift' was recognised as an issue by many educational leaders, who developed strategies aimed at retaining the important characteristics of their institutions.

The very nature of the relationship between the professoriate and students has changed over this period as well. Whereas the academic role was traditionally one of knowledge production and transmission through research, the role has expanded over the past two decades to embrace a much broader notion. This notion values the theoretic knowledge and the context for implementation, as well as the pedagogic skills—not least since the student body is no longer as highly selected academically as in the past and is, therefore, far more heterogeneous in ability, and the demand for graduate employability has increased. All this (and much more) has served to change the dynamic of the education experience for young people seeking degrees.

Issues of public good and private benefit have also arisen. Where once education at all levels was deemed to be 'a public good' and was, therefore, largely financed through government sources, the last quarter century has seen this perception shift. The requirement to invest in one's education through the payment of tuition fees has become widely accepted—the so-called principle that 'the beneficiary pays'. Higher education is often viewed as a public benefit, but it also has a private benefit. As the introduction of tuition fees became more widespread, the locus of power began to shift somewhat. Students (and their parents), as stakeholders, claimed a louder voice in demanding better infrastructure and laboratories, and an education that prepared students for entry to the workforce.

This move—to what some have euphemistically called 'co-financing' of education—has often been fraught and fractious. This was evidenced when, in November 2010, the UK Government faced over 50,000 demonstrators on London's streets, protesting against the proposed tripling of university tuition fees. To a significant extent, this mirrored the student protest in 1997 against the introduction of tuition fees, which came close to bringing down the then UK Labour Government. In May 2012, students in the Canadian province of Quebec took to the streets to demonstrate against a 75 per cent increase in tuition fees. Mass protests involved up to 250,000 Canadians. For some protestors, the argument is about access and equity, making the case that higher fees decrease access to higher education—especially for prospective students from the lower socio-economic income groups. This phenomenon was certainly not confined to Commonwealth countries: similar demonstrations took place in Chile in 2011 (Canadian Broadcasting Corporation, 2012; *Chronicle of Higher Education*, 2012; *University World News*, 2012).

Financing: The Consequences of Change

While issues surrounding tuition fees are clearly important, there have been many other changes in the financing of higher education, which have had far-reaching consequences.

In the developed economies, the funding available directly from governments has been under substantial pressure, and this has inevitably led to reductions (in some cases significant reductions) in the 'unit of resource'. The response of the universities to this has been principally through the growth of diversified sources of funding. In countries like the UK, Australia, and New Zealand, a significant contribution to university development has come from the funding associated with the growth of the numbers of fee-paying international students.

Additionally, the universities have been astute at pursuing funding from commerce and industry, not least through increasingly professional exploitation of their intellectual property, and through the income coming from the provision of continuing professional development courses. They have also built upon their widening alumni base, both through the pursuit of philanthropic contributions and through the enhancement of other forms of direct research, such as contract research, to the benefit of both the universities and the sponsors. It is also important to note that universities in developed economies have benefited significantly from comparative national research funding, which has often assumed a very high priority in the economic and social development of their communities.

In the context of the changed research agenda, there have been other developments of significance. In the UK at the start of the 1990s, the funding bodies initiated processes of evaluation of research within individual universities at a discipline-based level. This became the now accepted (albeit reluctantly, in some cases) Research Assessment Exercise (RAE).

This commitment to the 'quantified' evaluation of research spread quickly across the developed Commonwealth, with effective local variations. There are now parallel exercises—largely under the umbrella of Performance Based Research—in Australia and New Zealand. In Canada, there have been very important local initiatives, also based principally upon research evaluation, both at individual and group level, which have changed the policy landscape. One outstanding initiative was the creation of the Canada Research Chairs, which led to the creation of 1,600 new research chairs with significant associated resources in areas of both national and international importance. There is no doubt that this type of initiative fuelled the global competition for academic, and especially research staff.

Among the unexpected consequences of the RAE was the way in which the quantification of academic behaviour led to the ubiquity of university league tables and rankings. To the great regret of many, this development has assumed an importance that is not, for a great part of the academic community, a benefit; rather, it is seen as a distraction, albeit one which is driving new behaviours in institutional funding and decision-making in an effort to gain higher standing in the global league tables. The most significant criticisms of the league table rankings were that they were largely based on research performance, with scant regard for the quality of undergraduate education.

In the emerging economies, the most important issue, without doubt, has been the need to build higher education and human capacity. While many governments have given serious commitment to increasing capacity strategically, within their limited resources they have not been able to meet the growth in demand coming from their communities. Inevitably, this has meant that capacity-building has increasingly come to depend on support from private providers. While it is the case that in some parts of the world outside the Commonwealth, especially in Latin America, the provision of higher education by private providers has become commonplace (in some countries exceeding 90 per cent of higher education provision), this is not the case for most Commonwealth jurisdictions. There is a growing shift of emphasis, with the private providers playing an increasingly important and necessary role in building capacity in both the developed and the developing Commonwealth.

One manifestation of the growth in private providers has been the significant growth of offshore campuses in many parts of the Commonwealth, supported as 'private' endeavours by established public sector universities; for example, the UK's University of Nottingham in Malaysia and Australia's Monash University campus in South Africa. While branch campus growth prevails, increasingly there are examples where local entrepreneurs have taken on the responsibility of establishing private universities to meet their country's requirements, such as Ashesi University in Ghana and Manipal University in India.

Measuring the Grip of the State

As governments struggled to meet growing numbers in education, in the later decades of the twentieth century there was much greater intervention on their part, principally through demanding an ever-increasing level of accountability by universities for the financial support that those governments provided:

> Education as a whole became a growing concern for the state, verging on an obsession: between 1944 and 1979 there were four Education Acts passed [in the UK]; between 1988 and 2007, there were seventeen.
>
> (Meadway, 2011: 18)

In 1993, the ACU, with the support of the Commonwealth Secretariat, anticipated the needs of its members in responding to this increase in government intervention, by establishing the Commonwealth Higher Education Management Service (CHEMS). In 1997, CHEMS published the results of a research study, *Measuring the Grip of the State: The Relationship between Governments and Universities in Selected Countries* (Richardson and Fielden, 1997). This report examined the level of state control in eight Commonwealth regions across a continuum ranging from 'state supervising' to 'state control'. The report concluded that

> here is no doubt that some systems are much more paternalistic than others. The more sophisticated the Government controls are through planning mechanisms, buffer bodies, financial controls, the less interest Government seems to have in being directly involved with University governance. These systems seem to be drowning under a proliferation of paper returns and statistics.
>
> (Richardson and Fielden, 1997)

Subsequently, the ACU undertook an analysis of the role of quasi-governmental 'buffer bodies', to examine the developments across the Commonwealth as governments responded to the changing circumstances in regulation. To a certain extent, these bodies were intended to provide space between what government identified as its needs for higher education and the universities and colleges, which had the responsibility of meeting those needs. These bodies took various forms, such as:

- the Higher Education Funding Councils in the UK
- the Tertiary Education Commission in New Zealand
- the All India Commission for Technical Education in India

At the same time, there was a growth in the number of regulatory bodies, particularly addressing institutional quality assurance processes in response to increased student numbers. These bodies became widespread across the Commonwealth, and included:

- in the UK, the Higher Education Quality Council and the Academic Audit Unit, which were later merged to become the Quality Assurance Agency
- in Australia, the Australian Universities Quality Agency, now the Tertiary Education Quality and Standards Agency
- in South Africa, the Council on Higher Education
- in Hong Kong, the Council for Accreditation of Academic and Vocational Qualifications and the Quality Assurance Council of the Hong Kong University Grants Committee

This resulted in a managerial 'quality culture', whereas once such issues were relatively unconsidered or were left to the devices of the individual member of academic staff. As a consequence, universities were exposed to a wide range of audit assurance instruments—not always sensitively designed—which frequently caused deep concern in the academic community. This even led, from time to time, to protests associated with perceived threats to academic freedom.

The Rise of Managerialism

The changing circumstances described above required a much more managerial approach to leading an institution and, ultimately, a new cadre of university leadership evolved to meet the need for leaders to exhibit both academic and managerial skills.

This in turn led to the development of more formalised training in management practices for heads of institutions. This training was frequently provided by agencies with experience in general management education in other sectors. However, it became increasingly the case that sector-specific requirements were not provided for adequately. As a result, more specialist bodies soon emerged.

Across the Commonwealth, the sector representative bodies (such as the New Zealand Vice-Chancellors' Committee, the South African Universities Vice-Chancellors Association, the Australian Vice-Chancellors' Committee, the Association of Universities and Colleges of Canada, and Universities UK) took responsibility for the provision of sector-specific training. While doing this, there was recognition that managerial training needed to penetrate further down into the senior structures of universities—even going so far as preparing aspiring leaders in a structured way.

A very good example of this is the Top Management Programme, currently the province of the Leadership Foundation for Higher Education in the UK. The programme is

> intended to be challenging, providing an opportunity to broaden perspective and act as a force of change at a personal and professional level . . . [and] is designed to provide long term benefit to both the individual [as a strategic leader], the university and the wider higher education sector.
>
> (Leadership Foundation for Higher Education, 2012)

Another similar development is the establishment of the Higher Education Leadership and Management Programme within Higher Education South Africa, which has the express purpose to

> improve the quality of leadership of South African Universities in the light of the rapidly changing landscape of the higher education system and in the context of diminishing resources.
>
> (Higher Education South Africa, 2012)

In parallel, the changing demands of university governance led to attention being given to the developmental needs of the non-academic (lay) individuals involved in university councils and governing bodies.

In support of this rise in managerialism, the ACU (through CHEMS) developed an innovative Commonwealth-wide benchmarking programme to support member universities in addressing some of the growing challenges in professionalising institutions. The programme began in 1996 and brought together universities from across the Commonwealth on an annual basis. Each year a new set of topics was addressed, as chosen by the participating institutions. Over the years, a wide range of topics were covered, including:

- strategic planning
- human resources management
- student services
- managing information technology
- multi-campus management
- commercialisation
- change management

The benchmarking programme took a programmatic and process approach versus a more quantitative focus. The view is that

> [i]t enables members to learn from each others' experience of difficulty and success, across international boundaries. Its mode of operation has been designed by university people solely for use in universities, and has been refined, year on year, in the light of experience.
>
> (ACU, 2012)

There is no doubt that the increasing complexity of the higher education environment, the enhanced demands of both the government and students, the need for clear accountability, and changes in the funding regimes will put more pressure on both institutional leaders and institutions. This can only lead to more managerialism, not less. Efficiency and academic autonomy are often now posed as being in tension.

Universities in Society

As indicated above, in the last quarter century higher education's 'mission' has expanded, moving from the ivory tower 'elite' model to embrace an economic imperative, in which human capital development is an equally strong (if not stronger) driver for participation in higher education. This is frequently referred to as 'massification', an ungainly term that pointed to fundamental change in university missions.

It was in this context that the ACU initiated a project in 2001 to explore the nature of universities' engagement with society. Through consultations with stakeholders across the Commonwealth, a pulse was taken, exploring how universities understood the role of institutional engagement (Bjarnason and Coldstream, 2003).

The ACU paper circulated prior to the consultations set out a clear statement for the contexts in which universities needed to be engaged:

> Engagement implies strenuous, thoughtful, argumentative interaction with the non-university world in at least four spheres: setting universities' aims, purposes and priorities; relating teaching and learning to the wider world; the back-and-forth dialogue between researchers and practitioners; and taking on wider responsibilities as neighbours and citizens.
>
> (Bjarnason and Coldstream, 2003)

In this debate, the ACU was seeking to address the rising dialogue coming from the many pressures that university leaders faced—from changing financing mechanisms to demands to move curricula closer to the needs of industry. This was not a new debate in some institutions, whereas for others it was a challenge to the very core of academic freedom and the nature of the student experience. The challenge now extends in some institutions to the appointment of senior institutional officers, at deputy vice-chancellor level, with responsibility for community engagement.

In some countries, these processes of engagement were driven by partnership groups of academic leaders and leaders from commerce and industry—for instance, the Policy Roundtables in Australia and the Council for Industry and Higher Education in the UK. The nature of the discussions differed across the Commonwealth in terms of emphasis. In emerging economies, the focus tended towards direct employability of graduates through changing curricula, including the enhancement of work experience and internships; whereas, in more developed economies, the focus embraced research as well.

The ACU's then Secretary General, Michael Gibbons, wrote extensively about the emergence of Mode 1 and Mode 2 types of knowledge and research, powerfully illustrating the move from curiosity-driven research to mission-driven research, and which embraced the nature of engagement with society through research. Research centres are also identified as being critical in new modes of enquiry, and also as being significant in changing the research culture of universities themselves:

> In the prevailing contract, science made discoveries and offered them to society. The new contract will be based upon the joint production of knowledge by society and science. The prevailing contract produces knowledge, reliable in the restricted context of specific laboratory conditions; the new contract must produce socially robust knowledge; knowledge demonstrably reliable in a broader range of contexts.
>
> (Gibbons, 2003)

The emphasis on universities engaging productively with society continues through a variety of mechanisms, including the Talloires Network, which was formed in 2005 and presents itself as 'a global coalition of engaged universities' and undertakes and promotes a wide range of activities in support of university civic engagement (Talloires Network, 2012). The Talloires Network connects a number of regional networks, which encompass Commonwealth institutions such as the

Australian Universities Community Engagement Alliance, the South African Higher Education Community Engagement Forum and, most recently, the Asia-Talloires Network.

University Networks

The financial, operational, and governance pressures on universities led them to explore new ways of pursuing their goals.

One development, which has been slowly expanding, is the setting up of structured strategic networks of institutions. This builds on, and formalises on an institutional basis, the long-established practice of the sharing of research (and, in some cases, teaching) between individual academics.

One such example is Universitas 21 (U21), which was established following initial discussions at the ACU's Executive Heads meeting in Malta in 1996. This group brought together, in the first instance, a select group of 12 research-intensive universities from across the Commonwealth to establish partnerships beyond the standard bilateral structures. Over the succeeding years, it expanded to become an international network of 23 leading research-intensive universities in 15 countries, both within and outside the Commonwealth. Collectively, its members (Universitas 21, 2012)

- enrol over 830,000 students
- employ over 145,000 staff
- have approaching 2.5 million alumni
- have collective budgets amounting to over US$25bn
- have an annual research grant income of over US$4bn

The intention in establishing the structure for the U21 activities was to create benefits for both staff and students supported at the highest level.

- The exchange of academic and administrative staff was facilitated.
- Collaborative groups of colleagues from the same (or similar) disciplines were formed, who met either in person or virtually to discuss topics of mutual interest, with a focus on issues of importance within their field.

- Research partnerships outside the normal one-on-one links were facilitated.
- New initiatives were encouraged, including the setting up of U21Global, an online graduate school.

The relationship provided more highly structured and focused opportunities for students at all levels of study through activities such as summer schools, research conferences and semesters abroad. However, as a sign of the wider market pressures, and as one example of the influence of the changing landscape in global higher education, U21Global is now majority-owned by Manipal Education, a large private university based in India. Nonetheless, it is generally accepted that U21 has largely achieved many of its core goals.

Other global networks have developed, each with a slightly different raison d'être, and indeed with some institutions sharing membership in more than one network in order to benefit from the widest possible group of institutions and activities. Among these are

- the Worldwide University Network, which comprises 19 research-led institutions from nine countries
- the ASEAN University Network, involving 26 universities from the constituency of the Association of Southeast Asian Nations (ASEAN)
- the International Network of Universities, with 11 members from nine countries

In all cases, the aims and intentions of the networks parallel those of U21, with attention being given to the needs and aspirations of both staff and students.

It may be thought difficult to identify unequivocally the benefits coming from the development of these networks, and especially the benefits for student education. With the widespread acceptance that the future is 'global', the international experience that students gain from exchanges (which are largely credit-bearing) within the networks must be helpful both for personal development and for their future careers. There will, of course, be a need for the situation to be monitored over the longer term, in order to seek to identify and enhance benefits.

But not all university networks are global in nature. As government sought to harmonise the higher education sector in many countries, the institutions sought to differentiate. Thus, a number of networks grew up within national sectors, which aimed to provide a distinctive 'voice' to lobby government and to attract students. These include (and are certainly not limited to) the Russell Group in the UK, the U15 in Canada, and the Group of Eight in Australia, all of which are groupings of large, research-intensive institutions.

It seems sensible to expect this type of collaboration to expand in the future, both within the Commonwealth and outside, as the need to share best practice and build excellence grows in priority. There are clearly lessons to be learnt from the early history of these networks.

The Increasing Internationalisation of Higher Education

While universities have historically been international by nature, the last decades of the twentieth century and the first decade of the twenty-first have brought very significant growth in the pace of international activity.

The globalisation of higher education has included very marked increases in the mobility of students and, with it, commitments from established universities (both public and private) to set up provision in overseas territories. This globalisation has now become the topic of conferences and political debate, with some extolling its virtues and others dwelling on its evils.

As regards student mobility, the numbers are remarkable. Most recent estimates indicate that there were some 3.5 million international students studying outside their home countries—with an estimated one in five of these students coming from either China or India (IIE Open Doors, 2011). The four leading destination countries remain the US, the UK, Australia, and Canada, but increasingly there are moves from governments in various parts of the world to develop educational hubs to attract international students such as those in Singapore, Malaysia, and Dubai.

Most recent data from the UNESCO Institute of Statistics (2011), covering the period from 2002 to 2009, indicates that enrolments in the four leading destination countries have increased significantly.

- US numbers grew by 13 per cent, from roughly 583,000 to 661,000.
- The UK has increased its numbers by 62 per cent, from 227,000 to 369,000.

- Australia saw an increase of 43 per cent, from 180,000 to 258,000.
- Numbers in Canada were up by 67 per cent, from 53,000 to 88,000.

These growth figures, however, hide substantial changes in market share. For instance, in the US, while there was an absolute growth in numbers as indicated above, the market share fell from 27 per cent to 20 per cent over the same period.

In all cases there is the important issue of the ability of the host country to absorb the growing international numbers. Increasingly, the flow of students is being influenced by immigration and visa policies. Some countries have quite deliberately implemented immigration-friendly policies to facilitate access from abroad (for example, Canada and Australia); in other countries, the internal political climate has led to more stringent visa requirements (for example, the UK and the US). There is evidence that the latter development diverts students to other countries and with it the financial resources accruing to the host institutions.

One illustrative case in point concerning the volatility of the globalisation of higher education can be found arising from the Malaysian economic crisis in 1997. The Malaysian currency suffered a singular devaluation, associated with the broader Asian financial crisis. In the subsequent three years the number of Malaysian students studying abroad fell by 41 per cent in the UK and nearly 50 per cent in the US. This was largely because the Malaysian Government chose to bring Malaysian students home, as they could not afford to support them abroad. At an individual institutional level, this repatriation created significant upheaval in those institutions with significant Malaysian cohorts, as their income from overseas tuition fees was lost.

Thereafter, the Malaysian Government made a strategic decision to develop the country as a net importer of foreign students, while at the same time, building enhanced capacity for higher education for young people in the country. Part of the solution was to entice large foreign universities to establish campuses in Malaysia, which the UK's University of Nottingham and others have done. This included opening the sector to a large number of private education providers in order to meet demand. The Malaysian Government's commitment has most recently been extended, by creating new educational opportunities and incentives to entice large private education providers in the Iskandar Development Region and the South Johor Economic Region.

The Business of 'Borderless Education'

The many changes in the nature and provision of higher education has created an environment that has increasingly 'porous' boundaries. The education world has become 'borderless'.

This has been evidenced in various studies over the last decade or so, including landmark studies in Australia and the UK in the late 1990s. The Observatory on Borderless Higher Education (OBHE), set up in 2001 by the ACU and Universities UK, has produced many reports and documents dealing authoritatively with all the salient issues associated with 'borderlessness'.

The World Trade Organization challenged the very bedrock of education as a 'public good', by putting forward the case for education to be considered a tradable commodity. The General Agreement on Trade in Services (GATS), introduced as part of the Doha Round of trade negotiations in 2001, introduced education as an element in the liberalisation of trade. This issue was examined by the ACU's Policy Research Unit, which explored the implications that such a development had for universities across the Commonwealth and beyond. The GATS fuelled heated debate globally and in the end had little impact beyond igniting (often polarised) discussion. The ACU report posits:

> Knowledge has become a key commodity of global exchange and the trade in education services is one of the visible manifestations of this exchange. The trade in education services is driven not only by financial imperatives but is a broader reflection of a sector that has become more international and more globally networked in its core functions and outlook.
>
> (Kubler and Lennon, 2008)

However, there is no doubt that higher education is 'big business'. In the *Education Sector Factbook 2012* (GSV EDU, 2012), it is estimated that the current market size is US$10 trillion, which is predicted to grow to US$15 trillion by 2017. This is up from an estimated US$2.2 trillion turnover a decade ago.

The porous nature of the new-style university has had an impact at a variety of levels, many of which have been addressed earlier in this chapter. A pervasive theme in the study of universities has been the changing nature of higher education and, ultimately, what constitutes the very idea of the 'university'. Thus, for example, while for centuries education has been dominated by traditional public sector provision, the early twenty-first century is bringing a strong emergence of private sector involvement, both at institutional level as well as through services provided to the sector.

The United Nations Millennium Development Goals (MDGs) have placed a governmental premium on investing heavily in primary education in order to achieve the MDGs for education. As a result, many governments have few funds remaining to invest in secondary education—and even less for postsecondary and higher education.

This has led to the emergence of private sector provision in response to the demand from society for greater access to higher education provision. This is not without controversy. National debates reflect differing views on the relative merit of private provision. India has been debating its Foreign Education Providers Bill since 2010, but it has yet to be formally introduced to Parliament. Meanwhile, the Indian Government—and that of Nigeria, Africa's most populous country—has pledged to increase access to higher education very significantly, seemingly without corresponding increases in spending on education.

The late 1990s saw the rise of the 'corporate university', primarily in the US, which focused on the education and training needs for particular sectors or industries (CVCP, 2000: 10). There was also extensive experimentation in the delivery of higher education. Pearson, a large, UK-based publishing company and, among other things, owner of the *Financial Times* and the *Economist*, invested heavily in the provision of education—to the extent of establishing its own Academic Board and Quality Assurance structures. Today their promotional mission statement is clear:

> At Pearson, we believe in learning—whether it's at home, at university or in the workplace. In a world where knowledge and skills are increasingly important, we like to think we help people live and learn, to get on in their studies, progress their careers and make the most of their lives.
>
> (Pearson website, 2012)

Pearson, and many others like them, will bring pressure to bear on the higher education landscape that will undoubtedly lead to further changes in the way in which the established universities respond to these perceived threats of the university's role in providing education to society.

The OBHE researched the emergence of some of the private education providers through the Global Education Index, to determine whether the new players were in fact complementing and adding value to 'traditional' universities, or whether they were engaging in new, more competitive activities that could eventually threaten the nature of a university education.

Experimentation with institutional structures continues. However, evidence suggests that private providers have tended to pursue areas of provision that are less research-intensive (thus requiring less investment in infrastructure and fewer research-active academic staff) and to offer courses in disciplines that are employment-led. There is also evidence that private providers (both large and small), with their flexibility and academic agility, have challenged many of the traditional aspects of higher education so often associated with on-campus provision.

However, many of the long-established universities have worked assiduously to increase flexibility in their teaching by, for instance, making detailed information on curriculum content publicly accessible and by embracing web-based open learning to create (very effectively) concepts of 'blended' learning that are of real benefit to the student cohort. The most famous of these is the US MIT OpenCourseWare initiative at the Massachusetts Institute of Technology, which placed the curriculum from 50 of its courses on the web in 2002, increasing this to cover over 1,800 courses by 2007. It launched its own iPhone application ('OCW LectureHall') in 2011. This initiative was the forerunner of the now Massive Open Online Course developments which are attracting widespread attention (see Chapters 5 and 15).

Conclusion

The ACU Secretary General's observations in the late 1980s (Christodoulou, 1988) were indeed prescient. But it is unlikely that he could have foreseen some of the key factors that have shaped the sector in the decades since that time.

While the physical infrastructure of a university campus has remained relatively unchanged, much else has experienced considerable—and some would say revolutionary—change. The vice-chancellors of the 1980s would find many of the issues that currently preoccupy their contemporaries as unfamiliar on many fronts: global rankings, managing international campuses, and significant numbers of international students on campus, coping with the 'audit culture' for quality and research—and much more besides.

The pendulum has swung quite markedly away from the ivory tower, theoretically driven university experience, towards providing an education that includes new disciplines—new pedagogies with a syllabus that reflects both theory and practice, not to mention the commercialisation of research.

It is undeniable that we are in a time of enormous and ongoing institutional change, and the most informed observers expect the rate of higher education change to increase substantially. It is hard to resist the conclusion that, in future years, the landscape of higher education will look significantly different, as it continues to evolve and embrace innovation in content and structure, while at the same time navigating its way through increasing managerialism and more intrusive audit cultures. It is tempting to try to forecast those areas in which the greatest change is likely to occur; but the current breadth and complexity of higher education sectors across the globe militate against such a forecast being either accurate or sufficiently far-seeing. Perhaps, the only constant is change itself.

Bibliography

ACU (2012) Benchmarking Programme. Available online at www.acu.ac.uk/member_services/benchmarking_programme/benchmarking_programme (last accessed on 23 May 2012).

Altbach, P.G., Reisberg, L., and Rumbley, L.E. (eds) (2009) *Trends in Global Higher Education: Tracking an Academic Revolution.* A report prepared for the UNESCO 2009 World Conference on Higher Education. Paris: UNESCO.

Barnett, R. and Bjarnason, S. (1999) The Reform of Higher Education in Britain. In *Higher Education in a Post-Binary Era: National Reforms and Institutional Responses*, 87–109. ed. D. Teather. Higher Education Policy Series 38. London: Jessica Kingsley Publishers.

Bjarnason, S. and Coldstream, P. (eds) (2003) *The Idea of Engagement: Universities in Society*. London: Association of Commonwealth Universities.

Canadian Broadcasting Corporation (2012) Montreal Protest Simmers after Tuition Crisis Law Passes: Police Fire Tear Gas, Noise Bombs at Thousands of Demonstrators. Available online at www.cbc.ca/news/canada/montreal/story/2012/05/18/montreal-protest-declare-illegal-after-molotov-cocktail.html (downloaded on 4 April 2013).

Christodoulou, A. (1988) A Forward Look. New Challenges, New Responses. In *The Commonwealth of Universities: The Story of the Association of Commonwealth Unversites, 1963–1988*, 95–115, ed. H.W. Springer. London: Association of Commonwealth Unversities.

Chronicle of Higher Education (2012) With Student Strikes Creating Havoc in Quebec, Talks Aim to Resolve Impasse, 24 April 2012. Available online at http://chronicle.com/article/with-student-strikes-creating/131651/ (downloaded on 4 April 2013).

CVCP (2000) *The Business of Borderless Education*. London: Committee of Vice-Chancellors and Principals (now Universities UK).

Gibbons, M. (2003) Engagement as a Core Value in a Mode 2 Society. In *The Idea of Engagement: Universities in Society*, eds S. Bjarnason and P. Coldstream. London: Association of Commonwealth Universities.

GSV EDU (2012) *Education Sector Factbook 2012*. Available online at http://gsvadvisors.com/wordpress/wp-content/uploads/2012/04/GSV-EDU-Factbook-Apr-13-2012.pdf (last accessed on 23 May 2012).

Higher Education South Africa (2012) Higher Education Leadership and Management Programme. Available online at www.hesa.org.za/helm (downloaded on 4 April 2013).

IIE Open Doors (2011) *Report on International Educational Exchange*. New York: Institute of International Education.

Kubler, J. and Lennon, M. (2008) *International Trade in Higher Education: Implications for the Commonwealth*. London: Association of Commonwealth Universities.

Leadership Foundation for Higher Education (2012) Top Management Programme. Available online at www.lfhe.ac.uk/support/tmp/ (last accessed on 23 May 2012).

Meadway, J. (2011) The Rebellion in Context. In *Springtime: The New Student Rebellions,* eds C. Solomon and T. Palmieri. London: Verso.

Pearson website (2012). Available online at www.pearsoned.co.uk/AboutUs/ (last accessed on 23 May 2012).

Richardson, G. and Fielden, J. (1997) *Measuring the Grip of the State: The Relationship between Governments and Universities in Selected Countries*. London: Association of Commonwealth Universities.

Talloires Network (2012) Available online at www.tufts.edu/talloiresnetwork/?pid=35&c=2 (last accessed on 23 May 2012).

UNESCO Institute of Statistics (2011) *Global Education Digest 2011: Comparing Education Statistics across the World*. Canada: UNESCO.

Universitas 21 (2012) Available online at www.universitas21.com/ (last accessed on 23 May 2012).

University World News (2012) Quebec student protests. *University World News Global Edition*, Issue 222, 20 May. Available online at www.universityworldnews.com (downloaded on 4 April 2013).

4

From 'Imperial Bureau' to 'International Network', 1913–2013: Capacity-building in a Global Era

John Kirkland and Nicholas Mulhern

Change and Continuity for an International Network of Universities

When writing the first history of the Association of Universities of the British Commonwealth (AUBC) in 1963, Lord Ashby was struck by the similarity of the agenda of its foundation Congress—some 50 years previously—with that of contemporary higher education (HE). Specialisation among universities, reciprocal recognition of qualifications, international mobility, extension work, the place of technical and vocational education, and the role of women in universities—these were all cited to support the assertion that while 'the topics seem timeless; the voices only have changed' (Ashby, 1963: 7).

A further 50 years on, at the 2013 centenary of this oldest of global university associations and networks, this chapter considers the balance of change and continuity in the transition from the Universities' Bureau of the British Empire—the product of that first Congress—to the Association of Commonwealth Universities of the present day. As Ashby noted, there is a surprising degree of continuity, not only in specific topics, but also in an ethos firmly rooted in notions of international co-operation and the philosophy (more radical in 1912 than today) that this should involve a two-way sharing of knowledge and personnel.

It is not surprising that Ashby stressed continuity in 1963. Twenty-five years later, Sir Hugh Springer described the enlargement of the ACU in its first 50 years as 'gradual, almost leisurely' (Springer, 1988: 20), growing from 56 on the establishment of new Articles of Association in 1932 to 132 three decades later. Continuity characterises the period covered by Stringer's history, too. Although the pace of membership growth increased rapidly, from 132 in 1962 to 319 some 25 years later, core aspects of the Association's work remained stable over the period. In particular, the 'three main areas of the Association's work—publications and information, appointments and the administration of awards—all became more active in the period under review because what they offered was so clearly needed' (Springer, 1988: 41).

Not all universities joined, but many regarded membership as automatic, although their reasons for doing so varied. While 'membership of any prestigious body may well be thought to bestow a certain cachet… institutions joining the ACU have always been motivated both by their commitment to the ideals of the Commonwealth and by strictly practical factors' (Springer, 1988: 41). Whatever the reasons, the network proved incredibly durable. Despite the global economic crisis, the rapid decline of HE in Africa towards the end of the period, and the economic stringency of the 1980s, the ACU showed a financial surplus in each of the 25 years covered by Springer's history.

More recent historians would be more inclined to emphasise change over continuity. At face value, membership has continued to grow steadily, further increasing from the 319 reported by Springer to 536 by January 2012. In reality, the situation has been more complex. The proliferation of universities worldwide, as well as their size and diversity in the past 25 years, has been very significant, and therefore those joining the ACU now represent a much smaller proportion of the sector overall.

Moreover, the upward figures mask increased turnover. Institutions resign, as well as join, in significant numbers; in practice, some resign and rejoin within a relatively short period of time. The shift in regions and countries represented has also been marked; many of the new institutions joining are based in Asia (with that region as a whole constituting over half of the ACU's current membership).

Although the historian at the turn of the century would find the three core functions described by Springer still operative, by 2012 a very different picture has emerged: the eighty-second (and last) edition of the *Commonwealth Universities Yearbook* appeared in 2008; there was rapid decline in revenues from advertising and recruitment services; and scholarships were subject to increased scrutiny by their funding bodies.

Expansion and technological change represent a threat as well as an opportunity to the ACU. In 1913, the Association was one of the few mechanisms available to support international collaboration. Helping to organise programmes for academic visitors was cited as one of its first functions. As late as 1987, Springer could still describe the *Yearbook* as a 'unique source of information' (Springer, 1988: 30). By 2012, universities are inundated with collaboration opportunities. Yet most collaboration is formed without the aid of any formal association, often developing from individual (and perhaps informal) links and contacts. Many universities establish their own network of like-minded institutions, and for those that do value the role played by national and international associations, there are several to choose from. (The *Handbook of International Associations in Higher Education* [Schneller et al., 2009] lists a hundred or so, many of which were established over the last decade.) Some of these have a more limited geographical focus than the Commonwealth. Others operate on a subsidised basis, and some either do not charge or adopt a relatively lax attitude towards subscriptions. A few have very precisely defined missions or audiences, or alternatively are more informal groupings, which have developed perhaps with reference to a specific project. None of these is the case with the ACU.

The extent and nature of change required to meet these different circumstances forms the basis of this chapter. Rather than attempting a chronological history, this will be briefly assessed under five separate headings, corresponding to several key functions of the modern organisation. For each, the study considers how its present-day role has evolved, the main factors that have determined change, and the extent to which the Association of today can be meaningfully linked to its predecessors.

Five Key Functions of the Organisation

1. *The ACU as an information source*

In one sense, the role of the ACU as a provider of information is stronger than ever; in another, it is in steep decline.

The information source formerly most instantly recognised with the ACU—the *Commonwealth Universities Yearbook*—is no longer published. Other products of previous decades, such as its series of directories on scholarships and awards, its indices of research (for example, *Research Opportunities in Commonwealth Developing Countries*) or its guides to courses, have also long disappeared. The *ACU Bulletin of Current Documentation* (known as *ABCD*), established in 1971 to provide 'factual information about some of the more important books, reports and other documents that have recently been issued on matters affecting universities and are of more than local interest' (ABCD, 1 [June 1971]: 1), continues as simply the *Bulletin*. The need to distil information remains as strong today as ever.

However, the ACU now publishes far more than it has ever done, whether as regular series or occasional reports, as its own or commissioned material, and in varying formats (print, electronic, both print and electronic together). The Association has contributed to the development of new products: it was, for example, a partner in a project funded by the UK's Department for International Development (DFID) to establish the *Research Africa* database—the first funding service specifically for African universities—and in the late 1990s worked with the Community of Science (COS) funding service. Its library continues to provide information and support for the ACU's projects and publications, particularly the *Bulletin* and the professional network magazines.

Over recent years, information has been provided through an increased range of routes. During its first eight decades, the Association produced relatively few reports on policy-related matters, focusing mainly on directory-type publications, the main exception being the proceedings of the periodic conferences and congresses. The establishment of the Commonwealth Higher Education Management Service (CHEMS) in 1994, as part of a funded Commonwealth Higher Education Support Scheme (CHESS), helped to redefine the ACU's role and association with more active HE policy debate, not least in showing what effective HE management and planning involves. Performance indicators, resource allocation, government/university relationships, mergers, and outsourcing were among its published themes.

The commitment to policy reports continued with the development of the ACU's Policy and Research Unit in 2000 which, while maintaining established series (for example, academic staff salary surveys) also initiated debate, including a new emphasis on university engagement, for example. The ACU's gender programme also produced influential papers, drawing attention to the continuing under-representation of women at senior levels throughout the Commonwealth (see Chapter 6).

In recent years, the ACU has also worked with research organisations (such as the British Academy) and charities (for example, Arcadia), in analysing and contributing to policy change for specific needs. Examples include:

- *The Nairobi Report: Frameworks for Africa-UK Research Collaboration in the Social Sciences and Humanities* (British Academy and ACU, 2009)
- *Growing Knowledge: Access to Research in East and Southern African Universities* (ACU for Arcadia, 2010)
- *Foundations for the Future: Supporting the Early Careers of African Researchers* (British Academy and ACU, 2011)

The ACU's research profile has also been maintained by regular publication by staff in journal articles and book chapters, particularly in research management.

2. *The ACU as facilitator*

The ability to help members to do things that they could not achieve alone is critical to any membership organisation. Perhaps the most traditional means of achieving this in academic circles has been through the organisation of conferences. The nature of these has changed radically, from the large and formal congresses now largely abandoned (at the 15th Congress [1993] in Wales there were 733 attendees, of whom 510 were official delegates) to modern-day specialist networks and benchmarking sessions, often in conjunction with other educational and development organisations. It seems paradoxical that, in an age of virtual contact, the range and number of physical conferences staged by the Association has risen significantly in recent years.

At the time of the ACU's inception, contact between universities (as institutions) was limited. International contact required great sacrifice and advance planning; many of the conferences were over several days, if not longer, and were hosted by a number of institutions. The latter need can be seen from the fact that plans for a meeting in 1917 were circulated to members on 27 July 1914. Even planning at this range did not make the Association immune from unforeseen circumstances. As a result of the outbreak of the First World War, seven days later, a further circular was issued on 7 August, postponing the conference 'until conditions are more favourable' (Ashby, 1963: 16).

The format of ACU conferences, if not their content, followed a clear pattern. The main forum, the Congress, was held every five years, excepting during periods of war. The published Congress proceedings testify not only to the continuity of their themes, and their ambition as representative gatherings, but also to the aim of communicating with member institutions from the outset. As an example, planning for the Third Congress (Cambridge, 1926) refers to the 'eighty titles of subjects…the large majority…suggested by universities overseas' (Universities' Bureau of the British Empire, 1926: ix) that were received following an invitation for proposals in autumn 1924.

Introduced in 1948, to parallel these events, were the Conferences of Executive Heads of member universities—for 'private discussions', as explained in the 1963 Proceedings (ACU, 1964: x)—and the commitment to hold Congresses in alternate years outside the UK, the first being the Eighth Congress (Montreal, 1958).

The guiding themes of the meetings became more prominent and more focused, first as Congresses—for example, 'Commonwealth Universities and Society' in 1973; 'What Can We Do for Our Countries? The Contribution of Universities to National Development' in 1988; and then subsequently as Executive Heads meetings ('New Configurations in Globalisation' in 2001, with 'Universities and the MDGs' in 2010). The redefined 'General Conferences' ('Leadership and the Management of Change', Ottawa, 1998; 'Universities Engaging with Their Communities', Belfast, 2003) increasingly involved speakers from outside the university sector. They have since been continued by the ACU in co-organising or paralleling its events with those of associated groups.

In the past decade, these have been supplemented by smaller, more focused events. Those held on behalf of the various professional networks since 2004, research management perhaps being the most well-established, enable the exchange of information, just as those of the Bureau's first aimed to achieve. As some areas of university work have become more segmented and professionalised, so the need to communicate within universities, as well as between and on behalf of them, has become more pressing. The ACU's more recent involvement in the hosting of workshops, and latterly of summer schools, also shows how the ideals of universities can be practically applied.

A further example of the smaller, more focused type of meeting now favoured by the Association was the introduction, in 1996, of the ACU benchmarking programme. While the ACU tradition of membership surveys has continued in recent years, benchmarking in this sense has a more precise meaning. The programme is intensive, and concentrates on a small number of member universities (who normally pay an additional fee to take part). It is unashamedly based on discussion of processes, university-wide rather than departmental, and does not emphasise quantitative indicators. It seeks to be co-operative, avoiding the temptation to rank participating institutions simply on the basis of their performance, but instead providing each with an agenda for implementation according to local circumstances. The formula has proved attractive, with annual events taking place for university leaders, and occasional ones for subject specialists (such as an international exercise supported by the Higher Education Funding Council for England for research managers in 2005–06). Processes benchmarked in recent years have included the management of league tables, HR, student experience, and internationalisation.

3. *The ACU as advocate*

Established in an age when universities guarded their independence even more jealously than today, both the Bureau and the Association have been nervous of assuming a direct 'representational' role.

The 1912 meeting resolved that 'it will at no time be the business of the Bureau committee to pass judgement on University policy' (Ashby, 1963: 13). In these circumstances, the Bureau would probably not have regarded its early successes—such as its role, described by Ashby, in the introduction of the doctorate to the UK after the First World War—as lobbying.

Given the growth of national and regional university bodies, some might question whether ACU lobbying has a natural target. Influencing the Commonwealth authorities would not rank high in importance to most members, compared with influencing their national governments, or the more powerful and well-funded intergovernmental bodies. As with many other university associations, its ability to find a common line is hindered by diversity of interests among the membership itself. On many of the issues affecting members, there are difficulties in finding an agreed position between member institutions—and one that is both independent and can be effectively articulated. As the membership profile has changed in terms of location, size, funding, and governance, should the ACU be seen to represent its most powerful or its most vulnerable institutions?

In these circumstances, ACU lobbying has tended to be discreet and practical in nature. Springer describes how, following a paper which it presented to the 1980 Conference of Commonwealth Education Ministers, the Association 'played a key role…in sustaining the argument' (Springer, 1988: 81) against the policy of charging full-cost fees for overseas students. The Commonwealth Standing Committee on Student Mobility was effective from 1982 for nearly a decade in articulating this case; the ACU's Secretary-General was a member throughout. Political circumstances ensured that this argument was lost—in most developed countries as well as the UK—but the campaign did enjoy some success. Springer notes that it was partly due to ACU advocacy that 'the situation was partially retrieved by the announcement, in 1983, of the so-called "Pym Package"' (Springer, 1988: 81), which announced increased support for overseas students, through an expansion of Commonwealth Scholarships, and the development of a new programme, now the Chevening Scholarships.

More recently, the Association actively lobbied against a UK government decision to end support for Commonwealth Scholarships to developed countries in 2008, arguing that such financial support was integral to the scheme being seen as genuinely Commonwealth-wide in nature. Again, its efforts enjoyed some success, with the announcement of funding to continue some of the awards through another source.

Another topic to which ACU lobbying is likely to be well suited is the role that HE can play in development. Of obvious interest to universities in developing countries, acceptance of this argument affects developed countries too—through increased opportunities for research, student recruitment, staff exchange, and partnerships. ACU publications such as *The Role of Universities in National Development* (1978), *Roles and Responsibilities* (1985), and *Universities and Development* (2000) helped to restate the critical role that HE had to play in developing economies at a time when this argument was out of fashion. The Association lobbied for, and went on to manage, practical approaches to the problem, such as the (British) Overseas Development Administration Shared Scholarship Scheme, and it increasingly worked with development agencies and funders (for example, the Commonwealth Fund for Technical Co-operation and the Canadian International Development Agency). It also endorsed and helped to implement the CHESS in 1989, which was specifically 'directed to the qualitative improvement of colleges and universities in developing Commonwealth countries' (ACU *Annual Report 1988/89*: 25).

In recent years, the Association has helped to ensure that HE regains its prominence in Commonwealth education policy, through presenting papers to the 2006 and 2009 Conferences of Commonwealth Education Ministers and, in 2009, even organising a parallel HE event (a Vice-Chancellors' Forum) to draw attention to the contribution of universities in response to the economic recession.

One area where the ACU sought to shape debate more directly was in the role and contribution that universities make to society, whether in teaching, research or their community—however that is defined. *Engagement as a Core Value for the University: A Consultation Document* was issued in 2001 to prioritise this responsibility [community or regional engagement is not seen 'as a third leg or third strand of activity, but as one which is a core element in *all activities*' (ACU, 2001: 40)], and to prompt questions to help implement it. A further study, *The Idea of Engagement: Universities in Society* (Bjarnason and Coldstream, 2003), reflected on its widening implications and the potential that this offered beyond a familiar formulation of HE/industry links.

Finally, some of the themes considered at ACU conferences also show an ability to identify issues that express common interest among the membership, and to project the importance of HE to a wider audience. Among topics included at congresses/conferences have been:

- the social consequences of technological innovation (Birmingham, 1983)
- social and cultural factors as constraints in university development (Swansea, 1993)
- the impact of universities on national, regional, and international priorities (Jamaica, 2012)

None of these would have been considered by the Association to be primarily advocacy, but in an age when universities have constantly been asked to justify the public investment that they receive, all could be included in this category.

4. *The ACU as service provider*

A need to justify subscriptions has been another common theme over the century—from the reluctance of the University of Cambridge to pay £50 in 1913 since its finances were 'in a parlous condition' (Ashby, 1963: 13), to the universities who resign, renew, and take up membership annually today. Expansion of membership to its present level has required regular attention to members' needs, which in turn have changed rapidly.

As in the areas highlighted above, core services have been replaced by a more diverse set of activities. Since 2004, the Association has been able to save members in developing countries a significant amount through negotiating discounts on hard-copy journals, and has entered the wider debate about the role of publishers in development. This work has coincided with the aims of the ACU's Libraries and Information Network (established in 2007), and that for Research Management (2004), in encouraging research through access to effective resources.

The ACU also worked with the British Council on a DFID-funded programme to broker development-oriented inter-university partnerships (DelPHE); from this an ACU University Extension Network has emerged, initially to help disseminate project outcomes. New networks and contacts have been developed in other areas, and services have been undertaken on a cost-recovery basis for a range of external organisations. Such external work, however, has remained focused on areas relevant to members' interests.

- Since 2005, the ACU has provided the management of the UK's SEDA (Staff and Educational Development Association).
- From 2006 to 2010, it provided a home for the Africa Unit, a UK government initiative to help develop innovative partnerships between UK and African universities.
- CAAST-NET, an EU-funded network for science and technology co-operation between the EU and sub-Saharan Africa at a policy level, has also been based at the ACU since 2008.

A variant on this model was the establishment in 2001 of the Observatory on Borderless Higher Education, in conjunction with Universities UK and with support from the HE Funding Council for England. This initiative aimed to provide information and analysis on HE which crosses traditional boundaries (whether by location, level, or control). It became a successful subscription service in 2002, and has since been transferred to private ownership. Meanwhile, the work of the Policy Research Unit and that of its predecessor, CHEMS, continued consultancy in HE research, particularly management and governance, with projects funded by a wide range of international agencies.

5. *The ACU as funder*

The founders of the Bureau did not intend it to be a funding body—and yet elements of this role have developed over the last half-century. It does this in two distinct ways:

- by managing funds on behalf of other bodies
- by developing its own endowment funds, to provide grants as a direct benefit to members

In both cases, activity has been largely confined to the second half-century of the Association's work, with a quickening pace of change over the last decade.

The Association's first major venture into managing scholarships funds began in 1953, when it started to manage a programme which brought American scholars to the United Kingdom. At the time when the Marshall Aid Commemoration Commission—a 'thank you' from the British government for US Marshall aid—was established, the Association was still home to the Committee of Vice-Chancellors and Principals of the Universities of the United Kingdom (CVCP). The relationship with the United States dates back almost to the origin of the ACU. Two representatives from US universities were present at the 1912 Congress, while US delegates were invited in some numbers to the 1948 and 1953 Congresses, at the latter to 'participate in the general deliberations and also to commence discussions on questions of relationship and co-operation between the Universities of the Commonwealth and those of the United States' (ACU *Annual Report 1952/53*: 12–13). The Marshall link has been guarded jealously to the present day.

A larger and more obvious role for the Association was created with the development of the Commonwealth Scholarship and Fellowship Plan (described more fully in Chapter 8). The importance of Commonwealth Scholarships to the ACU cannot be overestimated. Ashby argues that with the instigation of the Plan in 1959 'the dreams of half a century came true' (Ashby, 1963: 85). The founding Congress had, after all, recognised the importance of the 'question of student migration from one University to another' (Universities' Bureau of the British Empire, 1912: 313). Springer notes that the growth of the Plan 'put the Association in a direct relationship, for the first time in its history, with large numbers of Commonwealth students', going as far as to say that 'the Plan brought many of the smaller nations of the Commonwealth directly within the

Association's orbit' (Springer, 1988: 41). Particularly since the creation of a Commonwealth Scholarship Commission (CSC) evaluation programme in 2008, the extent to which links between award-holders and their home countries can be demonstrated has been reinforced. Yet the relationship between Commonwealth Scholarships, the ACU staff, and ACU member institutions is complex and often misunderstood.

For many ACU members, Commonwealth Scholarships represent their most direct and visible contact with the Association. This is all the more so since universities are one of the routes invited to nominate candidates, and since many scholars have ultimately taken up positions in HE. Yet, as a government-funded programme, ACU membership has never been a condition of applying for or receiving scholarships; it is a competitive scheme open to all. Likewise, although ACU staff have contributed hugely to the development of the Commission, they have largely done so in their capacity as officials of the CSC in the United Kingdom, the government body responsible for the programme which funds the ACU to provide the secretariat. A formal distinction between the ACU and the CSFP has, therefore, always existed.

However synonymous the ACU is with Commonwealth and Marshall Scholarships, the funds that they distribute are not those of the ACU, while the basic selection criteria are those of the sponsors. Similar conditions have existed, to a greater or lesser extent, to grants and commissions from other donors—such as the Carnegie Corporation of New York, the Leverhulme Trust, the Commonwealth Foundation, and the Canada Memorial Foundation.

The most significant contract recently undertaken by the ACU is that for the administration, since April 2012, of the Chevening Scholarships. It represents a marked change from other ACU-based schemes in size (it supports over 700 postgraduates in the UK), in its geographical range (it is not Commonwealth-based but extends, instead, to some 110 countries), and in its profile (it is the government's global scholarships scheme, is funded by the Foreign and Commonwealth Office, and involves co-operation with UK embassies worldwide). The opportunity to co-ordinate an independent and international scheme centrally, however, reflects the original and continuing aims of the ACU.

In recent years, the emphasis has moved from grant to contract-based funding. The potential that these offer in deepening the ACU's work has been substantial, though they have, nevertheless, brought with them constraints of their own. The growth of project funding, in particular, has been significant—particularly over the past five years. In July 2012 the Association holds contracts from:

- the UK's DFID to work with 24 universities in Africa on research utilisation
- the European Union to forge stronger links between African and European students
- other EU and Carnegie Corporation projects to help the development of research management

All of these add real benefits for members which the Association alone could not provide, but all come with their own constraints, and all are time-limited.

The ACU has, however, generated its own endowment funds, which can give long-term financial support for selected projects. The most substantial was built up from donations by universities, business, government, and charities as part of its 75th anniversary appeal in 1988 (over £2 million was initially pledged); the main beneficiary is now the Development Fellowship scheme. This supports international staff mobility, by funding short-term awards among members and between, variously, universities, those working in industry, commerce or public service. The scheme's general ambition (echoing one of the Bureau's for the 'interchange of university teachers' (Universities' Bureau of the British Empire, 1912: 321) was 'to enable the universities of the Commonwealth…to develop the human resources of their countries… through the interchange of people, knowledge, skills and technologies' (ACU *Annual Report 1988/89*: 17).

A comparable, Commonwealth commemorative endowment—marking the 50th anniversary of the Commonwealth Scholarship and Fellowship Plan in 2009—was one in which the ACU played a leading role. It enables Commonwealth Scholarships to be hosted in low- and middle-income countries that have not previously been able to afford them. Such funding, although at a much lower level than external and contracted awards, allows greater control and flexibility in supporting academic co-operation; plausibly it also raises the ACU's profile, as distinct from work on behalf of other agencies and donors.

The balance between the different functions of the ACU—information, conferences, advocacy, services, and funding—has shifted over the past 100 years, reflecting wider social and technological change as much as the needs of member institutions. The initial emphasis on the *Yearbook* as an institutional directory, the advertising of appointments, and the first Congresses, all addressed the need to keep in contact through shared information. New technology has made such co-operation both more immediate and more individual. Yet the underlying ambition—to centralise, compare, and then redistribute information—remains in the conferences, publications, networks, and websites that the ACU maintains. Similarly, the exchange of staff and students, though now formalised through scholarships, fellowships, and workshops, is rooted in the hope of the opening Congress in 'widening the outlook of the teachers themselves, and of those whom they instruct' (Universities' Bureau of the British Empire, 1912: 313).

The most significant difference now lies in how the ACU is funded, specifically the value of contract income, and above all for scholarships administration. The need to diversify income sources has meant that expertise, thematic or regional, has been built up for specific projects, but over a period in which representing the interests of the membership collectively has become less straightforward. Nevertheless, although the membership may have increased ten-fold since 1912, it was acknowledged from the outset that the Bureau comprised different institutions with different aims: it was 'of the utmost importance that this distinction [between large and smaller universities] should be clearly recognised, and that each class of institution should endeavour to place itself in a true relation to the other' (Universities' Bureau of the British Empire, 1912: 315).

In this context, members' interests have been served selectively at different times, but such prioritisation has perhaps become more visible, as the competition for external funding has intensified. The current challenge is the need to undertake projects which are not just intrinsically valuable, but which can also be seen to address 'the wide range of problems which are common to all' (Universities' Bureau of the British Empire, 1912: 316).

Key Relationships and Strategic Partnerships

The changing balance of the ACU's work has had an impact on its relationships, both internally (if we can describe member universities as being 'internal') and with the external world. As with the functions described above, these have changed over the past century, with the pace of change increasing rapidly over the last decade.

Now, more than ever, the ACU is an 'Association' rather than a 'Bureau'. The original title indicated its role as, fundamentally, a co-ordinating, office-based, and perhaps, reactive organisation. The current title portrays the critical nature of coming together, the voluntary, loose, flexible, and sometimes informal nature of the relationship, but most of all the belief that the simple act of 'knowing each other' can bring mutual benefit.

The ACU has been an Association, rather than a Bureau, since 1948 (though, like the Commonwealth of Nations, it is often described as a network). Within the Association, relationships have changed. For long periods of its history, the ACU was essentially a club of university leaders. From the outset, the ACU was regarded as 'political'-level activity. As it evolved, and university administrative structures also developed, so the vice-chancellor increasingly represented the institutions at ACU meetings and served on the Council. From 1948, additional Executive Heads meetings began to be introduced specifically for university leaders, reflecting the view that Congresses (now typically involving registrars and council members also) were too infrequent and on too large a scale to be the sole means of meeting. It is no coincidence that the representative body of British universities—which grew out of the ACU and remained formally part of it until 1968—evolved into the Committee of Vice-Chancellors and Principals (CVCP). To this day, 'membership' of the ACU formally rests with university leaders.

This model, which served the Association well for the first three quarters of its existence, is no longer tenable in 2013. Representing a university has become a more complex function, involving multiple audiences, detailed arguments and more sophisticated communication skills. The channels available for such communications are more numerous. University leaders have to establish priorities, and a range of senior management functions have developed to help them in these tasks. The proportion of university leaders attending ACU Executive Heads conferences reflects these trends. Two decades ago, such meetings were relatively infrequent and attendance was the norm (and, with a relatively small membership, it was also more practical to offer some support for developing country members). Today, such meetings are more frequent, more targeted, and can still be ranked among the most impressive gatherings of university leaders—but attendance is decided by members on a case-by-case basis, and against much greater competition from other events. It is now rare for more than half of the (much enlarged) membership to gather in one place.

Even 20 years ago, the decision on whether to take out ACU membership was invariably one for the vice-chancellor or university president. Now, it is more typically devolved. The extent of these changes varies between regions, and the model described is perhaps more prevalent in the 'developed' Commonwealth. The implications for international university associations generally have, nevertheless, been profound.

The ACU has evolved an effective (although not always explicit) strategy to meet this challenge. A common theme has been to develop programmes which touch as many parts of the institution as possible. The assumption that where the vice-chancellor or president actively supports the ACU then the university will retain its membership, can no longer be relied upon. A more realistic target is to ensure that there are at least one or two contact points within the senior management, willing to testify to the value of, and direct benefits from, ACU activities. The most commonly cited reason for withdrawal is not a lack of support for the objectives of the Association, or even dissatisfaction with the services provided, but a statement that the university had not been able to 'use' its membership. The more the points of contact, the greater the awareness of what the ACU is doing and encouraging.

The increased breadth of programmes during the 1980s and 1990s—including gender, policy reports, and the development of direct funding through the ACU Endowment Fund—all played their part in developing the contact base at institutional level. Since 2004, however, the approach has crystallised with the development of ACU 'professional networks'. These have been targeted on managerial functions, at a level where universities have recognised the need for specialist knowledge, but which can be expected to have a profile at senior management level. As with all ACU activities, the aim has been to find issues of common interest between developed and developing country members, rather than to assume that day-to-day operations will be directly compatible.

Early examples of this approach were research management and human resource management. Both represented areas in which developed—as well as developing—country universities were already rethinking their structures. In each case, a separate network membership has developed, including 400–500 specialists across member institutions. This is serviced by hard-copy and electronic communications and specialist biennial conferences.

Access to institutional specialists has also attracted external donors.

- The ACU's research management network initiative has undertaken substantial projects for the Carnegie Corporation, the UK DFID and the European Union.
- The Human Resources Network collaborated with the University Grants Committee in India to stage a specialist conference on international HR practices.
- The Library and Information Network has linked with other aspects of the ACU's project work, namely, publishing and journal provision.

More recently, similar networks have been developed in the areas of public relations, marketing, and communication, extension work, and graduate employment. Each represents an additional point of contact for the ACU within its membership.

Such contacts are also important because of the size of the membership. During its first 50 years, with membership only gradually reaching three figures, and a much more limited range of countries, the ACU could almost 'touch' each individual member. During the next 25 years, attempts were made to maintain this relationship, reinforced by a larger Council, whose members were given the responsibility of promoting the Association within their 'constituencies', with frequent turnover of membership. This, together with the extraordinary level of detail collected for publication in the *Yearbook* based on direct contact every year with each university, still justified the Association's claim to an individual relationship with each member well into the 1980s.

Today, such a relationship is not possible. With membership at over 500 and growing, ACU member institutions make pragmatic judgements about the value of the ACU through services and benefits provided, and by hard-copy or electronic communication rather than personal contact. The balance of altruistic and self-interested reasons for joining the ACU, identified by both Ashby and Springer, remains, but as personal communication has declined, and the financial demands on universities have increased, so the emphasis has moved towards self-interest.

While it was able to rely on personal contact and had few competitors, income from subscriptions, conferences, and publications was adequate to maintain the presence of the ACU in members' thinking. Today, it is hard to see how membership subscriptions alone could fund the range of activities that members expect. This is all the more so, given the high overheads of maintaining a single office in London (a structure that has remained surprisingly unquestioned by members, perhaps because most of its events are hosted internationally). Externally funded projects both facilitate products that can be presented to members, and allow the Association to maintain a presence in a wider range of countries than would otherwise be possible.

The wider range of external activities can also be seen in a growing range of governmental and global relationships. While the idea that the ACU needs to look beyond its membership and the Commonwealth to fulfil its objectives dates back to its inception, the extent of such relationships has increased markedly. Many proposals have been advanced to increase the global presence of the ACU, including developing membership links outside the Commonwealth or outside the formal HE sector, and strengthening ties with other inter-university groups and organisations. Some have involved co-operation with international and regional agencies, with EU-funded work being among the most prominent in recent years. Projects to support research and innovation management in Africa and the Caribbean (RIMI4AC), and to promote links and discussion between African and European doctoral researchers (DocLinks), are recent examples. Though financed by the EU, such programmes serve long-standing ACU commitments and interests, whether regional or strategic, and confirm that opportunities to help member universities can be in projects which are shared and collaborative in how they work as well as in what they do.

An idea was even floated by the then Secretary General prior to the 2006 Conference of Commonwealth Education Ministers, that the ACU should strengthen its status and reach by itself considering becoming an inter-governmental organisation. In practice, there is little evidence that Council, or the membership, would support a change from the conventional membership structure; but improved relations with governments and other key networks remain an essential element in future strategy.

At the time of writing (July 2012),

- 10 Commonwealth governments had contributed to an Endowment Fund, mentioned above, to mark the 50th anniversary of the Commonwealth Scholarship and Fellowship Plan;
- direct contact is maintained with many African governments through the CAAST-NET programme;

- two specific projects have been undertaken in recent years for the Australian government;
- relations have been developed through a series of projects with the Agence universitaire de la Francophonie (AUF);
- the ACU has been an active partner in WISE (the World Innovation Summit for Education), established by the Qatar Foundation;
- the ACU plays an active role in the Talloires Network, a global alliance established to enhance the social responsibility of universities.

Each of these activities reflects the belief that the modern ACU can best serve its membership by developing a wider range of networks, contacts and funding sources.

The Dynamics of a Global Network and Its Future Role

Finally, what of relationships *within* the ACU structure?

The unique nature of the membership base—embracing the leading universities in the developed Commonwealth but with two-thirds of the membership coming from low- and middle-income/developing countries—is often cited as a distinctive feature of the ACU. But how far has this been incorporated into its structures and decision-making processes?

For much of its early existence, the Bureau could be characterised as reflecting colonial structures of power. An initial plan refers to its committee as having six representatives for the British Isles and six for the Overseas Dominions (Universities' Bureau of the British Empire, 1912: 320). The first seven Congresses were held in the United Kingdom (though the idea for them to be hosted elsewhere had been mooted earlier), and in practice the meetings continued to alternate between the UK and overseas until 1993 (15th Congress in Swansea).

Although over the last 20 years the ACU Council Chair has been held by a UK-based vice-chancellor more than any other country, the international representation on Council overall has become far more inclusive. Some institutions were represented on Council relatively early after their foundation; for example, University College Ibadan (1950), Makerere University College (1952), and Mauritius (1969). Moreover, the early date at which several new national universities became members, for example, Guyana (1967), Malawi (1968), Namibia (1993), and Zambia (1967), showed that education strategy was identified with, and perhaps helped to define, independence itself. In more recent years, a smaller Council ('with different electoral constituencies and longer periods of office') was introduced (ACU *Annual Report*, 2009: 4).

The extent to which the ACU is representative ultimately depends on how the issues it addresses are relevant and meet acknowledged needs. Together with its history of identifying new and emerging topics for discussion, the ACU has a strong record in embracing—and in some cases leading—change. There is, however, one important caveat to this statement, without which no commentary would be complete. That is its attitude to members whose countries have, for whatever reason, not met the political standards expected by the wider world.

Throughout the last 50 years, at least, the ACU has adopted a consistent position on such circumstances. It has severed relations with member institutions for political reasons only with the greatest reluctance. The main example was South African universities, which did leave the Association when their country ceased to be a Commonwealth member in 1961, although even here informal relations and inclusion in the *Yearbook* and conference attendance were maintained, until 1973, only being ended after what Springer describes as 'one of the most difficult meetings…in the history of the Association' (Springer, 1988: 67). When Zimbabwe resigned from the Commonwealth in 2003, there was no question of their universities being asked to leave the ACU. Nor has there been any sanction taken against individual universities in those countries—modern examples include Nigeria, Pakistan, and Fiji—which have had their participation in the formal Commonwealth fully or partially removed. When Hong Kong left the Commonwealth in 1997, the ACU charter was deliberately amended to allow the three universities in membership to remain so. They remain active to this day, jointly hosting the ACU Conference of Executive Heads in 2011.

This reluctance might appear controversial to future historians. It does not, however, reflect a lack of concern with conditions in the countries and regions affected. In the most recent example, the Association has been actively working with the Council for Assisting Refugee Academics to help ensure the continued support of Zimbabwean academics, announcing a formal partnership in this area at its 2011 conference. Nor has it weakened the long-term ACU presence in the regions concerned. It is significant that universities in post-1994 South Africa have generally been enthusiastic members of the Association, and among its most active ones in recent years. Indeed, several African nations have looked to an associate membership of the Commonwealth itself, with their universities then having the opportunity to join the Association.

The history of the ACU reflects a belief that universities cannot be fully responsible for the ills of the societies in which they operate, and in many cases they represent one of the most effective routes to change. Perhaps, too, it demonstrates a confidence that political change, when it does come, will need effective universities more than ever. An international university network of association across the Commonwealth (and beyond) is a positive reinforcement of that social vision.

Bibliography

ACU Histories

Ashby, E. (1963) *Community of Universities: An Informal Portrait of the Association of Universities of the British Commonwealth 1913–1963*. Cambridge: University Press.

Springer, H. (with Niven, A.) (1988) *The Commonwealth of Universities: The Story of the Association of Commonwealth Universities 1963–1988*. London: ACU.

Universities' Bureau/AUBC/ACU Publications

ACU (1964) *Ninth Congress of the Universities of the Commonwealth, 1963: Report of Proceedings*. London: ACU.

——— (1974) *Commonwealth Universities and Society: The Report of Proceedings of the Eleventh Congress of the Universities of the Commonwealth*, Edinburgh, August 1973. London: ACU.

——— (1976) *Research Strengths of Universities in the Developing Countries of the Commonwealth*. London: ACU.

——— (1984) *Research Opportunities in Commonwealth Developing Countries*. London: ACU.

——— (1985) *Roles and Responsibilities: Seminar Papers Presented during the ACU Council Meeting Held in Nigeria*, 25 February–7 March 1985. London: ACU.

——— (1988) *What Can We Do for Our Countries? The Contribution of Universities to National Development: The Report of Proceedings of the*

Fourteenth Congress of the Universities of the Commonwealth, Perth, February 1988. London: ACU.

ACU (1994) *People and the Environment: Preserving the Balance: The Report of Proceedings of the Fifteenth Congress of the Universities of the Commonwealth*, Swansea, August 1993. London: ACU.

——— (2001) *Engagement as a Core Value for the University: A Consultation Document*. London: ACU.

Bjarnason, S. and Coldstream, P. (eds) (2003) *The Idea of Engagement: Universities in Society*. London: ACU.

Bourne, R. (ed.) (2000) *Universities and Development: A Report on the Socioeconomic Role of Universities in the Developing Countries of the Commonwealth*. London: ACU

Dore, R. (1978) *The Role of Universities in National Development*. ACU Occasional Paper (ABCD Extra). London: ACU.

Universities' Bureau of the British Empire (1912) *Congress of the Universities of the Empire, 1912: Report of Proceedings*. London: University of London Press.

——— (1926). *Third Congress of the Universities of the Empire, 1926: Report of Proceedings*. London: G. Bell & Sons.

Universities' Bureau of the British Empire/AUBC/ACU (1932 to date) *Annual Reports*. London: Universities' Bureau of the British Empire/ AUBC/ ACU.

——— (1914–2008) *Commonwealth Universities Yearbook*. London: Universities' Bureau of the British Empire/AUBC/ACU. (Originally *The Yearbook of the Universities of the Empire*; later *The Yearbook of the Universities of the Commonwealth* [1948–57]; then the *Commonwealth Universities Yearbook* [1958 onwards]).

Joint ACU Publications

Harle, J. (2009) *The Nairobi Report: Frameworks for Africa–UK Research Collaboration in the Social Sciences and Humanities*. London: British Academy and ACU.

——— (2010) *Growing Knowledge: Access to Research in East and Southern African Universities*. London: ACU (commissioned and funded by Arcadia).

——— (2011) *Foundations for the Future: Supporting the Early Careers of African Researchers*. Paper commissioned by the British Academy as part of the Nairobi Process. London: British Academy and ACU.

Additional ACU Publications

ACU (1997 to date) *Academic Staff Salary Survey*, ACU Policy and Research Unit.

——— *ACU Bulletin of Current Documentation (ABCD)*, 1–139 (June 1971–June 1999); *Bulletin*, 140–160 (October 1999–August 2004), 161 (August 2007 to date).

——— (1988–2008) *Who's Who of Commonwealth University Vice-Chancellors, Presidents and Rectors* (various titles).

——— (2000) *International Awards 2001+: Scholarships, Fellowships, Grants* (replacing a series of awards guides: *Awards for First Degree Study at Commonwealth Universities*; *Awards for Postgraduate Study at Commonwealth Universities*; *and Awards for University Teachers and Research Workers*).

——— (2006) *Trends in Academic Recruitment and Retention: A Commonwealth Perspective*, ACU Policy and Research Unit.

Kubler, J. and Tarrant, J. (2008) *Shifting Horizons: Issues Facing Universities in the Commonwealth: An ACU Consultation.*

——— (2010) *Working in Tandem: Identifying and Responding to the Issues Facing Our Members—2009 ACU consultation.*

Additional Reference

Schneller, C., Lungu, I., and Wachter, B. (2009) *Handbook of International Associations in Higher Education: A Practical Guide to 100 Academic Networks World-wide.* Brussels: Academic Cooperation Association (supported by Asia Europe Foundation and Asia-Europe Meeting Education Hub).

PART II

Transformations: Instruments and Symbols of Change in Higher Education

Prelude

In the next two parts of the book, key issues at the heart of the higher education 'revolution' are examined in close detail: Part II critically addresses some of the major driving forces that have animated the 'academic revolution' globally, while Part III takes a 'bottom-up' approach, examining the story from within a social sample of the major nations and communities that make up the pluralistic Commonwealth of peoples and cultures.

The approach here is critical and interrogative. Rather than recounting the processes by which change came to higher education at a macro level (which is covered in many of the fine books listed below in the Bibliography section at the end of this Prelude), the chapters that follow look to 'problematising' the policies, issues, and forces that have defined the ongoing transformation of post-secondary education.

Change in higher education can mean gains as well as losses: good intentions with unintended consequences; idealistic ambitions and disappointing outcomes; complex strategies and baffling problems of implementation; strategic goals which were lost within contested politics; rational choices that face irrational cultural biases; human hopes confronted by embedded gender discrimination; greater educational provision, which serves only established classes and elites; a revolution that is apparently 'global' but which actually has to confront a protean world of local, ideological, and cultural differences.

The issues that we have selected for critique are representative as key forces, rather than comprehensive of the totality of higher education; and they draw especially from the rich experience of the ACU network and its strategic partners. While appreciating the more general theoretical literature on higher education, the emphasis here is on the enormous challenges to policymaking, implementation practice, and problem-solving. The chapters draw on the deep experience of executive leaders, educational directors, policy researchers, and educational researchers.

Equity

Equity has been at the heart of the university transformations of recent decades. Great advances have taken place in gender participation, in pedagogies of learning, and in challenging class strictures through social mobility. But, as our authors here demonstrate through incisive chapters of bold analysis, the challenges remain; and many of those are still fundamental to the ideal of a higher education of opportunity for all humanity, and not merely for elites or the developed societies.

Moreover, as the major new *UNESCO World Atlas of Gender Equality in Education* (UNESCO, 2012) has mapped, there remain considerable global inequalities—rooted in structural socio-economic factors, governance capacity, and legitimacy, not to mention local cultural norms. Recent comparative international studies suggest that widened access broadened enrolments, rather than deepening socio-economic involvement (UNESCO, 2009: 22).

The eLearning revolution—for example, see Chapter 5—and the arrival of open learning as a major dimension of higher education access and provision now faces the steeper slopes of costs and fees, where new technologies alone are not the solution. The Commonwealth of Learning has an admirably comprehensive and strong impact statement: 'A substantial and equitable increase in the number of Commonwealth citizens acquiring the knowledge and skills for leading productive and healthy lives, through formal and non-formal open and distance learning opportunities' (COL website, 2013). And yet in its very successes—which have been so very considerable—can be discerned the sheer scale of the challenges (and needs) at issue globally.

Inclusivity

Developing a multidimensional outreach capacity becomes imperative for all equity programmes and projects. The early successes in access and gender equality are no longer a sure guide to future progress. Throughout the range of national jurisdictions it has been found that increasing access and institutional enrolments may often reflect success among the elites and middling classes, leaving out lower socio-economic groups and ethnic minorities.

The powerful Spellings Commission (Spellings, 2005) in the US both celebrated the remarkable 60 per cent or so participation rates in a diverse American tertiary sector and lamented the extent to which the nation was still not tapping the talents of many minority and regional groups. The major recommendations pressed the imperative of greater access, to ensure that the Republic was not 'left behind' in the global moves towards 'knowledge nations'.

Fees and Loans

Likewise, in the general move towards student fees and student loans (to supplement the enormous costs of state expenditure on expanding systems), it would seem that fears of debt are much more prevalent as a detriment to higher education enrolment among the very social classes that education might empower. The introduction of income-contingent loans, such as the noted Australian 'Higher Education Contribution Scheme' (HECS), has been deemed a singular success, but concerns persist about how inclusive is that approach when it comes to socially and culturally disadvantaged families. At a political level, HECS also relies fundamentally on the gearing of a highly efficient national income tax regime—something that is not always replicable in other jurisdictions where government is less effective.

Gender and Equality

Great strides have been made in the participation of women in higher education over the last decades. From an abysmally low level, dramatic progress has been palpable in recent years, to the extent that the majority of first-degree candidates are probably women. And yet, as a creative and rigorous gender equity programme at the ACU has established—in findings outlined in a powerful chapter of this book (Chapter 6)—there are hugely challenging issues still at play. The participation rates vary considerably from one nation (and culture) to another; the flow on from undergraduate to postgraduate study has been so much lower than in the male enrolment data; and female students are hardly distributed equally across the disciplines.

If the now legendary STEM subjects—science, engineering, technology, and mathematics—are the key to the future of universities and their societies, there are simply not enough women in their classes. Men still cluster around the sciences, engineering, and technology, while women are often found in the social sciences and the humanities. The links between tertiary graduations and employment are also stronger for men than for women.

Moreover, the greatly increased female participation in higher education is not being reflected in similar proportion among the academic staff, let alone at the executive leadership level. The latter is a great deal better than in the proportion of women serving on private sector boards and in corporate administrations; but, after an initial increase in women academic leaders, the progress appears to have slowed markedly. Universities are sometimes seen to be 'chilly environments' for aspiring female leaders. Feminist critiques rightly speculate about how the university of the future might be different and enhanced by greater gender equality among the staff, including the top management and executive positions of leadership.

Student Mobility and Access

With globalisation has come an enhanced focus on student mobility, especially through trans-border educational opportunities. The ACU as a network has been strongly involved in this development, not least through its administration of the remarkable Commonwealth Scholarship and Fellowship Plan—one of the great student equity programmes in modern higher education. The Plan was bold in conception and its financing has been challenging throughout its existence, given the inequality in the resources of its national stakeholders. At its centre was the truly internationalist ideal of exchanging students among the societies of the Commonwealth, and not merely of providing access to British metropolitan institutions. But, as an expert chapter here indicates (Chapter 8), with all its successes, history has ultimately overtaken the scheme as the politics of targeted national funding intruded; as the emphasis shifted somewhat to 'development' (over individual educational opportunities); as the global flows of students seeking education became more regional (for example, more students from the

EU to the UK than from the Commonwealth; more students from Asia to Australia).

Globalisation has also meant freer movement not only of goods but also of people: the fee-paying international student mobility movement grew way beyond the annual 2,000 or so Commonwealth Scholarship and Fellowship holders. Of the 1 million students at, say, Australian universities, nearly 25 per cent are overseas, international, fee-paying students. In total, there are now several million students across the Commonwealth who fall into that category, supported by an eclectic range of fees, scholarships, part-awards, and work experience income.

'Internationalisation' has become an educational goal for many universities who see 'cultural competencies' as a key part of global citizenship in the twenty-first century. In complex ways, the global education market has moved the equity debate beyond state-funded student mobility programmes.

Private Philanthropy

Private philanthropy has also been involved and has increased over time. The oldest Empire–Commonwealth student scholarship programme began that way through a remarkable act of visionary philanthropy in 1903: the 'Rhodes Scholarships' have since then been administered by the Rhodes Trust, being based on the estate legacy of Cecil John Rhodes (1853–1902), mining magnate, imperialist, and African colonial politician.

Over 7,000 Rhodes Scholars have attended Oxford University for an undergraduate education, with an increasing number undertaking a Master's or research degree. It is an elite programme, which avowedly looks to shape future leaders (and has so far produced a highly successful American president, many prime ministers and politicians, senior public servants, professors, and vice-chancellors, as well as leaders in science and engineering, business, and the arts). What is less commented upon is its equity face: scholars have often come from humble homes and poor nations; Africans and Asians have been prominent alongside Americans; women have been eligible since 1977; new scholarships have been added, in order to address special social needs.

In addition, the Rhodes Trust has worked to help create the new Mandela Rhodes Foundation, which has a major equity and enhancement mission, by supporting postgraduate study and leadership development training for outstanding Africans. The chair of its board is currently a most distinguished former South African vice-chancellor and public intellectual, Professor Njabulo Ndebele. The Rhodes scheme has also been indirectly important, in embedding the notion of trans-national scholarships in global development.

The Carnegie Trust and the Fulbright Commission work within that tradition of valuing international education and cultural interactions. Many more such schemes now operate, with some becoming a feature of national strategies in an era of globalisation.

Quality Assurance

'More must mean worse', Kingsley Amis once shockingly remarked of mass education. But as the Quality Assurance (QA) movement globally has shown, more does not have to mean worse; and it can indeed just mean 'different'. There is no absolute in testing excellence over time and across global cultures. But in some circumstances—delivered through poor teaching in mass environments—it certainly can mean worse when it is delivered.

A comprehensive chapter below (Chapter 7) by a leading authority on the character, origins, and practice of QA across the entire Commonwealth, shows how the role of the 'external examiner' and then of 'benchmarking' served earlier systems, and pointed the way to more universal and structured means of assessing processes and outcomes of the expanding higher education jurisdictions.

But as QA matured, so questions arose over its efficacy and purpose: did it really test outcomes or the processes that defined the operations of the new 'multi-versities', as Clark Kerr famously described the modern university (Kerr, 2001)? Or even, more recently, how could 'quality' be embedded in the professionalism of the staff and rely on 'trust' rather than compliance targets? Was 'enhancement' not a better goal than satisfying frameworks of complex performance indicators—which may or may not be aligned with the actual educational aspirations of institutional providers?

A new external phenomenon has also entered the Quality paradigm in recent years: the role of 'university rankings'. What began as a relatively minor dimension within the debate over measuring performance, outcomes, and reputation has now become serious business, with a wide range of organisations involved in publishing lists that gain considerable attention, even notoriety. There has been a heavy barrage of criticism directed at 'rankings'—on methodology and sampling evidence especially—but universities have been their own worst enemies in the debate. Institutions that have strongly critiqued the validity and usefulness of rankings are often found to be promoting their own position on the ranking lists when those happen to turn in their favour. The impact of rankings is now probably so widespread that it is not unreasonable for some to argue that 'rankings are the new QA'.

That is but one of the issues impacting on the development of QA in the future. Other issues also raised by Chapter 7 include developing appropriate QA in response to the fast-changing modes of education and new types of providers; working to reduce the burden of QA on institutions, while assuring stakeholders; strengthening global systems of recognition and mobility; and ensuring that QA systems develop to match the changing world in which they operate.

The Policy Nexus

Higher education has become a key aspect of modernisation in societies of both the developed and the developing world, even if the policies and funding which frame that role are not always given the highest priority. It is in that context that higher education institutions have become increasingly proactive through interventions in public debate and in lobbying stakeholders for policy reform. The final chapter in this section (Chapter 9) accordingly offers a bold 'agenda for change', by focusing the debate around the need for a new 'mindset' towards driving change.

In particular, given the intensifying interconnectedness of global education systems in the twenty-first century, coupled with the new modes of communication and knowledge transfer, 'there are new opportunities for harnessing the power of higher education to Commonwealth development'. And this particularly involves the setting of new agendas and strategies that can be furthered through exploiting and strengthening the partnerships between the higher education community and its key stakeholders.

The ACU may well be the oldest global network, but it has tremendous opportunities in a new century to play a vital role in that bold new global vision. The lives and well-being of many millions in its member nations could be the direct beneficiaries.

Bibliography

Equity and Access

ACU (2007) *Commonwealth Universities Yearbook*, 2 vols, 81st ed. London: ACU. (An index of 2,700 institutions and centres, 23,000 academic departments, 186,000 academics.)

Altbach, Liz Reisberg and L.W. Rumbley (eds). *Trends in Global Higher Education: Tracking an Academic Revolution*, P.G. A report prepared for the UNESCO 2009 World Conference on Higher Education. Executive Summary. Paris: UNESCO.

Canadian International Development Agency (1997) *The Why and How of Gender-sensitive Indicators—A Project Level Handbook*. Quebec: CIDA.

D'Hombres, B. (2010) *Inequality in Tertiary Education Systems: Which Metrics Should We Use for Measuring and Benchmarking?* Washington: World Bank.

Morley, L. (2010) Gender Equity in Higher Education: Challenges and Celebrations. In *International Encyclopaedia of Education*, 629–35, 3rd ed., eds P. Peterson, E. Baker and B. McGaw. Elsevier Ltd.

Morley, L., Sorhaindo, A., Burke, P.J. (eds) (2005) Researching Women: An Annotated Bibliography on General Equity in Commonwealth Higher Education. London: Institute of Education.

OECD (2012) *OECD Indicators: Education at a Glance*. Paris: OECD Publishing, especially pp 60–86.

Spellings, M. (Chair) (2005) *A Commission on the Future of Higher Education*. Education Department, United States of America.

UNESCO (2012) *World Atlas of Gender Equality in Education*. UNESCO: Paris.

Websites (General)

Commonwealth Scholarship Commission in the United Kingdom (Commonwealth Professional Fellowships): http://cscuk.dfid.gov.uk/apply/professional-fellowships (downloaded on 2 April 2013).

OECD website: www.oecd-ilibrary.org/education/education-at-a-glance-2012_eag-2012-en (downloaded on 2 April 2013).

Scholarships and international mobility: www.acu.ac.uk/focus-areas/scholarship-administration (downloaded on 2 April 2013).

ACU Professional Networks

Graduate and Employment Network
Human Resources Management Network
PR, Marketing, and Communication Network
Research Management Network
University Extension and Community Engagement Network

ACU Capacity-building Services

Commonwealth Higher Education Management Service (CHEMS)
Commonwealth Higher Education Support Scheme (CHESS)

Specialised Publications

Bentley, M. (2005) *Producing Gender-Sensitive Materials for Open and Distance Learning*. The Knowledge Series. Vancouver: Commonwealth of Learning.

Kerr, C. (2001) *The Uses of the University*, 5th ed. Cambridge, Mass.: Harvard University Press.

Lindsay, B. and Justiz, M.J. (eds) (2001) The Quest for Equity in Higher Education: Toward New Paradigms in an Evolving Affirmative Action Era. New York: SUNY Press.

Morley, L. (2011) *Sex, Grades and Silence: The Impact of Feminist Research on Higher Education Globally*. Ideas and Issues in Higher Education Series, November. Centre for the Study of Higher Education, University of Melbourne.

Murism, S. (2004) *Elements of Gender Mainstreaming—A 14 Point Framework*. The Development Equity Group, Inc.

Thomas, P. (2004) Gender and Development—Bridging Policy and Practice. *Development Bulletin* (ANU Development Studies Network, Canberra), 64.

Touchton, J., Musil, C.M., and Campbell, K.P. (eds) (2009) *A Measure of Equity: Women's progress in Higher Education*. Report of the Association of American Colleges and Universities. Washington, DC: Association of American Colleges and Universities.

Institutional Centres and Websites

Association of American Colleges and Universities: Program on Status and Education of Women. Available online at http://www.aacu.org/psew/ (downloaded on 21 May 2013).

Commonwealth of Learning, Vancouver, Canada: Equity and Learning. Available online at www.col.Org/progServ/3YR/Pages/default.aspx (downloaded on 2 April 2013).

Equity101: Foundations for Social Inclusion in Education. Available online at www.equity101.info/content/welcome-equity101 (downloaded on 2 April 2013).

Institute of Education, University of London: Gender Equity in Commonwealth Higher Education Research Project. Available online at www.ioe.ac.uk/about/16509.html (downloaded on 2 April 2013).

University of Cape Town: African Gender Institute.

University of Nairobi: Institute of African and Gender Studies.

University of Pretoria: Institute for Women's and Gender Studies.

University of Sussex: Centre for Higher Education and Equity Research (CHEER).

World Bank: Global Study to Explore Issues of Equity in Higher Education Around the World. Available online at http://blogs.worldbank.org/education/global-study-to-explore-issues-of-equity-in-higher-education (downloaded on 2 April 2013).

Equity and Open Learning

Bates, A.W. (2011) 2011 *Outlook for Online Learning and Distance Education*. Sudbury, Ontario: Contact North.

Carnegie Commission on Higher Education (1968) *Quality and Equality: New Levels of Federal Responsibility for Higher Education*. New York: McGraw Hill.

Commonwealth of Learning/UNESCO (2011) *Guidelines for Open Educational Resources (OER) in Higher Education*. Vancouver/Paris: Commonwealth of Learning.

Gallagher, S. (2013) MOOCS means more time for different kinds of learning. Higher Education Supplement, *Australian*, 20 March 2013, 32.

Kanwar, A.S. and Taplin, M. (eds) (2001) *Brave Women of Asia: How Distance Education Changed Their Lives*. Vancouver: Commonwealth of Learning.

Naidu, C.G. (2007) *Manual on Financing Distance Education*. New Delhi: Commonwealth Education Media Centre for Asia.

Walsh, T. (2011) Unlocking the Gates: How and Why Leading Universities Are Opening Up Access to Their Courses. Princeton: Princeton University Press.

WikiEducator (2011) OER University (#oeru). Available online at http://wikieducator.org/OER_university/About (downloaded on 2 April 2013).

Equity and Global Studies

King, R. (ed.) (2003) *The University in the Global Age*. London: Palgrave Macmillan.

——— (ed.) (2010) *Inequalities and Higher Education—Whose Interests Are We Serving?* London: Palgrave Macmillan.

Vincent-Lancrin, S. (2009) An OECD Scan of Public and Private Higher Education. In *Globalisation's Muse: Universities and Higher Education Systems in a Changing World*, eds J.A. Douglass, C. Judson King, and I. Feller. California: Berkeley Public Policy Press.

Student Mobility

Commonwealth Scholarship Initiatives

Maxey, K. (2000) *Student Mobility on the Map: Tertiary Education in the Commonwealth on the Threshold of the 21st Century*. London: UKCOSA.

Perraton, H. (2009) *Learning Abroad: A History of the Commonwealth Scholarship and Fellowship Plan*. Newcastle upon Tyne: Cambridge Scholars Publishing.

Impact and Equity

Ilchman, A.S., Ilchman, W.F., and Tolar, M.H. (eds) (2004) *The Lucky Few and the Worthy Many: Scholarship Competitions and the World's Future Leaders*. Bellagion Conference Papers on Erasmus Program and Equity. Bloomington: Indiana University Press.

Maiworm, F. and Teichler, U. (1986) *Study Abroad and Early Career: Experiences of Former ERASMUS students*. London: Jessica Kingsley.

Opper, S., Teichler, U., and Carlton, J. (1990) *Impact of Study Abroad Programmes on Students and Graduates*. London: Jessica Kingsley.

Volkman, T.A. (ed.) (2009) *Origins, Journeys and Returns: Social Justice in International Higher Education*. New York: Social Science Research Council (Ford Foundation international fellowships program).

The Rhodes and Mandela Trusts

Kenny, Sir Anthony (ed.) (2001) *The History of the Rhodes Trust*, 2 vols. Oxford: Oxford University Press.

The Rhodes Trust. The Mandela Rhodes Foundation (from 2003). Available online at www.rhodeshouse.ox.ac.uk/rhodes-alumni/mandela-rhodes-foundation (downloaded on 2 April 2013).

Ziegler, P. (2008) *Legacy: Cecil Rhodes, the Rhodes Trust and the Rhodes Scholarships*. New Haven: Yale University Press.

The Pursuit of 'Quality'

Brown, R. (October 2012) Quality assurance 1992–2010. Perspectives: Policy and Practice in Higher Education, *Journal of the Association of University Administrators (AUA)*, 16(4): 113–17.

International Network for Quality Assurance Agencies in Higher Education (INQAAHE), The Hague, Netherlands. Available online at www.inqaahe.org./main/about (downloaded on 2 April 2013).

Marginson, S. (2007) Global University Rankings. In *Prospects of Higher Education: Globalization, Market Competition, Public Goods and the Future of the University,* ed. S. Marginson. Rotterdam/Taipei: Sense Publishers.

Quality Assurance Agency for Higher Education (2004) *Code of Practice for Assurance of Academic Quality and Standards in Higher Education*, Section 4: External Examining. Gloucester: QAA.

Schreuder, D.M. (2006) Hamlet's challenge—'Come show us your quality'. *Proceedings of the Australian Universities Quality Forum*. Melbourne: Australian Universities Quality Agency.

Schreuder, D.M. and Woodhouse, D. (2007) Through a Glass Darkly. Paper presented at the Annual INQAAHE Conference, Toronto, Ontario. Melbourne: Australian Universities Quality Agency.

Woodhouse, D. (2012) *A Short History of Quality*. Abu Dhabi, UAE: CAA Quality Series.

Agenda for the Future: Commonwealth Challenges

Commonwealth Secretariat (2011) *A Commonwealth of the People: Time for Urgent Action*. The report of the Eminent Persons Group to the Commonwealth Heads of Government. London: Commonwealth Secretariat.

Varghese, N. (2011) Globalization and Cross-border Education: Challenges for the Development of Higher Education in Commonwealth Countries. IIEP Research Paper. Paris: International Institute for Educational Planning.

Williams, P. and Urwick, J. (eds) (2012) *Educational Co-operation: Jewel in the Commonwealth Crown*. London: Commonwealth Consortium for Education.

5

Q: Will E-learning Disrupt Higher Education? A: Massively!

John Daniel, Asha Kanwar, and Stamenka Uvalić-Trumbić

Chapter Overview

The ACU celebrates its centenary at the time when political, economic, and technological trends are converging to create major change in higher education. This chapter is about the impact of evolving technologies, notably online learning or 'e-Learning'. The impact of online learning will go far beyond simply changing pedagogy because, like the Internet itself, it is a disruptive technology—and disruptive technologies rarely favour existing providers.

Paradoxically, early signs suggest that e-learning is not causing major change. Currently, at least in public higher education institutions, e-learning is raising (rather than cutting) costs, is not improving student performance, and is often of poor quality. However, this will change as e-learning takes an ever larger share of student enrolments. More and more students are opting for the online mode, and course enrolments in e-learning are expanding much faster than in campus-based courses. Projections suggest that over 80 per cent of US students will be taking courses online in 2014.

The disruptive paradigm will not be e-learning per se, but the combination of online technologies, lower-cost provision and for-profit corporate structures. Already in the US the for-profit higher education sector has a much higher share of the online market (32 per cent) than of the overall market (7 per cent). Such institutions are better placed to expand online, because they have access to capital, they are used to managing technology and they do not have to worry about resistance from academic staff, nor about exploiting their earlier investment in campus facilities.

The large for-profit educational corporations are expanding overseas, by acquiring local institutions and moving their teaching online. Countries still have time to develop indigenous models of online provision, although they will need to adopt some of the habits of the for-profit sector to do it successfully. As competition to offer online courses increases, prices should tumble, which is good news for expanding access.

Higher education will follow other business sectors in moving from full-service to self-service models of provision. An example is the new Open Education Resource University (OERU), described in the final section of this chapter. Yet, in a reminder that history sometimes repeats itself, the OERU has distinct echoes of the University of London External System that was created in 1858—half a century before the ACU!

Introduction

The following aphorism, coined by Clark Kerr's Carnegie Commission in 1968, should give us pause before predicting substantive change in universities:

> Taking, as a starting point, 1530, when the Lutheran Church was founded, some 66 institutions that existed then still exist today in the Western World in recognizable form: the Catholic Church, the Lutheran Church, the parliaments of Iceland and the Isle of Man, and 62 universities... They have experienced wars, revolutions, depressions, and industrial transformations, and have come out less changed than almost any other segment of their societies.
>
> (Carnegie Commission on Higher Education, 1968)

Here are just six examples of the predicted threats to universities that have failed to materialise.

- In 1997, the management guru Peter Drucker predicted that in 30 years the big university campuses would be relics (Lenzner and Johnson, 1997)—yet 14 years before his deadline, few appear to be on their last legs and most are as vibrant as ever.
- Enrolment growth has been consistently underestimated, particularly of women. Forecasts suggest the addition of another 80 million students worldwide by 2025. The desire for access to higher education is stronger than ever.
- When higher education was declared a tradable commodity under the General Agreement on Trade in Services in 1995, academics panicked about imminent commercialisation—yet most of the world's universities are still public institutions with an educational ethos.
- Quite recently, received wisdom held that the coming cohorts of students were a new breed of digital natives, who would create a generational divide in study habits—yet recent research on thousands of students of all ages finds no such divide (Jones and Hosein, 2010).
- The hype around the dotcom frenzy in 1999–2000 claimed that all education would soon go online—yet today it seems that universities have absorbed the virtual world, rather than letting it absorb them (Bates, 2011).
- Despite the efforts of some governments to restrict the research function to a limited number of institutions, most universities aspire to continue and expand the research function.

While this list supports the notion that higher education develops by gradual evolution rather than by revolution, it is too soon to dismiss all these forecasts as illusions. We shall examine four drivers of change.

In 1971, US President Richard Nixon asked the Chinese leader Zhou Enlai what he thought had been the impact of the French revolution. Zhou replied that it was too early to tell. Commentators, assuming that the leaders were talking of the storming of the Bastille in 1789, seized on the story as a charming illustration of China's propensity for long-term thinking. However, Nixon's interpreter insists that Zhou was referring to the recent student uprising in France in 1968 (*les évènements de mai 1968*) (McGregor, 2011).

One of the authors of this chapter (JD) was finishing his doctorate at the University of Paris in 1968. The protests inspired some of the most telling slogans and graffiti of the mid-twentieth century, although the students were less succinct about the reforms they actually sought. In 1971, it was indeed much too early for Zhou to provide Nixon with an impact analysis.

Four decades on, however, higher education has changed markedly, although not in the ways that the students in Paris campaigned for, nor as a result of their actions. The reality is that three of the key drivers of change in contemporary higher education (see below) were barely present in 1968, and the fourth, internationalisation, has taken on new dimensions.

Drivers of Change

The Internet

The first driver of change is the Internet. A year after the Paris riots, at the launch of the UK Open University (UKOU) in 1969, Lord Geoffrey Crowther, its founding Chancellor, said:

> The world is caught in a communications revolution, the effects of which will go beyond those of the industrial revolution of two centuries ago. Then the great advance was the invention of machines to multiply the potency of men's muscles. Now the great new advance is the invention of machines to multiply the potency of men's minds. As the steam engine was to the first revolution, so the computer is to the second. It has been said that the addiction of the traditional university to the lecture room is a sign of its inability to adjust to the development of the printing press. That, of course, is unjust. But at least no such reproach will be levelled at the Open University in the communications revolution. Every new form of human communication will be examined to see how it can be used to raise and broaden the level of human understanding.
>
> (Northcott, 1976)

Lord Crowther could scarcely have imagined where this communications revolution would have taken us four decades later. Online and mobile communications have lessened the significance of national borders and disrupted many business models. When refuelling their vehicles, buying books or arranging travel, consumers are opting increasingly for self-service models made possible by online and mobile communications. This trend is now impacting on universities.

The Cost of Higher Education

The second force for change is a greater concern, across society, about the cost of higher education and a growing reluctance on the part of hard-pressed governments to meet all this expenditure from public funds.

In 1968 only a small proportion of young people—and very few older ones—had access to universities in most countries, and governments were content to underwrite the costs of these relatively small systems. Newly independent countries copied this policy of their former colonial powers and did not charge tuition fees when they established national universities. The persistence of this policy, even after the former colonial powers began to introduce fees in their own countries, has handicapped the expansion of provision in many developing countries where, in a carryover of the socialist thinking that inspired much of their nation-building, the idea of charging fees for education was long taboo.

With hindsight, this attitude may have been partly justified, because where universities are free to set tuition fees, the fees tend to rise faster than inflation. The US may be an extreme case, but since 1986 college fees there have risen by 467 per cent compared to inflation of 107 per cent in the economy overall (Archibald and Feldman, 2010). The impact of the post-2008 recession on US household incomes, combined with public concern about the debt burdens on students and graduates, is finally putting downward pressure on fees and creating incentives to offer less expensive options. In the UK, strategies to reduce government debt have included steep increases in university fees, as well as policies to encourage for-profit institutions to play a larger role in the provision of higher education.

It is pointless, however, to exhort institutions to charge less unless they can cut costs without losing quality and limiting access. Online learning provides one means to do this.

Private Higher Education

A third driver of change is the growth of private higher education, including institutions that operate for profit. This is changing the pattern of corporate structures in higher education.

Private provision is now the fastest-growing subsector, with some 30 per cent of students enrolled in private higher education institutions globally. Some countries (Japan, South Korea) enrol around 80 per cent of their students in private higher education institutions. In parts of Latin America, for example, Brazil and Chile, the proportions top 70 per cent, and over 90 per cent of Chilean higher education institutions are private (PROPHE, 2012). In aggregate, 30 per cent of India's enrolments in 2005 were in the private institutions, which accounted for over 40 per cent of all institutions, supplying 53 per cent of the requirement for general higher education and 80 per cent of the requirement for technical education (PROPHE, 2012). In Malaysia, private institutions account for 50 per cent of all enrolments in higher education (Arokiasamy, 2010).

Within the private sector, for-profit higher education is developing its own business models. For example, India's Manipal Academy is a diversified private institution offering programmes in technology management and sciences to a student body of over 30,000 students. Its close interaction with industry enables it to place almost 100 per cent of its students in employment, giving it great pull in the market, despite high fees. Often, however, private sector business models have not yet been well documented because, in countries where the legal framework does not make for a clear distinction between private for-profit and private not-for-profit institutions, both tend to operate in a non-transparent way.

In other places, strong new institutions are emerging as public–private partnerships, a specific example being the Open University Malaysia, a private institution that pays dividends to its shareholders, which are Malaysia's public universities.

A key feature of the private higher education sector is its diversity. Large private providers of distance education, such as Phoenix Online with over 100,000 students, are the exception rather than the rule. Most private institutions are relatively small and conduct teaching face to face, although this is changing fast, as in the case of India's Symbiosis Centre for Distance Learning, which is barely 10 years old but now enrols 250,000 students in some 40 countries.

Internationalisation

Two icons of academic exchange remind us that internationalisation has been a feature of universities from their earliest days. Xuanzang was one of the many Chinese Buddhist scholars in the first millennium who studied in India at Nalanda University. This, the world's first international university, is today being re-established by the governments of India and Bihar with foreign support. Erasmus of Rotterdam, who studied at the University of Paris (the great international academic centre of the second millennium) and who also travelled to other European seats of learning, has given his name to the student exchanges that are helping to reintegrate academic Europe.

For most of the twentieth century, internationalisation referred primarily to students taking degree courses in other countries (an experience that all three authors of this chapter enjoyed). Student mobility was seen as a contribution to international understanding and as a catalyst for valuable exchanges when students returned home. Indeed, in the 1980s, when the richer Commonwealth countries raised tuition fees sharply and caused a precipitate drop in the number of students coming from developing countries, the Commonwealth Secretariat raised the alarm and set up a Standing Committee on Student Mobility. Its series of reports exploring alternative ways of maintaining and expanding opportunities for Commonwealth students to have access to higher education abroad triggered the appointment of an expert group chaired by Lord (Asa) Briggs, which recommended that if the students could not move to the courses, the courses should move to the students (Commonwealth Secretariat, 1987).

One approach is for universities to offer their courses overseas, by creating branch campuses in other countries. The Observatory on Borderless Higher Education reported that there were 200 degree-awarding international branch campuses in 2011, and the number was continuing to grow.

The Briggs group proposed a different approach. Its report stated: 'Our long term aim is that any learner, anywhere in the Commonwealth, shall be able to study any distance teaching programme available from any bona fide college or university in the Commonwealth'. It called for the creation of a new institution that 'would seek to achieve this by working in a co-operative partnership with existing colleges, universities and other institutions of post-secondary education' (Commonwealth Secretariat, 1987).

Commonwealth Heads of Government agreed to establish such a new institution, the Commonwealth of Learning (COL), in 1987. The Memorandum of Understanding was signed by governments at Lancaster House on 1 September 1988 and COL opened its doors in January 1989. Over the last quarter century, COL's work has spurred substantial growth in the provision of distance learning across the Commonwealth. Today it is promoting the creation and re-purposing of open educational resources

(OER) and encouraging the emergence of the OERU, a mechanism for co-operative partnership (to which we shall return later in this chapter).

The Disruption of Higher Education

The four drivers above, operating in combination and feeding on each other, are likely to recast the higher education systems of most countries. We can best understand their interplay by examining them individually.

Trends in E-learning

In his report *2011 Outlook for Online Learning and Distance Education*, Bates (2011) identified three key trends in US higher education. Other countries are likely to follow similar paths as connectivity expands.

The first trend is the rapid growth of online learning. Enrolment in fully online (distance) courses in the USA expanded by 21 per cent between 2009 and 2010, compared to a 2 per cent expansion in campus-based enrolments.

Despite this growth, institutional goals for online learning in public sector higher education lack ambition. Bates argues that the intelligent use of technology could help higher education to accommodate more students, improve learning outcomes, provide more flexible access, and do all this at less cost. Instead, he found that costs are rising because investment in technology and staff is increasing without replacing other activities. There is no evidence of improved learning outcomes, and there is often a failure to meet best quality standards for online learning. It seems that the traditional US public higher education sector has little heart for online learning. Some institutions charge higher fees to online students, even though the costs of serving them are presumably lower, perhaps to discourage this development.

A third finding, which should stimulate the public sector to take online learning seriously, given its rapid growth, is that the US for-profit sector has a much higher proportion of the total online market (32 per cent) than its share of the overall higher education market (7 per cent). Seven of the ten US institutions with the highest online enrolments are for-profits. For-profits are better placed to expand online, because they face less resistance from academic staff and need not worry about exploiting an earlier investment in campus facilities. Furthermore, the for-profits adopt a team approach to the development of online learning courses and student support, whereas most public institutions simply rely on individual academics to create and support online versions of their classroom courses. Bates calls this the 'Lone Ranger' model and argues that it is less likely to produce sustainable online learning of quality than the team approach (Bates and Sangra, 2011).

Finally, Bates projects that over 80 per cent of US students are expected to be taking courses online in 2014, up from 44 per cent in 2009. The for-profit providers that are already well established in this delivery mode are likely to gain the advantage.

Indeed, a UK report, *Collaborate to Compete: Seizing the Opportunity of Online Learning for UK Higher Education* (HEFCE, 2011), recommends that public higher education institutions should link up with for-profit companies in order not to get left behind in online learning. This is already a trend in the US. For example, Best Associates, a Dallas-based merchant bank with investments in education, operates an Academic Partnerships programme with a growing number of state universities. The aim is to help these institutions offer high-demand and socially important programmes (for example, MEd, BSc Nursing) online at scale. The public institution sets the fees, of which it retains 20–30 per cent with the rest going to Best Associates. Since the system has significantly lower costs than traditional teaching, some institutions have reduced their fees substantially—but others have not.

Bates concludes his report by alerting Canadian institutions to a growing market that campus education is not serving well. Canadian public higher education is not moving into online learning fast enough to meet the demand: 'If public institutions do not step up to the plate, then the corporate for-profit sector will' (Bates, 2011). This statement suggests that online learning could disrupt higher education systems globally. Will they split over the coming years into a public sector focused on research and a private sector doing most of the teaching online? Would this matter?

Some governments would like to distinguish between research universities and teaching institutions. An extrapolation of these trends could make this wish come true, with the added difference that research would take place in public institutions, while most teaching would be carried out by for-profit enterprises.

Why Does Higher Education Cost So Much?

US tuition fees have been rising faster than inflation for several decades. Other rich countries where fees used to be zero or nominal have either introduced or raised them. Parents and students have begun to object to rising fee levels, which inspired Robert Archibald and David Feldman (2010) to justify high fees in their book *Why Does College Cost So Much?*

These economists write about the US experience, but their arguments have broader relevance. They place the higher education enterprise in the wider economy and make careful comparisons with the evolution of prices in a range of industries over half a century. The prices of manufactures have gone down in real terms; those of many services, such as hairdressing, have stayed roughly constant; whereas, the prices of personal services by professionals with high training requirements have risen. They cite academics, dentists, horn players, and stockbrokers as examples of such professionals.

Are such comparisons valid? The link between the high prices of certain services and the cost of training the professionals who deliver them was labelled the 'cost disease' in the 1960s by William G. Bowen and W.J. Baumol in research on the economics of the performing arts (Baumol and Bowen, 1965). They argued that salaries in such areas are pushed up, even if productivity remains static, by productivity-linked salary increases in other sectors of the economy. Archibald and Feldman (2010) adopt this reasoning in their book, dismissing summarily the possibility of increasing productivity in higher education with technology.

Bowen himself, however, is no longer so sure. In a foreword to Taylor Walsh's book *Unlocking the Gates: How and Why Leading Universities Are Opening Up Access to Their Courses*, he writes that he is rethinking his scepticism about the potential of new technologies to improve productivity in higher education (Bowen, 2011).

It is not surprising that the price of dentistry rises faster than inflation because, despite increasingly sophisticated equipment, it is a personal service with little scope for automation. The case of horn players, as examples of orchestral musicians, is more debatable. They are rare and specialised professionals, but technology has increased their productivity dramatically because most people now listen to them, with equal enjoyment and at much lower cost, on iPods and CDs instead of in concert halls. The most interesting comparison is with stockbrokers. Their prices went up more rapidly than those of higher education until the 1980s and then fell steadily to a relatively much lower level. This was when brokerage services went online, giving individual punters more control.

Brokerage services are a better comparator for higher education. Technology now allows institutions to deliver their programmes through media and to give students more control as distance learners. This can cut costs substantially without loss of effectiveness, and the cost advantage of distance learning is increasing steadily. This is because in large distance education systems the cost of learning materials production has remained almost constant as a proportion of the total cost, while that of learner support services has almost doubled (Naidu, 2007).

How Does Technology Cut Costs?

Most governments want to widen access to education, while improving its quality and reducing its cost. We can visualise this challenge as a triangle of vectors (see Triangle A in Figure 5.1), which makes the simple point that in conventional classroom teaching there is little scope to alter these vectors advantageously. Improving one vector worsens the others. Pack more students into the class, and quality will be perceived to suffer (see Triangle A1 in Figure 5.1). Improve quality by providing more learning materials or better teachers, and the cost will go up (see Triangle A2 in Figure 5.1). Cost-cutting may endanger both access and quality (see Triangle A3 in Figure 5.1).

We call this the 'iron triangle' and it has constrained the expansion of education throughout history, by creating in the public mind an insidious link between quality and exclusiveness. If this were the end of the story, Archibald and Feldman (2010) would be correct that the cost of higher education must rise inexorably. However, technology is able to stretch this triangle to achieve, simultaneously, wider access, higher quality, and lower cost (see Triangle B in Figure 5.1).

Asian studies show that costs per learner in technology-based distance learning systems are a third of those for conventional learners (Dutt and Gaba, 2006). The open universities have been exploiting this advantage for years. They enrol millions of students and some achieve impressive ratings for the quality of their teaching. For example, the most recent national quality assessments for teaching in England put the UKOU in fifth place out of 100 institutions, one place above Oxford (see Figure 5.2).[1]

Figure 5.1:
The 'Iron Triangle' of Scale (Access), Quality, and Cost

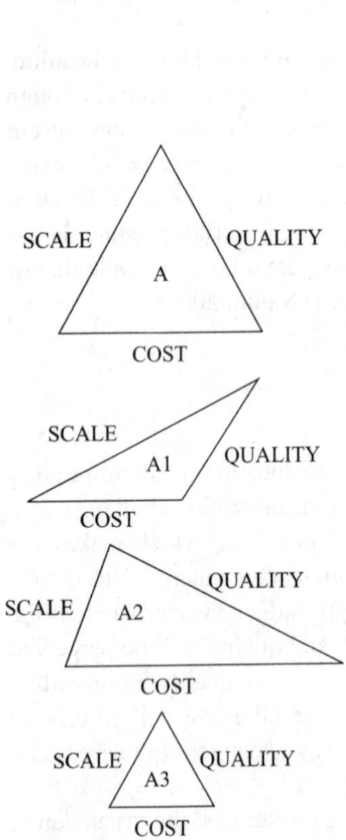

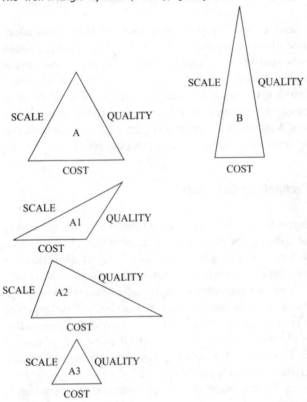

The UKOU has also come top—and never lower than third—in national surveys of student satisfaction conducted with a large sample.

This revolution of providing high-quality teaching to large numbers at low cost was originally achieved with traditional learning technologies (print, audio, video, and stand-alone computers). It was based on the principles of industrial production, which were identified two centuries ago by Adam Smith as division of labour, specialisation, economies of scale, and the use of machines and media (Smith, 1776).

Today's new generation of digital technology is characterised by the concepts of networks, connectedness, collaboration, and community. As well as increasing economies of scale, since digital material costs almost nothing to distribute, this technology also speeds up and intensifies the

Figure 5.2:
National Rankings of Teaching Quality in England

BRITAIN'S TOP NINE UNIVERSITIES
Quality Rankings of Teaching

based on all subject assessments 1995–2004
(Sunday Times University Guide 2004)

1	CAMBRIDGE	96%
2	LOUGHBOROUGH	95%
3=	LONDON SCHOOL OF ECONOMICS	88%
3=	YORK	88%
5	**THE OPEN UNIVERSITY**	**87%**
6	OXFORD	86%
7	IMPERIAL COLLEGE	82%
8	UNIVERSITY COLLEGE LONDON	77%
9	ESSEX	77%

Source: Sunday Times University Guide 2004.

interactions possible between students and their teachers. As a result, technology-mediated learning now reaches far beyond the confines of the open universities. Most campus universities in countries with a basic IT infrastructure are now dabbling in distance education online, and more and more students are opting for this form of teaching. Forecasts that digital technology would create a generation gap, with young 'digital natives' seeking online learning while older students avoiding it, have been proved wrong.

Research on UKOU students shows that, although older and younger people use technology differently, there is no clear break between two separate populations (Jones and Hosein, 2010). The research was conducted on 7,000 students aged between 21 and 100 with 2,000 between ages 60 and 69; 1,000 aged 70 and over; and, for comparison, four 1,000-member groups of students in their twenties, thirties, forties, and fifties, respectively. The results showed that while there are differences in the use of digital technology with age, the change is gradual from group to group. There is no coherent 'net generation'.

One important discovery was a correlation—independent of age—between attitudes to technology and approaches to studying: 'Those students who had more positive attitudes to technology were more likely to adopt a deep approach to studying, more likely to adopt a strategic approach to studying and less likely to adopt a surface approach to studying.' This evidence that, at any age, a good attitude to technology correlates with good study habits is also important in giving the lie to the view that online learning tends to trivialise instruction. The intelligent use of technology can improve the quality of learning.

Changing Corporate Structures

A key question is whether these changes herald a new—and less costly—business model that will transform corporate structures in higher education as the for-profit sector expands.

The US is a good place to see trends emerging. Although Americans have accepted tuition fees that rise faster than inflation for decades, there are signs of a tipping point. The fees bubble will not suddenly burst, but lower-cost alternatives will steadily take market share. Some US states are pressurising institutions to cut costs and fees, some institutions (for example, the University of California) are taking online learning seriously, and models such as Best Associates' Academic Partnerships are spreading. The Western Governors University, which was viewed as a marginal and idiosyncratic initiative at its creation in the late 1990s, charges fees of US$5,000 per annum, makes no demands on public funds, and is attracting increasing numbers of students.

What does an expanded role for the for-profit sector imply? It has room to cut fees and still make good profits, so as the public sector starts to reduce fees it will be able to follow suit. In countries where tax codes and charitable status are clearly defined, the distinction between private for-profit and private not-for-profit provision is easy to make. In Western countries, most not-for-profit private providers are religious organisations or charitable foundations. In much of the world, however, the distinction is not so clear, so in this discussion we shall use the term 'private' to designate both types of institution. All private providers try to make a surplus, and they appear similar on the ground, especially in developing countries.

Public institutions aim to break even and to reinvest any surpluses. How are these surpluses spent? All institutions make cross-subsidies between units, but the private sector may be more disciplined about investing for the future and may pay more attention to student perceptions of the balance between costs and benefits. Hence the interest of the private sector in taking advantage of online technology to cut costs and in trying to ensure that its graduates secure employment.

The private sector can be either home-grown or international. Indeed, all providers—public and private—become private providers once they offer programmes across borders. A public university is a private provider when it operates in another country, even though it may not initially repatriate its surpluses. The growth of private provision is essential for the expansion of postsecondary education in many countries. No government can any longer fund all the postsecondary education that its citizens want, so the choice is either a public sector monopoly giving inadequate provision or meeting the demand through a diversity of public and private institutions.

The Middle East, for example, is seeing rapid expansion in the private sector. Egypt needs 100 new universities, and student numbers there are forecast to double by 2030. In the United Arab Emirates the proportion of students in private institutions jumped from 23 per cent to 60 per cent in 2011 alone. Partnerships are a common vehicle for expansion. For example, a major Indian private institution has partnerships with 180 universities in China. In China and in Africa, where the Indian institution works with a UK university, the partner universities confer awards based on the Indian institution's courses and materials.

A country such as Malaysia, which encourages private provision, has many lively home-grown postsecondary education businesses, the best of which also conduct research. Thailand and Vietnam have private campuses of foreign public universities as well as local commercial providers. In Kenya, some private providers have international links, both to secure capital and to gain credibility by association with foreign institutions.

The World Bank's private sector arm, the International Finance Corporation, estimated the private higher education market worldwide to be already worth some US$400 billion in 2006 (Bjarnason, 2009). The current challenge, if the aim is a major expansion of postsecondary education, is that most private providers, both local and foreign, still cater expensively to an elite market. They do not contribute much to expansion, because they are not usually scalable. This is the central dilemma of private higher education: can it be combined with equity of provision?

This role of the private sector in expanding equitable provision is a question that exercises many developing country governments, even when their existing public systems, catering as they usually do to a small proportion of the population drawn largely from the urban elite, can hardly be described as equitable. The key question is whether governments can regulate the private sector without strangling it. Is it possible to develop some common principles of accountability and transparency for all providers of higher education? Quality assurance is a relatively recent concern in higher education in some countries. The issue is whether public and private institutions should be treated in the same way for quality assurance purposes. Ownership is important for the tax authorities but is not, in principle, relevant to quality. There are good and bad actors in the public sector and there should be the same quality thresholds for all.

Legitimate for-profit institutions welcome strong quality assurance frameworks, but ask that they be applied fairly across the whole higher education sector. Legitimate areas for regulation are the avoidance of excessive student loans, ground rules for acquiring accredited institutions, and processes for eliminating bad actors. The main plea is for a level playing field.

For the private sector, as for postsecondary education generally, the key challenge is to serve the 4 billion people at the bottom of the world economic pyramid. As C.K. Prahalad (2004) demonstrated in the case of other businesses, to serve such people, postsecondary education will require 'radical innovations in technology and business models', aspiring to 'an ideal of highly distributed small scale operations married to world-scale capabilities'.

The likeliest candidate for a new business model is the combination of increasing connectivity and OER.

A Disruptive Model: The OER University

We end with a proposed model that combines online learning with lower costs and new corporate structures. This is the OERU that is being explored by an international group of public universities (WikiEducator, 2011).

OER are materials used to support education that may be freely accessed, reused, modified, and shared by anyone (Butcher, 2011). They may well be the most radical technology-based tool poised to disrupt higher education. How might they help to widen access and cut costs?

Some institutions already have policies that encourage the use of OER, so that teachers do not have to reinvent each of their courses from scratch. For example, once academics at the Education Faculty of the Asia eUniversity in Malaysia have agreed on course curriculum outlines, they do not develop any original learning materials, because good-quality OER for the topics they require are already on the web—they simply adapt them to their precise needs. Likewise, Canada's Athabasca University will not approve the development of a course until the proposing department has shown that it has done a thorough search for relevant openly licensed material that can be used as a starting point.

But some would go much further. Paul Stacey has outlined the concept of *The University of Open* (Stacey, 2011). He believes that the combination of open source software, open access publishing, OER, and the general trend to open government creates the potential for a new paradigm in higher education. In February 2011, the Open Education Resource Foundation convened a meeting in New Zealand to operationalise the OERU, a concept developed from this thinking (WikiEducator, 2011).

The idea behind the OERU is expressed in Figure 5.3 (adapted from Taylor, 2011). Students find their own content as OER; get tutoring from a global network of volunteers; are assessed, for a fee, by a participating institution; and earn a credible credential. Such a system would reduce the cost of higher education and has echoes of the University of London External System that innovated 150 years ago by declaring that what mattered was performance in examinations, not how knowledge was acquired. That programme has produced five Nobel laureates.

OER are unquestionably being used. Millions of students and informal learners access the OER put out by Massachusetts Institute of Technology, the UKOU, the OpenCourseWare Consortium, and others, to find good teaching. A total of 32 Commonwealth small states work together within the Virtual University for Small States of the Commonwealth to develop OER that they can all adapt and use (Daniel and West, 2009).

The UKOU's OpenLearn site has 11 million users. Hundreds of courses, some 80,000 hours' worth of study can be downloaded, some as interactive eBooks. With 300,000 downloads per week, the UKOU alone accounts for 10 per cent of all downloads from iTunesU, and there is a worldwide viewing audience of hundreds of millions for OU/BBC TV programmes. UKOU Vice-Chancellor Martin Bean argues that universities should provide paths from this informal cloud of learning

Figure 5.3:
The Open Education Resource University (OERU) Concept

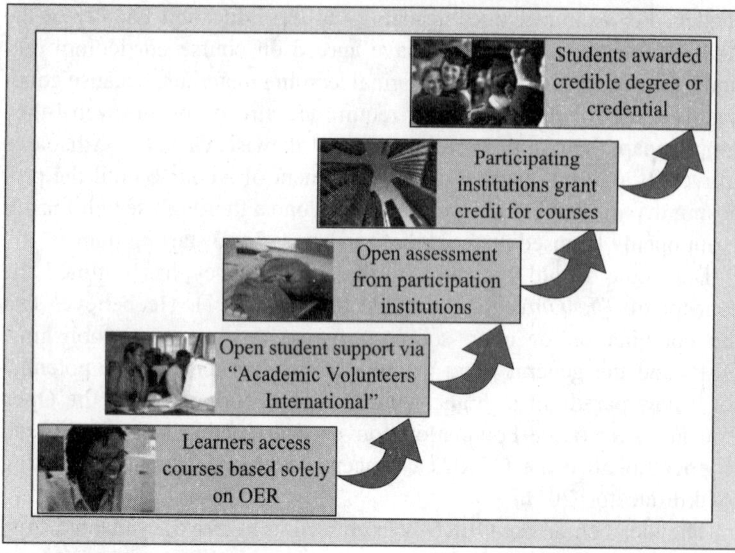

Source: Adapted from Taylor (2011).

towards formal study for those who wish to take them (Bean, 2010). Such paths should provide continuity of learning technologies, because millions of people around the world first encounter higher education institutions such as the UKOU through iTunesU, YouTube, TV broadcasts, or the resources on university websites.

What are the implications of the OERU concept? The institutions best equipped to make a success of it are probably reputable public universities that offer distance learning successfully. They must also have the right mindset, because it would be difficult for a university that has put exclusivity at the centre of its business model suddenly to embrace openness.

To examine how the OERU would work, we juxtapose Martin Bean's remark about leading learners gradually from the informal cloud of learning to formal study with Jim Taylor's representation of the five steps in the OERU concept (Taylor, 2011; see Figure 5.3).

The first step (access to OER) is increasingly solid. The OER pool is growing fast and it is progressively easier to find and retrieve these resources.

For the second step (student support), distance teaching institutions have the skills necessary. They already manage extensive networks of tutors or mentors. A few institutions, such as the State University of New York's Empire State College, also have long experience of mentoring students to develop their own curricula. This approach has close parallels with a situation where the students construct their programmes from OER that they have discovered for themselves. Taylor envisages the emergence of a body rather like Médecins sans Frontières (Doctors without Borders) or Engineers without Borders, which he calls 'Academic Volunteers International'. Having students buy support on a pay-as-you-go basis would also work, and might make for a more sustainable model. Furthermore, social software is enriching the possibilities for student support and interaction. The UKOU's OpenLearn website, for example, is not just an OER repository, but also a hive of activity involving many groups of learners. Digital technology is breathing new life into the notion of a community of scholars, and social software gives students the opportunity to create academic communities in ways that go well beyond the page-turning approaches to online learning that sometimes give it a bad name. Some of this social learning activity involves various forms of informal assessment that can be helpful in preparing students for the formal kind.

At step three (assessment), payment is essential, but this is well-travelled territory. It takes us back 150 years to recall the University of London External model—with the difference that some assessments would need to be designed for curricula developed by the student, not the institution.

With credible assessment by reputable institutions, the next step (the granting and transfer of credit) is straightforward, and leads to the top step.

The solidity of the top step (credible credentials) depends on the involvement of existing, reputable, accredited institutions that espouse this approach.

The discussions around the OERU assume that it will not be a single institution, but rather an umbrella organisation for a network of participating universities. No established institution is likely to adopt the OERU model for its core operations in the foreseeable future, since the revenues—and the costs—would be much lower than conventional approaches. It will be necessary to test the waters. The University of Southern Queensland, which has a strong track record in open, distance, and blended learning, intends to do this, by offering study on this model, initially as part of its community service function.

Conclusion

Historically, higher education has progressed by evolution, rather than revolution. That pattern will likely persist, but we have argued that the steady expansion of online learning will severely disrupt current arrangements and practices. An ever growing proportion of higher education will be provided online in response to student demand for more convenient and personalised instruction, and this will have a much broader impact, notably on the nature of academic work and the corporate structures of institutions. This will make it possible to offer quality options at low cost to address the burgeoning demand for higher education.

The achievement of consistent and sustained quality in online learning requires teamwork, so academics will have to relinquish some of the individual autonomy that they have traditionally exercised in the teaching function. Organising such teamwork may prove more difficult for the public sector than for private institutions, which can also adapt more readily to the large-scale, quasi-industrial processes required for online learning at scale.

Once higher education does most of its teaching online, a new—and much lower cost—structure will emerge. By the time this happens, connectivity will be effectively global, which will make it possible to bring higher education to the billions at the bottom of the pyramid (Prahalad, 2004) for whom it is now only a faraway aspiration. Symbolising the direction of change towards inexpensive online education has been the innovation of MOOCs (Massive Open Online Courses). The University of Manitoba enrolled 2,300 learners in the first free MOOC in 2008. They became news when MIT and Stanford attracted worldwide audiences of tens of thousands to MOOCs in 2012 (Daniel, 2012). So far MOOCs are mostly non-credit, but structures like the OERU will soon allow students to count them towards degrees. The engagement of elite institutions with online learning will greatly accelerate its adoption in higher education generally.

Note

1. These national assessments of teaching quality were discontinued, at the request of the 'elite' universities, after this table was published, so there is no more recent data.

Bibliography

Archibald, R.B. and Feldman, D.H. (2010) *Why Does College Cost So Much?* New York: Oxford University Press.

Arokiasamy, A. (2010) *The Impact of Globalization on Higher Education in Malaysia*, p. 6. Available online at www.nyu.edu/classes/keefer/waoe/aroka.pdf (downloaded on 11 March 2012).

Bates, A.W. (2011) *2011 Outlook for Online Learning and Distance Education*. Sudbury, Ontario: Contact North. Available online at on www.contactnorth.ca/trends-directions/2011-outlook-online-learning (downloaded 11 March 2012).

Bates, A.W. and Sangra, A. (2011) *Managing Technology in Higher Education: Strategies for Transforming Teaching and Learning*. San Francisco, CA: Wiley.

Baumol, W.J. and Bowen, W.G. (1965) On the performing arts: The anatomy of their economic problems. *The American Economic Review*, 55(1/2): 495–502.

Bean, M. (2010) *Informal Learning: Friend or Foe?* Available online at http://cloudworks.ac.uk/cloud/view/2902 (downloaded on 11 March 2012).

Bjarnason, S. (2009) A New Dynamic: Private Higher Education. *Proceedings of the World Conference on Higher Education*. Paris: UNESCO.

Bowen, W.G. (2011) Foreword to *Unlocking the Gates: How and Why Leading Universities Are Opening Up Access to Their Courses*, by T. Walsh, vii–xvi. Princeton University Press.

Butcher, N. (2011) *A Basic Guide to Open Educational Resources (OER)*. Vancouver: Commonwealth of Learning and Paris: UNESCO. Available online at www.col.org/PublicationDocuments/Basic-Guide-To-OER.pdf (downloaded on 11 March 2012).

Carnegie Commission on Higher Education (1968) *Quality and Equality: New levels of Federal Responsibility for Higher Education*. New York: McGraw-Hill.

Commonwealth of Learning/UNESCO (2011) *Guidelines for Open Educational Resources (OER) in Higher Education*. Vancouver: Commonwealth of Learning and Paris: UNESCO. Available online at www.col.org/resources/publications/Pages/detail.aspx?PID=364 (downloaded on 11 March 2012).

Commonwealth Secretariat (1987) *Towards a Commonwealth of Learning (The Briggs Report)*, 60.

Daniel, J.S. (2012) Making Sense of MOOCs: Musings in a Maze of Myth, Paradox and Possibility. *Journal of Interactive Multimedia Education*. http://jime.open.ac.uk/article/2012-18/htmml (last accessed 7 July 2013).

Daniel, J.S. and West, P. (2009) The virtual university for small states of the Commonwealth. *Open Learning: The Journal of Open and Distance Learning on OERs* 24(2): 67–76.

Dutt, R. and Gaba, A. (2006) Cost of Dual Mode and Single Mode Distance Education. In *Four Decades of Distance Education in India: Reflections on Policy and Practice*, 380–91, eds S. Garg, V. Venkaiah, C. Puranik, and S. Panda. India: SAGE Publications.

HEFCE (Higher Education Funding Council for England) (2011) *Collaborate to Compete: Seizing the Opportunity of Online Learning for UK Higher Education*. Report of the Task Force on Online Learning, London. Available online at www.hefce.ac.uk/pubs/hefce/2011/11_01/ (downloaded on 11 March 2012).

Jones, C. and Hosein, A. (2010). Profiling university students' use of technology: Where is the net generation divide? *The International Journal of Technology Knowledge and Society* 6(3): 43–58.

Lenzner, R. and Johnson, S.S. (1997). Seeing things as they really are. *Forbes*, 10 March 1997, 122–31. Available online at www.forbes.com/forbes/1997/0310/5905122a_7.html (downloaded on 11 March 2012).

McGregor, R. (2011) Zhou's cryptic caution lost in translation, ft.com, 10 June 2011. Available online at www.ft.com/intl/cms/s/0/74916db6-938d-11e0-922e-00144feab49a.html#axzz1jI1U7N91 (downloaded on 11 March 2012).

Naidu, C.G. (2007) *Manual on Financing Distance Education*. New Delhi: Commonwealth Educational Media Centre for Asia.

Northcott, P. (1976) The Institute of Educational Technology, the Open University: Structure and Operations, 1969–1975. *Innovations in Education & Training International* 13(4): 11–24.

Prahalad, C.K. (2004) *The Fortune at the Bottom of the Pyramid*. Upper Saddle River, NJ: Wharton School Publishing.

PROPHE (2012) *International Databases—Program for Research on Private Higher Education*. Available online at www.albany.edu/dept/eaps/prophe/data/international.html (downloaded on 11 March 2012).

Smith, A. (1776) *An Inquiry into the Nature and Causes of the Wealth of Nations*. London: Methuen.

Stacey, P. (2011) Musings on the EdTech Frontier: The University of Open. Available online at http://edtechfrontier.com/2011/01/04/the-university-of-open/ (downloaded on 11 March 2012).

Taylor, J. (2011) Towards an OER University: Free Learning for All Students Worldwide. Available online at http://wikieducator.org/Towards_an_OER_university:_Free_learning_for_all_students_worldwide (downloaded on 11 March 2012).

WikiEducator (2011) OER University (#oeru). Available online at http://wikieducator.org/OER_university/About (downloaded on 11 March 2012).

6

Equity and Leadership: Evaluating the ACU's Gender Programme and Other Global Initiatives

Jasbir Singh and Dorothy Garland

Rwanda is the first country in the world to boast a majority of 56 per cent women in its parliament. This small African country, which (as at June 2011) could also claim that 50 per cent of its cabinet members were women, is an example of what can be achieved with commitment from the head of state combined with effective laws, strategies, and monitoring processes.

Conversely, in a country with all the supposed advantages of the UK, it was reported in January 2012 that '14.9 per cent of UK directors at Britain's 100 largest public companies are women, up from 12.5 per cent in 2010' (Wearden, 2012).

There are many such examples in the global media of conflicting images about the balance of men and women in positions of power and influence across the various sectors of society. As far as the global higher education sector is concerned, however, the picture is almost uniformly one of women being poorly represented in positions of leadership and management.

It was in 1985 that the ACU first began to play its part in addressing the serious inadequacy of opportunities for women to develop effectively within their universities, an initiative that was recognised and applauded in *The Commonwealth of Universities* (Springer, 1988: 108). Twenty-six years later, while the gender balance at the undergraduate (and even the postgraduate) level has changed beyond all recognition in most countries of the Commonwealth, the advancement of women into senior and leadership positions does not reflect that change. Disheartening though that is, the ACU, alongside many other national and international agencies, continues to strive for a more equitable representation of women and men at every level of the academy.

The Status of Women in Commonwealth Universities since 1993

Data from many countries has made it apparent that the domain of administrative leadership and key decision-making in higher education remains the domain of men. The proportion of women decreases significantly as women move up the academic and occupational ladder. A 1993 UNESCO–Commonwealth report on women in higher education management showed that

> with hardly an exception the global picture is one of men outnumbering women at about five to one at middle management level and at about twenty to one at senior management level…Women deans and professors are a minority group and women vice-chancellors and presidents are still a rarity.
>
> (Dines, 1993: 11)

As Lund put it, while it is hoped that 'academic life…is a sphere where, in theory, women should find few barriers to opportunity', the reality seems to be that 'academia…has been perceived as traditionally elitist, male and patriarchal in its workplace culture, structure and values' (Lund, 1998: 1).

In response to this situation, the ACU initiated a series of studies to monitor the status of women in Commonwealth universities. In September 1998 the Commonwealth Higher Education Management Service published a report on the under-representation of women in the academic and administrative hierarchies of Commonwealth universities, *A Single Sex Profession? Female Staff Numbers in Commonwealth Universities* (Lund, 1998). The ACU viewed this report as an important benchmark to measure progress and changes in the status of women in

Commonwealth universities. The findings of the 1997/98 survey confirmed that in Commonwealth universities women academics were significantly under-represented at nearly all levels.

A second ACU survey, *Still a Single Sex Profession?* (Singh, 2002a), showed that by 2000, the situation had improved only marginally.

The most recent update in 2008, *Whispers of Change* (Singh, 2008), was based on 2006 data. With data in 2000 and 2006 limited to academic staff above the level of senior lecturer, the surveys revealed that women were severely under-represented at all upper levels of the academic and administrative hierarchies of Commonwealth universities.

Women in Senior Leadership and Management Positions

These three surveys (which analysed gender-disaggregated data collected by the ACU from its member universities) demonstrate that the situation pertaining to the status of women in senior leadership and management positions in Commonwealth universities had not improved significantly between 1997 and 2006.

- Men continued to dominate the top executive positions in the universities of the Commonwealth. In 2006, across the Commonwealth, 9.8 per cent women were executive heads, marking a very small improvement from 9 per cent in 2000 and 8.3 per cent in 1997. Of the 35 countries surveyed, 23 countries had never appointed a female chief executive.
- Head of administration remained largely a male domain, with only 16.2 per cent women in this position in 2006, marking a small increase from 2000 (14.9 per cent). Twenty-one countries had no woman head of administration.
- Better representation of women was seen in the senior management teams (SMTs). In 2006, Commonwealth university SMTs comprised 22.3 per cent women. This showed an improvement over 2000 and 1997, when 19.8 per cent and 15.9 per cent women, respectively, were included in these teams. Among the developed Commonwealth countries, SMTs comprised more than 25 per cent women.
- The post of finance officer or bursar continued to be seen very much as a 'man's job'. In 2006, 15.4 per cent women held this position in Commonwealth universities, up from 10.1 per cent in 1997 to 12.0 per cent in 2000.

- In 2006, there were 17.0 per cent women deans in Commonwealth countries, an improvement of 4.0 per cent since 1997. The developed Commonwealth countries had, on the whole, appointed more women deans than universities in the Asian and African regions, ranging from 23.5 per cent in Australia to 17.2 per cent in Canada.
- Women chief librarians enjoyed the highest representation at the senior management level. In 2006, some 41.5 per cent of chief librarians in the Commonwealth were women, an increase from 36.4 per cent in 1997. In the developed Commonwealth countries, nearly 50 per cent of chief librarians in their universities were women, with a marked increase since 1997.
- Women have continued to make advances in taking up many administrative positions within universities, taking charge of personnel, public relations, equity/equal opportunity, and international offices, as well as quality assurance/accreditation, staff development and strategic planning. In 2006 (as in 2000), women enjoyed the highest (65.3 per cent) representation as heads of equal opportunity/equity offices. This was followed by leadership in staff development and training, where 40.9 per cent women were heading all staff development training units in 2006, a slight decline from 42.5 per cent in 2000.
- Since 2000, more women had entered the fields of personnel (32.6 per cent in 2000 compared with 37.4 per cent in 2006), quality assurance (32.2 per cent in 2000 compared with 35.6 per cent in 2006), international affairs (32.9 per cent in 2000 compared with 35.0 per cent in 2006), and development or fundraising (28.2 per cent in 2000 compared with 31.7 per cent in 2006). While strategic planning was still very much in the hands of men, women had made inroads into this area of male dominance with an increase from 19.7 per cent in 2000 to 26.8 per cent in 2006—an increase of 7.1 per cent. However, computing remained very much the domain of men, seeing no more than 13.1 per cent women in 2000 and 13.8 per cent in 2006.

Women Academic Staff

Similarly, the statistics relating to women academic staff in Commonwealth universities revealed only modest improvements between 1997 and 2006.

- In 2006, 15.3 per cent women were professors in Commonwealth universities, a slow and steady increase from 9.9 per cent in 1997. Overall, developed Commonwealth countries and countries in the Asian region demonstrated better performance, with an average of 18.8 per cent professors in Asian countries (where there are several women-only universities) and 15.3 per cent women professors in the developed Commonwealth countries. The presence of women professors in Africa was very low, ranging from 0.0 per cent to 14.1 per cent, with minimal changes since 1997.
- Overall in the Commonwealth in 2006, there were 29.1 per cent women associate professors, readers, principal lecturers, and senior lecturers, a small increase from 23.3 per cent in 1997 and 27.0 per cent in 2000. The data showed that, at this level, women were beginning to play an important role in their universities.
- More women were appointed as heads and directors of academic departments and institutes than as deans of faculties. There were 21.4 per cent women heads and directors in 2006, an increase of 6.2 per cent since 1997. On the whole, there was no marked difference in these appointments between developed and developing countries.
- Women's participation in all academic disciplines had improved since 2000, but women were still under-represented in all the disciplines. Women had taken a few steps forward in moving into the scientific and technological fields, but there was still much room for improvement. Even in the humanities and the social sciences, in the majority of departments women composed less than 40 per cent of the academic staff.

Small Improvements

The studies demonstrate that the developed Commonwealth countries made the greatest progress in appointing women to senior management positions, especially at the middle management level. The majority of developing countries revealed that they had a long way to go to redress the male/female imbalances in the management of academic institutions. Asian countries performed better in appointing women to academic leadership positions as professors and heads of academic departments than in appointing women to senior management positions or even middle-level management positions. There seems to be the perception that management and administrative jobs were too demanding for women and were best handled by men. In African countries, too, the situation showed little improvement over the period 1997 to 2006. Even in the middle-level administrative positions women played a very small role. The surveys revealed an almost complete absence in Asian and African countries of equal opportunity/equity offices that might be able to promote women's interests as well as keeping track of women's performance at the different levels. Nor were there well-established women's networks or leadership programmes that could train and empower women to play a more prominent role in the management of their universities.

Unable to break through the existing conservative traditional cultures and systems, women were generally reluctant to put themselves forward for appointments into management positions, concurring with the predominantly male view that these were truly men's jobs, while women's skills and talents were best suited to teaching and perhaps research, allowing them time to attend to their family, caring and nurturing roles.

How did the situation in 2006 measure up to the 1993 conclusion by Dines? The 2000 survey noted small improvements over 1993, with men outnumbering women at about three or four to one at middle management level and at almost ten to one at senior management level, while women vice-chancellors/presidents, deans and professors were still a rarity. The situation prevailed for both developed and developing countries, though it could be seen that it was in the developed countries that women had made the greatest advances into middle management. In 2006, while some improvements were noted in women's representation in middle management, on the whole, men still outnumbered women at about three to one, and at very senior management levels (executive heads and presidents) men still outnumbered women at about ten to one. However, much improvement was noted at the SMT level, where men now outnumbered women only at about five to one, and at the associate professor, reader and senior lecturer level, where men outnumbered women at about three to one.

International and National Efforts to Promote Women

The educational needs and interests of girls and women, at all levels, have been placed firmly on the agenda of Commonwealth national governments and development agencies.

The Commonwealth Secretariat and the ACU, together with the Commonwealth of Learning (COL) in Canada, are the principal Commonwealth agencies that have made a significant contribution to closing the gap in disparities in the opportunities for higher education and training between the sexes. Through a range of their own programmes and through collaborative efforts with other international development agencies, especially UNESCO and the Carnegie Corporation of New York, these agencies have focused on women and development in higher education as a priority concern in their consultative and functional activities.

A range of leadership programmes across the Commonwealth (including those described below) attempt to address the problem of women's poor participation from several perspectives:

- policy changes
- raising awareness of the problem
- improving the skills and competencies of women
- changing university structures and procedures
- changing attitudes of men and women
- creating a more enabling, women-friendly environment

The Commonwealth Secretariat

To raise the profile of women in higher education management, the Commonwealth Secretariat initiated a Women in Higher Education Management Programme, for which the ACU offered to be the implementing agency.

In 1991, the Secretariat and the ACU entered into a Memorandum of Understanding with UNESCO for the establishment of a co-operative programme of activities, which aimed to

> facilitate the development of women in Commonwealth universities so that they could use their academic, administrative and, above all, their management skills in contributing to the institutional development of universities, thus securing a significant increase in the number of management positions women hold, as universities redefine and develop their role to face the twenty-first century.
>
> (Commonwealth Secretariat, 1993: 3)

These three organisations collaboratively planned, and gave financial support to, a wide variety of projects.

The programme opted to make interventions on two fronts:

- endeavouring to change the management structures of universities
- enhancing the capacity of women in universities to 'break through the glass ceiling' into top management positions

Between 1993 and 1995, the Secretariat commissioned six training modules to provide basic training materials for workshops for women in higher education management. These were trialled at two workshops sponsored by the Secretariat: at the University of Papua New Guinea (1995); and at the Gender Institute of South Africa at the University of Cape Town (1996). During 1997, the Secretariat held the first training workshops in collaboration with the University Grants Commissions (UGC) in Sri Lanka and India. Subsequently, in 1998, the responsibility for taking forward this workshop programme was handed over to the ACU.

The Association of Commonwealth Universities

The Rationale for Establishing a Gender-specific Programme

Initially called the ACU's Women's Programme, this initiative was established in 1985 in response to a recognition of the extent to which women, both academic and administrative, were under-represented at senior levels throughout the Commonwealth university sector; and as an expression of the ACU's commitment not only to natural justice but also to ensuring that universities have access to the entirety of their human resource potential.

It was underpinned by awareness of two key Commonwealth concerns at that time: equity, with particular reference to the enhancement of the participation of women and girls in development; and issues around educational access and quality, pertaining in particular to higher education.

The improved recruitment of women into, and retention of women at, all levels of management and leadership in higher education was seen as integral to overall institutional development in terms of both equity and quality.

Objectives

The objectives of the programme are to enhance the career profiles of, and prospects for, women academics and administrators through the provision of leadership and management training, gender sensitisation (for both men and women), seminars, and workshops. Inherent in the training programmes is a strong element of advocacy for the development of gender-equitable policies and practices.

The linked objectives of the programme are:

- to empower women with the confidence and competence to bid for, assume, and sustain positions of leadership and management in their institutions
- thereby to increase both the quantity and quality of women managers and leaders in higher education institutions in the Commonwealth
- to develop and provide for women in higher education a range of training strategies and materials that are replicable or may be adapted for use in the various Commonwealth regions
- to assist in the development of networks whose members will provide each other with professional and moral support
- through all of the above, to help universities better reflect—and serve as exemplars of good practice to—the societies they serve

Principal Activities

The principal activities of the programme, which operated initially in tandem with the Commonwealth Secretariat and/or UNESCO, have included:

- the publication in 1993 of a book, *Women in Higher Education Management*, edited by Elizabeth Dines, which analysed the career paths of women in higher education within the context of national higher education environments
- training workshops in: Bombay, India (1986 and 1988); Jamaica (1990); Botswana (1991); Kuala Lumpur, Malaysia (1991); The Gambia (1992); Suva, Fiji (1994); Port Moresby, Papua New Guinea (1995); Cape Town, South Africa (1996); Colombo, Sri Lanka (1997); New Delhi, India (1997); Malacca, Malaysia (1999);

Kandy, Sri Lanka (1999); Lagos, Nigeria (1999); Bridgetown, Barbados (2001); Nairobi, Kenya (2002); Rawalpindi, Pakistan (2002); Lokoja, Nigeria (2004); Entebbe, Uganda (2005); Bagamoyo, Tanzania (2006); Dar es Salaam, Tanzania (2007); Pakistan (2007 and 2011); and Botswana (2008)

- training modules, which address the key problems encountered by women in higher education management. As well as a facilitator's handbook, a total of eight themes has been developed: academic leadership; managing personal and professional roles; university governance; women's studies; research; developing management skills; mentoring; and gender mainstreaming universities
- sponsorship of an MA in Women and Management in Higher Education at the Institute of Education, University of London, between 1998 and 2001, during which period four cohorts of students (15 in total) graduated and are currently playing a crucial role in developing and implementing gender policies in their countries. Several of the former MA students went on to study successfully for their PhD and at least two are known to have attained professorial appointments
- commissioning/sponsoring: surveys and reports on gender management systems, equal employment opportunity offices, and gender-disaggregated statistics; *A Good Practice Handbook* (Singh, 2002b); and *An Annotated Bibliography on Gender Equity in Commonwealth Higher Education* (Morley et al., 2005)
- a regular feature on gender issues and initiatives which appeared, for many years, in the ACU's *Bulletin*
- establishing pan-Commonwealth and national-level networks to provide mutual support and information to women in higher education in the Commonwealth.

Commonwealth Scholarships and Fellowships

As is well documented elsewhere in this volume, the ACU plays a significant role in the implementation and monitoring of the Commonwealth Scholarship and Fellowship Plan (CSFP), the flagship scheme of Commonwealth higher education co-operation. Its awards are for 'men and women of high intellectual promise who may be expected to make a significant contribution to life in their own countries on their return from study overseas' (Commonwealth Relations Office, 1959: 6). In recent years, attention has increasingly been given to the low level of participation of women and to measures for alleviating the obstacles that have prevented better uptake of the awards by women.

Throughout the early operation of the Plan, female participation was extremely poor. In 1962, only 10.4 per cent of the scholars were women. The First Ten-Year Review of the Plan took note of this and proposed the removal of discrimination based on sex in the payment of marriage allowances. The concern with the continued poor representation of women at about 20–25 per cent level was expressed in the Second Ten-Year Review of the Plan. By the time of the Third Ten-Year Review (1993), it was reported that 33 per cent of the scholars were women. There was some evidence of affirmative action succeeding. In 1991/92, 25 per cent of scholarship applications were submitted by women, the percentage of female nominations was 31 per cent and the percentage of women among those actually taking up awards was 33 per cent. Since then, the situation has improved a little and the percentage of women scholars now stands at about 40 per cent.

The Commonwealth of Learning (COL)

As COL's strategic plan is located within the framework of the United Nations Millennium Development Goals, the organisation strives to contribute to the achievement of gender equality and women's empowerment (Millennium Development Goal 3). A gender equality perspective is promoted at all stages of the programme cycle (planning, implementation, monitoring, and evaluation), to ensure that the initiatives offer equal opportunities, benefits, and participation to girls/women and boys/men.

For COL, gender equality is a cross-cutting corporate goal, which requires that both women's and men's views, interests, and needs shape its programmes and organisational policies and processes. COL is committed to removing barriers to women's access to education through delivery of gender-balanced programmes and projects, as well as through initiatives that are specifically targeted to benefit women and girls. By making learning available at times and places suitable to the particular needs of the student, distance education overcomes many of the barriers faced by girls and women trying to access conventional education systems.

As an example, COL assisted Makerere University, Uganda, in establishing a Bachelor of Education programme implemented with open and distance learning methodologies, and this has resulted in an increased proportion of women enrolling on that programme. In the awarding of Fellowships, COL has paid special attention to ensuring an equitable gender balance, by requesting that those submitting nominations give particular consideration to nominating women.

The Forum for African Women Educationalists (FAWE)

The work of FAWE is to encourage governments, international organisations, and local communities to enact policies and to provide positive learning environments that treat girls/women and boys/men equally.

FAWE has systematically:

- documented and publicised the areas that women find problematic on campus
- developed strong support networks among individuals (men and women) committed to change on and off campus
- installed a series of equal opportunity and affirmative action activities
- provided targeted scholarships and other financial assistance
- attempted to change existing structural, organisational, and institutional practices in order to accommodate the needs of women

FAWE recognises that it is imperative to invest in developing research and to use up-to-date relevant data to buttress its advocacy and demonstration work in education policy and practice. The organisation believes that without applied research into the gender perspectives of development that are specific to the African context, planned development may be seriously compromised or even retarded. It is therefore important to ensure that initiatives that target women are based on gender-sensitive research and that they equip women with relevant knowledge and skills that are responsive to the needs of girls and women at individual, social, political, and economic levels.

To promote women's access and professional development in higher education (2009/10), FAWE partnered with the Rockefeller Foundation on an initiative that aims to enable access, professional development, and promotion of women in higher education through gender-responsive research, innovative advocacy strategies, and leadership training. The FAWE–Rockefeller initiative seeks to:

- determine gender trends in staff recruitment, promotion and retention in universities
- influence policymakers and administrators to take action on the gender gaps in employment and leadership identified within their institutions
- monitor, track, and report on implementation of proposed gender-responsive actions
- improve the capacity of women academics and managers to advocate and influence institutional leadership for greater gender equality
- facilitate women's access and promotion to leadership and management positions in universities

Uganda

Makerere University, Uganda, has introduced a significant programme to mainstream gender into all aspects of its management. The overall objective of its gender management system is to ensure gender sensitivity in the governance and administration of the university.

The process has:

- analysed the issues that have given rise to concerns about gender inequality in university governance, management, and administration
- explored women-specific issues in diagnosing gender inequality at Makerere
- developed an appropriate action plan for a gender management system to support the mainstreaming of gender at Makerere

South Africa

In 1996 the Gender Institute of South Africa at the University of Cape Town hosted the second Commonwealth Secretariat/ACU workshop to trial the training modules prepared by the Secretariat for its Women in Higher Education Management Programme (see 'The Commonwealth Secretariat', above). The goal of the institute is to strengthen African-based researchers', writers', and scholars' understanding of gender analysis and its importance to social transformation on the continent.

HERS-SA is a small, self-sustaining, non-profit organisation, which is dedicated to the advancement of women in the higher education sector in South Africa. Since 2004, it has advocated for, and contributed to, the career development of women—not least by means of the annual HERS-SA Academy, which attracts participants from all over sub-Saharan Africa.

Universities Australia (UA)

In representing the interests of women in higher education, the Colloquium of Senior Women in Australian Higher Education, together with the then Australian Vice-Chancellors' Committee (AVCC), took a major step forward in formulating an Action Plan for the five-year period 1999–2003.

The AVCC spelt out concrete measures and a timeframe to achieve the objectives of its Action Plan. Under the plan, the AVCC:

- developed a policy statement
- collated baseline quantitative data on the position of women employed in higher education
- recommended that all universities include gender equity performance measures in institutional plans and quality assurance processes
- monitored and promoted more equal representation of women to men on AVCC committees

The AVCC encouraged training programmes for senior staff, to enable them to provide more effective leadership in gender equity in their institutions; and supported the development of an information, communication, and mentoring network for women. The Action Plan also supported relevant research projects, including a trend analysis of graduate outcomes and a study of gender and promotion. The Colloquium and the AVCC revised the Action Plan in 2005 to operate for a further five years.

The AVCC, since renamed Universities Australia, has continued this commitment with a Strategy for Women: 2011–14. UA is committed to 'fully utilising the skills and capabilities of all members of its workforce' and continues to address the challenges facing women who enter and contribute to higher education. It supports ongoing efforts by its members to bring about employment equity and an inclusive culture, building on the equity achievements of past years.

Numerous examples of leadership programmes for women in higher education come from Australia [for example, the Leadership Development for Women Program at the University of Western Australia; the Australian Technology Network (of Universities) Women's Executive Development Programme model of women's executive management and leadership development; and the Changing Academic Profession project at the LH Martin Institute, University of Melbourne]. They share a focus on skills development, on recognition of existing strengths and capacities, on increasing the numbers of women in leadership roles, and on visibility and support networks. There is also a consciousness of transforming cultures and gaining organisational support. Most aim both to enhance participants' skills and professional development/leadership potential; and to build a culture and structure in the organisation that encourages women's full participation.

Senior Women Academic Administrators of Canada (SWAAC)

SWAAC holds an annual conference, which addresses major issues facing women and development in higher education. SWAAC also publishes and distributes an electronic newsletter to its members; and posts online research and conference papers on numerous topics relevant to the issues of women in higher education. Because women administrators experience conditions that are distinctive to them, SWAAC exists as an avenue for collegial support, innovation, and action.

University Grants Commission (UGC), India

The UGC's programme on capacity-building of women in higher education management had its origins in a Commonwealth Secretariat/UGC 'Training of trainers' workshop for women in higher education management held in Delhi in 1997. This workshop decided to modify the training modules better to suit the Indian context, so that they could be used to support the first set of five regional workshops on gender sensitisation, awareness, and motivation, which were held with support from the National Accreditation and Assessment Council under its quality improvement programme in 2003. Over 150 participants were trained, and facilitators for the next round of regional workshops were identified.

In 2004, the UGC took over this programme and decided that it should reach the regional and local level and should be decentralised to be cost effective and to help establish a critical mass of trained women faculty in colleges and universities. The programme is conducted under the guidance of an apex committee, the National Consultative Committee, constituted by the UGC.

There are two levels of workshops: gender sensitisation, awareness, and motivation; and training of trainers. The target group is senior and middle-level women faculty and administrators from all disciplines and subjects from public and private universities that have UGC recognition.

The programme is currently carried out in ten regions and, to date, about 240 workshops have been run for about 4,000 women participants.

Fatima Jinnah Women University, Pakistan

In Pakistan, Fatima Jinnah Women University has provided exceptional leadership in holding ACU-sponsored 'Training of trainers' workshops, which have been followed in turn by a number of local workshops.

Their first international workshop was held in November 2002, co-sponsored by the British Council and the ACU. The resource team comprised four women from Australia, Canada, and the UK and two from the host university. Participants from both public and private universities attended, including representatives from Bangladesh and Sri Lanka.

A second ACU workshop, designed to develop a regional group of key women trainers, was held in late 2007 in association with the Higher Education Commission, Pakistan, and with additional support from the Carnegie Corporation of New York.

A third workshop was held in January 2011, in which training was extended to a wider group of women in universities in Pakistan.

All these ACU workshops have been followed by locally organised workshops at institutional levels.

University of Papua New Guinea

In 1995, the University of Papua New Guinea hosted the first Commonwealth Secretariat/ACU workshop to trial the training modules prepared by the Secretariat for its Women in Higher Education Management Programme (see 'The Commonwealth Secretariat', above).

Sri Lanka

The UGC, Sri Lanka has provided leadership in arranging ACU/Commonwealth Secretariat-sponsored 'Training of trainers' workshops for their senior academic women.

Trainers from these workshops have used ACU training materials to conduct further workshops for women in their own institutions/regions. Gender work has also been carried forward by the Centre for Women's Research, a non-governmental, non-profit organisation founded in 1984 by a group of women academics, researchers, and activists to facilitate the realisation of the full potential of women in all spheres of life.

In 2011, the University of Kelaniya established a Gender Centre to promote the cause of women in Sri Lankan universities. At the time of writing, the ACU is co-organising with that university, for the first time in the ACU's first century, an international conference to explore a number of key equity, educational, and development issues from a specifically gendered perspective.

The (then) Committee of Vice-Chancellors and Principals (CVCP), UK

The CVCP's 'Room at the top' programme for senior women in higher education in the UK focused on the development needs of those occupying or aspiring to second- and third-tier academic/administrative roles involving a leadership and strategic management dimension.

The broad aims of the programme were to:

- increase the pool of potential women leaders in higher education
- provide an extended programme of personal/professional development to help individuals achieve career progression to positions of institutional leadership
- influence leadership styles and management styles and models in UK universities and colleges

The CVCP also established the Commission on University Career Opportunities to look into all aspects of diversity, including gender disparities in higher education.

The CVCP is now known as Universities UK and, while neither the 'Room at the top' programme nor the Commission on University Career Opportunities still exists, the Equality Challenge Unit, which supersedes the latter, works to further and support equality and diversity for staff and students in higher education in the UK.

Strategies That Have Advanced the Status of Women

Although little evidence can be adduced about women's inability to perform on the job, real inequities exist in many areas that affect their performance and the opportunities for their advancement in higher education, including:

- absence of enabling conditions
- discriminatory salary scales and fringe benefits
- publishing productivity
- recruitment policies
- segregation
- cultural and structural barriers
- the 'chilly climate' for women in universities

Nevertheless, many lessons may be drawn from the reviews by the ACU and by PricewaterhouseCoopers LLP of initiatives that enhance the status of women in the higher education sector. Some of the key factors that have helped to improve women's participation in higher education leadership and management are discussed below.

The Role of National Agencies

In some countries, key drivers for change are initiatives led by national agencies.

For example, the Equal Opportunity for Women in the Workplace Agency in Australia recognises higher education institutions that are leaders in their field with regard to embedding equality and diversity initiatives by listing them as an 'Employer of choice'.

The American Council on Education seeks to provide leadership and a unifying voice on key higher education issues and to influence public policy through advocacy, research, and programme initiatives. Its Office of Women in Higher Education provides the national direction for women's leadership development and career advancement through programmatic initiatives and activities that aim to:

- identify women leaders in higher education
- facilitate leadership development activities for women in higher education
- encourage women leaders to make full use of their abilities
- advance women to senior-level positions
- link women leaders at all levels to one another
- support the retention of women in higher education

Legislative Drivers

While gender equity policies and programmes represent good intentions, it is the provision of legislative and infrastructure support that underpins the creation of an enabling environment for women. Among these are:

- the United Nations (1979) Convention on the Elimination of all Forms of Discrimination against Women, which sets out (in legally binding form) internationally accepted principles and measures to achieve equal rights for women everywhere
- the 1995 Commonwealth Plan of Action on Gender Development, which provides a framework for Commonwealth governments and identifies for planners and practitioners 15 areas that are considered desirable components of gender equity
- the National Policy of Education, India (1986), a landmark in the approach to women's education, which attempted for the first time to address the basic issues of women's equality
- legislation in Australia—the 1984 Sex Discrimination Act, the 1986 Affirmative Action (Equal Employment Opportunity for Women) Act and the 1988 National Agenda for Women—which laid the foundations for women's equity, setting out guidelines for selection, promotion, training, and development, as well as reporting to an Affirmative Action Agency

It is clear from research that statutory requirements have increased awareness about equality and diversity. What is less clear is the extent of their impact on the implementation of the equality and diversity agenda. It has been observed that compliance has been a major activity of equality personnel in most higher education institutions studied. This is evident in the types of activities and in the data collected at institutions. Often no more than the categories which are required by the legislation are actually collected in higher education institutions. For example, in Australia, mandatory annual reporting on a national level to the Equal Opportunity for Women in the Workplace Agency since 1986 has focused on women only, and has probably been the most significant consistent driver behind the introduction and maintenance of programmes aimed at increasing the level of participation of women in the workplace.

Importance of Supporting Structures

Gender policies and legislation are assured of greater success with the establishment of mechanisms and support structures.

Support structures that are helpful include the:

- preparation and distribution of clear guidelines on gender-related topics
- setting up of clear reporting procedures
- establishment of a monitoring and reporting agency
- establishment of equal opportunity offices
- setting up of special agencies and commissions to assist with achieving set objectives and targets

Commitment and Support from the Top

Commitment and support from the top levels of the agency, organisation, network, or institution is vital. Agencies that are making an impact have the mandates of the governments they represent and the support, both moral and financial, of the agencies and their top management.

Integration into Strategic Plans

The most critical factor in the success of women's programmes is the extent to which these programmes are linked into the strategic plans of their country or institution and are seen to be integral to the overall development aims of the country/institution.

Setting of Targets

Success in bringing about any significant change is more assured if targets are set. While determining the aims and objectives of policies and programmes is important, their outcomes remain uncertain and are difficult to measure or monitor without clear targets.

Transparency of Procedures for Recruitment and Promotion

Women often do not make headway in their careers and institutions because there is a lack of transparency and/or clarity about such opportunities as and when they arise and about the required procedures/processes for gaining employment, further training, or promotion.

When women (and men) do not succeed in promotions, they need to know what has held them back—whether they have failed to present themselves well or have not met all the promotion criteria (and, if so, which criteria they have failed to meet, and by what margin). Transparency at all levels would greatly help to provide clear evidence of the standards which should be reached and by which women may assess themselves.

Improving the Supply of Women Who Meet the Employment Criteria

There is an ongoing, pressing need for institutions to take greater responsibility for ensuring that women are able to meet the strong qualifications barriers embraced by the sector. Strategies and (flexible) programmes to ensure that greater numbers of women are able to enrol in and complete postgraduate research degrees are essential, and greater recognition must be given by the academy to the value of the different kinds of research that may be undertaken by women.

Training Programmes and Courses

Training programmes for women represent an important strategy for enhancing their knowledge about higher education, as well as sharpening their skills and competencies in a range of activities, such as research and management.

While the Commonwealth Secretariat–ACU Gender Programme has focused on enhancing leadership and management skills for senior women in higher education, many successful women's programmes address the problem from a number of perspectives. These include a range of initiatives—mentoring, training, networking, work-shadowing, and advocacy, as well as some affirmative strategies—which are implemented in a structured way over a specific timeframe.

Evaluation reports of training programmes point to positive outcomes, such as:

- increased consciousness of the issues facing women
- the formation of networks
- increased motivation
- increased knowledge, competencies, and confidence
- significant career moves

Establishing Special Networks for Women

It has been the experience of many institutions that women are not privy to the information networks from which men benefit through their sports, 'old boys' associations, or other networks. Often carrying multiple roles, women tend to miss out on these informal opportunities to hear the latest news of research grants, training, or promotions.

The establishment of networks that are specifically designed to provide women with access to vital information and to the critical encouragement, counselling, and advice they may need to support their research and enhance their performance can greatly help not only to overcome a perception of isolation but also to advance their careers.

Mentoring

Recognising the important role of mentors in the careers of successful people has led an increasing number of organisations to establish formal mentoring programmes to orient new employees, foster executive development, assist in career advancement, improve job performance, lower employee turnover, enhance creativity, and increase leadership potential.

Mentoring programmes created specifically for women have proved to be particularly supportive and effective.

Establishment of Women's Universities and Colleges

As a step towards enabling more female students to obtain the benefits of higher education, a number of countries have encouraged the establishment of all women colleges and universities. In gender-segregated societies, such as India (which has several women's universities and colleges) and Pakistan (which has two), women's universities play a significant role in promoting women's education and developing their self-reliance.

The focus and curriculum of these universities provide high-quality professional and academic education to women, comparable to that available in the co-educational universities and colleges; and their courses meet the challenges of modern times. All-women universities also, of course, provide opportunities for more women to be appointed to positions of leadership.

Women's Studies

Women's studies programmes have played an important role: as a catalyst in enhancing the participation of girls and women at all levels of the education system; in the generation of knowledge; and in policy design and practice.

In many countries, women's studies programmes have proved to be a successful vehicle for achieving change both in their higher education institutions and in the societies they serve.

An Integrated and Holistic Approach

The principal lesson emerging from all the literature is that policies and programmes should not be conceived in a vacuum or unrelated to other key ingredients. It is not sufficient to adopt policies—action plans need to be drawn up; targets with measurable indicators need to be set; positive action needs to be set in train; and monitoring processes must be established to track progress.

Key Performance Indicators

The use of key performance indicators to embed equality and diversity is not present in every country. It is recommended that equality and diversity be a key performance indicator to which a system of reward and penalties be tied—the hypothesis being that if there were a system which gave incentives for the mainstreaming of equality and diversity, it might generate innovative initiatives. Moreover, innovation in equality and diversity could be rewarded nationally.

The Challenges Ahead

While this chapter is able to refer to only a representative sample of the Commonwealth-wide programmes and strategies that have been introduced to address the imbalance between men and women in leadership and management in higher education, what seems clear from the statistical evidence is that, despite such interventions, progress in redressing the imbalance is snail slow.

Certainly, it is clear that legislative frameworks and compliance, targets and key performance indicators, institutional commitment and training, and networking and mentoring—all play a key part in bringing about change; but, unless and until the whole academy is brought to an understanding of the individual, institutional and societal benefits of gender equality, there will be no real desire to make change happen.

In the meantime, the ACU, along with many of its members and with other organisations, will continue to do what it can to foster greater equality. One area in which the ACU's intervention appears to be valued and valuable is in the provision of training programmes in less developed countries; and one of the challenges will be to identify those countries in which this work is likely to make the greatest impact and in which it should be introduced or extended.

The ACU could also consider launching a number of partnerships in which universities with richer experience of promoting gender equality collaborate with institutions which lack the expertise to commence gender-related initiatives. Links leading to the exchange of scholars and researchers among institutions working on gender leadership would also advance the objectives of the programme.

Advocacy will, however, continue to be both a challenge and a necessity. The ACU has the capacity to set an example, and make representations, to all member universities about the importance of gender equality, particularly at leadership and management levels; but the case could be made more persuasively if sustained by statistical evidence—and this is where the challenge lies, as the ACU no longer collects gender-disaggregated data from its members. The three reports on female staff in Commonwealth universities from which the data at the beginning of this chapter is drawn are uniquely valuable resources; but, without a huge investment of staff time and resources, it would not be possible to maintain or update these records in the future.

A more realistic aim might be to initiate a benchmarking project among member universities, to facilitate the collection of data about, and to monitor the changes in, defined areas (such as appointments, promotions, and participation and presence in decision-making committees and university councils). In this way, universities could benchmark their own progress in promoting gender equality, as well as permitting Commonwealth-wide comparisons.

In that universities are, in essence, equipped to undertake, report, and distribute research about gender disparities in education, some members may be encouraged to create and maintain databases about gender in education. There are still wide gaps, for instance, in the understanding of pedagogy as it affects men and women and of the extent to which gender plays a role in educational achievement. Some universities may even be persuaded to adopt a total gender mainstreaming approach to their development, and to be vigilant not only of numbers of women at different levels, but also of the gender dimension of a range of other elements, such as the curriculum, support services, infrastructure, and budget.

It remains a matter of wonder and concern that, as bastions of liberal thinking, upholders of human rights and nurturers of innovative thinking, universities should be—but are not yet—trendsetters in recognising the fundamental issues around gender equality and dealing with them creatively.

Bibliography

Australian Technology Network (of Universities) Women's Executive Development: http://atn.edu.au/wexdev/

Commonwealth Relations Office (1959) *Report of Commonwealth Education Conference: Oxford, 15–28 July 1959*. London: Her Majesty's Stationery Office. Cmnd 841.

Commonwealth Secretariat (1993) *Report of the ACU-CHESS Steering Committee*. London: Commonwealth Secretariat.

Dines, E. (ed.) (1993) *Women in Higher Education Management*. Paris: UNESCO/Commonwealth Secretariat.

LH Martin Institute, The Changing Academic Profession. Available online at www.lhmartininstitute.edu.au/research-and-publications/research/20-the-changing-academic-profession (downloaded on 4 April 2013).

Lund, H. (1998) *A Single Sex Profession? Female Staff Numbers in Commonwealth Universities*. London: Commonwealth Higher Education Management Service.

Morley, L., Sorhaindo, A., and Burke, P.J. (2005) *Researching Women: An Annotated Bibliography on Gender Equity in Commonwealth Higher Education*. London: Institute of Education, University of London.

Pricewaterhouse Coopers LLP (2004) *Overview Report for Cross-national Study*. London. Part of the Higher Education Funding Council for England's Equal Opportunities Research Programme.

Singh, J.K. (2002a) *Still a Single Sex Profession? Female Staff Numbers in Commonwealth Universities*. London: ACU Gender Equity Programme.

——— (2002b) *Women and Management in Higher Education: A Good Practice Handbook*. Prepared for ACU/UNESCO. Paris: UNESCO.

——— (2003) Gender in Education: Overview of Commonwealth Strategies. In *Education in the Commonwealth—The First 40 Years: From Oxford to Halifax and Beyond*, ed. L. Bown. London: Commonwealth Secretariat.

——— (2008) *Whispers of Change: Female Staff Numbers in Commonwealth Universities*. London: ACU Gender Equity Programme.

Springer, H.W. (1988) *The Commonwealth of Universities*. London: ACU.

University of Western Australia, Leadership Development for Women Program: www.osds.uwa.edu.au/programmes/ldw/story/programme (downloaded on 4 April 2013).

Wearden, G. (2012) Record number of women in UK boardrooms. *Guardian*, p. 19, 11 January 2012.

7

Quality Assurance: Practice and Critique

David Woodhouse

Introduction

The great worldwide expansion of attention to external quality systems has taken place in the last 25 years, and therefore its occurrence in former colonies, including those in the Commonwealth, is almost entirely a post-independence phenomenon.

Before that, the founding of universities in the Commonwealth followed the outflow of colonisation, as did the London external system, the external examiner system, and (to a lesser extent because in a later period) the Commonwealth Benchmarking Club (see under 'Central influences', below).

Largely, though, there is no single narrative of quality assurance (QA) in the Commonwealth. Rather, QA developments in Commonwealth countries have been driven by the same varied causes as have affected other countries, and have taken place over similar time periods and drawn on the same stock of ideas (see, for example, Woodhouse, 2012).

Many influences on Commonwealth countries have been regional rather than Commonwealth-based, and there are more similarities within regions than across the Commonwealth. Therefore, this chapter addresses the quality history of Commonwealth countries in several regions, before offering some concluding remarks.

Central Influences

The University of London External Programme

The University of London played a significant role in the quality of universities throughout the Commonwealth.

In 1828, a new higher education institution was founded in London, and caused a stir by calling itself a university. The consequent debate centred on which institutions had degree-granting powers, and which did not. The compromise solution, reached in 1836, was that a new entity called the University of London would be the examining body for a number of London colleges (initially University College and King's College). Successful students would receive a University of London degree.

The colleges soon extended their system to embrace the concept of distance learning. The University of London External Programme was established in 1858 to make University of London degrees accessible to students who could not come to the University to study in the conventional way. This service rapidly spread throughout the Commonwealth, and External Programme students were graded to the same standards as internal students, to ensure uniformity of credentials.

It is intriguing to contrast the respect for University of London qualifications gained through the External Programme with the suspicion shown in many parts of the world (particularly by governments) for distance qualifications; and the requirement of many institutions that a significant proportion of a student's study time must include attendance at the institution.

The University of London External Programme played an important role in the development and quality of higher education institutions throughout the Commonwealth. Many universities, in England and abroad, started out as 'university colleges' and prepared students for external University of London degrees. Hence the quality systems in place for University of London degrees were exported along with the education (Kenyon Jones, 2008).

When these institutions gained their own degree-awarding powers, they continued to link to the British system through the use of British external examiners.

In 2007, the name was changed from the University of London External Programme to the University of London External System; and then in 2010 to University of London International Programmes.

The External Examiner System

When the University of Durham was established in 1832, additional examiners were appointed to help with the load of setting and marking examinations. An ancillary benefit to Durham of using Oxford University examiners was the confirmation to the outside world that their degrees were of a comparable standard.

In the 1880s, a further expansion in the number of British universities was accompanied by a requirement that examinations should be conducted by internal and external examiners. The Council for National Academic Awards (CNAA), established in 1965, maintained a system of external examining in the non-university sector.

External examiners came to be seen as an essential element in British higher education. In the 1990s, however, growth of the higher education system, modularisation of courses and diversification of the student body led to questions about the feasibility and efficacy of the system. It was also an essentially amateur system that lacked training of the examiners, and included wide variations in practice between institutions and between examiners, which detracted from its effectiveness.

The National Committee of Inquiry into Higher Education (1997) (the Dearing Committee) commented on the external examiner system within its comprehensive review of higher education. It was

> not convinced that it would be the best use of scarce resources to continue the system in the long term…for the longer term we see the way forward lying in the development of common standards, specified and verified through a strengthened external examiner system, supported by a lighter approach to quality assessment.
>
> (Dearing Report, 1997)

The committee therefore recommended that:

- teams be convened, within disciplines, to provide benchmark information on standards, in particular threshold standards, operating within the framework of qualifications
- there be created a UK-wide pool of academic staff from which institutions must select external examiners

The benchmark information was to be used by external examiners to validate whether programmes were within the agreed standards for particular awards.

The former recommendation led, ultimately, to the creation by the Higher Education Quality Council (HEQC)—and then by the Quality Assurance Agency for Higher Education (QAA)—of subject benchmark statements.

The latter recommendation was picked up by the QAA, which overplayed its hand, by proposing that the examiner's report to the QAA as well as to the institution. In response to the negative backlash, the QAA decided instead to produce subject reports, every few years, which would draw, inter alia, on external examiner findings in that subject. The QAA also produced a code of practice on external examining (QAA, 2004), and summaries of external examiners' reports are published.

Hannan and Silver (2006) found that external examiners often receive little or no support from their own institution for this activity, and that the home institution does not make systematic use of the learning that the examiner could bring back. They conclude that examiners:

- value the role for reasons of reciprocity and information- or intelligence-gathering
- are resistant to attempts to make it more formal in function
- generally oppose attempts to impose a national system of training

Perhaps for this reason, the training of external examiners is still not systematic, but external examining survived the scare of its possible abolition in the early 1990s, as it was seen to have value—even if not the extensive value often claimed. Perhaps a certain realism crept in, as expressed by Barnett (1998), who questioned whether it was 'ever possible to maintain a broad comparability of standards across the system. In truth we do not know with any sureness what the real picture was.'

British practice has influenced members of the Commonwealth to a greater or lesser extent. Canada turned to accreditation, and Australia has used a variety of systems over the years. New Zealand had external examiners within the unitary University of New Zealand, and it continued to some extent between the institutions into which the University divided. In these countries, external examiners are used at postgraduate level. Most of the other former colonies maintained the system for many years after independence, until the costs of frequent international visits became prohibitive.

The Commonwealth Benchmarking Club

As the UK's Graduate Standards Project reported in 1997 after a two-year investigation (HEQC, 1997), standards in any discipline are what are collectively determined at any time by the professionals in that discipline. This suggests that standards:

- are not absolute
- are not immutable over time
- are not determined in isolation; it is by interaction with others that an institution can determine what standards it is achieving, and hence whether its purposes are sufficiently stringent and demanding

This observation has led to an increasing emphasis on 'benchmarking' in higher education. Whatever its origin, the term 'benchmarking' is now used in higher education to denote a comparison with some selected aspect of performance in another institution or organisation. In this context, benchmarking sometimes means simply a comparison of data about one's own institution with analogous publicly available data about another institution. More usefully, however, the term is reserved for a much more extensive process of systematic comparison of data with one or more selected partners, looking in depth at the processes that gave rise to the data under scrutiny, with the aim of learning how to improve one's own practice and outcomes in some aspect of one's own operations.

Systematic benchmarking is therefore clearly a major contributor to the achievement of quality in higher education. The ACU has run a benchmarking programme for over 15 years. The Commonwealth University Management Benchmarking Club was formed in 1995 by the Commonwealth Higher Education Management Service (CHEMS), working in collaboration with benchmarking advisers from PricewaterhouseCoopers. Its work commenced in 1996, led by John Fielden (Fielden, 2004), and was subsequently taken up by Cliff Wragg.

The club's purpose and aims were: 'To measure and promote excellence in university management'. In the first year (1996), membership was canvassed via the ACU networks, and this produced nine inaugural members of the club from six countries. The club has been run every year since then (except in 2000) with between 10 and 16 participating institutions each year, from a range of countries. In 2012, the three topics were:

- financial management
- managing league tables
- managing graduate outcomes

The key feature of this scheme was (and is) to make comparisons at institutional level, not at the level of sub-units.

By encouraging debate of the issues, and highlighting problems relating to the variations in context, culture, etc., elements of best practice have emerged or been identified. Members can take away that knowledge and use it to implement appropriate changes back at their own university.

This process may be of most use to institutions that have not previously done systematic self-review, so this is their first experience of it; or to institutions 'at the other end', which realise that they should plan through to an 'improvements' step. The ones in the middle, which hoped to have improvement handed to them on a plate as a result of going through the review and meeting process, are probably disappointed.

Africa

Following independence, there was a rapid growth in student enrolment at most higher education institutions in Africa during the 1980s and 1990s, with some governments explicitly indicating that access was more important than quality.

This led to a proliferation of private providers in the 1990s. While the number of African public universities doubled from roughly 100 to nearly 200 between 1990 and 2007, the number of private tertiary institutions in Africa surged during the same period from two dozen to an estimated 468 (Saint et al., 2009). This explosion brought with it problems of unqualified staff, sub-standard curricula, and lack of facilities (in both the public and private institutions).

Furthermore, while the enrolment growth rate was increasing, 'the average public expenditures per student in higher education fell tremendously during this period with detrimental effects on quality' (Hayward, 2006). The situation was not helped by the explicit decision of the World Bank in 1988 to favour the support of schools rather than higher education (Mkude, 2010). Eventually, however, the pressures became too much. 'The decline in quality, growing internationalisation, need to monitor the private sector, and other concerns, contributed to the emergence of a small number of quality assurance agencies, initiated by ministries of education, encouraged by academic staff' (Materu, 2007; see also Sey, 2010).

The earliest universities in Africa tended to affiliate to a university in the imperial country. With affiliation, the institutions became part of the British, French, Portuguese, or other systems of QA through their partner universities (Hayward, 2006). In the UK, the University Grants Committee (UGC), which advised the British government on the distribution of grant funding among the British universities from the early twentieth century until 1989, also influenced the colonies. In Africa, as tertiary education expanded from a handful of public institutions to hundreds of public and private institutions, many governments looked for ways to oversee these increasingly large and complex systems. It is noteworthy that buffer bodies for this purpose are more commonly found in the English-speaking countries, perhaps influenced by the UGC model. (In contrast, within the French-speaking countries, the tendency has been to create separate ministries of higher education to manage their growing tertiary systems [Saint et al., 2009].)

The history of QA in the Commonwealth in Africa can conveniently be addressed in three or four regions, namely, eastern, southern, western, and possibly central, although the last is usually associated with either the eastern or southern regions (see also Mkude, 2010). Three countries stand out in these regions, and they are Commonwealth countries in the form of Kenya, Nigeria, and South Africa.

Eastern Africa

In British colonial times, the three east African countries of Kenya, Tanzania, and Uganda formed the East African Community, with EA Airways, EA Railways, and so on. This tradition of co-operation has served the countries well, despite the break in the East African Community from 1980 to 1999.

In 1970, the University of East Africa, consisting of colleges in each country, split into three universities, but an Inter University Committee was formed for co-ordination of academic programmes in universities in the region. In 1980, the Inter University Committee was re-established after the break-up of the East African Community, and transformed into the Inter-University Council of East Africa (IUCEA) to continue the work of the Inter University Committee (Lenga et al., 2010).

Kenya became the first country in Africa to have a national QA agency, when the government established the Commission for Higher Education in 1985 to accredit private universities (but not those established by Parliament) (Materu, 2007). Subsequently, quality agencies were created in the other two countries (the Tanzania Commission for Universities, Acts of 1995 and 2005; and the National Council for Higher Education, Uganda, Acts of 2001 and 2003).

In 1999, the East African Community was revived and, in 2000, the IUCEA was revitalised. Its mandate was increased to include strengthening of research capacity in universities and other higher education institutions. This was followed by signing of a protocol in 2001, giving the IUCEA the mandate to work in collaboration with regulatory agencies, and the national quality agencies themselves became members of the IUCEA (Lenga, 2010), which therefore functions as the region's QA network.

The IUCEA also aimed at promoting harmonised and well-structured internal QA systems in the East African universities (by now numbering far more than the original one). The first step was to have a harmonised external QA system, and the three agencies participated in an IUCEA QA project to do this, conceived by the IUCEA and the German Academic Exchange Service (DAAD) in 2006. The subsequent improvement in internal QA systems led to a leap in the attention of East African institutions to matters such as self-review, peer review, and continuous quality improvement.

West Africa

Nigeria is perhaps second in the pioneers of university-level accreditation in Africa. Three national regulatory agencies are statutorily empowered to assure quality in the higher education system in Nigeria. These are:

- the National Universities Commission (NUC), established in 1964 as an oversight body
- the National Board for Technical Education, established in 1977

- the National Commission for Colleges of Education, established in 1989

From 1980, the National Board for Technical Education carried out accreditation, and in 1990 the NUC was given accreditation responsibilities in higher education (Materu, 2007).

In the early days of these organisations' activities, the quality of Nigerian universities was seen to be good (Okebukola, 2010), but then there was a deterioration. The quality of graduates from the Nigerian university system was assessed by the NUC in 2004 through labour market surveys. They found a pervasive deterioration of social values of truth, honesty, and dedication, 'affecting the processes of examinations conducted by the West African Examinations Council…and more recently the Nigerian Examinations Council…; and the Joint Admissions Matriculation Board…examinations/admissions processes' (Okebukola, 2010).

Another negative factor has been the extensive activities of degree mills. 'In a dramatic national "raid", NUC (backed up by the force of the anti-riot wing of the Nigeria Police under orders of the Inspector-General), took steps physically to close the illegal campuses' (Okebukola, 2010).

Regionally, a quality network is emerging in West Africa. In 2009, members of QA agencies from Nigeria, Ghana, and Sierra Leone held a consultative session in Ghana. A forum to plan the various national QA mechanisms and qualifications frameworks was held in November 2012.

Southern Africa

In South Africa until the 1980s, the typical British-tradition binary line existed between universities, which were assumed to be good by definition, and a more technical sector—the 'technikons'—which were subject to external review.

In the early 1990s, a few interested people (for example, Professor Kalie Strydom) tapped into the global movement and saw its relevance for South African universities. This resulted in the Committee of Vice-Chancellors and Principals creating a Quality Promotion Unit to carry out quality audits of all the universities in South Africa. The first auditors were trained in 1996, and the first audit was of Rhodes University. Although this was a good start, the unit also made errors.

The post-apartheid government had a thorough review of higher education, and in 2001 created the Council for Higher Education, which included the Higher Education Quality Committee (HEQC). The HEQC took over from both the Quality Promotion Unit and the Technikon Quality Agency. It now audits all higher education institutions and reviews their programmes, and also carries out system-wide, special-purpose reviews.

A major feature of South Africa's attempt to achieve quality in higher education has been the South African Qualifications Framework (SAQF), overseen by the South African Qualifications Authority. Many countries have qualifications frameworks, but the SAQF was created in the dying days of apartheid and the early days of the 'rainbow nation'—in a spirit of idealism, democratisation, and access for the excluded many—with an immensely complex structure to achieve a new national integrated framework to transform education and training in the country (Hay, 2011, personal communication).

The SAQF was intended to help transform South Africa's deeply fragmented and unequal education and training system, and to increase access and make education more democratic, while ensuring that education played a role in improving South Africa's economy. The SAQF was based on the ideas of competency-based education and outcomes-based education, with the aim that workers could get formal credit for competences achieved through experience, and move up a career path through the provision of approved training modules. Unfortunately, considerable faith was placed in arguments without evidence (Allais et al., 2009). Ideas were borrowed from Australia and from New Zealand (which had a prescriptive framework) and were made even more prescriptive.

For these reasons, although the SAQF and the South African Qualifications Authority have had a tangible impact, the overall value, and the cost–benefit balance, is still somewhat debated.

The Southern African Development Community (SADC) was established in 1992 as a collaboration between 15 member nations, from as far north as Tanzania. There were stirrings of the creation of a southern quality network in 1997, when the International Network for Quality Assurance Agencies in Higher Education conference was held in South Africa, but nothing materialised. Now there is nominally a quality network under the aegis of SADC, but it does not appear to be very active.

Central Africa

In Central Africa, developments are still at an early stage, and there is a very great deal to be done in establishing an effective and extensive QA system. Higher education itself is fragile in provision, with an understandable emphasis on mass school education. It will be important to invest in tertiary education for the future of this large and resource-rich region of Africa.

South Asia

For the purposes of this section, this region extends from Nepal in the north to the Maldives in the south, and east–west from Bangladesh to Pakistan.

Nations in this region collaborate through the South Asian Association for Regional Cooperation, comprising Afghanistan, Bangladesh, Bhutan, India, the Maldives, Nepal, Pakistan, and Sri Lanka. For example, in April 2007, they agreed to set up the South Asian University in India.

The region is composed almost entirely of Commonwealth countries, so regional and Commonwealth histories are synonymous. Universities on the British model were established in the sub-continent in Calcutta (1857) and the Punjab (1882), and others followed in the twentieth century.

As elsewhere, systematic attention to QA is a feature of the last 20 years.

India

The National Assessment and Accreditation Council (NAAC) of India, founded in 1994 under the UGC, was the first quality agency in the region.

As the Indian higher education system is so large, programme-level review was infeasible, so the NAAC carries out institution-level audit. Again, because the system is so large, the NAAC felt it appropriate to 'band' the institutions. The NAAC therefore uses the terminology 'institutional assessment and accreditation', and locates institutions on a nine-band scale on the basis of the audit.

The Indian higher education system comprises some 500 universities and 25,000 colleges, which means that the NAAC has an almost impossible task—especially as it is now working through second- and third-cycle audits. The only reason why the ostensible load is manageable is that NAAC audit is voluntary, and not all institutions come forward to be audited. The Indian government is now considering legislation to make audit compulsory, but to permit a plurality of quality agencies. In the pattern that has become familiar in India, it is taking years from proposal to enactment of legislation.

India benefited from Jawaharlal Nehru's strong commitment to education from the time when India obtained independence from Britain. That commitment led to the establishment and generous funding of the Indian institutes of technology, which are still highly regarded on the global scene.

More recently, the NAAC has held the responsibility for quality. However, history can take one only so far, and further developments are needed to deal with new realities, such as foreign institutions, low participation, effectiveness of affirmative action, and so on.

Pakistan

From having a single university at independence in 1947, Pakistan now has 132 recognised higher education institutions, of which 73 are public and 59 are private, with 7.4 million students. Pakistan also had a UGC, but this was superseded in 2002 by the Higher Education Commission (HEC).

The main purpose of the HEC was to enhance the quality of Pakistani universities, so they became reputed centres of education, research, and development. To this end:

- the HEC developed QA policies, standards, criteria, and guidelines, in consultation with international agencies and domestic stakeholders
- higher education institutions were expected to establish internal QA systems, to integrate quality into the institution's academic activities
- the HEC assisted the institutions to set up quality enhancement cells as the main instrument of implementing internal QA

Only at the third stage did an external QA system emerge. This is an interesting bottom-up approach to QA. It is noteworthy that many Pakistan higher education institutions are active on the world scene in ways that are more reminiscent of external quality agencies in other countries. The external QA system took the common form of programme and institutional accreditation (Batool and Qureshi, 2010).

In 2009, the HEC established a Quality Assurance Agency (QAA), to be an independent, autonomous body responsible for the QA of higher education in the country. The QAA accredits the accreditation councils in professional fields (such as engineering) and oversees the accreditation of academic programmes. The HEC has also produced a ranking of its institutions within defined categories.

There are many reports of improvements in Pakistan higher education in the first years of the HEC (Hayward, 2009). There are also criticisms that the rapid increase in the number of institutions—and hence the rapid increase in the number of academics—has led to a significant drop in quality (Hoodbhoy, 2011). This may not be the fault of the HEC in itself. If India has suffered (and is suffering) from the unwieldiness and hence slowness of the Indian democratic process (and political corruption), Pakistan has suffered from the destabilising effects of military dictatorships and power politics (Zehra, 2011). These have led to missed opportunities, including in higher education—and in QA in higher education.

In 2011, the government of Pakistan decided to devolve the responsibilities of the HEC to the provinces. It is not clear whether this was primarily due to genuine constitutional issues relating to the respective powers of the state and provincial governments, or whether it was because the HEC had been so thorough in investigating and confirming allegations of politicians claiming fake degrees. The proposal generated protests from the HEC itself and from academia—even from some who had been critical of the HEC (for example, Hoodbhoy, 2011). At the time of writing (late 2011), the matter is before the Supreme Court. The government appears likely instead to replace the HEC with a more regulatory (and perhaps more amenable) body.

Bangladesh

The University Grants Commission (UGC) of Bangladesh was established in 1973 to oversee university education. It is also responsible for maintaining standards and quality in all the public and private universities in Bangladesh.

In 1992, a Private University Act was passed. Its purpose was to encourage the establishment of further universities, in order to meet the evident demand (Bangladesh Government, 1992). The Act contains criteria that must be satisfied by any proposed private university (though there are none for public universities), but even now the higher education institutions and their programmes are still largely operated without the sustained introspection and periodic external review that is needed for QA and improvement (Aminuzzaman, 2010). The QA systems that do exist tend to be subjective.

In 2003, the UGC drafted a proposal for an Accreditation Council for Private Universities, but this stalled in the Ministry of Education. Late in 2005, the UGC renewed its efforts, but political problems supervened as a caretaker government came to power at the beginning of 2006, and the parameters for caretaker governments did not allow it to act on this matter during its two-year regime.

Eventually, a new Private University Act was passed in 2010. It requires each private university to have an internal QA cell, and for each university to report annually on measures taken to ensure quality. The Act also provides for the government to establish a separate, and fully independent, accreditation council (Khaled, 2011, Secretary, UGC). Whether this will happen is yet to be seen.

Sri Lanka

In Sri Lanka, work on QA was started in 2001 by the Committee of Vice-Chancellors and Directors and the University Grants Commission. A handbook was published, and reviewers were trained to carry out external assessments.

By the end of 2004, the Quality Assurance and Accreditation Council (QAAC) was established, to carry out institution-level and programme-level (or subject- or discipline-level) reviews. Sri Lanka drew on the UK's QAA in developing its system. The QAAC, initially funded by the World Bank, is an independent body under the University Grants Commission. There are plans to convert it to a legally autonomous board (Peiris, 2013, personal communication).

The QAAC's constituency is the 15 universities, 17 affiliated institutes, and the non-state higher education institutions. Plans are under way for the QAAC to review foreign institutions operating in Sri Lanka on a voluntary basis (Peiris, 2011). As with the other nations in this region, the agency has strongly emphasised the need for each university to create its own internal QA unit. That has yet to happen and the challenges remain large.

East Asia

The Commonwealth countries in east and south-east Asia are Brunei Darussalam, Malaysia, Singapore, and formerly Hong Kong. This section concentrates on the last three of these, all of which share some similarities in the quality realm, but with differences also.

Similarities include the British-derived attitude that universities are 'good by definition'. Hence, it is relatively straightforward to set up external quality or registration systems for non-universities, but universities have to be dragged, kicking and screaming, into the process. This occurred at different times in the three countries. Another similarity is that all have been attractive targets for educational exports since the early 1990s, especially from Australia and the UK, drawing on the Commonwealth heritage and the English language medium.

Differences include their reactions to this attention.

- Malaysia, like many other countries, experienced a rapid growth of private providers, and established (in 1996) an agency to control both these and the imports from overseas.
- Hong Kong was more concerned to maintain its positional advantage as a free trade area, and set up an agency to ensure that the quality of the incoming education was similar to that attained by the institution 'back home'—even if neither quality was very good.
- Singapore took tight control of the Singaporean public institutions but adopted a 'caveat emptor' approach to the private sector, which it saw as being in the commercial (or even tourist) sector.

Hong Kong

Like the south Asian nations, Hong Kong drew on British practice and established a UGC (in 1965). The UGC was responsible for advising the government on the development and funding of the then two institutions of higher education, namely, the University of Hong Kong and the Chinese University of Hong Kong. Later, a third university, two polytechnics and two colleges came within its ambit.

Even so, the universities and non-universities were treated differently in relation to external QA. The universities received a very polite annual visit from members of the UPGC, with a follow-up letter, whereas the non-universities were reviewed by the UK's CNAA (see under 'United Kingdom', below) and were required to comply with its findings.

In 1990, with the imminence of the handover of Hong Kong to China, it was seen as inappropriate to have institutions reviewed by a non-local agency, so the Hong Kong Council for Academic Accreditation (HKCAA) was created to review the non-universities and their programmes. Early in the 1990s, the majority of the HKCAA's clientele were renamed as universities, and hence left its purview. Recently there has been a rapid increase in the number of associate degrees, growth in the vocational sector and the creation of a qualifications framework. Oversight of all these was allocated to the HKCAA and its name changed (in 2007) to the Hong Kong Council for Accreditation of Academic and Vocational Qualifications.

Also early in the 1990s, the UGC decided to do something more formal and stringent about QA with respect to the universities. It carried out some focused reviews of the eight institutions under its jurisdiction. Each of these reviews, with international panels, looked at all the UGC institutions, variously focusing on research, teaching, and management. The UGC made it clear that these reviews 'could inform funding', and in fact withheld new postgraduate places from one university until the recommendations of a particular review had been implemented.

More recently, the external QA arrangements have proliferated.

- In 2005, the universities established the Joint Quality Review Committee to review the QA processes of their self-financed, sub-degree programmes. The committee was intended to forestall other external review of these programmes.
- In 2009, however, the UGC created the Quality Assurance Council to systematise the intermittent UGC reviews, by carrying out audits of each individual institution. The first cycle of audits was concluded in 2011. There might not be a second cycle, as the Hong Kong government has recommended that all the external

> QA arrangements of higher education be brought together under the Hong Kong Council for Accreditation of Academic and Vocational Qualifications.

Hong Kong requires overseas institutions operating in Hong Kong to be reviewed, to ensure that their Hong Kong–offered programme will be comparable with the one back home. There is a loophole, however: if the overseas institution is operating in partnership with a Hong Kong UGC institution, the review is waived. A successful review (or exemption) grants the programme 'recognition' and registration, but not accreditation. Accreditation of overseas programmes in Hong Kong requires a further check, to see whether the Hong Kong–offered programme is comparable with equivalent indigenous Hong Kong programmes. Overseas institutions may voluntarily seek accreditation.

Singapore

Like Hong Kong, Singapore is a small country/territory with no natural resources. Hence, it is dependent on the initiative and industry of its people, and on trade with the rest of the world. A difference is that the former Hong Kong government saw its task as providing the context in which private enterprise could flourish, whereas in Singapore the government saw its task as controlling the lives of its citizens so that all could flourish. This control extended to higher education.

Public education in Singapore is seen to be mainly for Singaporeans. Students leaving school may go to university (the top 25 per cent in performance on the end-of-school examination) or polytechnic (the next 40 per cent). Standards in the public sector are largely handled by input and output, with little explicit concern with process. The main approach to quality, particularly for the universities, has been through international benchmarking and attracting top staff through generous salaries. Singapore's lack of a national accreditation body for the qualifications awarded by the higher education institutions was explained by a senior Ministry of Education official in 2004 as being because 'we believe the employers are in the best position to determine the value of these qualifications'. However, a more formal external QA system was introduced for universities in 2004 and for polytechnics in 2006.

Private education is left to the market ('caveat emptor'), is seen as an economic activity, and is largely for overseas students. It is left to the Ministry of Trade and Industry to introduce voluntary controls—with carrots rather than sticks.

Although Singapore is a small country, its higher education quality system involves a large number of agencies and procedures, including:

- the Ministry of Education
- the Ministry of Trade and Industry, which oversees a voluntary 'business excellence' scheme for private institutions, known as Singapore Quality Class for Private Education Organizations (or SQC-PEO)
- CaseTrust (CASE is the Consumer Association of Singapore, and CaseTrust [later EduTrust] is a form of fee guarantee)
- the Singapore Tourism Board, which has a role here because the government regards education (and health) provision for foreigners as being a tourist matter

In 2004, the Ministry of Trade and Industry created the Singapore HE Accreditation Council for the private sector. In 2006, however, the minister decided that higher education did not properly belong in his Ministry, so the council was dissolved and the task of external QA for the private sector passed to the Ministry of Education.

In 2009, a Private Education Act was passed, setting up a Council for Private Education.

Malaysia

In 1996, the Malaysian government established a National Accreditation Board (Lembaga Akreditasi Negara, LAN) to monitor the standards and quality of higher education provided by all private higher educational institutions in Malaysia (Government of Malaysia, 1996). LAN was established in view of the expected rapid increase of such institutions to meet access demands from society.

All certificates, diplomas, and degrees were required to satisfy the minimum standards as determined by LAN. The criteria for the determination of the compulsory minimum standard level of achievement, as well as the higher optional level of accreditation, were based on the courses of study, teaching staff, syllabus of all subjects, available facilities, management system, and rationale for conducting the course of study. Institutions meeting the 'minimum standard' level of achievement were allowed to give the courses and to graduate students. Those courses that obtained accreditation certificates additionally could enable their students to seek employment in the public sector.

Approval for government employment required recognition of the qualification by the Department of Private Education in the Ministry of Education. Department of Private Education recognition therefore related to accreditation rather than minimum standards. Especially in view of this double level of approval by LAN, there has often been some confusion over whether a course was—or was not—recognised for the purposes of government employment.

Malaysia encouraged foreign institutions to set up schemes where the foreign institutions offered the first one or two years of a degree in Malaysia, in collaboration with a local partner organisation, with the student completing the degree at the home campus. This was more economical for the students and used less of Malaysia's foreign exchange. However, the Malaysian Ministry of Education oscillated in its attitude to these awards, sometimes being most conscious of their value, and at other times being doubtful about their quality.

In the late 1990s, the government began a campaign to bring the public universities under a QA process, and created the Quality Assurance Division of the Ministry of Education. Gradually the concept of external QA and systematic internal QA took hold in Malaysian universities, and in 2007 the Malaysian Qualifications Agency succeeded both LAN and the Quality Assurance Division to be a single national consolidated body for all higher education institutions and, most importantly, to implement the Malaysian Qualifications Framework, of which it is the custodian.

Like Singapore, Malaysia is a country that over the decade of the 1990s was increasingly seen by other countries (notably the UK and Australia) as a place to which to export education, but which in more recent years has itself moved into the business of educational export. It has high targets for the number of foreign students, and is positioning itself as an open and welcoming environment for students from Muslim countries, after the 11 September 2001 attacks in New York resulted in the USA being less welcoming. As with other educational exporters, this goal requires enhanced attention to QA for education.

UK and the Dominions

It is convenient to consider these countries together, although they are not very homogeneous. They do share the British attitude, mentioned in the section on East Asia, that universities are 'good by definition', so universities were included in the respective QA systems later than other institutions.

United Kingdom

In the UK, for example, the CNAA was established in 1965 to oversee the 'colleges of advanced technology' and to assist them to develop into 'technological universities' by validating the institutions and their qualifications. In fact, the awards were CNAA awards, not awards of the teaching institution. Polytechnics and colleges were also subject to inspection by Her Majesty's Inspectorate.

In the late 1980s, the universities noted that questions about the quality and standards of higher education were becoming increasingly frequent, and they established the Academic Audit Unit to look at institutions' QA processes. But this had only just begun work when the government's intention to abolish the binary line was announced in May 1991.

The following year, the government decided that the QA regime for the new single sector should comprise:

- a new sector-owned body, the HEQC, building on both the CNAA and the Academic Audit Unit and auditing at institutional level
- teaching quality assessment, building on Her Majesty's Inspectorate practice, implemented by the funding councils and linked to funding

Within a few years, the government responded to institutional concerns about overload and agreed that a single body could implement both the institutional audits and the programme-level teaching quality assessments (later known as 'subject review'), carrying out the latter on behalf of the funding councils (Brown, 2012). The single body set up in 1997 as a successor to the HEQC to carry out the external QA tasks is the Quality Assurance Agency for Higher Education (QAA). It spent several years in creating a new single quality regime. However, the universities felt that the only decrease in external bureaucratic load that they could detect was that all submissions could be sent to the same address, rather than to two addresses!

In 2001, responding again to pressure from the universities, the government suddenly announced that the scale of subject review should be reduced, and audit—now known as 'institutional review'—became the main quality mechanism. In return, the institutions agreed to produce and publish a much greater amount of information about quality (Brown, 2012).

The QAA has varied its emphases from cycle to cycle, and operates slightly differently in the four countries of the UK. It bases its work on an 'academic infrastructure', which includes codes of practice and subject benchmark statements. In 2011, it thoroughly reviewed the infrastructure, and a revised system is beginning in 2013.

New Zealand

In New Zealand in the 1980s, it became increasingly apparent that postsecondary qualifications were not readily recognised by institutions or employers in different parts of the country. The government therefore created a National Qualifications Framework (NQF) to provide a common national structure and content for all postsecondary qualifications, both higher and vocational.

The designers of the NQF took the philosophical position that all postsecondary education could be fitted into the same framework, in the same way. The universities objected to this, and sought to be excluded from the NQF. The legislation establishing the NQF in 1989, therefore, explicitly delegated responsibility for quality in the universities to the New Zealand Vice-Chancellors' Committee (NZVCC).

Over the next few years, the NZVCC considered various models for a QA system for the universities. It was attracted by the quality audits being carried out by the UK's Academic Audit Unit, and decided to create a New Zealand Universities Academic Audit Unit (NZUAAU). When the NZUAAU began operation in 1994, therefore, its aim was to create 'an AAU adapted for New Zealand'. The NZUAAU has continued to carry out quality audits of the eight NZ universities (institutional level, not programme level), and it now completes its fifth cycle. In some cycles, the scope has been the whole institution, while in others it has been more focused.

To address programme-level quality, the NZVCC has a Committee on University Academic Programs. This has a representative from each university (plus a few other people), and the universities have jointly agreed not to introduce a new programme before it is approved by the committee.

Meanwhile, the New Zealand Qualifications Authority (established in 1989) has developed institutional and programme-level accreditation processes for all other postsecondary institutions. The universities' primary objection to the NQF was that it required a fragmentation of their programmes in order to express them as the atomic 'unit standards'. In the early 2000s, agreement was reached that there would be a common 'register of qualifications' containing those qualifications on the NQF and those approved by the universities. The system was unified in July 2010, when the New Zealand Qualifications Framework was established to replace the NQF and the New Zealand Register of Quality Assured Qualifications.

Australia

The binary system (of colleges and universities) was abandoned in Australia at about the same time as in the UK (1988–90), but without the same thought being given to a post-unification quality system. Instead, suddenly all the colleges and institutes that had been subject to external checks were called universities, and were under no external QA regime. This was a challenge created by the major higher education reforms associated with the so-called 'Dawkin's revolution' under the Hawke-Keating Government.

In 1992, the federal government ultimately created a Committee on Quality Assurance in Higher Education, and between 1993 and 1995 it audited each university annually. The incentive for the universities was that the government allocated a small sum (about 2 per cent of the higher education budget) to reward institutions differentially on the basis of the committee's judgements. There were significant defects in this process, including rushed preparation, overload on review panels, and little chance to act on any findings. Nonetheless, there was a positive effect of making institutions think actively and systematically about quality. With the election of a new federal government, the committee was disbanded in 1996.

Later in the 1990s, Australia's increasing involvement in the export of education, and its dependence on the consequent student fees, made the absence of a national quality agency a significant drawback in its marketing efforts. In 1999, the federal government announced the creation of a new national agency, the Australian Universities Quality Agency (AUQA). AUQA was a not-for-profit company, owned jointly by all the federal and state ministers of education. This company status, under an independent board of directors, gave AUQA significant freedom of movement, and it avoided charges of political and bureaucratic interference.

AUQA carried out two cycles of institution-level quality audits from 2001 to 2011 of over 40 universities and other institutions. The quality of Australian education overseas (transnational education) was a major emphasis, and AUQA review panels visited almost 200 overseas campuses and partners in that decade. Significant improvement in the quality of transnational education operations could be seen in that time. AUQA panels also included members from overseas, to stress the openness of the process and to bring external views to bear on Australian higher education.

In addition to the universities, there were (in 2011) about 160 other higher education institutions. These were subject to quality control by the respective state government. They were also subject to multiple state requirements if they operated across state boundaries. Then, in 2007 about half of them became subject also to AUQA audit in order to access federal funds. As a result, a country with only 200 higher education institutions had 10 QA agencies with overlapping responsibilities.

Therefore, in 2009 the federal government decided to replace AUQA and the state agencies with a single new federal statutory body, the Tertiary Education Quality and Standards Agency, which would emphasise standards (of many sorts) and operate through a risk management lens, using the oversight of the financial sector as its model. The new framework of assessment is based on 46 indicators of 'risk', against which institutional performance will be scrutinised. Three areas of risk have been highlighted:

- risk to the students and their education
- the risk of the provider collapsing
- the risk to the sector's reputation for quality

Existing data on the sector will be supplemented on the basis of 'risk profiles' identified for each provider. The initial main foci are offshore course delivery and any serious student complaints. The thresholds for risk are not yet made public (Lane, 2012).

South Africa

South Africa has already been discussed in the African context, but since it was often included among the Dominions, it merits a brief observation here that it continued the genealogy running through what has already been described above. It based its qualifications framework and its QA system for the universities on the respective bodies in New Zealand.

Canada

Canada, however, does not fall within this genealogy. Canada is not a single jurisdiction (as New Zealand is), nor is it as tight a federal policy environment as Australia. There is no national or federal minister of education, and the current chair of the Council of Ministers of Education, Canada (CMEC) (the group of provincial ministers of education) fulfils that role for international purposes.

Hence, QA development in Canada has varied greatly between provinces (Baker and Miosi, 2010).

- In some cases, the government is directly involved through quality assessment agencies; in others, there are joint government/institutional committees or the responsibility falls to individual institutions.
- In some cases, there are written learning outcome standards and peer reviews; in other cases, there are peer reviews alone.
- In some cases, peer review includes wholly external experts; in others, a mix of in-house and external consultants is used.
- In some regions, universities have established collaborative bodies to undertake reviews or to audit them; in other regions, the practices remain rooted in single institutions.
- In Alberta, British Columbia, and Ontario, where new private institutions and out-of-province institutions are permitted, arm's-length

quality assessment agencies review and recommend on the quality of the institutions and programmes.

- In New Brunswick, the Maritime Provinces Higher Education Commission coordinates the assessments for private institution applicants.

In 2007, CMEC endorsed a statement on QA for three main purposes (CMEC, 2011):

- to provide public assurance that institutional standards are assessed
- to provide a context for identifying how degree credentials compare in level and standard to those in other jurisdictions
- to improve student access to further study

The statement is used as a guideline in decision-making relating to new degree programmes and new degree-granting institutions within a province or territory. It contains three sections:

- Canadian Degree Qualifications Framework
- Procedures and Standards for New Degree Program Quality Assessment
- Procedures and Standards for Assessing New Degree-Granting Institutions

A player on the national scene is the Association of Universities and Colleges of Canada (AUCC). This is an advocacy body, primarily for Canadian public universities. Nonetheless, and in the absence of a national approach, some public universities have declared that they will recognise only degree programmes offered by members of the AUCC on the grounds that membership is a 'proxy' for accreditation.

Small States

There are various definitions of the term 'small state'. It usually (but not always) refers to size of population, and usually sets a population figure in the range of 5 million to 10 million.

Small states have problems in implementing external QA systems of common current form.

- External QA is usually based on peer review, but the peers must be close enough to the reviewed programme or institutions to understand it, yet far enough away not to have a conflict of interest. In a small system, this duality is difficult to achieve.
- One way of achieving independent views is to bring in peers from abroad, but that is expensive and small states typically have small budgets. (There are exceptions, for example, Brunei.)
- A third problem is that the peers are often from the university system, but a small state may have only one university—so who will review that?

Small states have adopted a variety of measures to overcome these problems. Linking in a regional network is the most popular.

- The most obvious network of small states is the Caribbean Area Network for Quality Assurance in Tertiary Education (CANQATE), the Caribbean regional network for quality in the Anglophone Caribbean. Jamaica has long had a QA agency, and Trinidad and Tobago established one in the mid-1990s. The other tiny islands are using CANQATE to achieve the necessary growth and interaction. (To an outside observer, the right solution is a single Caribbean QA agency, but national pride supervenes, no matter how small the nation.)
- The other region with many small islands is the Pacific. Some of these islands fall under US systems, but 11 nations jointly own the University of the South Pacific, headquartered in Fiji. The University of the South Pacific contracted the Australian and New Zealand quality agencies to assist in developing its QA procedures and to carry out a quality audit.

What Now?

It appears that QA agencies will continue for the foreseeable future, although the leading educational and policy thinkers are pointing to the need to:

- pay attention to new modes of education and to new types of provider

- reduce the burden of QA
- strengthen global recognition and mobility
- ensure that QA systems develop to match a changing world

Will the Commonwealth have a specific role in this? It is likely that, as heretofore, some Commonwealth countries will be in the forefront of these developments, though operating regionally rather than through the Commonwealth itself. There is an opportunity for the Commonwealth to generate comparative and connectional studies in the development of an application across its jurisdictions globally.

Bibliography

Allais, S., Raffe, D., Strathdee, R., Wheelahan, L., and Young, M. (2009) Learning from the first qualifications frameworks. Employment Working Paper No. 45, Employment Sector, International Labour Office, Geneva.

Aminuzzaman, S.M. (2010) Quality Issues of Higher Education in Bangladesh, referenced in NUFFIC International Policy Documents, 18 November. Available online at www.nuffic.nl/international-organisations/international-education-monitor/country-monitor/asia-and-the-pacific/bangladesh/documents (downloaded 6 March 2012).

Baker, D.N. and Miosi, T. (2010) The quality assurance of degree education in Canada. *Research in Comparative and International Education*, 5(1).

Bangladesh Government (1992) An Act made to provide for the establishment of private universities: Act No. 34 of 1992, *Bangladesh Gazette Extraordinary*.

Barnett R. (1998) The Idea of the External Examiner: Myth or Legend? In *Making the Most of the External Examiner* (SEDA Paper 98), ed. G. Wisker. Birmingham: Staff and Educational Development Association.

Batool, Z. and Qureshi, R.H. (2010) Quality Assurance Framework for Higher Education: Pakistani Context. Presentation to Quality Congress of Dubai, Sultan Hamadan bin Muhammad University.

Brown, R. (October 2012), Quality assurance 1992–2012. Perspectives: Policy and Practice in Higher Education, *Journal of the Association of University Administrators (AUA)*, 16(4):113–17.

Council of Ministers of Education, Canada (CMEC), website entry (accessed on 24 December 2011).

Fielden, J. (2004) Association of Commonwealth Universities Initiatives in Benchmarking: University-wide Quality Management. In *Consortia:*

International Networking Alliances of Universities, ed D.C.B. Teather. Melbourne, Australia: Melbourne University Press.

Government of Malaysia (1996) Lembaga Akreditasi Negara Act, 1996 (Act 556). Government of Malaysia, Kuala Lumpur.

Hannan, A. and Silver, H. (2006) On Being an External Examiner. *Studies in Higher Education*, 1470–174X, 31(1): 57–69.

Hayward, F.M. (2006) Quality Assurance and Accreditation of Higher Education in Africa. Presentation at the Conference on Higher Education Reform in Francophone Africa: Understanding the Keys of Success, Ouagadougou, Burkina Faso, 13–15 June.

——— (2009) Higher education transformation in Pakistan: Political and economic instability. *International Higher Education Quarterly*, 54, Winter.

HEQC (1997) *Graduate Standards Programme Final Report*. London: Higher Education Quality Council.

Hoodbhoy, P. (2011) Should the HEC live or die? *Express Tribune*, 8 April 2011, Pakistan.

Kenyon Jones, C. (2008) *The People's University: 150 Years of the University of London and Its External Students*. London: University of London External.

Khaled, M. (2011) Roadmap to Formation of an Accreditation Council for Quality Assurance in Bangladesh. Presentation to seminar on 'Approaches for Quality Needs in Higher Education: Bangladesh perspective', Bangladesh University of Professionals, Mirpur, 22 March.

Lane, B. (2012) Tertiary regulator issues risk list. Higher Education Supplement, *Australian*, Sydney, 29 February 2012, 29.

Lenga, F.K. (2010) East African Quality Assurance System: The Role of and Experiences from National Regulatory Agencies. Presentation to AfriQAN/IUCEA Capacity Building Workshop on Quality Assurance in Africa, Naura Spring Hotel, Arusha, Tanzania, 29–30 November.

Lenga, F.K., Okae, P.G., and Damian, V. (2010) Recognition of Academic Qualifications: The East African Initiative. Presentation to AfriQAN/IUCEA Capacity Building Workshop on Quality Assurance in Africa, Naura Spring Hotel, Arusha, Tanzania, 29–30 November.

Materu, P. (2007) Higher Education Quality Assurance in Sub-Saharan Africa: Status, Challenges, Opportunities and Promising Practices. World Bank Working Paper No. 124, Africa Human Development Series, The World Bank, Washington DC.

Mkude, D.J. (2010) HE Landscape and Quality Assurance Dynamics in Africa. Presentation to AfriQAN/IUCEA Capacity Building Workshop on Quality Assurance in Africa, Naura Spring Hotel, Arusha, Tanzania, 29–30 November.

National Committee of Inquiry into Higher Education (1997) *Higher Education in the Learning Society* (the Dearing Report). London: HMSO.

Okebukola, P. (2010) Fifty Years of Higher Education in Nigeria: Trends in Quality Assurance. Presentation to the International Conference on the Contributions of Nigerian Universities to the 50th Independence Anniversary of Nigeria, 27–29 September, Abuja. Available online at www.unilorin.edu.ng/publiclectures/Final-Okebukola-AVCNU-50-Years%20of%20Higher%20Ed.pdf (downloaded on 7 March 2012).

Peiris, C.N. (2008) *Quality Assurance and Accreditation (QAA) in Higher Education*. Asia Pacific Quality Network. Available online at www.apqn.org/files/virtual_library/articles/quality_assurance_and_accreditation_in_higher_education.pdf (downloaded on 6 March 2012).

Quality Assurance Agency for Higher Education (2004) *Code of Practice for the Assurance of Academic Quality and Standards in Higher Education, Section 4: External examining*. Gloucester: QAA.

Saint, W., Lao, C., and Materu, P. (2009) Legal Frameworks for Tertiary Education in Sub-Saharan Africa: The Quest for Institutional Responsiveness. World Bank Working Paper No. 175, Africa Human Development Series. Washington DC: The World Bank.

Sey, A. (2010) Quality Assurance Practices in African Universities. Presentation to AfriQAN/IUCEA Capacity Building Workshop on Quality Assurance in Africa, Naura Spring Hotel, Arusha, Tanzania, 29–30 November.

Stella, A. (2002) *External Quality Assurance in Indian Higher Education*. Paris: International Institute for Educational Planning, UNESCO.

Woodhouse, D. (2012) *A Short History of Quality*, CAA Quality Series, Abu Dhabi.

Zehra, N. (2011) Nusrat Bhutto's enduring legacy. *Gulf News*, October.

Personal Communications

Personal communications from Z.M. Fahmi, M. Hay, E. Ko, C. Lok, T. Okafor, C.N. Peiris, A. Stella, and C.Wragg are also gratefully acknowledged.

8

International Student Mobility: Lessons from the Commonwealth Scholarship and Fellowship Plan

Hilary Perraton

In hindsight, the late 1950s marked the 'apogee of the Commonwealth idea'.[1] It demanded political attention: of the 360 files that crossed Harold Macmillan's desk in 1958, a total of 58 (or 16 per cent) concerned the empire or Commonwealth; only foreign affairs came higher on the British Prime Minister's list. By 1965, imperial and Commonwealth affairs had moved to first place on this list, with 20 per cent of the total (Hennessy, 2001: 92–94).

Across the Atlantic, John Diefenbaker, who had unexpectedly come to power in 1957, saw the Commonwealth as so important for Canada and its economy that he called for a Commonwealth trade conference, the first in 26 years, which was duly held in Montreal in September 1958.

Half a century later, the significance of the Commonwealth had shrunk to the point where the word 'Commonwealth' appeared only once (in the heading) in a list of Foreign and Commonwealth Office priorities. With yet more hindsight, the seeds of its insignificance were already visible at the time of the 1958 Montreal conference, when the British, at least, would have nothing of Canada's hopes for imperial preference or grand plans for a Commonwealth development bank.

By 1958 plans for a free-trade competitor to the European Economic Community were eroding, and within two years Macmillan was ready to start on the slow and painful path towards joining the Community. British trade followed that economic flag, and Europe was to replace the Commonwealth as Britain's major trading partner—just as Asia did for Australia. But, curiously and from far down its agenda, the Montreal trade conference produced two lasting effects that had little to do with trade: a Commonwealth telecommunications network; and the creation of a Commonwealth Scholarship and Fellowship Plan (CSFP).

Both Canada as host, and Britain as the still-imperial power, agreed over the summer of 1958 that the conference should address wider issues than trade, and that education might therefore also get onto the agenda. Britain wanted something positive out of the conference. A civil service brief for the Commonwealth relations minister complained that:

> A difficulty is the Prime Minister's insistence on some new 'institution' emerging from Montreal...The trouble is that the Commonwealth very largely operates on the 'old boy net' and there is pretty strong aversion in most Commonwealth countries to institutionalising our flexible arrangements, unless there is real practical advantage in doing this.[2]

For Sidney Smith, the Canadian Foreign Minister, there was just such a practical advantage. As a former president of the University of Toronto, as well as a government minister, he made two speeches in September 1958, to the quinquennial Commonwealth universities congress and to the trade conference, both in Montreal, arguing for a 'fellowship project' to increase academic exchange within the Commonwealth (Smith, 1968). Earlier in the year he had asked Tom Symons, then a junior academic at the University of Toronto but also a founding member of a student organisation called 'Friendly Relations with Overseas Students', to sketch plans for a 'great Britannic initiative' that would expand opportunities for postgraduate studies within the Commonwealth. Smith argued that '[i]t would be a great thing for this proposal to come from Canada'.[3] The Montreal conference approved the proposal in principle and, with one conference begetting another, recommended that the details should be worked out at a Commonwealth education conference within a year.

The proposals were woven from several contrasting strands. One was a post-war belief in internationalism: Symons, like other Canadians of his generation who were backing the plan, had themselves travelled in Europe on scholarships (Perraton, 2009: 8–9). Another was the assumption that scholarships could, even should, be set up for political ends: Rhodes, competing European scholarship programmes in the 1930s, and Fulbright had all paved the way. The idea of Commonwealth cohesion—part of the everyday political jargon of the time—provided its own political strand. It was seen as a major aim of British foreign policy, was cited by Smith in his speech to Commonwealth universities, and quoted by academics in Britain as a defining characteristic of the scholarship proposals (Perraton, 2009: 36–37).

Inevitably, the cold war tinged the fabric: British ministers were interested in 'presenting the overall project as an important initiative in the West in the educational field, comparing favourably with the facilities offered by the Communist bloc in this sphere'. However, in Symons' view, Smith's concern was mainly about 'opening windows between countries' so that his 'speech [to Commonwealth universities] would have been much the same if the world weren't polarised east and west at that point'.[4]

Launching the Plan

Between September 1958 and July 1959, Commonwealth governments reached agreement on the shape of the plan, which was endorsed at a Commonwealth education conference in Oxford.

There was no unanimity. Australia and New Zealand saw the training of civil servants as a higher priority than academic exchange. Teacher training was more important for Britain. Canada conceived the plan as mainly for students in the humanities, India in the sciences. In Britain, the ACU had to fight to become the plan's implementing agency and even then had to agree that the British Council would look after the money. (British civil servants claimed to be concerned that the money might not be safe when the ACU had a non-British chairman.[5])

But despite the differences, the Oxford conference—with participants from the nine Commonwealth members, and colonial representatives from Fiji to Zanzibar—agreed on behalf of their governments to set up what was now formally named the CSFP.

Five principles were endorsed (Commonwealth Relations Office, 1959: para. 14). The plan was:

1. to be distinct from other scholarship plans
2. to be based on mutual co-operation
3. to be flexible
4. to work through bilateral agreements between states
5. to recognise 'the highest standards of intellectual achievement'

The principles have remained unchanged and were formally re-endorsed at three 10-year reviews undertaken by the Commonwealth Secretariat in 1972, 1982, and 1993.

Of the five principles, perhaps the last two have been the most important. Respect for bilateralism left each Commonwealth country to decide how many awards to offer, and to set up its own arrangements for selecting candidates. There was no central or coordinating mechanism. In practice, the selection of scholars and fellows was shared between sending and receiving countries, with the former producing long lists and the latter making the final choice. The principle of seeking intellectual achievement meant that, for many years, applicants were selected purely on academic merit. This differentiated the plan from programmes of technical assistance and led to criticism that some awards failed to match developmental needs: one chairman of the Commonwealth Scholarship Commission in the United Kingdom complained that '[s]ome of the things students are coming here to do are not justified as a form of economic aid. Some are even ridiculous. It is a world of "flannel".'[6]

The Oxford conference made a series of recommendations, alongside the five principles, that were to shape the plan. From the outset it was open to men and women. Awards would be made at two levels: scholarships to relatively young scholars, mainly for postgraduate degrees; and fellowships to more established academics. It was hoped to build up to 1,000 awards, with half provided by Britain and a quarter by Canada. Each country was expected to establish an agency to nominate candidates, or (if it was making awards) to make the final selection. Above all, the plan was based on reciprocity—something for which Canada had argued consistently at Montreal and Oxford—on the grounds that

> educational interchange between all the countries of the Commonwealth is essential if we are all to get the best out of the Plan and to share to the full the benefits of the special experience and facilities which our countries possess. Each has something to learn from the others; each has something to give.
>
> (Commonwealth Relations Office, 1959: Annex I)

Commonwealth governments moved quickly to set up the necessary mechanisms for the plan. Within six months of the Oxford conference, Britain had created a Commonwealth Scholarship Commission, which was to be responsible for the selection of scholars and fellows. Australia, Canada, and New Zealand gave this job to committees of academics. India (which had explained to the Oxford conference that it already had machinery that was dealing with 1,000 scholarships a year) added this task to the work of the government scholarships department.

Within five years, awards were on offer from 16 Commonwealth territories—Australia, Britain, Canada, the Central African Federation, Ceylon, East Africa, Hong Kong, India, Jamaica, Malaya, Malta, New Zealand, Nigeria, Pakistan, Sierra Leone, and even South Africa before it left the Commonwealth in 1961.

Within five years, too, numbers had built up to exceed the total of 1,000 agreed at Oxford. As predicted, Britain and Canada provided the lion's share of the awards, and by 1966 were hosting 813 (78 per cent) of the total. While Commonwealth scholars made up only about 6 per cent of the total number of Commonwealth students in Britain, the totals look significant when set against the total number of university students within some parts of the developing Commonwealth: in 1960, with the exception of South Africa, Commonwealth Africa had fewer than 4,000 students, while the Caribbean had fewer than 1,000.

The wind of change, which Macmillan heard blowing across Africa, was to invigorate higher education throughout the developing Commonwealth in the 1960s; the CSFP was to play its part in that process.

The First 20 Years of the Plan (1959–79)

The Commonwealth itself was to change dramatically in the plan's first 20 years. In 1959, there were only two independent states in Commonwealth Africa: Ghana and South Africa. By 1979, Southern Rhodesia, under an illegal government, was the only remaining colony. Independence had by then come to the whole of the rest of the Commonwealth with the exception of small and awkward anomalies, like Anguilla, the Falklands, Gibraltar, and Montserrat. Apartheid had driven out South Africa.

The process of decolonisation changed the relationship between the industrialised and developing Commonwealth, with a measure of disillusion for Britain:

> It was splendid when India, Pakistan, Ceylon, Ghana, Malaya and Nigeria joined the Commonwealth, hitherto a white man's club. But far from the Commonwealth proving to be a buttress in its post-colonial era, as was confidently expected, it turned out to be instead a new, unplanned, and quite major area in which Britain found itself pilloried.
>
> (Low, 1991: 330)

New patterns of trade were to reinforce the changes. As Britain edged towards joining the European Economic Community, the government went from claiming in 1964 that 'the first responsibility of the British government is still the Commonwealth' to the much more limited commitment three years later 'to negotiate for a period of transition to enable Commonwealth countries to adjust' (quoted in Barclay, 1970: 163, 185). The abandonment of fixed exchange rates in 1971/72 marked the demise of the sterling area and with it the idea of the Commonwealth as a major economic or trading bloc.

It would, however, be wrong to write off the Commonwealth as lacking any political significance by the 1970s. At this time, Australia, Britain, and Canada all had prime ministers with personal sympathies for, and commitment to, the Commonwealth. Fraser played a major role in keeping the Commonwealth together over Rhodesia, and later tried unsuccessfully to become Commonwealth Secretary General. Wilson had felt warmly towards the Commonwealth since a childhood visit to Australia. Trudeau was described by his own foreign secretary as an 'ardent advocate' for the Commonwealth (MacGuigan, 2002: 126).

Ironically, too, the institutions of the Commonwealth grew stronger as the bonds linking its members grew slacker. The Commonwealth education conference of 1959 was followed by another in Delhi in 1962 and was to become a triennial meeting of ministers. As the CSFP was a Commonwealth-wide educational activity, a report on the plan went to the Delhi conference, which set up a working party to consider it, inaugurating a process that remained in place for succeeding conferences. Other ministerial meetings were introduced on their own regular cycles.

In 1965, the Commonwealth Secretariat was established and took over responsibility for servicing Commonwealth meetings from the British government. But it made no claim on the CSFP which, with six years' experience behind it, seemed to be working effectively without any coordinating body, as a multilateral activity based on bilateral agreements. The secretariat, along with the ACU, collected information about the plan but remained at arm's length from it, observing but not managing.

Along with a new politics, decolonisation brought new demands for higher education within the independent Commonwealth. By later standards, Commonwealth universities were modest in size—and even in ambition—in 1960. Britain was enrolling 4 per cent of the age group in its universities, Canada 11 per cent. India had some 40 universities with just over a million students. Commonwealth Africa had only seven universities and university colleges outside South Africa (Perraton, 2009: 29). In the extreme case of Malawi, then Nyasaland, as it approached independence, it had 22 African graduates, of whom 12 were in prison.[7]

Universities in the north and the south were poised to expand, in response to three pressures: public demand, reinforced by the expansion of secondary education; the need for professionals and administrators, felt with particular urgency by new governments in the south; and the requirements of the universities themselves, needing to grow their own seed corn by producing the next generation of academics.

Over the next 20 years, British university numbers increased almost five-fold, India's more than three-fold, while Commonwealth Africa's tertiary numbers rose from their low base to 180,000.

The CSFP grew more slowly. The total number of scholars and fellows grew from 341 in 1961 to 1,040 per annum within five years, and then remained at slightly over 1,000 per annum for the 1960s and 1970s. The bulk of awards went to scholars rather than mid-career fellows; in the plan's first decade, Britain usually provided between 200 and 250 scholarships a year, Canada about 100, Australia 30–40, India about 20, and New Zealand about 12. Most were studying for a higher degree but, throughout the plan's existence, there have been a handful of undergraduate awards, almost all of them for small territories with no national or regional university. Fellowship numbers rose slowly to just over 100 in the first 10 years, most of them offered by Britain.

In the plan's first few years, the main awarding countries began to widen the variety of awards. Britain introduced a programme of medical awards, announced at a Commonwealth medical conference in 1965, and followed this three years later with a programme of academic fellowships, both designed to support capacity-building, mainly within the developing world. A number of awards were targeted to people working in education: Australia ran a programme of fellowships for them from 1960 to 1996; New Zealand provided fellowships for educational administrators from 1966 to 1988; India offered visiting fellowships between 1962 and 1978, to encourage the exchange of experience among educators; the Central African Federation provided two awards in total between 1960 and 1964, to support education in the federation. Basic details about the types of award are given in Table 8.1 and about numbers of scholars and fellows in Table 8.2.

Table 8.1:
Commonwealth Scholarships and Fellowships

Awarding country and type of award	*Dates*	*Purpose*	*Numbers*
Australia			
Scholarships	1960–98	Mainly postgraduate	Usually 25–50 p.a.[a]
Visiting fellowships	1960–86	For persons prominent in education	Usually 4 p.a.
Visiting professorships	1964–86	Research and teaching	Usually 2–3 p.a.
Britain			
Scholarships	1960–	Mainly postgraduate	Usually 200–250 p.a.
Distance-learning scholarships	2002–	Postgraduate	Usually 150–300 p.a.
Fellowships	1960–80	To support research	2–7 p.a.
Medical and senior medical fellowships	1965–95	Capacity-building in overseas medical schools	Usually 40–60 p.a.
Academic fellowships	1968–	To strengthen developing-country universities	50 p.a.
Professional fellowships	2003–	Short-term awards for mid-career professionals	60–70 p.a.
Canada			
Scholarships	1960–	Mainly postgraduate	Usually 75–150 p.a.
Distance-learning scholarships	1998–2002	Undergraduate degrees in four areas	67 in total
Visiting fellowships	1960–96	Various fields in education	About 4 p.a.
Research fellowships	1965–97	Bring scholars of established reputation for research with mutual benefits	Usually 3–7 p.a.
India			
Scholarships	1961–	Mainly postgraduate from selected countries	Usually 20–30 p.a.

(Table 8.1 Continued)

(Table 8.1 Continued)

Awarding country and type of award	*Dates*	*Purpose*	*Numbers*
Visiting fellowships (later short-term visits by senior educationalists)	1962–78 1988–89	Encourage exchange of experience among senior educators	31 awards in total
New Zealand			
Scholarships	1960–	Mainly postgraduate	Usually 10–20 p.a.
Prestige fellowships	1960–87/8	Bring scholars of eminence to research and lecture in New Zealand	About 3 awards p.a. in total
Administrative awards	1960–87/8	For administrators in education expected to occupy key role in the future	As above
Other			
Scholarships awarded less regularly by Botswana, Brunei, Ghana, Hong Kong, Jamaica, Malaysia, Malta, Nigeria, Pakistan, Sierra Leone, South Africa, Sri Lanka, Tanzania, Trinidad and Tobago, Zimbabwe			
Fellowships awarded by Central African Federation	1960–64	To support education in the Central African Federation	2 in total

Source: Perraton (2009) and information from the Commonwealth Scholarship Commission in the United Kingdom.
Note: a = Occasional awards after 1998.

In the plan's first two decades, nearly 80 per cent of scholarships were provided by the industrialised countries of the Commonwealth to developing country students, while about 20 per cent were for exchanges between the industrialised countries. Most were men. A review of the plan carried out for the Commonwealth Secretariat for the education ministers' conference in 1974 found, with little surprise or apparent dismay, that the proportion of women was fairly stable at between 10 and 12 per cent. Hong Kong and Singapore provided more than the average, Ghana and Nigeria less (Commonwealth Secretariat, 1972: 44–45).

Awards were spread across the disciplines, but with a tendency for scholars from developing countries to favour science, medicine, and technology and for those from Australia, Britain, Canada, and New Zealand to be in the arts and humanities. Canada had assumed that the internationalist purpose of the plan would lead most scholars to be in the humanities and was concerned that in the plan's first years the modal

Table 8.2:
Numbers of Commonwealth Scholars and Fellows by Region

	Africa	*Caribbean*	*East and South-East Asia*	*Pacific*	*Mediterranean*	*Old Commonwealth*	*South Asia*	*Others/ not specified*
By nominating region								
1960s	981	346	329	80	82	1,234	1,226	22
1970s	1,201	363	435	142	118	1,279	1,577	0
1980s	1,882	533	443	157	174	1,325	1,656	0
1990s	1,514	534	221	72	125	923	1,471	170
2000–05	1,190	211	72	39	33	374	797	0
Total	**6,768**	**1,987**	**1,500**	**490**	**532**	**5,135**	**6,727**	**192**
By hosting region								
1960s	80	5	51		2	3,914	248	
1970s	64	10	43		1	4,719	278	
1980s	33	18	48		1	5,844	226	
1990s	24	14	38		0	4,737	217	
2000–05	3	11	63		0	2,501	138	
Total	**204**	**58**	**243**		**4**	**21,715**	**1,107**	

Source: Perraton (2009: 124).

student proved to be an Indian scientist (Levi, 2009). The small number of students who went from the north to the south were almost all working in the humanities, with the exception of a small group studying life sciences. (One explained how Malaysia was the obvious place to study gibbons, 'the most appealing of the apes' [Perraton, 2009: 149].)

Scholars were expected to go home on completing their award although, except where they were bonded, there was no way of requiring them to do so. While this was a topic of concern to education ministers at their conferences in the 1970s, and to the ACU itself, the limited evidence available suggests that the majority of early scholars did return home. Those from industrialised countries were more inclined to stay in their country of study than those from developing countries. Australia complained about this: the ministers' conference in 1964 heard that 'the net result has been loss rather than gain: good men had not returned to Australia and Britain had done a very good thing in buying their brains' (Perraton, 2009: 32). A high proportion of those who went home to the south took up academic posts in the expanding universities. While numbers were relatively small, by 1972 the supply of 'better qualified faculty members [had] had the most profound effect upon the strength of Commonwealth universities'; in some places, the plan had become 'almost part of the system' of university development. Those scholars who did not go into university posts were generally to be found in the public sector. Many scholars from the industrialised countries, too, moved into academic posts: 37 per cent of the British, 43 per cent of the Canadians, and about 60 per cent of the Australasians (Commonwealth Secretariat, 1972: 62–65).

There were always tensions in the operation of CSFP, as well as unfulfilled promises. Despite its status as a multilateral programme, the British, Canadians, and Australians paid most of the pipers and felt entitled to call the tunes. While their interest in Commonwealth cohesion led to the emphasis on postgraduate awards, many countries in the south had development as a higher objective and, in the early years, argued strongly for more awards at undergraduate level. Ghana, India, Kenya, and Pakistan, for example, made this case at the Commonwealth education conference in New Delhi in 1962, though to no avail. The argument was stilled only as university expansion increased the flow of graduates capable of taking up postgraduate awards.

A disappointment, at least for ministers of education, was that the plan never became fully reciprocal. The number of developing countries offering awards steadily declined, as did the number of award-holders. Africa, for example, hosted 80 awards in the 1960s but only 24 in the 1990s. The Commonwealth Fund for Technical Co-operation attempted to bolster the number of south–south awards through an offer to supplement their costs, made at the ministers' conference in Jamaica in 1974 and repeated in 1977, but apparently never taken up. Scholars in the south were more convinced of the value of metropolitan degrees than moved by the ideology of south–south exchange. In part, too, bureaucratic obstacles, and the slowness of intercontinental communication, hindered south–south awards.

The Commonwealth Secretariat carried out a review of the plan's second decade in 1982. Its rather anodyne report noted that women now made up 20 per cent of award-holders, regretted that the plan had not expanded as ministers of education had wanted, but concluded that the plan had been 'an outstanding success' and that it was 'highly desirable that the CSFP should continue as a distinctive scheme of Commonwealth co-operation' (Commonwealth Secretariat, 1982). Changes to student mobility within the Commonwealth, and to the plan, were to come not from that process of review but from political changes at the end of the 1970s.

The Plan in the Years of Ideological Change, 1979–93

The tectonic plates of world politics were to move in the next 15 years with the rise of neo-liberalism in the west, the collapse of the Soviet Union in the east, and poverty in the south (so that public expenditure on education in developing countries fell, in real terms, from 1980 to 1985 and had still not recovered by 1990). Britain edged closer to Europe, endorsing the Maastricht Treaty in 1993. The politics of southern Africa, which had embittered relations between Britain and the rest of the Commonwealth, were transformed as Zimbabwe gained independence in 1980, Mandela was released from jail 10 years later, and South Africa could rejoin the Commonwealth in 1994.

Britain had a new government under Margaret Thatcher in 1979, which was to reshape British policy and society; policy towards overseas students was transformed within three months. Ministers in the previous government had, with little success, tried to restrict the flow of overseas students, whom they saw as reducing opportunities for home students and as imposing a financial burden: university fees were then set at a level which meant that all students were subsidised by government. In a search for expenditure cuts, the (then) Department for Education and Science suggested charging overseas students full-cost fees—an easier political move than domestic alternatives, such as cutting education for the under-fives. While some criticism was expected, overseas student fees were not identified as presenting particular difficulties.[8]

The interests of the Commonwealth do not appear to have been discussed as the British government worked out its budget cuts. As students from the Commonwealth made up more than half the overseas total, any concession to them would have driven a coach and horses through the new policy. Europe was a different matter, with numbers so low that a concession to them would reduce a planned £100 million of savings by only £5 million. British officials were reluctant to move away from European policy, which was to charge the same fees to all students from any member country.[9] European students got their concession, Commonwealth students did not. From this time, students outside the European Community, and later the European Union, were required to pay fees that would recover the full cost of their degrees.

The policy had short-, medium-, and long-term effects—all apparently unintended. In the short term, there were protests by universities, by overseas governments (where Malaysia led the way, with a 'Buy British last' slogan), and by the Commonwealth. The Commonwealth Secretary General set up a standing committee on student mobility which tried, over seven meetings and 10 years, to get concessions for Commonwealth students. Appropriately enough, its last report was entitled *The Final Frustration*. In the short term, too, overseas student numbers fell, but were again rising within five years.

In the medium term, the British government made some concessions. Following pressures from its own overseas departments as well as its external critics, the Foreign Secretary, Francis Pym, announced increased but targeted funding for overseas students. Initially carrying his name, the 'Pym package' provided an additional £46 million for overseas students over a three-year period (Renton, 1985). The bulk of this went on a new Foreign and Commonwealth Office programme, later renamed as Chevening awards, after the foreign secretary's official country house. Awards were made through ambassadorial patronage and matched to diplomats' perceptions of national needs. But some of the additional funding went to the Commonwealth Scholarship Commission, which saw its annual income rise from £5.3 million to £9.6 million over the next four years.

There were, however, no concessions on the principle of full-cost fees. In the medium term too, the other industrialised countries followed Britain's lead, so that within a decade full-cost fees were the norm in Australia, Britain, Canada, and New Zealand.

There were longer-term effects on the patterns of student mobility. Universities began with a near-universal denunciation of the policy. But as time went on, universities saw international postgraduate students as an important source of income, and one that was under their control, rather than government's. Meanwhile, as fees for European students were set at the home-student level, Britain became increasingly attractive for them. The proportion of students from the European Community are reported to have risen from 9 per cent in 1979 to 29 per cent in 2004, while the Commonwealth figure fell from 55 per cent to 29 per cent (Maxey, 2000 and 2006).

The controversy about full-cost fees meant that student mobility became a major issue for debate at the Commonwealth ministers' education conferences in 1980 and 1984. While Britain was criticised for its policies, the 'Pym package' meant that it could announce an increase in the number of its awards in 1984. Meanwhile, following urgings from the Commonwealth Secretary General, Canada came to the 1984 conference with a commitment to increase the number of its awards. The conference agreed a target of 1,500 awards, as compared with the original 1,000. A third 10-year review of the plan was able to announce in 1993 that this target was met in most years (Commonwealth Secretariat, 1993: 2).

The same review duly reported on modest but steady progress in the 1980s. Some 14,000 scholars and 3,000 fellows had benefited from the plan, and awards had gone to 56 of the 60 territories within the Commonwealth. There had been an increase in the number of women on the plan, so that they took up 33 per cent of all awards even though making up only 25 per cent of the applicants. Exchanges between the industrialised countries of the Commonwealth continued to make up about a fifth of all awards, maintaining the plan's distinction as a structure for international co-operation rather than for aid. The review regretted that the number of countries making awards had fallen from 19 to nine; there were hopes, but not much more, that the number might rise again (Commonwealth Secretariat, 1993).

Despite the generally upbeat note of the report, the plan was by this time coming under increasing external scrutiny. In Australia, as policy shifted from regarding international student mobility as aid towards treating it as trade, it encouraged universities to recruit full-cost (rather than subsidised) overseas students. The Australian programme also narrowed in 1986 with the abolition of professional fellowships, no longer seen as being good value for money. Canada, too, launched a series of reviews into the working of the plan and its funding, and saw its national priorities as lying in the former Soviet bloc and in countries with high growth potential rather than in the Commonwealth (Levi, 2009). In Britain, the government carried out a financial management review of the commission, though without recommending major changes (Perraton, 2009: 64). In 1993, the ACU decided to save money, by stopping the collection of statistics for the plan. All of the above may have been small financial clouds, but they threatened to darken the future.

By now, the plan had been in existence long enough for there to be some evidence of its effects, although with little formal evaluation much of this is anecdotal. A large proportion of the plan's alumni had gone home to work in universities. Before setting off on a visit to Malaysia,

Singapore, and Sri Lanka, Edgar Temple, the administrator of the plan at the ACU, prepared a list of alumni and met 104 of these, many of whom were now 'heads of department or other leading members of their universities'. The British review in 1987 claimed that the plan had some 27 vice-chancellors among its alumni; over half of the Canadian alumni from the 1980s whom it was possible to trace went on to academic posts, including vice-chancellors in Kenya, Nigeria, Sri Lanka, and Swaziland (Perraton, 2009: 64, 106–7).

While the influence of the plan on university development was bound to shrink, as its numbers grew far more modestly than university numbers as a whole, the evidence consistently shows that it was helping to form the academic elite of the Commonwealth.

Doubts, Threats, and Changes, 1993–2011

The political significance of the Commonwealth continued to decline in the 1990s and 2000s. The end of the cold war meant that it could no longer be regarded as a (flawed) bulwark against the Soviet bloc. Trade patterns had shifted: the North Atlantic Free Trade Area moved Canada closer to the United States, British trade with Europe expanded, and Australian trade with Asia assumed ever-greater importance.

The Commonwealth's own institutions were changing. The Commonwealth Secretariat grew smaller and no longer employed a staff member devoted solely to higher education; neither it nor the ACU called for a fourth review of the CSFP around 2000 or for a fifth review 10 years later. Policy towards education, student mobility, and scholarships were all to reflect these changes.

In contrast with the 1980s, these two decades were ones of educational expansion. Numbers in basic education grew, bolstered by new international commitments made at world conferences at Jomtien in 1990 and Dakar in 2000. Aid agencies switched their energies and attention from higher education to basic education, with the result that it became increasingly difficult to make the case for spending aid funds on universities. But at the same time, investment in higher education gained new credibility, as the route to prosperity was increasingly seen as lying in the development of knowledge economies.

The upshot was a worldwide increase in the numbers of students in tertiary education, which went from 69 million in 1990 to 88 million in 1997 and 151 million in 2007. The numbers of students studying abroad rose, so that by 2008 there were some 3 million foreign students in higher education, making up 2 per cent of the world total. In Britain, the proportion of overseas students, which had remained steady at between 8 per cent and 12 per cent of the total for much of the twentieth century, had risen to 16 per cent in 1991 and reached 20 per cent by 2008. Australia, which successfully and aggressively marketed its higher education in the 1990s, doubled the number of foreign students between 2000 and 2007, when they made up 212,000 (or 20 per cent) of its total student population.

The CSFP had mixed fortunes in these years, to be explained mainly by policy changes on the part of the industrialised Commonwealth countries. (These changes did not follow from doubts about the value of scholarships or about the value of higher education in general. In Britain, both Conservative and New Labour governments introduced scholarship programmes for the solid political reasons of strengthening relations with China and India in the 1990s and 2000s.)

Prompted by the British government, the Commonwealth Scholarship Commission sought guidance on government priorities for the plan. The Overseas Development Administration, which funded the larger part of the programme, did not reply, but in 1995 the Foreign and Commonwealth Office spelt out that it wanted to find 'future leaders, decision makers and opinion formers' and 'influential friends overseas' for its awards to industrialised countries (quoted in Perraton, 2009: 71). Intellectual strength was no longer enough by itself. Changes to the aid programme were to be more far-reaching. By the mid-1990s, the aid budget was being cut, with consequent reductions to the commission's grant, which was to fall each year from 1996 to 1999.

While it may have been battered in Britain, the CSFP was bowed in Australia and New Zealand. By 1990, Australia required all overseas students to pay full-cost fees, although the effect of this was mitigated by scholarships and subsidies. At the Commonwealth ministers' conference in 1994, Australia announced plans to increase the number of its awards, but this all changed two years later when government decided to rationalise and merge scholarship programmes. In future there would be a single Australian Development Scholarship for developing countries: the Commonwealth no longer had salience in its policy for international education. An attempt by Australian vice-chancellors to reverse the policy was unsuccessful, although, in the new century, a small number of targeted scholarships—one or two a year in designated disciplines and offered by individual universities—were to continue. The reciprocal nature of the plan was weakened as Canada, though not Britain, stopped offering awards to Australians. While New Zealand followed in Australia's wake and withdrew government funding for the plan in 1998, their vice-chancellors were more successful and themselves continued to fund the plan, making 57 awards between 2003 and 2006 and 70 in the following three years (Perraton, 2009: 97; Commonwealth Secretariat, 2009, Table 1). Despite doubts about the plan, Australia and Britain could both applaud the award of a Nobel prize in 2009 to the former scholar Elizabeth Blackburn, who had studied molecular biology at Cambridge.

Canada and Britain were to follow Australasian examples in the new century. The 2006 election in Canada brought a cost-cutting government into power, which announced that there was no guarantee of continued funding for a number of scholarship programmes, including the CSFP. The commission in Britain was instructed, by clearly embarrassed Canadian diplomats, to stop the process of recruiting the next year's scholars.[10] The new policy got a bad press in Canada—it may have helped that the editor of the *Globe and Mail* was an alumnus of the plan—and was reversed by Christmas 2006. Canadian awards were to continue after all, although in a reshaped form. Canada now invited graduate students and faculty members from Commonwealth Africa, Asia, the Caribbean, and the Pacific to spend periods of four to six months in Canada and a small number of postdoctoral scholars from Britain and New Zealand, but not Australia, to spend a year in Canada. In 2011/12 Canada made 189 developing-country awards and gave eight each to Britain and New Zealand.

The British government then blew hot and cold. The commission had carried out its own review of activities in 2000 and proposed a number of new developments, which received government endorsement; by 2007, the commission was assured of three years' funding, from 2008 to 2011, which was to rise from £15.9 million to £17.5 million per annum. But, as the overall development budget grew, that of the Foreign and Commonwealth Office shrank. It promptly ended all support for scholars from the rich Commonwealth countries, which now included Bermuda, Cyprus, Malta, and Singapore as well as Australia, Canada, and New Zealand. Protests, including motions in parliament and an electronic petition on the website for the prime minister's office, made noise, drew public attention to the CSFP, and got nowhere. As in New Zealand, universities came to a partial rescue, with a new tranche of awards, jointly funded by themselves and by the government Department for Innovation, Universities and Skills, which brought to the UK a dozen scholars a year, who were seen as potentially benefiting British research.

The loss of government confidence in the CSFP came despite changes of direction in both Canada and Britain. Concerned about charges of elitism, the Canadian committee introduced in 1998 an experimental programme of distance-learning awards for students in the Caribbean. It was acclaimed as a success, although it remained a one-off.

In Britain there were changes in the commission's practice and its programmes. It was clear by 2000 that expenditure from the aid budget could be justified only if this could be seen as related to reducing poverty or supporting sustainable development, words written into the 2002 International Development Act. The commission therefore, for the first time, required applicants to explain how their proposals met these requirements, and they were assessed on this criterion alongside their academic strengths. (Rich-country applicants were assessed against much more debatable evidence of their leadership potential.) A programme of work with alumni was launched, which may have raised the plan's political profile and certainly improved the information available about it. Refugee organisations were now invited to nominate candidates alongside governments. Professional fellowships were offered to match the longstanding academic fellowships. Following the Canadian example, Britain introduced a distance-learning programme, which by 2009/10 brought in 140 scholars, as compared with 414 for conventional awards. A minority of these awards allowed scholars to spend one term in Britain, following the rest of their course at a distance and online.

The Commonwealth education ministers' conference in 2009 heard that while the 1990s had been a period of general decline (so that only six countries offered awards in 1999 and the total of award-holders had fallen to 1,021), numbers increased in the next decade, with some new initiatives. A target of increasing the number of awards by 20 per cent each year, set by ministers in 2000, had been achieved and there was a modest increase in the number of countries making awards (Commonwealth Secretariat, 2009, paras 10–11). Attempts were, at the same time, being made once again to widen the number of countries offering awards, which brought Ghana, Jamaica, Malaysia, Malta, South Africa, and Trinidad and Tobago into the list as regular providers. India continued to make awards, as it had consistently done from the launch of the plan.

Ministers also approved the launch of an endowment fund, designed to support south–south and north to south scholarships and set up to mark the plan's fiftieth anniversary. It attracted funding from round the Commonwealth, with significant tranches from three unexpected countries: Malaysia, which hosted the education ministers' conference in 2009; the Foreign Office in Britain, perhaps embarrassed at the bad publicity on its withdrawing funding for industrialised countries; and in 2011 from Australia, host of Commonwealth heads of government that year, even though it declined to rejoin the plan. The first five awards took one fellow from Britain to Nigeria and four scholars from Ghana to Kenya, Canada to Tanzania, Sri Lanka to Samoa, and Tanzania to Mauritius. Though 'Commonwealth cohesion' was no longer a political catchphrase, the plan could still claim some credibility as a Commonwealth-wide activity.

Conclusion

International student mobility has never been simply a function of scholarship programmes. While reliable figures are scarce, it seems likely that privately funded, and family-funded, students have always exceeded those on scholarships. This makes the assessment of a programme like the CSFP particularly difficult: without counterfactual speculation, we cannot say whether a particular individual would have got a different scholarship, or found some other means to study abroad.

However, leaving counterfactuals aside, there is solid evidence of the benefits that the plan has brought to individual award-holders and to their countries. Their effects are more discernible in small countries—which always had a disproportionate share of awards—than in large, and are most clearly visible in universities where many of the plan's alumni have worked. At the same time, it has remained modest in size, with total numbers that doubled from about 1,000 to 2,000 per annum, while the Commonwealth's university numbers grew exponentially.

As the plan was set up to foster an almost forgotten ideal of Commonwealth cohesion, it may be appropriate to ask about its achievements for the Commonwealth. Survival is something: the plan has adapted and survived, although it has become much more a vehicle for technical assistance than a mutual programme of Commonwealth co-operation. The plan has continued almost in the shadow of other Commonwealth institutions, drawing services from the ACU without having a major influence on its policy, keeping away from the Commonwealth Secretariat—at times a bête noire for the rich Commonwealth countries—and appearing at Commonwealth ministerial conferences essentially to get nods of approval. That may well have been a strength for the plan, if a weakness for its original ambitions.

Finally, as the political significance of the Commonwealth has fallen away, so student mobility within the Commonwealth has been overshadowed by other flows of students. For example, Britain now attracts more from Europe than from the Commonwealth; and Australia's students come mainly from its Asian trading partners. The almost tangible benefits of studying within universities with something of a common heritage are, inevitably and for many, outweighed by the economic and political benefits of going with the increasingly regional flow.

Notes

1. This was the view of Lord Garner (Garner, 1978: 378), who should have known, as he was at various times British High Commissioner to Canada, Permanent Secretary in the Commonwealth Relations Office, and Chairman of the Commonwealth Scholarship Commission.
2. H.A.F. Rumbold, brief to secretary of state, 27.6.1958, NA, DO 35/8477. (In this and other references, files in the British National Archives are prefixed 'NA'.)
3. Symons went on to become founding vice-chancellor of Trent University. Interview, Symons/Perraton, London, 7.5.2008 and Symons, 'Draft notes for Dr Sidney Smith for a Commonwealth Scholarship Plan, May 1958'.
4. Minutes, ministerial committee of Commonwealth trade and economic conference, 1.9.1958 (GEN 650), NA, CAB 130/148; Interview, Perraton/Symons, 7.5.2008.
5. H. Lintott to R. Aitken, 5.6.1959, NA, CAB 21/3108.
6. D. Houghton to R. Prentice, 14.12.1967, NA, OD 40/35.
7. Hansard Commons, 19.11-1962 col. 837.
8. Prime Minister in Cabinet, 17.5.1979, NA, CAB 128/66/2; Public expenditure 1980/1 to 1983/4: The scope for reductions, 6.7.1979, NA, CAB 129/206/25; Cabinet minutes, 24.7.1979, NA, CAB 128/66/11.
9. A. Thompson to Mr Wilson, 24.10.1979; C.A. Clark to A.H.A. Judd, 25.10.1979, NA, ED 212/167.
10. In the absence of the chair of the commission, I hosted the meeting at the ACU on 8 August 2006.

Bibliography

Barclay, G. St J. (1970) *Commonwealth or Europe*. St Lucia: University of Queensland Press.

Commonwealth Relations Office (1959) *Report of the Commonwealth Education Conference* (Cmnd 841). London: HMSO.

Commonwealth Secretariat (1972) *Commonwealth Scholarship and Fellowship Plan: Ten-year Review 1969–70*. London: Commonwealth Secretariat.

——— (1982) *Commonwealth Scholarship and Fellowship Plan: Report of the Second Ten-year Review Committee*. London: Commonwealth Secretariat.

——— (1993) *Commonwealth Scholarship and Fellowship Plan: Report of the Third Ten-year Review Committee*. London: Commonwealth Secretariat.

——— (2009) Report on the Activities of the Commonwealth Scholarship and Fellowship Plan 2006–2009: Results and recommendations from a survey of national nominating agencies. Paper presented at the 17th Conference of Commonwealth Education Ministers, Kuala Lumpur, 15–19 June.

Garner, J. (1978) *The Commonwealth Office 1925–68*. London: Heinemann.

Hennessy, P. (2001) *The Prime Minister: The Office and its Holders since 1945*. London: Penguin.

Levi, C. (2009) *Canada: The CSFP*. Cambridge: Von Hügel Institute.

Low, D.A. (1991) *Eclipse of Power*. Cambridge: Cambridge University Press.

MacGuigan, M. (2002) *An Inside Look at External Affairs during the Trudeau Years*. Calgary: University of Calgary Press.

Maxey, K. (2000) *Student Mobility on the Map: Tertiary Education in the Commonwealth on the Threshold of the 21st Century*. London: UKCOSA.

——— (2006) *International Student Mobility in the Commonwealth: 2006 Update*. London: Council for Education in the Commonwealth.

Perraton, H. (2009) *Learning Abroad: A History of the Commonwealth Scholarship and Fellowship Plan*. Newcastle upon Tyne: Cambridge Scholars Publishing.

Renton, T. (1985) *Government Policy on Overseas Students (Foreign Policy Document No. 143)*. London: Foreign and Commonwealth Office.

Smith, S.E. (1968) 'Universities and the Commonwealth', address at the VIII Quinquennial Congress of the Association of Universities of the British Commonwealth, Montreal, 1 September.

9

Developing Policy Priorities: Commonwealth Agendas for Tertiary Change

Peter Williams

Introduction

Education has always been salient among Commonwealth concerns. Well over 90 per cent of Commonwealth citizens live in developing countries and, in many of these states, half the population is aged under 25—in sub-Saharan Africa in 2010 this age group accounted for over 60 per cent of the total (United Nations, 2011). In this Commonwealth of young people, provision of universal educational opportunity is naturally a preoccupation of political leaders. Member countries greatly prize basic education for its important role in nation-building, given that so many are comparatively new as political entities. These shared concerns underlie the Commonwealth's avowed commitment to Education for All[1] and to achievement of the two educational targets (completion of primary school and gender equality in education) under the United Nations Millennium Development Goals (MDGs).

The ambition to extend educational provision is not confined to basic education, and after an extended period of focus on the first stages, international attention is reverting to upper secondary and tertiary education. From the earliest days, inter-university collaboration has been a prominent feature of Commonwealth educational co-operation. Commonwealth countries at all levels of development have aspired to expand and deepen learning opportunities at post-basic levels of education, to enlarge their skills base, and to keep abreast of others in moving towards the creation of 'knowledge societies'. Academic interchange of staff and students, and the exchange of ideas and knowledge, are important means of achieving this.

The ACU's Centenary coincides with this new Commonwealth-wide interest in tertiary education and a growing sense of its importance. The intensifying interconnectedness of education systems, mirroring processes of economic globalisation, and the rapid development of communications technologies offer new opportunities for harnessing the power of higher education to Commonwealth development. Success in this area will require changed mindsets, new agendas and strategies, and the rebuilding of partnerships on the part both of the Commonwealth academic community and of its friends outside.

The discussion below briefly charts the evolution of Commonwealth thinking and action on these issues, outlines possible ways forward, and makes proposals for significant change.

The ACU and the Official Commonwealth: An Evolving Relationship

The ACU is a prominent member of the wider Commonwealth family, but for the first half-century of its existence, its antecedent body, the Universities' Bureau of the British Empire, had few counterparts with remits to promote interchange across the countries of the present-day Commonwealth. That was true not only on the official plane, but even in the context of civil society where, in education, only the Imperial Institute (later the Commonwealth Institute) and the League of the Empire (more recently the League for Exchange of Commonwealth Teachers) had come into existence.[2] The original Bureau operated in what might be described in modern parlance as an 'institution-lite' Commonwealth.

It was only in 1960, when the ACU was already nearly halfway to its centenary, that new programmes of inter-governmental Commonwealth co-operation in higher education transformed the context of its work. In that year the publicly financed Commonwealth Scholarship and Fellowship Plan (CSFP) and an inter-governmental Commonwealth

Education Liaison Unit (CELU) began operations. Five years later, in 1965, the Commonwealth Secretariat came into being.

From that point, the ACU's relations with the official Commonwealth ceased to be through Britain's Commonwealth Relations Office and were instead mediated through the Commonwealth Secretariat based at Marlborough House in London. Thenceforth the ACU had to position itself in relation to Commonwealth governments' agreed priorities and collective policies on educational development and co-operation, as articulated at triennial Commonwealth Heads of Government Meetings (CHOGMs) and triennial Conferences of Commonwealth Education Ministers (CCEMs), and implemented through the Commonwealth agencies.

Hand in Glove: The ACU and Marlborough House 1960–97

In the 1960s and 1970s the development of secondary and post-secondary education was prominent in the education activities first of the CELU and later of the Commonwealth Secretariat. Two-thirds of the Commonwealth's present membership of 54 (including the suspended Fiji) joined the Commonwealth as newly independent countries in the 1960s and 1970s. Their political agendas were dominated by the need to staff local public services with nationals, to acquire the specialised skills needed for economic expansion, and to create capacity in higher-level education and training. The agendas of the first eight CCEMs (held between 1959 and 1980) reflected such preoccupations, and the composition of national delegations to the Conferences frequently included senior university representatives.

The CSFP and the shorter-lived Commonwealth Bursary Scheme for teacher education catered to these concerns. Oversight of the pan-Commonwealth aspects of the CSFP was entrusted jointly to the ACU and the Commonwealth Secretariat, and the working partnership between the two bodies in relation to Commonwealth Scholarships has been a core element in their ongoing relationship. The Commonwealth Secretariat took main responsibility for mobilising support from governments for the Plan and commissioned 10-year reviews in 1970, 1981, and 1993. Annual reports of progress were prepared jointly, with the ACU's contribution to this process being made on a goodwill basis.

Staffing of the Commonwealth Secretariat's Education Division, headed by an Assistant Secretary General, reflected the focus on higher education at that time. The first four incumbents—Hugh Springer, Yusuf Lule, James Maraj, and Khan Sarwar Murshid—were all recruited from senior academic positions in their home countries. There was also a particularly close interchange between the Secretariat, the ACU, and UK and Commonwealth university leadership in this period. John Foster (the ACU Secretary General for 23 years from 1947 to 1970) was also Secretary General of the UK's Committee of Vice-Chancellors and Principals (CVCP). At the ACU he was succeeded by Hugh Springer, moving directly from the Commonwealth Secretariat. Among Foster's successors at CVCP were Roy Marshall, a Barbadian who was Vice-Chancellor of the University of the West Indies and later of Hull, and who was to undertake important committee-chairing assignments for the Commonwealth Secretariat; and Geoffrey Caston, whose career spanned the Colonial Office, Registrar of the University of Oxford, and Vice-Chancellor of the University of the South Pacific.

From the late 1970s, development of higher education slipped down the agenda of many bilateral and international agencies. Thanks to the expansion of universities in developing countries, and substantial overseas scholarship and training programmes, localisation of national leadership cadres had become almost complete. The 'manpower requirements'[3] justification for higher education expansion had diminishing force. Meanwhile, the burgeoning number of cost-analysis studies of returns to educational investment tended to show that, especially in Africa, unit costs of higher education exceeded those in the lowest levels of education by factors of 20, 50, or (in some cases) 100; and that rewards in employment, reflecting differential education qualifications, were very unequal. Critics started to brand higher education as elitist. Such considerations led to a decline in resources provided for higher education development.

The Commonwealth Secretariat and its assistance arm, the Commonwealth Fund for Technical Co-operation (CFTC), was under less pressure than others to respond to these new currents of thinking for two reasons. Its principal clients included many small and micro-states still graduating to independence through the 1960s and 1970s, and needing help with skill development both at national level and in respect of shared regional institutions, like the University of the West Indies and the University of the South Pacific. The Commonwealth also acknowledged a special moral commitment to support liberation movements and other exiled groups from the countries of Southern Africa—Rhodesia, South-West Africa, South Africa, and even non-Commonwealth Mozambique—all passing through their liberation struggles en route to majority rule and independence.

Even allowing for these special considerations it seems likely that—but for a political thunderbolt—higher education development might well have disappeared from Commonwealth Education Ministers' agendas a decade and a half earlier than turned out to be the case. This 'thunderbolt' was the 1979 decision by the incoming British Conservative Government to introduce full-cost fees for students from abroad attending UK tertiary institutions. The impact on Commonwealth education agendas turned out to be substantial and far-reaching—for Education Ministers, the Secretariat and also the ACU.

This is not the place to rehearse the reasons or to debate the justification for the British Government's decision, nor to revisit the heated exchanges on this issue within the UK and between the British Government and its international partners. Strong as the criticism of UK policy was, and in many quarters remains, it has to be acknowledged that:

- the change that the British Government introduced should not have been perceived as quite such a bolt from the blue as it was represented to be; there had been many straws in the wind under the pre-1979 Labour administration
- although Britain incurred most opprobrium among opponents of the high fees, Australia and later New Zealand were in fact pursuing very similar policies of raising fees for students from abroad to market levels
- retrospectively, it can be plausibly argued that this 'commodification' of higher education was, in fact, the driver of the enormous expansion in global student mobility that has subsequently taken place. Charging of market-level fees created strong incentives for universities and colleges to engage in active recruitment wherever fee-paying students could be found

The Commonwealth Secretariat's immediate response to the fees crisis was to establish a Consultative Group on Student Mobility, chaired by Hugh Springer. This was succeeded by a Standing Committee under the leadership of (by now Sir) Roy Marshall, which issued seven reports between 1982 and 1992. The Standing Committee's original remit was confined to student mobility, but later in the 1980s this was extended and became 'Student Mobility and Higher Education Co-operation'.

One outcome at the Secretariat was creation of a Commonwealth Higher Education Unit within the Education Programme.

The Standing Committee was the vehicle for especially close collaboration between the Secretariat and the ACU in the 1980s, and this continued into the 1990s. The ACU Secretary General (Anastasios Christodoulou) and Treasurer (Thomas Symons) were members, as was Hugh Springer. Roy Marshall and Walter Kamba (another member) had both chaired the ACU's Council. The Secretary of the Australian Vice-Chancellors' Committee and the Chair of the University Grants Commission in India both served.

In successive phases, the Standing Committee:

- initially focused its efforts on searching for 'favourable fee regimes for Commonwealth students', including formulae that would provide concessionary access for Commonwealth students to member-country universities, and increased student support through scholarships and bursaries.
- explored promotion of reciprocal exchanges of students. One result was the launch of the Commonwealth Universities Study Abroad Consortium (CUSAC) with a joint secretariat shared between Marlborough House and the ACU.
- promoted experimentation with the various options for reducing the length of time for which students had to reside abroad for their studies, including various formulae for split-site studies. Of particular interest were the possibilities of cross-border study by distance education, where the Committee's deliberations paved the way for the establishment of the Commonwealth of Learning (COL).
- examined ways to strengthen the capacity of universities in developing countries. The Committee's work led to the establishment of a Commonwealth Higher Education Support Scheme (CHESS), endorsed by Education Ministers in 1990 (Commonwealth Secretariat, 1990). Subsequently proposals were developed and activities initiated for strengthening higher education management; enhancing opportunities for career development of women in higher education; and supporting libraries and improved access by developing country universities to affordable books and journals.

The Standing Committee was stood down in 1993. In its final report it expressed its frustration at the very limited progress made with moderation of fee policies by the main host countries. It could, however, take pride in its role in the creation of COL and in a string of other institutional developments in higher education, of undoubted benefit to the ACU and its members.

- The expansion of the CSFP, and particularly the UK contribution (administered by the UK Commonwealth Scholarship Commission serviced by the ACU), was heavily influenced by the Standing Committee's work.
- The CUSAC programme referred to above and continuing to this day, but now serviced directly by the ACU, was a direct product.
- The ACU's programmes on women in higher education management were partly inspired by the CHESS initiative, and Professor Jasbir Singh has continued as lead consultant to the ACU for more than a decade.
- The CHESS proposal for a Commonwealth Higher Education Management Unit was carried forward with the help of a grant from the CFTC. The ACU operated a highly regarded service, with John Fielden as Director, for six years between 1994 and 2000.

This period of intensive activity by the Commonwealth Secretariat in higher education lasted until the late 1990s. A final throw that temporarily kept higher education on the agendas of Education Ministers and Heads of Government was the Report of the Commission on Commonwealth Studies, whose Chair was Professor Symons (Commission on Commonwealth Studies, 1996).

The watershed in the orientation of Commonwealth Secretariat education activity coincided with leadership change at the ACU and personnel moves in the Secretariat itself. Anastasios Christodoulou's retirement as Secretary General in 1996 ended quarter of a century during which the ACU had been headed by Secretaries General closely familiar with education in the 'Third World' (Springer from Barbados, and Christodoulou from his lengthy earlier period of service as a colonial administrator in Tanganyika)—and familiar too with the Secretariat and its ways of working. Simultaneously, all the three Secretariat staff who had worked most closely with Christodoulou and his ACU colleagues on distance education, higher education development, and student mobility—Peter Williams, Hilary Perraton, and Jasbir Singh—completed their service between 1993 and 1997.

The year 1997 marked the closure of the Secretariat's Higher Education Unit with the retirement of Jasbir Singh. From then on, the Secretariat reduced its engagement with higher education issues, even to the point of ceasing to play any substantive role in partnering the ACU in reporting the pan-Commonwealth aspects of the CSFP. It instead focused its efforts on education at the basic level.

At the ACU, meanwhile, the baton passed to Secretaries General cast in a different mould: Gibbons from Canada followed by Rowett, Tarrant, and Wood from the UK. Given changes in Secretariat agendas and personnel described above, it was perhaps inevitable that these Secretaries General were less frequent visitors to Marlborough House and less well known there.

New Commonwealth Agendas—Poverty Reduction and Basic Education

In the last quarter of a century, the international agenda in educational co-operation has switched to the global pursuit of universal primary education, following the 1990 World Conference on Education for All in Jomtien, Thailand, and the follow-up gathering in Dakar 10 years later.

In September 2000 the international community signed up to the MDGs, with their focus on education at the basic level (primary and lower secondary schooling),[4] as part of an international consensus embracing poverty eradication as an overriding objective of development policy.

As noted earlier, if it had not been for the 1980s crisis over full-cost student fees, Commonwealth education agendas would probably have switched towards a more exclusive concentration on basic education much sooner than when it actually occurred. Indeed, even while the political traumas were focusing Ministers' attention on creating new Commonwealth tertiary education structures to address the problems thrown up by the student mobility crisis, the Commonwealth Secretariat had been doing solid work on extension and improvement of schooling, including the management and support of teachers, the quality of education, small schools and multi-grade teaching, and issues of mobilisation and effective deployment of resources. The Secretariat was also represented on the International Working Group on Education, through which inter-agency consultations on convening the Jomtien Conference took place in the late 1980s.

As the 1990s progressed, the international co-operation agenda became ever more heavily concentrated on issues of poverty alleviation. Commonwealth countries were particularly under the spotlight. For, while most individual member states had achieved the two education objectives enshrined in the MDGs, the great majority of Commonwealth citizens lived in a few high-population Commonwealth countries in Sub-Saharan Africa (for example, Nigeria, Tanzania) and South Asia (Bangladesh, India, Pakistan) that were conspicuously far from achieving universal primary education and gender equality in education.

Unsurprisingly therefore, the themes of the 14th to 18th CCEMs zeroed in on Education for All at the basic level, with conference titles that have lately been repetitive in orientation and even wording:

- 14CCEM (2000) Education in a global era: challenges of equity, opportunities for diversity
- 15CCEM (2003) Access, inclusion and achievement: closing the gap
- 16CCEM (2006) Access to quality education for the good of all
- 17CCEM (2009) Education in the Commonwealth: towards and beyond global goals and targets
- 18CCEM (2012) Education in the Commonwealth: closing the gap as we accelerate towards the achievement of the Internationally Agreed Goals

This chapter focuses particularly on ACU–Secretariat co-operation. Discussion of Commonwealth priorities in education should not, however, be conducted exclusively in those terms. From 1989 onwards the Commonwealth of Learning (COL) has played an expanding role, collaborating closely with the ACU and with Commonwealth universities, and earning a high reputation for providing developing countries with valuable advice and practical help.

Anastasios Christodoulou had been the founding Secretary of the Open University for a period of 12 years before becoming ACU Secretary General, and so had much to contribute to the conceptualisation and planning of COL and, as a Board member, to its development in its early years. COL's first four Presidents—James Maraj, Gajaraj (Raj) Dhanarajan, John Daniel, and Asha Kanwar—have all come from academic backgrounds. COL played a major role as midwife to new distance-learning institutions in the developing countries of the Commonwealth, and in advising many existing universities on their transition to dual-mode institutions combining conventional and distance-learning programmes. Frequently, it undertook this work in partnership with major institutions like the UK Open University (where John Daniel was Vice-Chancellor for 10 years) and the Indira Gandhi National Open University (IGNOU) in India.

In the first decade of the twenty-first century, COL has made activity in support of poverty reduction and achievement of the MDGs the focus of its strategy and programming. Yet, unlike the Commonwealth Secretariat, COL has also concurrently remained closely engaged with the tertiary sector, focusing attention on the opportunities for expanding access through programmes available through distance learning and on the importance for scholarship of access to the Internet. In any future strategies for engagement of Commonwealth inter-governmental bodies with tertiary education, the players should not be a simple duumvirate of the ACU and the Commonwealth Secretariat, but a triumvirate with COL as a major partner.

A Time for Reappraisal?

Turning now to the present and future, a triple conjunction of events marks this out as an appropriate moment to reappraise future directions of Commonwealth educational co-operation and the place of higher education within it.

First, obviously, the Centenary of the ACU in 2013 directs attention to the Commonwealth's role in promoting and supporting higher educational development in member countries and to ways in which higher education co-operation in turn deepens and intensifies Commonwealth ties.

Second is the close scrutiny currently being applied to the Commonwealth's own future role, following the review of the role and future of the Commonwealth undertaken for Heads of Government by a Commonwealth 'Eminent Persons Group' (EPG), which submitted its report (Commonwealth Secretariat, 2011) to the CHOGM in Perth, Australia, in October 2011. Despite the report's encouraging title (*A Commonwealth of the People: Time for Urgent Reform*), the EPG appeared largely oblivious of the depth and breadth of Commonwealth connections in education, with the exception of the CSFP, on which it lavished considerable praise. The ACU, probably the most capable of all the Commonwealth's independent civil-society organisations, is listed among those making submissions to the EPG, but is not otherwise mentioned—not even by way of any appreciative acknowledgment of its pivotal role in ensuring the CSFP's success. The EPG report calls inter alia for the Commonwealth Secretariat to focus its work more sharply on defined priorities. The Commonwealth Secretary General's initial response was to propose a sharp reduction in the Secretariat's own direct involvement in the education and health sectors, dispensing altogether with a professional staff in education and relying instead on outsourcing of work to others and use of the Commonwealth Connects web portal for orchestrating co-operation. Education Ministers at their 18th Conference in Mauritius (August 2012) expressed their strong opposition to this (Commonwealth Secretariat, 2012), a stand reportedly endorsed by the Commonwealth Foreign Ministers Meeting a month later. The eventual outcome in terms of the place that education, and higher education especially, is accorded in the Secretariat's Strategic Plan in the post-2013 period will obviously impact considerably on the ACU's own work.

Third, as the 2015 target date for achievement of the MDGs approaches, the international dialogue on post-2015 agendas, led by the United Nations, is gathering momentum. An issue for the tertiary education sector is whether the education goals will be broadened out to address learning opportunities at secondary level and beyond. In addition, universities and colleges will undoubtedly be urged to engage through their teaching and research with agendas across the development spectrum, in science and technology, environment and climate change, social and economic challenges, governance and management, and international relations and globalisation.

Why Bring Higher Education Back to the Commonwealth Mainstream?

It is contended that the past 15–20 years represent a deviation from where the Commonwealth can best apply its strengths in education for promoting economic and social development, and that its best interests lie in bringing co-operation and development at tertiary education level back to centre stage. The issue is not whether basic education is more or less important than tertiary education, but rather where and how the Commonwealth can best deploy its educational strengths to benefit all its members.

First, education systems should be viewed holistically, recognising the interdependence of different levels, types, and modes of education. Learners progress through the stages, so that the efficacy of secondary and higher education depends largely on the quality of provision at earlier levels. Reciprocally, the availability and visibility of opportunities to continue studies at secondary and post-secondary stages constitute a powerful incentive to enrol and succeed in primary school.

Importantly, the teachers and managers required by pre-schools and primary schools are the product of upper levels of education. There are plentiful examples in contemporary Commonwealth Africa, for example, of primary school expansion having outrun the capacity of secondary schools to absorb primary school graduates, and the ability of higher education to supply primary school teachers in sufficient numbers or quality. These have been contributory factors in creating disillusionment among some parents and pupils about the value of primary education.

Short-term concentration of educational investment exclusively on basic education may thus not be the best way to promote its health in the medium and longer terms. Numerous conferences, projects and studies, including some sponsored by the Commonwealth Secretariat (Singh, 1998) and the ACU,[5] have addressed the contribution that tertiary education can make to improvement of education at the basic level through training, curriculum development, research, and advocacy.

Second, it is unclear whether the Commonwealth enjoys intrinsic comparative advantage in delivering support for basic education. Paradoxically, those more developed member countries that have been most vocal in urging Commonwealth agencies to concentrate in education exclusively on pursuit of the MDGs are the same ones that have more recently complained that the Secretariat lacks comparative advantage in education and has failed to demonstrate effective performance.

Here one needs to distinguish 'hard-power' influence (through deploying financial resources) from 'soft-power' leverage (in terms of convening power), and leadership in the realm of ideas (for example, through furnishing technical assistance). The Commonwealth's inter-governmental agencies certainly cannot bring their own 'hard power' to bear on global deficits in basic education. They do not command financial resources on a scale that can either impact significantly on the quantity of primary schooling that developing countries can provide or begin to compare with funds at the disposal of bilateral agencies (like the UK's Department for International Development) or of multilateral agencies (such as the World Bank, regional development banks or UNICEF).

At basic levels of education, even soft-power interventions—through delivery of technical support, for example—are problematical, given that control is in many places decentralised and that primary schools are often small in size and scattered, operate in indigenous languages, and deliver a curriculum reflecting the culture that is local to the area of the school. It is extremely challenging to provide effective external technical assistance on a scale necessary to bring about systemic improvement. The Secretariat has, however, been more effective in playing a leadership role in selected specialist areas of Education for All, where it has built up professional capacity and specialised contacts—for example, in the management and support of teachers at school level.

By contrast, networking in tertiary education has much greater potential. At this level, programmes in the Commonwealth frequently use English, and teach to a curriculum that has commonalities across national boundaries. There may well also be more institutional entry points—tertiary education commissions, grants committees and student loan institutions, quality assurance and accreditation agencies, admissions boards, staff/leadership development centres—for effective intervention by co-operation agencies in ways that may impact on whole national higher education systems. Given the connections between universities, government, business, and a nation's cultural life, the potential beneficial spin-off effects of help to the tertiary sector are especially attractive.

A third consideration is the purely pragmatic one of where member states stand in their development of education. Most Commonwealth countries—24 out of 43 for which data is available—have already substantially achieved the MDGs in education, having 90 per cent or above of children of the appropriate age enrolled in basic education (Packer, 2012: 28). This refers to 'net' enrolment—gross enrolment rates (which include under- and over-age children in primary school) would be much higher. Most countries have also attained rough parity in terms of gender at this level. Out of 42 Commonwealth countries for which Packer gives data, nine have a worse gender ratio than 0.98 (only 98 girls to 100 boys) and seven have a ratio better than 1.02, in favour of girls. The remaining 26 countries have ratios close to parity (1.00).

As members of the Commonwealth community, this 'achiever' group of countries certainly subscribes to the collective commitment to secure Commonwealth-wide attainment of the MDGs, and they are also doubtless conscious of their own domestic need to enrol the last few per cent of primary-aged children in their own systems. For them, however, the main imperatives and ambitions now lie elsewhere—in improving secondary education, in skill development through technical and vocational education and training, and in greatly expanding higher education and research capability, enabling them to compete in the emerging knowledge-based global economy.

It would be a mistake to think that these last-named agendas are important only to countries that have already achieved universal primary education enrolment and gender equality at basic level. Countries like Mozambique, Nigeria, or Pakistan, which ostensibly have furthest to go to reach the educational MDGs, have the same ambitions to extend opportunities beyond the primary level. For them, it is not a matter of 'either/or': indeed, even when they were far from universal primary education in the 1980s and 1990s, African universities at their Harare meetings in 1986 and 1987 castigated the World Bank and other donors for suggesting that for them higher education expansion was elitist and an unaffordable luxury (Sawyerr, 2004: Note 13).

A Commonwealth Higher Education Agenda for the Twenty-first Century

Where can the Commonwealth make a substantial difference in engaging with tertiary education in the twenty-first century? What issues can it most fruitfully pursue?

The starting point is recognition that today's context is quite different from that of yesteryear, even though the challenges of access, equity, relevance, quality, and affordability are the same now as then. The face of higher education has changed completely since, half a century ago, the Commonwealth first created its various institutions for co-operation and development (CCEMs, CSFP, CFTC, etc.), and since UNESCO held its great regional education conferences in the Arab States (Beirut, 1960), Asia (Karachi, 1960), Latin America (Santiago, 1962), and Africa (Addis Ababa, 1961; Tananarive, 1962).

The more obvious changes have included:

- a huge growth in the number of universities and other higher education institutions. Every Commonwealth country now has one or more universities of its own or else co-owns a regional university serving several small states.[6]

- a several-fold expansion of tertiary-level enrolments, at a pace exceeding the growth of population, and so resulting in rapidly rising participation rates. These remain modest in many parts of the developing world, at 5 per cent of the age group, or lower, in parts of sub-Saharan Africa, but in some countries they are closer to the 80 per cent mark (Varghese, 2011, Table 3.1). In university and college, attendance largely remains the privilege of the elite when it should be a universal experience. Tertiary education systems now cater for a wider range of talents, interests, and age range among their students. Individual university institutions have tended to become much larger—at the extreme, IGNOU serves four million students across India and 36 other countries.
- more diversified systems of higher education with a widening variety of tertiary institutions, both university and non-university. Ownership ranges between public, private for-profit and private non-profit (including institutions under religious sponsorship). A majority of institutions may still use only the conventional basis of face-to-face teaching, but an increasing number operate partly or completely in distance-education mode. Most higher education institutions offer their own degrees, diplomas, and certificates, but many have affiliated status with another awarding institution.
- creation of a web of institutions charged with the coordinated management and regulation of these complex new mega-systems of post-secondary education. Tertiary education commissions, university grants committees, clearing houses for student admission, quality assurance councils, accreditation bodies, national associations of vice-chancellors and academic staff and students have proliferated, and have been incorporated into the national institutional infrastructure.
- diversification of funding sources. As systems have expanded and public revenues have come under strain, governments have expected higher education institutions to supplement public institutional grants with user fees. In turn, universities and colleges have sought to enhance institutional income with contracted research and consultancy work, and all kinds of other revenue-earning activities.
- an accompanying managerial revolution at institutional level, which has resulted in many institutional heads finding their current work to be 75 per cent CEO of a 'business' and 25 per cent

leader of an academic team—the reverse of the situation many of their predecessors experienced half a century ago.

- greater internationalisation of institutions through recruitment of staff and students from abroad, and forging of partnerships with universities and colleges in other countries. As the world 'shrinks', some well-established universities even operate branch campuses across national borders. At the same time, the range of international contacts has widened, new players are making their presence felt on the international scene, and institutions no longer feel tied to Commonwealth apron-strings.
- the transformative effect of new information technologies on data processing and research, and of the Internet on access to knowledge and communication within and between institutions.

The last of these is of growing importance in determining both the quality and relevance of teaching and research in colleges and universities across the Commonwealth, and of their capacity to engage in co-operative ventures with partners in other countries. Infrastructure developments providing continuously improving access to broadband technologies have a key role to play in enabling staff and students to keep abreast of developments in scholarly activity and to participate in academic exchange across national boundaries.

For the future, one must be cautious about Commonwealth capacity to address the many agendas of higher education development. Its portfolio of specialist multilateral institutions—the Commonwealth Secretariat/Commonwealth Fund for Technical Co-operation, Commonwealth of Learning, Association of Commonwealth Universities, Commonwealth Scholarship and Fellowship Plan, Commonwealth Association of Polytechnics in Africa—is unique, has proved its worth and contains repositories of valuable experience. However, the institutions are modest in scale and the resources at their disposal are essentially of the 'soft power' variety of professional networks, ideas and influence, contacts and connections, convening power, rather than a 'hard power' capacity to deliver grants and loans on any large scale.

Much more substantial resources lie with the bilateral co-operation agencies of Commonwealth member states, not just of Australia, Britain, and Canada but also of rising new powers that are developing their own international co-operation programmes, such as India and Pakistan, Malaysia and South Africa. More should surely be done by Commonwealth agencies to familiarise themselves with the capacity, direction, and priorities of these new programmes and to examine the scope for joint operations.

Through co-operative programmes the Commonwealth can contribute further to building the capacity of tertiary education systems in member countries. Such programmes of support for capacity-building should have many different strands. These include resource transfers in capital and technical assistance to countries least able to effect development from domestic resources. It will involve special programmes to sustain the viability of the tertiary systems in the many small states of the Commonwealth. Much of this work will sensibly be undertaken with regional higher education institutions and associations that have been formed in the many regions and sub-regions (East and Southern Africa, South Asia, Caribbean, South Pacific) where Commonwealth countries are in a majority. And as the global balance of power shifts from West to East and from North to South, the development of a greater degree of polycentrism in the Commonwealth should be welcomed and encouraged. This should involve, for example, welcoming, assisting, and learning from the efforts of middle-income countries of the Commonwealth (India, Malaysia, Nigeria, Singapore, South Africa, Sri Lanka), as they move further and faster down the road they have already begun to tread in developing their own programmes of technical co-operation and establishing international student mobility hubs.

Allowing for the fact that national agencies in different Commonwealth member states have varying degrees of willingness to engage with education at tertiary level, opportunities should be explored for combining bilateral and multilateral approaches in supporting tertiary education development. Part of the success of the Colombo Plan[7] and the CSFP was based on the principle of bilateral programmes operating within a multilateral framework operated by a small central secretariat. The combination of the multilateral dimension of common programme ownership—providing enhanced prestige, legitimacy, and acceptability—with bilateral programming and resource provision appears to provide a formula that might usefully be applied in other areas of work.

Careful monitoring of the interests and activities of non-government organisations, whether for-profit or not-for-profit, will also pay dividends. In North America, the Middle East, the Indian subcontinent, and elsewhere, new private funds and charitable foundations are appearing, some of them with substantial resources derived from oil and mineral wealth or other commercial activity. Subject to obvious safeguards, partnerships that combine the ACU's contacts and expertise with resources that wealthy donors are ready to apply to tertiary education development, offer promise. Especially in Africa, the ACU has traditionally been able to work fruitfully with American charitable foundations, including Ford, Rockefeller, Carnegie, and Hewlett; and has already begun to follow the route proposed above with organisations like the World Innovation Summit for Education (WISE) Qatar Foundation. More opportunities of this kind will surely open up. Relations will also doubtless develop with private sector groups seeking to engage more closely with higher education in Commonwealth countries. In some instances, difficult judgements may have to be made as to whether profit or service is the main motivation of would-be partners.

Shortage of resources will compel a careful selection of priorities and areas of work. One criterion should be the presence of Commonwealth comparative advantage in the field in question. This may be based on accumulated experience and expertise, the uniqueness of a particular programme and absence of duplication on the part of other agencies, and the reach and range of contacts of the organisations or programme.

It is suggested that future Commonwealth higher education co-operation agendas, whether or not pursued with other external partners, could usefully have the following four main thrusts.

1. *Addressing tertiary education's internal concerns*

A first task is to assist tertiary institutions and systems to address their own internal concerns more effectively. Given similarities of structure and organisation in Commonwealth tertiary education, and commonalities in philosophies and approaches to higher education development, there appears to be plentiful scope for exchange of practical experience on issues internal to higher education. Areas of interest at institutional level would surely include:

- institutional management
- student support and counselling
- student and staff evaluation
- quality assurance
- new technologies of teaching and learning
- mobilisation of resources
- assisting local enterprises to improve their productivity

The base for activity of this kind is essentially already in place in the ACU's Strategic Management Programme, benchmarking good practice in higher education leadership and enabling universities to compare their key management processes. Complementing this are the ACU's various professional networks, currently embracing graduate employment, libraries and information, public relations, marketing and communications, research management, and university extension and community engagement.[8]

Moving beyond the individual college or university to the wider systemic level, the challenge of coping with diversity in tertiary education systems and forging beneficial relationships between the component parts of these systems is engaging increasing attention. At one time, the primary issue was coordination between the university and non-university segments of public sector provision, defining the respective roles of different types of institution and addressing issues of equivalence of qualifications and transfer of students, relative pay scales of staff, comparability of unit costs and per capita subventions, and issues of affiliation and accreditation, between university and non-university institutions. Relationships have become much more problematic as non-state university and college provision has expanded exponentially in some countries, propelled by the dearth of public supply relative to demand. Many new for-profit and non-profit institutions have sought recognition and licensing. There is plentiful scope for exchange of international experience in addressing the triple challenge of linking these different universities, colleges, and institutes into a single coordinated system; of developing a range of common procedures and services (in admissions, information, staff development, etc.) that can be applied to all; and of devising and operating regimes that combine enablement and encouragement on the one hand with quality control on the other.

Countries differ in their structures of management and administration of education of different kinds and at different levels. Among non-devolved systems, some combine all education and vocational training under a single ministry, while others separate off higher education and research; and in yet other cases, there is a three-way ministerial split between schools, vocational education and training, and tertiary education. This is an area where an exchange of experience between countries to identify benefits and challenges could be useful, especially as a number of Commonwealth countries have lurched uncertainly from one organisational model to another, and back again, in recent years.[9]

In the same way, Commonwealth countries located at similar points along the spectrum of country size might profitably collaborate in comparing and gaining insights from their varying approaches to the common issues affecting them. The several larger Commonwealth countries with federal systems (for example, Canada, India, Malaysia, Nigeria) encounter a set of organisational issues distinct from those in unitary states; while at the other end of the spectrum, the Commonwealth's many micro-states face their own special set of challenges.

2. *Assisting tertiary education in conducting international operations*
Tertiary institutions and systems increasingly find themselves involved in a web of international connections, as their staff and student bodies become diversified. New issues arise, like the evaluation of international qualifications, assessment of credit awarded by an institution abroad, approaches from an institution in another country to enter into partnership agreements for exchange of students or staff or the conduct of joint research, possibilities of accessing capital aid and technical assistance from international donors, thorny issues of staff earnings from consultancy for international organisations, or inward and outward international scholarship offers.

Entrepreneurial institutions use these contacts both to diversify and to enrich the institution's clienteles and programmes and, importantly, to diversify and increase sources of institutional income. International bodies like the ACU are well placed to offer advice and support, helping institutions to master good practice in the organisation of an office for external affairs, and to position themselves to bid for contracts, to attract research and consultancy funding, or to develop programmes that will attract students and income from abroad. Useful information and counsel can be provided on reaching out to new partners among the international agencies, foundations, and the private sector.

3. *Promoting a better world order in tertiary education*
The increasing globalisation of economies, labour markets, and education throws up many challenges that require a collective response from the international community. These challenges include:

- encouragement of the international mobility of academic staff, students, knowledge, and ideas.
- ways of ensuring that those who bear the costs of national investments in higher education also reap a fair share of the benefits. Difficult issues of trade-off between individual rights and

obligations to the community arise. For the moment, developing country taxpayers are the losers, while the migrating individual and the countries to which they migrate are the winners.

- devising systems to ensure that internationally mobile students on publicly funded awards meet their obligations to return home, and to repay advances and loans for international study.
- addressing the consequences of wide differences in tuition fees and public subsidy in different countries.
- quality assurance in relation to tertiary education programmes and qualifications offered across national borders, including distance education programmes.
- finding a productive balance between encouragement and regulation of cross-border investments in higher education, whether by public universities, non-state institutions, or individual/corporate private entrepreneurs.
- strengthening machinery for evaluating and accrediting qualifications earned in another country.
- means of securing and maintaining international access to knowledge on affordable terms, in the face of copyright and the enforcement of intellectual property rights.
- measures to assist refugee academics and students.

The Commonwealth's mix of more and less developed countries, its well-developed collective institutions, and its members' experience of accommodating strong local cultures and value systems with globalisation trends, equip it particularly well to make a constructive contribution to the development of a better and more sustainable global order, and to engage actively in developing agreed frameworks for tertiary education interchange.

The agenda outlined above does, however, present particular challenges for better endowed universities and higher education systems in wealthier Commonwealth countries. In this increasingly competitive age they may be called upon to choose between short-term commercial advantage and profitability, and the longer-term benefits to be derived from supporting capacity development for their less privileged partners abroad and from building a collaborative international higher education community. This will require a readiness on their part to actively promote and sign up to codes of good conduct on cross-border provision of tertiary education, on consumer protection in relation to quality of such programmes, and to operate favourable regimes in relation to intellectual property rights for universities and students in Commonwealth low-income countries, including the active promotion of open educational resources.

4. *Addressing Commonwealth development agendas*
The potential of universities and colleges to assist in addressing key Commonwealth developmental concerns through research, training, and consultancy could be better exploited than at present.

Recently the Commonwealth Secretary General has identified a number of focal areas for future Commonwealth activity, including: protection and promotion of the Commonwealth's political values (democracy, respect for diversity, good governance, and the rule of law, etc.); advancement of the development goals of Commonwealth countries, including capacity-building in government departments and public institutions; youth development, and so on. In turn, the Commonwealth Foundation has identified participatory governance as the focus for its work in the period ahead (Commonwealth Foundation, 2012). These are all areas that have been subjected to intensive study by Commonwealth academic researchers, and where the assembling of multinational teams to investigate specialised issues on which more detailed work is needed by policymakers would present no insuperable problems.

The ACU has a ready-made capacity to contribute in these areas through its already established professional networks of scholars. If appropriate machinery and procedures were established, there could be a fine-tuning to link up need and capacity in a purposeful way, through working parties and expert groups, or commissioning and contracts. A suggestion of this kind was advanced by the Committee undertaking the Third Ten-year Review of the CSFP (Commonwealth Secretariat, 1993). The Committee proposed that from time to time a tranche of Scholarships and Fellowships be awarded to mobilise international study and research teams to address selected issues of Commonwealth concern, as identified by governments and Commonwealth agencies.

Implications for the Commonwealth Secretariat and the Commonwealth Foundation

If the Commonwealth family is to exploit the opportunities presented by its comparative advantage in higher education co-operation, this will require creative strategic planning not only on the part of its academic community, but also through corresponding interest and support from the ACU's Commonwealth partners.

It implies far-reaching changes of perspective and culture in the Marlborough House institutions, deepening and broadening their interface with scholarship and the academic community. One would hope to see the Secretariat and Foundation proactively reaching out to the ACU and its members, sharing with them the Commonwealth's research and public policy agendas, seeking their advice and engagement, and inviting them to be partners in official programmes.

The necessary cultural change should start with Secretariat staffing. This would benefit from a return to the earlier practice of recruiting experienced professionals from different disciplines, often to be found in academia, to leadership positions in the Secretariat's operational divisions, as well as in the most senior management posts. Of late, the Secretariat's top management has lacked a sufficient infusion of persons with specialist expertise from outside the ranks of diplomats and economists, and this has restricted its access to professional networks and to the latest intellectual insights.

There are obvious limits to the range of expertise that the Secretariat can have represented on its own staff, and it should resort more frequently to tried-and-tested ways round this constraint. In the past, much of the most influential work that it has been able to undertake for addressing key issues facing the Commonwealth and global communities has been generated by convening authoritative expert groups. These have typically been presided over by a distinguished person of international renown, and have included in their ranks an appropriate mix of academic specialists, senior public servants, and representatives of the private sector and civil society.[10] The reports so produced command respect among outsiders, and the recommendations tend to carry conviction. This device has given the Secretariat access to authoritative advice from some of the best minds in the Commonwealth and has enabled it to extend its networks in a valuable way. At a time of resource shortage this can be a cost-effective way to move agendas forward.

The Commonwealth Secretariat and the Commonwealth Foundation should take a new look at the composition of the 'civil society' they claim to be mobilising and—in the case of the Foundation—representing. All too often the groups consulted in the name of civil society are drawn to an excessive degree from the ranks of grass-roots activists and professional Commonwealth associations. Both those constituencies indeed have their place as important parts of civil society, but this also embraces other constituencies, such as trades unions, faith groups, and recreational and sporting bodies. More relevantly for the purpose of this discussion, the world of research and scholarship—including think tanks, research organisations, professional societies and institutions, university centres and the like—needs to be drawn in; and can add intellectual authority and credibility to the advocacy statements issued in the name of 'Commonwealth civil society'.

Focusing now more narrowly on the education sector, four specific steps could be taken to re-engage Commonwealth universities more closely with the Commonwealth's public agendas.

1. Of prime importance is that the Secretariat should revert to pursuit of more holistic approaches to education development, according fuller recognition to tertiary education's role in development. Through its own professional education staff, assuming it decides to retain a team in the education sector, it should embrace agendas for developing and strengthening capacity in Commonwealth tertiary education and institutions, for mobilising the tertiary education sector's contribution to other levels of education, and for tapping academic expertise in relation to Commonwealth agendas. Tertiary education should find a central place in the Secretariat's future programmes of education support.
2. In its turn, the CFTC should reserve a portion of its funds for support to development of tertiary education infrastructure in member countries, and encouragement of regional and pan-Commonwealth networking and interchange. It should use the ACU as one of its prime sources of professional advice in responding to requests.
3. The Secretariat should take far more seriously its responsibilities towards the CSFP. In recent times it has largely defaulted on its responsibilities in relation to the CSFP, trading on the ACU's goodwill in filling gaps by providing coordination and reporting services from its own resources. A first step would be for the Secretariat to implement the recommendation made repeatedly by civil society representatives, and explicitly endorsed by the EPG in its 2011 Report, that the Secretariat should recreate a dedicated post on its own staff to handle coordination of the CSFP (Commonwealth Secretariat, 2011: 177).
4. The Secretariat should take the lead in creating a Commonwealth Education Forum, where the different organisations and agencies dedicated to promotion of education in the Commonwealth

can share information and consult with one another about their priorities, plans, and programmes on a regular basis. From these discussions, opportunities for improved collaboration and possible division of labour may emerge. The group would include the inter-governmental agencies (the Secretariat, the Foundation, and COL), the Commonwealth Education Trust, the ACU, and other Commonwealth professional associations in membership of the Commonwealth Consortium for Education.

Conclusion

It has been argued that the essence of the Commonwealth relationship lies in the affinity of its peoples, institutions, and cultures, and the ongoing links between them. Education is at the heart of Commonwealth personal and institutional networks, and in the education sector the infrastructure for Commonwealth co-operation is developed to an extent not mirrored elsewhere. Within that sector, the tertiary level is particularly well positioned to promote the well-being of Commonwealth peoples and the reinvigoration of Commonwealth relationships and connections.

Tertiary education seems likely to loom larger in the lives of individual Commonwealth citizens and their societies in the twenty-first century. In responding to their aspirations, the sector faces many constraints and challenges. A future of continuous adaptation and change, some of it painful, beckons. Co-operative programmes and exchange of experience within the Commonwealth may make a useful contribution to overcoming constraints and to finding productive ways forward.

The past hundred years of collective endeavour by institutions in membership of what is now the Association of Commonwealth Universities has demonstrated the potential. It is not enough, however, for potential to exist: the identified opportunities must be firmly grasped.

Notes

1. Education for All was the theme of an international gathering (World Conference on Education for All) held at Jomtien, Thailand, in 1990 and convened by the UN Development Programme, UNESCO, UNICEF, and

the World Bank. It became the rallying call for development efforts in education by the international community in the following two decades.

2. The Imperial Institute, later the Commonwealth Institute, was founded in 1886. In 2000 its assets (mainly a lease on its building in Kensington) were transferred to the Commonwealth Education Trust. The League for Exchange of Commonwealth Teachers was founded as the League of the Empire in 1901. After transferring its activities to the CfBT Education Trust in 2007, it closed down in 2011, when its funding support from the UK Government was withdrawn.
3. The 'manpower requirements' approach to planning education seeks to gear education expansion to the future skill needs of the economy. It is often contrasted with two alternative approaches—'social demand' and 'rate-of-return' approaches.
4. The Millennium Declaration adopted by the UN General Assembly promulgated inter alia the intention 'to ensure that, by the same date [i.e. 2015], children everywhere, boys and girls alike, will be able to complete a full course of primary schooling and that girls and boys will have equal access to all levels of education'.
5. See, for example, the papers for the Conference of ACU Executive Heads in Cape Town on Universities and the Millennium Development Goals.
6. Seychelles was the last to acquire its own university, in September 2009.
7. The Colombo Plan for Cooperative Economic Development in South and Southeast Asia was launched in 1950, initially with a mainly Commonwealth membership, and provided a framework for bilateral assistance in the region. In 1977 the Plan was redesignated 'The Colombo Plan for Cooperative Economic and Social Development in Asia and the Pacific', to reflect its expanded membership to include many more non-Commonwealth countries and a broader scope of activity.
8. For further details, see the ACU website (www.acu.ac.uk).
9. Namibia and Zambia are examples of countries that started with unified ministries of education, then for a period had separate ministries for higher education, but have now reverted to a single education ministry combining responsibilities for schools and for tertiary education.
10. There have been many notable examples, including the recent Commonwealth Commission on Respect and Understanding chaired by Professor Amartya Sen, whose report *Civil Paths to Peace* was published in 2007.

Bibliography

Commission on Commonwealth Studies (1996) *Learning from Each Other: Commonwealth Studies for the 21st Century*. London: Commonwealth Secretariat.

Commonwealth Foundation (2012) *Strategic Plan 2012–2016*. London: Commonwealth Foundation.

Commonwealth Secretariat (1990) *CHESS—Commonwealth Higher Education Support Scheme: Strengthening Capacity for Sustainable Development.* Report of a Commonwealth Expert Group (Chair: James Downey). London: Commonwealth Secretariat.

——— (1993) *Commonwealth Scholarship and Fellowship Plan: Report of the Third Ten-year Review Committee* (Chair: Sir Alastair McIntyre). London: Commonwealth Secretariat.

——— (2011) *A Commonwealth of the People: Time for Urgent Reform.* The report of the Eminent Persons Group to Commonwealth Heads of Government. London: Commonwealth Secretariat.

Packer, S. (2012) The Commonwealth and education for all. In *Educational Co-operation: Jewel in the Commonwealth Crown*, eds P. Williams and J. Urwick, 24–32. London: Commonwealth Consortium for Education.

Sawyerr, A. (2004) Challenges facing African universities: Selected issues. *African Studies Review* 47(1): 1–59.

Singh, J. (1998) Linking higher education to basic education (HEBE): A Commonwealth project to strengthen basic education. *NORRAG News*, 23, 28–29.

United Nations (2011) *World Population Prospects: The 2010 Revision.* File 1. UN Department of Economic and Social Affairs. Population Division. CD-Rom.

Varghese, N. (2011) Globalization and Cross-border Education: Challenges for the Development of Higher Education in Commonwealth Countries. IIEP research paper. Paris: International Institute for Educational Planning.

PART III

'Impact': Regional Case Studies in Access, Equity, and Social Change

Prelude

National policy development and implementation remain at the core of higher educational implementation. Given the underpinning importance of funding regimes and the imperative of political impulses within the leadership of states regarding higher education, institutions take government lightly at their peril. In the case of the members of the ACU network that involves a veritable plethora of jurisdictions. These are explored in Part III.

Indeed, this dimension of our book specifically works through major case studies, which examine the global themes we have been discussing from the perspectives of diverse societies—their institutions, peoples, and cultures. Selecting case examples in a global story is hardly easy, and is invariably debatable. But our choices have been guided by the theme 'Network membership', in drawing from the enormous social sample that is the Commonwealth of Nations; and within that, to a focus on a typology reflecting the broad character of the societies involved. Ideally, we would have had a chapter on all 54 nations of the Commonwealth (or at least every continent and oceanic region), but we would then have been projecting a huge and unrealistic multi-volume series; practicality called for compression.

Accordingly, as we wished to see Part III as essentially complementary to the thematic chapters that have preceded it, we have chosen to illustrate the global trends through 'thick descriptions' of regional societies in change. We opted to proceed through four large and capacious narratives, which draw in most of the largest and some of the smallest states—some of the most developed and many of the most aspirational of the developing nations.

This contextualising of the global academic revolution brings out both its complexity and the scale of the challenges involved. It also gives a human face to the otherwise disaggregated social science factors on higher education. Part III has also been written (proudly, it should be said) from within the societies involved; all of our authors call Africa, Asia, Australia, or the Caribbean 'home'. Here is a 'Southern' approach to higher educational history. The authors have also written in a manner that is mindful of their 'regional' story being part of an international process of change in higher education provision. There are, naturally, connections to (and comparisons with) developments elsewhere (such as in the Americas, or in China and Japan) in what is now a global story.

Part III duly covers:

- *Africa:* as a huge land mass of over 50 states, perhaps a billion citizens, a multitude of cultures living in distinct regions, and facing major human and developmental challenges in which education is critical for peoples living on what the *Economist* (2 March 2013) describes as a ' hopeful continent'
- *Asia:* through a close examination of the parallel but diverging trajectories of higher education systems in India and Pakistan, involving nearly 1,000 universities and 2 billion people, with a notable tilt towards private providers
- *Australia:* as one of the former migrant 'Dominions', but now increasingly an Asia Pacific state, small in population (23 million), with 41 universities, a high concentration of international, fee-paying students and a particularly entrepreneurial education system
- *The English-speaking Caribbean:* representative here of the 'Small States' of the Commonwealth, but which actually predominate in terms of numbers within membership of the global organisation and which are striving to add value through a regional solution to tertiary challenges

'Think global, act local' has become a modern catchphrase about development. This has a special meaning in education. Each of our major regions has its own dynamic in cultures and politics; each has drawn from a distinctive historical experience and developmental trajectory; all felt the impact of European imperialism, but each has charted its own post-colonial future; all have very distinctive features in the eyes of the outsider.

Africa has extreme variations in university provision across the great continent; the dramatic growth of private education in India and Pakistan is striking; the Caribbean has developed an especially subtle university system, which connects distinctive island states to a national university institution; while in Australia a public system of higher education dominates, despite the fact that its universities are 'enterprise institutions' with a fee-paying regime. Two of the great regions—Africa and South Asia—can point to ancient and pre-European institutions of learning and scholarship; all contain Commonwealth and ACU members, while diversifying their international linkages and networks.

And yet all have felt the impact of globalisation and the necessity of being global citizens; all have a variety of higher educational systems, which both connect them to the world at large, and to which they contribute in their own distinctive ways; and all are charting missions that recognise the importance of adopting and adapting major global trends in teaching and learning, e-education, and innovative research.

There is a significant lesson in the theory and practice of higher education in this sample of major regions. To make sense of what is happening within the Organisation for Economic Co-operation and Development's (OECD) academic revolution in higher education, we need to take cognisance of both levels of action and experience, which work in a dialectical fashion: the global and the local.

Bibliography

Regional Transformations and Global Challenges

General

Eastwood, D. (2012) Global tunes and national melodies: Being global and sounding local. In *The Globalisation of Higher Education*, 34–39, eds C. Ennew and D. Greenaway. Palgrave Macmillan.

Africa

Ajayi, J.F.A., Goma, L.K.H., and Johnson, G.A. (1996) *The African Experience with Higher Education*. Accra: Association of African Universities; Oxford: James Currey Publishers; Athens, Ohio: Ohio University Press.

Morley, L. (2011) Sex, grades and power in higher education in Ghana and Tanzania. *Cambridge Journal of Education* 41(1): 110–15.

Morley, L. and Lussier, K. (2010) Intersecting poverty and participation in higher education in Ghana and Tanzania. *International Studies in Sociology of Education* 19(2): 71–85.

Teferra, D. and Altbach, P.G. (eds) (2003) *African Higher Education: An International Reference Handbook*. Indiana: Indiana University Press.

Mazrui, A.A. (ed.) (1984) *The Cambridge History of Africa*, Vol. 8. Cambridge: Cambridge University Press.

UNESCO (1981) *General History of Africa*, Vol. VII (1985). California: Heinemann with UNESCO.

Asia: India and Pakistan

Agarwal, P. (2009) *Indian Higher Education: Envisioning the Future*. New Delhi: SAGE Publications.

Beteille, A. (2010) *Universities at the Crossroads*. New Delhi: Oxford University Press.

Guha, R. (2010) *Makers of Modern India*. New Delhi: Penguin/Viking.

Stein, B. (1998) *A History of India*. Oxford: Blackwell Publishers.

Talbot, I. (2012) *Pakistan—A New History*. New York: Oxford University Press.

Universities in Pakistan (2013) University Web Ranking. 4International Colleges & Universities. Available online at www.4icu.org/pk (downloaded on 30 March 2013).

Wolpert, S. (1999) *A New History of India*, 6th ed. New York: Oxford University Press.

Australasia

Bashford, A. and Macintyre, S. (eds) (2013) *The Cambridge History of Australia*, 2 vols. Cambridge: Cambridge University Press.

Horne, J. and Sherington, G. (2012) *Sydney: The Making of a Public University*. Melbourne: The Miegunyah Press.

Leong-Salobir, C. (2013) Striving for Equity and Diversity. In *Seeking Wisdom: A Centenary History of the University of Western Australia*, ed. J. Gregory. Perth: UWA Publishing.

Malcolm, W. and Tarling, N. (2007) *Crisis of Identity? The Mission and Management of Universities in New Zealand*. Wellington: Dunmore Publishing Ltd.

Marginson, S. and Considine, M. (2000) *The Enterprise University: Power, Governance and Re-invention in Australia*. Cambridge: Cambridge University Press.

Sharpham, J. and Harman, G. (eds) (2007) *Australia's Future Universities*. Armidale: University of New England Press.

Caribbean

Rogozinski, J. (2000) *A Brief History of the Caribbean*. London: Penguin Press.
Sherlock, P. and Nettleford, R. (1990) *The University of the West Indies: A Caribbean Response to the Challenge of Change*. London: Macmillan Publishers Ltd.
Wallace, E. (1977) *The British Caribbean: From the Decline of Colonialism to the End of Federation*. Toronto: Toronto University Press.

10

Out of Africa: The University Ideal Faces Challenge and Change*

Michael Omolewa

Introduction

Africa occupies a unique position in our discourse on 'Universities for a New World' for several reasons. First, it is the last region to have adopted the modern university system as we know it. Second, it is the least developed 'by international standards...in terms of higher education institutions and enrolments' (Teferra and Altbach, 2003: 3). And third, the progress of African universities reflects the nature and history of the continent.

It is also significant that, in the twenty-first century, only two African institutions are featured in *The Times Higher Education* ranking of 200 universities across the globe—an indication that the region has not made as much progress as it should have, given its resources.

---

* I wish to thank the librarians at the University of Ibadan, Nigeria, the Institute of Education of the University of London, the Association of Commonwealth Universities, the British Library and the Association of African Universities; and the following for the invaluable assistance they gave in the course of preparing this contribution: Mercy Ette, Matthew Grundy Haigh, Olugbemiro Jegede, Nicholas Mulhern, and Deryck Schreuder.

This chapter, in a mixture of chronological and thematic structure, examines how Western-type universities were established in Africa, and considers the response of Africans to the new system of education. The chapter is divided into 11 sections, each dealing with a pivotal factor in the emergence of these universities. It also explores the role of the Association of Commonwealth Universities (ACU) and other key educational institutions in the growth and development of universities in Africa.

The Precursor to Western-type Universities

Before the introduction of Western university education in Africa, the continent had its own thriving education programme, with an emphasis on the training of master craftsmen and artisans, traditional medicine practitioners, judges, and community leaders (Ajayi et al., 1996). While this system did not quite constitute what would today be described as 'higher education'—itself a relatively new concept, with an emphasis on mass education, state funding, research, and knowledge transfer—Africa can boast of Alexandria, with its noted library and museums: a 'city of the intellect'. As C.J. Potter, Public Orator at the University College, Ibadan, Nigeria, declared at the inauguration of the college in November 1948, 'the continent of Africa has a great and long tradition of learning' (Ajayi et al., 1996: 18).

J.A.B. Horton declared historical Africa as 'the nursery of science and literature' (Ajayi et al., 1996: 17). This is a sentiment echoed by Thabo Mbeki, former President of South Africa, in his 2004 Cape Town lecture: 'Africa has had great universities. Higher education in Africa, we should remember, stretches back to ancient Egypt, where the great Temple imparted knowledge not only to Africans, but also to many who were to play leading roles in the later civilisation of ancient Greece' (Mbeki, 2004: 5).

The old university system had been planted by Muslim missionaries, who founded the University of Sankore in Timbuktu with a focus on the promotion of Islamic and Arabic culture and influence. As such, the introduction of Western university education and its standardised procedures had considerable impact in Africa, leading inevitably to the transformation of the entire educational landscape of the continent.

In the new system, regarded by its founders as the university ideal, the emphasis was on teaching and research, the preparation of graduates through examinations and prescribed courses of study, and the promotion of European languages and Christian core values (Gasset, 1946). This constituted the new international academic currency, a veritable weapon for social and political transformation. Education remains crucial in the African response to modernity—both materially and intellectually.

The Missionary Factor

The introduction of modern university education in Africa in the nineteenth century was an innovation closely associated with the work of Christian missionaries. These pioneers recognised European education as a potent tool for the transformation of the traditional African society. They established Western-type educational institutions to promote the Christian message, and identified brilliant and promising young students who were sent to study at British universities before higher education institutions were established in Africa. The missionaries also sought the support of British universities for their work in Africa.

The Fourah Bay Institution, founded in 1827 by the Church Missionary Society (CMS) and located in Freetown, Sierra Leone, was the first Western education institution in West Africa. In 1845 it was upgraded to a grammar school, with the expectation that it would later develop into a university. The CMS was keen to establish an indigenous university as a strategy to reduce the number of young people sent to study abroad; many people were concerned about 'the injurious effects which the training of youths with tender minds in England was likely to have' (Ayandele, 1970: 72).

The vision for the establishment of local Western-style educational institutions was shared by the African educated elite, who themselves were mostly products of British university education. One of them, James Johnson, even cited the 'veritable danger of the English climate to the African' as a factor to be considered in the education of young Africans abroad. He cautioned that 'the Africans trained in Britain would acquire British tastes, traits and habits and indulge in a material living which their earnings might not be able to sustain' (Ayandele, 1970: 70).

Against this backdrop, some African intellectuals thus proposed the founding of a university that would be funded from the public purse, with an emphasis on scientific courses in preference to humanities and the social sciences (Ayandele, 1970: 72). The CMS, however, objected to the proposal of a secular, African-controlled university, despite the support of John Pope Hennessy, the Governor in Sierra Leone. The missionary society was wary of Hennessy's support and suspected that he was 'a dogmatic Catholic out to destabilise Protestants' (Ajayi et al., 1996: 22). The CMS also considered the proposal too expensive, and the Principal of Fourah Bay College, the Revd Metcalfe Sunter, concluded that the establishment of a university would be premature unless the 'White Man's money' established and maintained it (Ajayi et al., 1996: 23).

In 1874 the CMS proposed an affiliation with Durham University that would enable students of Fourah Bay College to sit for the examination of its degree in arts. The request was granted 'by a unanimous vote' by the Senate of the university on 16 May 1876 (Ashby, 1966: 166). Ashby explains that Durham University was chosen by the CMS because of its Christian credentials. The affiliation was also to forestall the establishment of a secular university by the British government (Ashby, 1964).

The objection by the CMS thus halted the effort of the Colonial Office and produced an affiliated university with limited staff and scope of studies. In spite of these limitations, Fourah Bay College initiated the perpetuation of university education and became 'the oldest Western-styled college in Africa' (Paracka, 2003: 3). Its alumni 'became the intellectual leaders of society' (Ayandele, 1970: 71) and the college was given the title of 'Athens of West Africa' (Paracka, 2003: 3).

The Colonial Factor

By its very nature, colonial rule would seem at odds with the facilitation of university education in Africa, as an emerging educated class could be a perceivable threat to its control of large portions of the region. And yet, while in some instances the Colonial Office impeded the development of universities, colonial rule supported the work of Christian missionaries and, arguably, the establishment of such institutions.

To some extent, the hoisting of the colonial flag in Africa had a positive impact on the emergence and sustenance of the Western university model in the region. In the first instance, the establishment of the colonies stimulated a need for the training of manpower in various administrative offices and positions that were introduced by European colonial administration. There was thus an attraction for many Africans to acquire higher education; a certificate was seen as a passport to recognition, employment and access to wealth, authority, and influence.

As touched upon above, the development of higher education institutions in Africa was shaped by its very history. For instance, while the indigenous people had neither the freedom of choice nor the control of the educational system in the colony, the settler communities of South Africa, with its Dominion status, had the freedom to pass acts of the legislature to establish and manage its own educational institutions.

However, in spite of this autonomy, the settlers were still expected to model their universities on British institutions because, as Ashby noted, the British had 'an invincible confidence in the efficacy of British education, not only for Englishmen but for Indians, Africans, and Malayans and—for that matter—Americans' (Ashby, 1964: 2). Thus the defeat by the British of the Boer republics of South Africa halted the move by the republics to 'offset the British- and English language-dominated UCGH [the University of the Cape of Good Hope] by establishing links with Dutch universities to prepare candidates for entry into that system' (Subotzky, 2003: 546).

The Colonial Office assisted the University of London with the administration of the external examinations that were to be introduced to the colonies and the Dominions (Namie, 1989). The consequence was that colonialism impacted deeply on the status and focus of university education. The response to the criticism in its reports on the educational initiatives in Africa by the Phelps-Stoke Commission, which was inspired by the Christian missionaries in the United States, led the colonial government in the 1920s to review its attitude to educational work in East, West, and Central Africa (Whitehead, 1987).

The Settlers Factor

The arrival in the seventeenth century of settler communities, mostly from Europe into parts of Southern and Central Africa, offered tremendous incentive for the development of modern institutions.

This population, who by the nineteenth century were 'long-established colonies with a considerable resident population of European stock' (Newton, 1924: 264), upheld the value of university education, and the settlers were eager to transplant to the colonies the familiar European system. They also had the advantage of an arrangement that gave them the freedom to establish social services—including education—and allowed their legislatures to establish universities.

There was a strong political will for quality investment in higher education, and many progressive citizens and philanthropists in Southern Africa were prepared to invest their resources to support educational development. As a result, the self-governing Cape Colony government established the UCGH in 1858, modelled after the University of London and offering examinations to candidates who were looking for civil service employment.

The UCGH started as the Board of Public Examinations in Literature and Science and in 1873 was incorporated by the Act of the Cape to a full university. It was granted a Royal Charter in 1879 and given full power and authority to regulate the management and governance of its programmes, including the appointment of the teachers and other officers. It was also 'eligible to award degrees' and was 'entitled to the same rank, precedence, and consideration as those of any university in the UK' (Universities Bureau of the British Empire, 1914: 109). The legislatures also passed various other Acts, which established university colleges in Bloemfontein, Cape Town, Grahamstown, Johannesburg, and Pietermaritzburg. The University of South Africa was created by the South Africa Act of 1909 to replace the UCGH (though it continued as an examination body to which other university colleges were affiliated).

It should be noted that while Fourah Bay College in West Africa was allowed to offer courses only in theology and liberal arts, colleges in South Africa specialised in disciplines ranging from mines and technology, to engineering and mathematics, and sciences and medicine. These were introduced to meet the developmental needs of South Africa.

The University of London

The University of London external examinations programme had a crucial effect on the development of university education in Africa.

First and foremost, the programme was secular and not influenced by the missionary factor. But it also allowed overseas candidates, who were not enrolled at the university, to sit in the examinations and obtain degrees and qualifications. This strategy was replicated in South Africa by the UCGH, which was established from its outset 'as a purely external examining and degree-granting institution' (Subotzky, 2003: 546). However, English-speaking settlers in Cape Town continued to present candidates for the University of London external examinations.

In parts of Africa where the British had established control, the colonial administration invited the University of London to offer its external examinations to local candidates. The Senate of the University of London approved the request for the holding of examinations overseas on the condition that 'the examinations were to be conducted in every respect on the same footing of the examination carried in Britain' (Namie, 1989: 115). The examinations were first held in 1865 in Mauritius, which had become a British colony in 1810 following the defeat of the French forces. The programme was part of a mission to anglicise the island (Namie, 1989). By 1873, several candidates from Mauritius had obtained the London Matriculation certificate and three candidates had obtained a full BA degree (Namie, 1989).

In 1887, the University of London external examination programme was introduced in Nigeria (Omolewa, 1980). The University of London external degree programmes were later expanded to all the regions of Africa and extended in scope beyond the London Matriculation examinations (Ajayi et al., 1996).

The Response of Africans

It should be noted that support for the Western system of education was not universal. In fact, many Africans rejected or avoided it (Molteno, 1984). Some Africans were also indifferent to the demand for universities and unimpressed by the argument that the salvation of the region was in this new educational system. Indeed, it has been argued that in West Africa there was 'no evidence that demand for university education was as popular as James Johnson and [Edward W.] Blyden attempted to make out' (Ayandele, 1970: 76). Moreover, Africans were not prepared to shoulder the financial burden of the new system (Ayandele, 1970: 77).

In the meantime, many Africans continued to take advantage of the provision of European-based university education. The provision was, however, limited because of a dearth of universities in most parts of the region. Thus, rich parents sent their children overseas and the Christian missionaries, mostly in West Africa, continued to use the limited facilities offered by Fourah Bay College in Sierra Leone.

The opportunities available for overseas students in many universities in Europe and America also attracted African students who could work while studying. As the number of educated Africans grew, the pressure for universities in Africa also increased. By 1920, the First Conference of Africans of British West Africa was held in Accra, and King George V was petitioned by delegates for the founding of 'a British West African University on such lines as would preserve in the students a sense of African Nationality' (Nwaowa, 1993: 251).

In December 1933, at its 49th meeting, the UK's Advisory Committee on Education in Tropical Africa received the 'memorable report' on higher education in the colonies sanctioning the establishment of local universities (Whitehead, 1987: 122).

Although the Colonial Office accepted the recommendations, the directors of education and the governors of East and West Africa were less enthusiastic. At their annual conference in 1935, the directors concluded that the subject was by no means a priority (Whitehead, 1987) and questioned 'the strength of African demand for universities and the wisdom of stimulating it' (Pattison, 1984: 11). Consequently, instead of fully fledged universities, the colonial government began to establish specialist colleges: Achimota College in Accra, Ghana; Gordon Memorial College, in Khartoum, Sudan; Yaba Higher College in Lagos, Nigeria; and Makerere College, in Uganda. However, these were considered inferior as international educational currency, and therefore did not meet the aspirations of the African intelligentsia (Nwaowa, 1993).

As the number of African students who were studying in the United States increased, there was a growing need for more institutions of higher education in Africa, to stem the flow. The Colonial Office acknowledged that if 'the Africans' thirst for higher education remains unabated…it can only lead to an increasing efflux of undergraduate African students towards the universities of Europe and America' (Pattison, 1984: 10). Against this backdrop, the Colonial Office suggested that 'the only right policy for the Government is to think out ahead a scheme of developing selected institutions in Africa up to real university standard, and that this policy, as soon as decided upon, should be publicly announced as officially adopted' (Pattison, 1984: 11).

It was therefore resolved that a further delay in founding universities was no longer justified. The UK's Advisory Committee on Education in Tropical Africa thus endorsed in 1940 the recommendation of the

West African governors for the appointment of a Commission on Higher Education in the Colonies. This was eventually set up in July 1943 under the leadership of Lord Asquith. The reports of the commission were published on 19 June 1945 and, soon after, university colleges (known as 'Asquith Colleges') were established in Nigeria, Ghana, Sudan and Uganda, and later in Tanzania and Kenya (Maxwell, 1980).

The British government also accepted recommendations for the establishment of the Inter-University Council and passed the Colonial Development and Welfare Act, which provided funds for the development of universities. The focus on quality of teaching and scholarship assured graduates that their qualifications were 'legal academic tender anywhere in the world' (Ashby, 1964: 17).

The Independence Factor

The decolonisation of Africa—and the attainment of political Independence by African countries as of 1957—had myriad consequences for the development of universities in the region.

The need for the training of personnel to replace the departing expatriate staff in the public service and private sector led to an increase in demand for universities and the mass production of graduates. Thus, higher education qualifications became valuable tools for social and economic growth.

The emerging political leaders of the region, who were themselves products of the university system, began to establish new national universities, sometimes as status symbols, but more importantly for the training of an indigenous workforce. These new institutions were also seen as strategies for tackling the educational imbalance of the colonial period. Acts of Parliament were thus passed in the UK to convert the Asquith Colleges into autonomous operations.

Political leaders also began to evaluate the relevance of universities and resolved to use them to promote studies of African culture and practices, and for African unity. For example, President Kwame Nkrumah of Ghana directed that all undergraduates had to take a course in the first year of their study that stressed 'the unity of the African continent in all its aspects' (Ashby, 1964: 63). He also established for that purpose the Institute of African Studies at the University of Ghana and argued that '[w]e must in the development of our university bear in mind that once it had been planted in African soil it must take root amidst African traditions and culture' (Ashby, 1964: 61).

In response to the unprecedented demand for access, and due in part to interest from Christian and Muslim missions as well as private individuals about making a contribution to the advancement of higher education, there has also been an upsurge in the growth of private universities in recent years. Of the 19 universities in Kenya, 13 are private (Teferra and Altbach, 2003). In Nigeria, 45 of the 117 universities are private, and this number exceeds the number of universities owned by the federal and state governments (National Universities Commission, 2010). There has been a notably rapid growth of the private sector in South Africa (Subotzky, 2003).

It is, however, important to note that the contribution of private universities has been relatively small, as enrolment by them has been low, thus leaving a large population of eligible students still without access. It is also interesting to note the new role being played by the World Bank in funding university education through its 'micro-loan' programme (see also Chapter 3 in this volume by Svava Bjarnason and Graeme Davies).

The British Universities Connection

In 1912, when delegates from 53 universities gathered in London for the inaugural Congress of the Universities of the Empire, out of which the ACU emerged, Africa was represented by just one institution: the UCGH. Nine years earlier, the same institution had represented Africa at the conference of Allied Colonial Universities and Colleges from the British Empire, which was attended by 31 institutions (Ashby, 1963). It is worth pointing out that those territories that were administered by the French, Belgian, Portuguese, and Spanish had no local universities, as higher education training was limited to the capital cities of the colonising countries.

The status of the university in Africa was still fledgling, and this was reflected in the representation of the continent at conferences. For instance, while the UCGH in South Africa had the status of a full university, Fourah Bay College in Sierra Leone was only an affiliate of Durham University. While the UCGH had King George as the Chancellor as well as various eminent professors and other teaching and non-teaching staff, Fourah Bay College had only a principal, a vice-principal, and the Bishop of Sierra Leone as its Visitor.

Although these conferences were designed as opportunities 'to develop the intellectual and moral forces of all the branches of our race wherever they dwell', and 'to strengthen the unity of the British people dispersed throughout the world', institutions located in the countries which had 'political connections with the British Empire' were also considered eligible to attend and belong to the 'British family of institutions' on payment of the subscription (Namie, 1989: 96). Under these conditions, Fourah Bay College may perhaps have been eligible for membership of this 'family' of universities and colleges, but for its affiliate status.

The conferences and administrative structures offered members a variety of benefits, particularly important in Africa where the university system was untried, and where guidance and direction were vital. For example, the universities and colleges were eligible for membership of the ACU, and could participate in congresses, enjoy staff exchanges, apply for scholarship and fellowship grants, and exchange information and experiences. Members now had open access to information about new opportunities for study and research.

The ACU also recognised the need to have the older universities in Britain assisting the new African institutions in their quest to maintain proper standards of education. This was reflected in an appeal by Kenneth Mellanby, appointed as the founding Principal of the University College, Ibadan, in Nigeria. At the Sixth Congress of the Association of Universities of the British Commonwealth (AUBC, which went on to become the ACU), held in Oxford on 19–23 July 1948, Mellanby thanked the organisers for giving him and his colleagues from 'the six embryonic university institutions' the opportunity of attending this and the previous conference at Bristol. He expressed the hope that his institution would receive the help and co-operation that were much needed. At the session of the Congress on 21 July 1948, Mellanby pleaded:

> I have come forward to do a little advertising. We hope that the University College in Nigeria will not be forgotten when people are trying to find places for young post-graduates and junior teachers overseas. We are having very considerable staffing difficulties. One of the troubles about people coming to these fairly small new institutions is that there are not very many people in their subject on the staff.
>
> (AUBC, 1951: 77)

The AUBC was thus poised to render all the assistance that was possible to younger universities, helping with the recruitment of staff and the upholding of standards.

South Africa and the Apartheid System

While opportunities for university education were opening up for Africans in different parts of the continent, a notable exception was in South Africa, where discrimination against the majority black population persisted—even within the context of an 'educational policy that had been crafted over the years since Union' (Kallaway, 2002: 3).

A South African Native College was established for the black population in 1916, and was to become the University of Fort Hare (Kerr, 1968). Although the Native College was allowed to present candidates for the examinations of the University of South Africa, it was not granted affiliate status (Subotzky, 2003).

This practice of discrimination was given legal sanction with the introduction of apartheid, which was

> characterised by the promotion of Afrikaner culture, language, and economic interests, the emergence of a powerful structure of state power designed to defend the privileges of the minority, the restriction of the political, social, and economic rights of the majority [which led to] racial inequality.
>
> (Kallaway, 2002: 1–2)

In this case, the apartheid system restricted the access of black students to white universities. Instead of promoting integration, the state built university colleges for Asians, 'the Coloured' and the different African ethnic groups: the Sotho, Venda, Zulu, and Swazi Africans. Fort Hare College also became a preserve for the Xhosa-speaking Africans (Ajayi et al., 1996). Many black South Africans had to flee the country for university education (Morrow et al., 2004).

The discrimination in South Africa was condemned by African leaders, liberal white South Africans and the international community. It was argued that 'to exclude black students from a university is an insult to their human dignity; it is inhuman' (Ajayi et al., 1996: 72). Eric Ashby described discrimination against black students as something 'we would uncompromisingly reject' because it was incompatible with the promotion of intellectual freedom (Ashby, 1966: 351). Consequently, South Africa became excluded and isolated from international organisations such as UNESCO and the International Association of Universities. The apartheid regime was forced out of the Commonwealth in 1961.

The AUBC, which was not used to getting involved in the domestic politics of member states, had to face up to the challenge posed by apartheid in South Africa. Following legal advice on the implications for South African universities, the Executive Council of the AUBC resolved that ordinary members could retain their membership, but associate members would lose theirs. Thus nine South African universities were to keep their membership in the Association, but the University of Fort Hare, an associate member, would no longer be recognised (AUBC, *Report of Executive Council, 1960–1961*).

However, following the review of the Royal Charter that governed the AUBC, and the inauguration of the ACU, the Executive Council of the AUBC noted at its last meeting that the nine universities in South Africa were no longer eligible as members. The Council, however, 'decided to offer to these universities forthwith an informal relationship with the Association outside legal membership carrying privileges similar to those which had been extended to other former members in countries which were no longer in the Commonwealth, such as the Republic of Ireland' (AUBC, *Report of Executive Council, 1962–1963*: 7).

The nine universities accepted the offer and maintained contact with the ACU by sending observers to conferences until 1973, when such contact was considered disruptive. The South African universities were thenceforth listed as former member institutions.

The Search for a Distinct African Identity

In the meantime, universities in other African countries continued to strive towards the transformation of the inherited university system, while not abandoning their international appeal, into an African institution with a distinct focus on the promotion of African languages and the development of a curriculum centred on African issues (Sicherman, 2005).

Africa's political and intellectual leaders attempted to formulate a response to international pressure for regional integration and the knock-on effects of the cold war. The English-speaking countries worked to improve relationships with the Arab countries and the French-speaking African countries. United by the common desire to fight apartheid, they also began to establish a platform for the discussion of issues related to the status and mission of African universities. Africans were reminded of the need to develop 'an indigenous self sustaining intellectual community…So long as large numbers of university professors working in Africa look to Europe or America as centres of gravity of their intellectual life, Africa will remain intellectually a province of Europe or America' (Ashby, 1966: xii).

African universities were brought together by UNESCO at a conference in Tananarive, Madagascar, in 1962 to consider matters of mutual interest and concern related to the growth of universities in the region. From this meeting emerged the Association of African Universities (AAU), which was inaugurated on 12 November 1967 in Rabat, Morocco (AAU, 1967). The aim of the association was to bring together all the universities in the continent. However, South African universities were excluded from membership because of the apartheid system, which had also cost them membership of the ACU. Ghana was eventually chosen as the headquarters (Ajayi et al., 1996) and Y.K. Lule, a British-trained Ugandan professor and former Principal of Makerere University, was appointed to lead the association.

At its first General Conference, held in Kinshasa in September 1969, the AAU declared its mission

> to identify and formulate a new philosophy of higher, particularly university education for Africa, in the hope of evolving institutions that are not only built, owned and sited in Africa, but are of Africa, drawing their inspiration from Africa, and intelligently dedicated to her ideals and aspirations.
>
> (AAU, 1969)

To this end, the AAU hosted a workshop in Accra on 'Creating the African University: Emerging Themes of the 1970s'. The workshop called on the AAU to

> widen and intensify its existing student exchange programmes, initiate staff exchanges between universities, as a means of cross-fertilization of ideas, bridging the language barriers, upgrading the staff concerned, and generally promoting African unity, undertake the publication of multilingual journals to disseminate research findings.
>
> (Yesufu, 1973: 5)

The AAU began to publish on a regular basis the *Bulletin of African Universities* and the *Guide to Higher Education in Africa*, as a means of sharing ideas and research product. It also began to focus on academic staff development and training, to promote research networks and to initiate staff and student exchange programmes.

Fortunately, this appetite for an authentic African identity in the universities persisted, as did the eagerness to make the university that 'of' Africa and not just 'in' Africa. It was agreed by the AAU that Africa must make its own mark on the development of the global university system:

> What is needed is that, despite the multiplicity of models of university systems, the universities in Africa should not only be relevant to the continent's situation, they should also be truly African and strive to make a specific contribution to the world of scholarship, research and knowledge, inspired by the African insight, historical experience and challenges.
> (Ajayi et al., 1996: 234)

It is important to stress that the establishment of the AAU was by no means an attempt to isolate Africa from global concerns. Nor was it intended to diminish the influence of the Commonwealth or the ACU. The AAU worked in partnership with the International Association of Universities, and also later with the Association for the Development of Education in Africa. It still works to this day with international partners interested in the development of higher education in Africa.

The ACU itself would continue to prove itself integral to the development of African universities. In its quest to celebrate diversity, the Council actively elected Africans as Chair of the Council, moved many of its meetings to Africa, and began to focus attention on vital areas of university governance and development. Thus, at its meeting held in Nigeria in 1985, the Council held seminars on 'The University as an instrument for achieving national objectives' and 'The impact of professional bodies on university programmes' (ACU, 1985). Nigeria's Minister of Education, Science and Technology seized the opportunity of the seminars to assess the work of the Commonwealth and the ACU, declaring: 'If anyone still needs to be convinced of the usefulness of the nebulous association of Commonwealth countries, a ready answer lies in the programmes which the ACU provides, particularly for its more than 140 member universities' (ACU, 1985). He was pleased that Nigeria had 'continued to benefit from the various ACU programmes' (ACU, 1985).

Towards the Renewal of African Universities

African universities could today be said to have come of age. From fielding only one member of the Congress of the Universities of the Empire (out of a total of 53 universities) in 1912 (less than 2 per cent), African representation in the ACU had increased to 110 members out of a total of 536 (over 20 per cent) by the beginning of 2012. As in other regions of the world, not all the universities in Africa are members of the ACU. For example, of the over 100 universities in Nigeria, only 36 are current members.

It must also be noted that there is considerable diversity in the status, quality, and orientation of the universities in Africa. As Ajayi and his colleagues have observed, 'diversity reigns in the African university community, as in African economies and political patterns' (Ajayi et al., 1996: 234). However, Africa is not universally in decline; some parts are witnessing major growth and investment, which will facilitate and support educational development and thus meet the needs of both the economy and the burgeoning young population.

Following the demise of South Africa's apartheid regime in 1994, its universities were able to address the issues generated by the inherited apartheid system. For example, there has been a strong determination by the universities in the region to serve Africa as a whole, with scholarships, research partnerships, and a curriculum which reflects their place in the world. Within the Southern African Development Community region, there are reports of real institutional growth, access and quality delivery through some 66 public universities in 15 nations.

Thus, South African universities became eligible for membership of the AAU, and for the first time in its history, universities from all parts of Africa could share a common platform to deliberate on issues of common interest. The ACU welcomed back the institutions that had left and admitted new universities into membership from 1995 onwards.

However, there is now a litany of challenges facing African universities in the new century, not least of which is the general decline in their relevance, quality, funding, and stature. It would appear that independence has unleashed a wave of unplanned and unhealthy politicisation in university development.

The problem has been further exacerbated as universities in Africa open up to the wider masses, leading to proliferation, with its inevitable consequences for staff quality, qualifications, and accreditation (Ngara, 1995).

As the Secretary of the AAU has boldly declared: 'Graduates of our universities hardly come out with any employable skills, they find communicating in English an uphill task, and those with master degrees cannot define what research is or means to a nation, let alone to themselves' (Jegede, 2011: 6).

Universities have also suffered from the economic crisis that has confronted the whole of Africa, leading to inadequate government funding (Zelesa and Olukoshi, 2004). This has been aggravated by the withdrawal of support from international stakeholders such as the World Bank and the United Nations agencies including UNESCO, which began to focus attention away from tertiary education to basic education.

In many cases, foreign staff and students have withdrawn from African universities due to an unacceptable deterioration in basic infrastructure and quality of education, increased government control, and an inability to pay attractive salaries. There has also been an exodus of local staff to universities in Europe, North America and the Middle East, where conditions of service have proved more attractive, resulting in a brain drain from Africa (Ajayi et al., 1996). Many African students sent overseas for further training have also refused to return. The age in which African academics could articulate the needs of Africa has disappeared, as it has been observed that 'Africa is absent everywhere it matters…its voice is inaudible' (Ajayi et al., 1996: 230).

In most African countries, there is little coordination between graduate production and the labour market. The inevitable consequence is mass unemployment in graduates, leading to discontent and anti-social behaviour. It is also known that, in the global development of universities, Africa no longer has a monopoly on knowledge production; the higher education industry worldwide offers stiff competition. Added to these challenges is the 'serious all-round decline' that the domestic status of the universities has suffered in recent times (Zelesa and Olukoshi, 2004: 597).

It also seems that African universities may have lain to rest the idea of using African languages as medium of instruction. For, as Kwame Anthony Appiah, a respected African intellectual, has observed, the 'Anglo-Saxon tongue' remains 'a language superior to the various tongues and dialects of the indigenous African populations; superior in its euphony, its conceptual resources, and its capacity to express the "supernatural truths" of Christianity' (Appiah, 1992: 1). Appiah then concludes that over a century after its introduction to Africa,

> more than half of the population of black Africa lives in countries where English is an official language; and the same providence has decreed that almost all the rest of Africa should be governed in French or Arabic or Portuguese.
>
> (Appiah, 1992: 1)

Unfortunately, many African leaders and universities seem unaware of the major challenges or are not prepared to solve them. But former South African President Mbeki is all too aware of the problems facing African universities and demands that they be solved as a matter of urgency: 'I would suggest that our entire continent remains at risk until the African university, in the context of a continental reawakening, regains its soul' (Mbeki, 2004). Strikingly, the Commission for Africa—established by the British Government—has reached a similar conclusion that 'without a renewal of Africa's universities there would be no sustainable development in the continent' (Commission for Africa, 2005).

The search for the renewal of the African university has also continued to attract the attention of the ACU. Working in partnership with the AAU, the ACU urges that a partnership with the universities, businesses and governments of the developed world would be invaluable. It also concludes that without such renewal, Africa will become increasingly marginalised in the world economy and will fail to meet the social and economic demands of their citizens.

Some countries have responded to the problem of falling standards by strengthening the quality control mechanism, establishing quality assurance institutions. Some nevertheless remain feeble and incapable of handling the matter effectively.

The AAU, however, has attempted to formulate a response. At its General Conference held in Nairobi on 9 February 2001, it issued a 'Declaration on the African University in the Third Millennium', and called for 'the revitalisation of the African University, and for a renewed sense of urgency in acknowledging the crucial role they should play in contributing to the solution of the many problems facing our continent'.

The Conference of Rectors, Vice-Chancellors and Presidents of African Universities, convened by the AAU, has also considered strategies for confronting the challenges of brain drain and brain gain (AAU, 2007). The Higher Education Research and Advocacy Network in Africa, and the Association for the Development of Education in Africa have conducted important studies on the state of African universities that could be helpful for the transformation of the African university.

The African Union, on its side, has proposed the establishment of a model university, a pan-African university, to promote the delivery of quality higher education. The university is to be located in Addis Ababa, the seat of the African Union, and is to have campuses in each of the sub-regions of Africa. The impact that this will make remains to be seen. The fact that 12 November annually is now celebrated as African Universities Day is perhaps also significant in pan-African university development.

Africa has demonstrated a capacity to face the challenge of the world university ideal and to make its own contribution. In the midst of the changes, Africans are encouraged to march on with confidence and dedication, and 'not feel apologetic about being African and being pre-occupied with things African as unambiguously deserving of intellectual endeavour at the highest level' (Ajayi et al., 1996: 234).

Bibliography

Ajayi, J.F.A., Goma, L.K.H., and Johnson, G.A. (1996) *The African Experience with Higher Education*. Oxford: James Currey Publishers.

Appiah, K.A. (1992) *In My Father's House: Africa in the Philosophy of Culture*. London: Methuen.

Ashby, E. (1963) *Community of Universities: An Informal Portrait of the Association of Universities of the British Commonwealth, 1913–1963*. Cambridge: University Press.

——— (1964) *African Universities and Western Tradition: The Godkin Lectures at Harvard University*. London: Oxford University Press.

——— (1966) *Universities: British, Indian, African: A Study in the Ecology of Higher Education*. London: Weidenfeld and Nicolson.

——— (1976) Reconciliation of tradition and modernity in universities. In *On the Meaning of the University*, ed. S.M. McMurrin, 13–27. Utah: University of Utah Press.

Association of African Universities (AAU) (1967) *Minutes of the Founding Conference of the Association of African Universities*, Rabat.

——— (1969) *Report of the Second General Conference of the Association of African Universities*. Kinshasa, Zaire: Lovanium University.

——— (2007) *Proceedings of the Conference of Rectors, Vice-Chancellors and Presidents of African Universities*. Accra: AAU.

Association of Commonwealth Universities (ACU) (2010), *Annual Report and Summarised Accounts, 1963–2010*. London: ACU.

——— *Quinquennial Reports of the Executive Council, 1948–73*. London: ACU.

Association of Commonwealth Universities (ACU) (1985) Roles and Responsibilities: Universities and the Professions. Papers presented during the 1985 meeting of the ACU Council. London: ACU.

Association of Universities of the British Commonwealth (AUBC) (1951) *Report of Proceedings of the Sixth Congress of the Universities of the British Commonwealth, 1948*. London: AUBC.

——— *Report of the Executive Council, 1949–63*. London: AUBC.

Ayandele, E.A. (1970) *Holy Johnson: Pioneer of African Nationalism, 1836–1917*. London: Frank Cass & Co Ltd.

Commission for Africa (2005) *Our Common Interest. Report of the Commission for Africa*. London.

Commonwealth Secretariat (1968) *Report of the Fourth Commonwealth Education Conference, Lagos, Nigeria, 26 February–9 March*. London: Commonwealth Secretariat.

Gasset, J.O. (1946) *Mission of the University*. London: Routledge and Kegan Paul Ltd.

Jegede, O. (2011) 'Go forth and soar', Keynote Speech at the 6th Convocation Ceremony at Covenant University, Ota, Nigeria, 22 July.

Kallaway, P. (ed.) (2002) *The History of Education under Apartheid, 1948–1994: The Doors of Learning and Culture Shall Be Opened*. New York: Peter Lang.

Kallaway, P.G., Kruss, G., Donn G., and Fataar, A. (eds) (1997) *Education after Apartheid: South African Education in Transition*. Cape Town: University of Cape Town Press.

Kerr, A. (1968) *Fort Hare 1915–1948: The Evolution of an African College*. London: C. Hurst & Co.

Maxwell, I.C.M. (1980) *Universities in Partnership: The Inter-University Council and the Growth of Higher Education in Developing Countries 1946–1970*. Edinburgh: Scottish Academic Press.

Mbeki, T. (2004) Renewing the African University. Inaugural Lecture at the University of Cape Town, Cape Town.

Molteno, F. (1984) The Historical Foundations of the Schooling of Black South Africans. In *Apartheid and Education: The Education of Black South Africans*, ed. P. Kallaway, 45–107. Johannesburg: Ravan Press.

Morrow, S., Brown, M., and Pulumani, L. (2004) *Education in Exile: SOMAFCO, the African National Congress School in Tanzania, 1978–1992*. Pretoria: Human Sciences Research Council.

Namie, Y. (1989) The role of the University of London Colonial Examinations between 1900 and 1939, with Special Reference to Mauritius, The Gold Coast and Ceylon, PhD Thesis, University of London.

National Universities Commission (2010) *Accreditation Results of Private Universities in Nigeria*. Abuja: National Universities Commission.

Newton, A.P. (1924) *The Universities and Educational Systems of the British Empire*. London: W. Collins Sons & Co Ltd.

Ngara, E. (1995) *The African University and its Mission Strategies for Improving the Delivery of Higher Education Institution*. Roma, Lesotho: Institute of Southern African Studies.

Nwaowa, A.O. (1993) The British establishment of Universities in Tropical Africa, 1920–1948: A reaction against the spread of American 'Radical' influence. *Cahiers d'Etudes Africaines* 33(2): 247–74.

Omolewa, M. (1980) The promotion of London's Universities Examination in Nigeria, 1887–1951. *International Journal of African Historical Studies* 13(4): 651–71.

Paracka, D.J. (2003) *The Athens of West Africa: A History of International Education at Fourah Bay College, Freetown, Sierra Leone*. New York: Routledge.

Pattison, B. (1984) *Special Relations: The University of London and New Universities Overseas, 1947–1970*. London: University of London.

Sicherman, C. (2005) *Becoming an African University: Makerere, 1922–2000*. Trenton, NJ: Africa World Press.

Subotzky, G. (2003) South Africa. In *African Higher Education: An International Reference Handbook*, eds D. Teferra and P.G. Altbach, 545–62. Indiana: Indiana University Press.

Teferra, D. and Altbach, P.G. (eds) (2003) *African Higher Education: An International Reference Handbook*. Indiana: Indiana University Press.

UNESCO (1963) *The Development of Higher Education in Africa*. Paris: UNESCO.

Universities Bureau of the British Empire (1914) *Year Book of the Universities of the Empire*. London: Herbert Jenkins Ltd.

——— *Report of the Executive Committee Together with the Accounts of the Bureau, 1930–63*.

Universities Mission to Central Africa (1908) *David Livingstone and Cambridge*. London: Universities Mission to Central Africa.

Whitehead, C. (1987) The 'Two-Way Pull' and the establishment of University Education in British West Africa. *History of Education* 26(2): 119–33.

Yesufu, T.M. (ed.) (1973) Creating the African University: Emerging Issues in the 1970. In *Proceedings of the Workshop of the Association of African Universities, 10–15 July 1972*. Ibadan: Oxford University Press.

Zelesa, P.T. and Olukoshi, A. (eds) (2004) *African Universities in the Twenty First Century*, Vol. 1. Dakar: Codestria.

11

Asia: Higher Education in India and Pakistan—Common Origin, Different Trajectories*

Pawan Agarwal

The advent of modern higher education in the Indian subcontinent can be traced to the setting up of the first college, the Hindoo College (now Presidency University) at Calcutta (now Kolkata) in 1817. The subcontinent's first universities were founded 40 years thereafter at Calcutta, Bombay (now Mumbai), and Madras (now Chennai) in 1857. This was also the year of a popular uprising against British rule. It is therefore ironical, but not surprising, that these universities later played a key role in the struggle for freedom and shaped the foundations of two nation states, India and Pakistan.

After their independence from the British Empire system in 1947, when India and Pakistan became sovereign republics in 1950 and 1956, respectively, they adopted for themselves democratic systems of governance based on universal adult franchise, a defining feature of the Western liberal tradition. While India began as a secular nation, Pakistan became an Islamic state in 1973, a distinction that defined the destinies of the two nations and their education systems in the following decades.

* When I wrote this chapter, I was an Emerging Leaders Fellow at the Australia India Institute at the University of Melbourne in November–December 2012. I gratefully acknowledge the Institute's support for this.

This chapter reviews the evolution and status of higher education in India and Pakistan, the two most populous countries of the Commonwealth. India with its population of 1.26 billion (as at 2012) is not only the most populous country of the Commonwealth, but also has many more people than other countries of the Commonwealth taken together. India will surpass China to become the most populous country in the world by 2025. Pakistan with 180 million people, though much smaller compared to India, is the second most populous country of the Commonwealth, with a large and growing young population.

Higher education in the two countries has a common origin and thus a similar academic and governance structure. However, after independence in 1947, higher education in India and Pakistan evolved along different trajectories. Today, there are significant differences in the reach and quality of higher education in both the nations. Despite being immediate neighbours, there is little interaction between their academic systems.

The approach in this chapter is chronological, with a focus on the commonalities and differences between the two countries. The first section covers the period up to 1947, when India and Pakistan attained independence. The second covers the post-independence period until 1980, when the process of economic reforms and privatisation began. The third reflects on the post-1980 period, when the rhetoric of the knowledge economy became dominant, particularly since 2000, and then tracks the recent developments. A significant juncture in history took place in 1971, when East Pakistan separated from West Pakistan to form an independent nation, Bangladesh. Since then, higher education in Bangladesh has evolved differently from West Pakistan (now Pakistan). Following the chronological review, critical issues affecting the two systems have been identified and discussed. The chapter ends with a short summary and conclusions.

The Foundation and Evolution to 1947

The Indian subcontinent has a long tradition of higher learning, going back to the Buddhist monasteries of the seventh century BC, and then to the third century AD Hindu Nalanda, together with the eleventh-century Islamic madrasahs.

That education was mostly religious and literary in character, based on ancient religious and philosophical literature in Sanskrit, Arabic, and

Persian languages. These institutions either collapsed or receded into the background as the British rule was firmly established on the Indian subcontinent by the end of the eighteenth century (Perkin, 2006).

The Foundations and Early Growth in the Nineteenth Century

The British came to India as traders through the British East India Company, established by Royal Charter in 1600. The Company confined itself to trade and establishing its presence on the subcontinent over the seventeenth century and much of the eighteenth century. Only in the latter part of the eighteenth century did it begin to support education. The Company founded the Calcutta Madrasah (now Aliah University) in 1781 and the Benaras Sanskrit College in 1792. This has sometimes been described as the beginning of modern higher education on the subcontinent. However, since these institutions actually encouraged classical learning in Arabic and Sanskrit languages on traditional lines, this analysis would appear to be inappropriate. A few more madrasahs and Sanskrit colleges were set up in subsequent years. But these languished for want of support from the people at large, while a growing recognition of the value of Western education was apparent among the rising Indian urban middle class.

By the turn of the eighteenth century, much of the subcontinent was under British rule. The society was constrained by orthodox Hinduism on the one hand, and by exploitative colonial rule on the other. Against this backdrop, Raja Rammohan Roy, along with a group of enlightened Indians and Englishmen, founded the first institute of Western-type higher education, the Hindoo College (now Presidency University at Kolkata) in 1817, aimed at meeting the rising aspirations of the nascent urban middle classes. This truly marked the foundations of modern higher education on the subcontinent. Raja Rammohan Roy, who is often referred to as the 'Father of Modern India', 'was unquestionably the first person on the subcontinent to seriously engage with challenges posed by modernity to traditional social structures and ways of being' (Guha, 2010: 26).

Soon after the setting up of the Hindoo College, several other colleges with English as the medium for instruction were established in different parts of the subcontinent by Christian missionaries or by the government. These colleges adopted the British style of higher education, and they catered to the demand of the urban middle class, who wanted access to prestigious appointments in the British bureaucracy or in the growing commercial sector. This served the interest of the British colonial government, which needed a class of educated Indians to manage secondary-level tasks in the government, and to act as intermediaries between the 'British Raj' and the local people.

By 1857, some 27 such colleges had been established on the subcontinent. With so many institutions in place, a need for standardisation of higher education, and maintenance of its quality, was felt. For this reason, the British established three universities in the presidency capitals of Calcutta (now Kolkata), Bombay (now Mumbai), and Madras (now Chennai). These institutions adopted the model of the University of London, which was emerging as a major new institution in England at that time. Under this organisational model, the three universities were primarily examining bodies that affiliated pre-existing colleges and subjected their students to examinations (Kolhatkar, 2012: 29). Since then, the 'affiliating university' has remained as the key organisational model for higher education on the subcontinent.

By 1882, when the fourth university, the University of Punjab, was established in Lahore (now in Pakistan), there were 80 colleges enrolling about 5,400 students. The University of Punjab was the first teaching university on the subcontinent. However, it was not until two decades later that teaching was included as a function of other universities, following the amendment of the Universities Act in 1904. In 1909, the Indian Institute of Science at Bangalore (now Bengaluru) was set up by the Tatas (a large industry house) for experimental science and for carrying out original research. Thus, while the modern colleges have existed for some 200 years, teaching and research were only added to the functions of universities much later.

Evolution during the Twentieth Century

In short, by the turn of the nineteenth century, there were four universities, 123 colleges, and 23,000 students enrolled in higher education across the subcontinent.

Another university was set up and more colleges were established in the first decade of the twentieth century. By 1913, when the Association of Commonwealth Universities was formed, there were five universities and 180 colleges enrolling 36,000 students, predominantly (90 per cent) male. Most of them were general colleges. However, four engineering colleges—at Guindy in Madras (1794), Roorkee in Uttar Pradesh (1847), Poona in Maharashtra (1854), and Shibpur in Bengal (1856)—had also been established by that time. In addition, some facilities for medical and legal education were also created.

Thereafter, higher education grew slowly but steadily, following an isomorphic pattern of growth until the independence of the two countries (Jayaram, 2006). Apart from the colonial government setting up new universities and colleges, a strong tradition of private philanthropy, plus active Christian missionaries on the Indian subcontinent, helped in setting up several institutions of higher education. Many of them are still the best institutions of higher education on the subcontinent.

The new universities were primarily established for linguistic, cultural, and politico-administrative considerations. A policy resolution was taken by the colonial government in 1913 to have a university for each province. This paved the way for setting up many more universities, mainly by the government and a few by the princely states, as well as through private philanthropy. The Princely State of Mysore set up the University of Mysore for the Kannada-speaking State of Mysore in 1916, and the Nizam of Hyderabad established Osmania University in 1918 with Urdu, the official language of the princely state, as its medium of instruction. Annamalai University was set up in Tamil Nadu, based on a philanthropic endowment (Kolhatkar, 2012: 31).

In sum, at the time of independence in 1947, India and Pakistan had quite a large system of higher education, comprising 19 universities and 420 colleges enrolling about 240,000 students. The system was, however, 'anaemic, distorted and dysfunctional' (Jayaram, 2006). In other smaller countries of the subcontinental region that were not under the colonial rule, such as Nepal, Bhutan, and the Maldives, there were no higher education facilities. Students from these countries accordingly came to undivided India for higher education.

Adoption of a Western-style Curriculum

In educational terms, the universities on the subcontinent followed the British classical curriculum set by the Universities of Oxford and Cambridge, with stress on English literature and European history. This ensured that a large part of middle-level appointees were actually from the local population, while almost all senior positions continued to be held by Britons, typically with an Oxbridge degree. In 1887, over 70 per cent of the middle-level civil service appointments were held by Hindus, Muslims, or Eurasians (European father and Indian mother).

Most local people accepted the Western model of higher education, even though there was some increasing disagreement about its acceptance due to nationalist and anti-colonial sentiments. Some Muslims even rejected foreign education on social and religious grounds. But overall, British-style higher education had become the de facto model of higher education on the subcontinent.

A significant exception was Visva-Bharati, set up in 1921 by Nobel Laureate and poet Rabindranath Tagore. Visva-Bharati, with its motto 'where the world makes a home in a single nest', aimed to revive the ancient Indian educational traditions. Its curriculum included music, painting, and dramatics—a significant departure from the other universities. Simplicity was its cardinal principle; classes were held in the open air in the shade of trees, where man and nature entered into an immediate harmonious relationship and teachers and students shared the single integral socio-cultural life. However, Visva-Bharati remained an isolated case and did not become a mainstream model for higher education, and nowadays this university is not very different from others.

Banaras Hindu University was founded by the great nationalist leader Pandit Madan Mohan Malviya in 1916. He wanted to blend the best of Indian education based on the ancient centres of learning—Takshashila and Nalanda and other hallowed institutions—with the best tradition of modern universities of the West. This experiment was also only partially successful. The modernist reformer Syed Ahmad Khan advocated Western education for the Muslims on the subcontinent and went on to establish the Mohammedan Anglo-Oriental College in 1875 (now Aligarh Muslim University) at Aligarh (today part of India). This university produced educated Muslims, who later provided political leadership for the independence movement and established Pakistan.

In sum, because most universities and colleges on the subcontinent followed the British style of higher education, they brought with them the strengths and limitations of metropolitan society. Whereas in the West, and particularly in England, the universities had lagged behind in the movement from hierarchy to equality, in India they were at the forefront of the social movement. Many leaders of the nationalist movement were educated in these universities and colleges, and some of them even went to London for further qualifications. Thus, the modern higher education that the British brought to India ironically helped Indians to arm themselves ideologically, and even to acquire the necessary intellectual and moral means towards gaining independence. They questioned the logic of colonial rule and held up, as a mirror to their British rulers, the ideals of liberty and justice that provided intellectual ammunition for the popular movement towards independence. Indeed, by the 1920s the student bodies had become hotbeds of Indian nationalist sentiment. According to sociologist Andre Beteille, 'the British themselves were not always happy when they thought of the political uses to which their Indian subjects might put the ideas to which they were increasingly exposed' (Beteille, 2010).

Foundation of Institutional Arrangements

Political geography was also important. When the British took control from the East India Company, they organised the subcontinent into various provinces. The Government of India Act 1919 transferred 'education' to the provinces. This position of education as a 'transferred' subject continued after the Government of India Act 1935. At the time of independence, the Constituent Assembly made no changes, in spite of the recommendation given by the Radhakrishnan Commission to make higher education a joint responsibility of the federal and state governments.

The foundations for institutional form—notably the separation of research from teaching—were also laid in the decades preceding independence. The following three key developments took place:

- The Imperial (later renamed as Indian) Council of Agricultural Research was established in 1930.
- The Medical Council of India was established in 1934.
- The Council of Scientific and Industrial Research was set up in 1944.

This completely isolated the university system from research. The Sargent Plan (1944) created a framework for a national system of education and recommended creation of a University Grants Committee and of a National Board for Technical Education. In post-independence India, these were converted into the University Grants Commission (UGC), and the All India Council for Technical Education.

More than a decade after the creation of the Association of Commonwealth Universities, the idea of creating an association of Indian universities came through a Conference of Indian Vice-Chancellors convened at Shimla in 1924 by Lord Reading, the then Viceroy of India. The following year, an Inter-University Board was established. This was, however, registered as a society only in 1967, and then assumed its present name, the Association of Indian Universities, in 1973.

Thus, it could be said that, in many ways, the underpinnings of modern higher education, of the overall contours of its institutional arrangements for governance, and of scientific research on the subcontinent were laid by the British prior to independence.

Divergent Trajectories after Independence: 1947–80

The post-independence period has witnessed a significant government-led expansion of higher education in both India and Pakistan.

By 1965, there were 1,686 private colleges, 527 government colleges, and 147 university colleges in India, while the number of students rose from 263,000 to 1.9 million, growing at an average of over 10 per cent per annum. The central and state governments in India not only set up new universities and colleges, but also took upon themselves the responsibility for funding private institutions through a grant-in-aid system, resulting in de facto nationalisation of higher education. Large-scale expansion favoured access, but there was a cost in deterioration of quality.

At the time of independence, Pakistan had just two universities and fewer than 50 colleges. By 1955, this number had increased to six universities and 191 colleges, including 46 professional colleges, and continued to grow thereafter, through both government and private efforts. Under the Education Policy of 1972, education was nationalised, resulting in government taking over all existing private colleges and technical institutions. This led to financial constraints, resulting in the enrolment growth slowing down significantly. Poor participation rates as a consequence of the nationalisation policy forced the government to recognise that it could not alone carry the burden of the whole educational process. Accordingly, in a policy review of 1979, private provision was again allowed in education at all levels. By 1980, there were 22 universities and 500 colleges in Pakistan.

Centralising Tendencies

The formative years since independence also saw constitutional and legislative changes rebalancing the relative roles of the federal and state governments in the sphere of higher education. Education is typically a state subject in all federal systems.

Under the Indian constitution of 1950, education at all levels was the responsibility of the state governments, except that the federal government was given the sole responsibility in matters relating to determination and coordination of standards in higher education. For this purpose, the federal government established the UGC in 1956. This body was also assigned the role of disbursing grants, a role that became its dominant role over time. Education, including vocational, technical, and medical education and universities, was brought to the 'Concurrent List' by constitutional amendment in 1976, meaning thereby that the responsibility for education was now to be shared between the federal and the state governments.

In Pakistan, after the breaking away of East Pakistan in 1971, it was recognised that education could play an important role in national integration and social cohesion. Education was brought under the Concurrent List in 1973, a UGC was established in 1973, and the federal government created a highly centralised structure—so shrinking the role of the provincial governments. As in India, the national government exercised its authority through the process of allocation of funding to universities by the UGC (Coffman, 1997). The curricula are devised by the UGC and it is mandatory for the universities to adopt them under the Federal Supervision of Curricula, Textbooks and Maintenance of Standards of Education Act enacted in 1976.

Deepening of Colonial Academic Arrangements

Structurally, expansion occurred mainly through colleges affiliated to existing and, in some cases, new universities in both India and Pakistan. Most of the colleges were set up without clear planning and proper regulations. In Pakistan and in a few states in India, colleges also imparted instruction for students in grade 11 and 12. In such colleges, the teachers taught both the grades 11 and 12 concurrently with the undergraduate classes, so raising a host of pedagogical issues. Streaming in rigid and narrow fields of study (right from grade 11 onwards) prevents students from exposure to a broad-based curriculum. This lacuna in the education systems of both the countries persists.

In the affiliating system, the university designs the syllabus, conducts exams, and grants degrees, while teaching is done in affiliated colleges that have no control over the academic content and minimal control over evaluation. While this type of standardisation has a 'pull-up' effect for lower-end colleges, it curtails innovation and change, and it also has a 'pull-down' effect on those colleges that can offer something superior to the standard.

In the 1970s, based on the recommendations of the (Indian) Education Commission (1964–66), the Indian government instituted the 10 + 2 + 3 system, a common and national pattern of study at the school and college level, in order to bring uniformity into the school system and to ensure mobility across states and comparability with the rest of the world. This replaced the four patterns of school and college study in operation in India until then: 10 + 2 + 3, 10 + 2 + 2 + 2, 11 + 3 and 11 (or 12) + 1 + 3. The approach was gradually adopted throughout the country. Higher secondary classes that were held in the colleges in some states were shifted from the jurisdiction of the universities to the boards of secondary education (Agarwal, 2012).

In Pakistan, efforts were made in the early 1960s to shift classes 11 and 12 from colleges to the boards of secondary education, and to increase the duration of the bachelor's degree to three years after 12 years of education. Both these efforts failed, however, due to nationwide unrest. Much of Pakistan still has a two-year bachelor's degree programme after 12 years of study, which is roughly equivalent to 'A' level in the British system (Gilani, 2012).

In the post-independence period, several new science research institutes and government laboratories were established outside the university system. The Indian Council for Social Science Research, the Indian Council for Historical Research, and the Indian Council for Philosophical Research were established in 1968, 1971, and 1977, respectively. Several independent institutes for social science research were additionally established. All this further distanced the universities from research, particularly from applied research.

It should be especially noted that the curriculum in higher education continued to be strongly influenced by British practices, with traditional emphasis on classics and humanities, and with very little stress on science or more practical subjects or applied technical fields. Thus, higher education increasingly had little relation to the needs of the newly emerged nations. This caused a rising concern about the growing graduate unemployment during the 1960s and 1970s. Taking cognizance of this, the Education Commission (1964–66) in India recommended a slowing of the rate of higher education expansion.

Language Impasse

Language issues and, in particular, the question of the medium of instruction, had been a highly emotive issue both in India and Pakistan, with a flavour of both nationalism and regionalism.

Soon after independence, several major efforts were made in India to change the language policy for higher education, by changing the medium of instruction from English to regional languages. A sense of regionalism, which became particularly dominant after the creation of linguistic states in the late 1950s, added to this pressure. A decision was taken that undergraduate education would gradually shift entirely to the regional languages. English would probably remain the main language of graduate education. There would be some emphasis on Hindi in non-Hindi-speaking areas. However, success has been limited.

The decision to impose Urdu as the language of instruction in Pakistan met with a similar fate.

Growing Student Activism in India

The student activism of the pre-independence period that was closely linked to the nationalist movement morphed into student 'indiscipline' in the post-independence period. It changed from a 'self-conscious, articulate, and unified movement' into more 'spontaneous usually locally oriented campaigns' (Altbach, 1971). In some states, West Bengal in particular, the student activism in the late 1960s evolved into left-wing extremism, referred to as the 'Naxalite movement', which aimed at establishing an Indian Marxist State, by overthrowing the democratically elected government. In a few places, students' activism was centred on larger political issues, such as language or reservations, but in most places students' activism was 'sporadic, unorganised and leaderless' (Altbach, 1971). Such activism has had a deleterious effect on the academic culture in the universities and colleges.

Relative Decline of Higher Education in Pakistan

Despite the common issues above, significant differences in emphasis on higher education in the two countries have become increasingly apparent.

With many Muslims rejecting British-style education on social and religious grounds, even prior to independence, this had resulted in the marginalisation of Muslim-dominated Pakistan in terms of its educational and social development. After independence, unlike India, Pakistan did not put educational and scientific development at the top of its agenda. Education was viewed as just one of several initiatives that the new Pakistan would eventually need, and no particular vision in this regard was articulated. Indeed, the allocations of the First Five-Year Plan were too small and wholly inadequate for producing universal literacy or a system of proper schools. Insufficient emphasis was given to technical and vocational education, and higher education continued to follow the template inherited from the British. In the early 1970s, education was nationalised, effectively ending private education in Pakistan.

In view of considerable political conflict and violence at the time of independence and the division of India and Pakistan, the primary agenda of political leaders in Pakistan was to create a common, homogenised, and purportedly Islamic national identity. Education was used as the key instrument for this purpose, by having a curriculum inspired by Islamic ideology, compulsory religious instruction for Muslim students, and Urdu as the medium of instruction.

The report of the Commission on National Education (1959), and subsequent planning documents, continued to focus on the Islamisation of education. The National Education Policy and its Implementation Programme 1979 made Islamic studies (Islamiat) and Pakistan studies compulsory at all levels of education, from class one to bachelor's degrees (Gilani, 2012). Around the same time, Pakistan was coming under the growing influence of radical Islam, which resulted in a ban on private higher education, while the medium of instruction was changed from English to Urdu.

In 1971, East Pakistan was separated from West Pakistan and an independent nation, Bangladesh, came into being. Faced with resource constraints, higher education in Bangladesh has been largely led by the private sector.

Emergence of US-style Institutions in India

While higher education was being marginalised in Pakistan, a significant and interesting development was taking place in India during the 1950s and 1960s. Between 1951 and 1963, several elite institutions for education in engineering, technology, and management were established by the federal government on the pattern of quality US institutions. The Indian Institutes of Technology and the Indian Institutes of Management, as they were called—with highly selective admissions and successful alumni—became a symbol of the country's progress, and represented the epitome of middle-class aspirations.

They were also, purposefully, established outside the university system. These institutions brought in a choice-based integrated curriculum, incorporating sciences and humanities for engineering education, and using a combination of lectures, tutorials, and self-study as the instructional mode. This was to move away from annual external evaluation and lectures as the main mode of instruction in the existing universities and colleges. Creating these institutions was a major innovation, by bringing in a more flexible curriculum, better pedagogic practices and improved governance, and by having improved career pathways for faculty (Subbarao, 2008). Over time, this became the dominant model for engineering and management education in the country.

In sum, while there were common issues in the modern history of India and Pakistan—centralising tendencies, structural issues of the affiliating system, irrelevance of the curriculum, separation of research from teaching, a language issue, and student activism—there was divergence in the growth and development of higher education in the two countries, not least due to continuing policy reversals in Pakistan.

The Era of Rapid Expansion: 1980 to the Present

Both India and Pakistan continue to have a young and growing population, reflecting their high fertility rates. Along with improvements in schooling and the rising aspirations of the growing middle class, this has put considerable pressure on higher education to expand capacity. Responding to this demand surge, enrolments in higher education have continued to grow in the two countries, but more rapidly in India than in Pakistan.

Accelerated Growth in India

In 1980, India had 110 universities, 7,000 colleges and a few hundred diploma institutions that in total enrolled about 5 million students. Since then, the number of universities has grown six-fold, and the numbers of colleges and of enrolments have risen five-fold. There are now 660 universities, and over 35,000 colleges. Further, there are about 12,000 stand-alone institutions outside the university system that offer diplomas in education, teaching, and nursing.

In addition, the open and distance education system that once enrolled only about 166,000 students in 1980, now has 4.2 million students enrolled in 13 open universities and 183 other institutions. (These include several regular universities that offer programmes both in conventional and distance mode.)

With an enrolment of 26 million students, India's higher education system is now the second largest in the world. India's enrolments recently surpassed those of the United States. With its significantly large and young population compared to China—374 million under the age of 15 years against 262 million in China—India could soon be the largest higher education system. India's progress in higher education in terms of numbers is simply exceptional.

However, there are several contradictions in this impressive growth story. Even though India can boast of the second-largest enrolment next only to China, it accommodates just about 18 per cent of the eligible age group, which is one of the lowest globally. Female participation rates are even lower. There are also large regional imbalances and wide disparities in enrolment of various socio-economic groups. The country's 48,000 institutions of higher education exceed the number of institutions in the rest of the world taken together. Average enrolment of fewer than 500 students makes many of them unviable and ineffective. Managing such a highly fragmented system is a huge governance challenge.

Enrolment is skewed in favour of certain subjects, like arts and humanities, and does not reflect the country's needs. Overall, higher education lacks vocational focus, and produces unemployable graduates. Vocational education and training that caters to low-level and medium-level skills is underused and is separated from higher education. Having low prestige and being of poor quality, there are few takers for vocational education, despite large unmet demand for flexible skills. In short, even though higher education in India has grown dramatically, it suffers from structural weaknesses that need urgent attention.

Moreover, as India's largely rural-based, agrarian economy was transformed into an urban, manufacturing-service economy, higher education is now seen as essential to meet a surge in demand for appropriately qualified professionals. Higher education is increasingly receiving wide-ranging support from the country's economic planners, who were earlier disinclined to invest in higher education. In 2006, a nationwide agitation over the quotas for admissions in national-level institutions paralysed the country for months. It became abundantly clear that higher education could potentially garner mass political support. Thus, there is now growing enthusiasm both from economic planners and from the political establishment for developing higher education in India.

In this context, several commissions and committees were set up by the Indian government to address the issue. Most significant have been the National Knowledge Commission and the Yashpal Committee. These and other committees have come up with several innovative ideas. Based on their recommendations, a series of regulatory and governance reforms have been initiated; and many of them are awaiting parliamentary sanction. Funding for higher education has received a significant boost with the Eleventh Five-Year Plan (2007–12). As many as 65 new central institutions have been established by the federal government over the past five years. Much larger expansion occurred in the state sector and the private sector than in the central institutions. The country's Twelfth Five-Year Plan (2012–17) for higher education has advanced several important and useful ideas, with a focus on greater quality in both the state and the private sector.

Expansion in Pakistan amid Policy Uncertainty

The Pakistan story has been less positive. Continuing poor performance by the economy in the 1980s resulted in significant underfunding of higher education. As a direct consequence, not only has the capacity of the system failed to keep up with national needs, but even existing institutions have not been appropriately resourced. Acceptable salaries could not be paid, libraries could not be maintained, physical facilities crumbled, and research was practically non-existent. Students and faculty alike became increasingly discontented. There was near unanimity among Pakistanis that the nation's public higher education system was close to being a tragedy of lost opportunities. This reflected the policy and funding hiatus, which continued throughout the 1980s and for much of the 1990s (Coffman, 1997).

From 1998, steps were initiated to rejuvenate higher education. This culminated in the setting up of a new Higher Education Commission (September 2002)—so replacing the erstwhile UGC. There followed a massive increase in the higher education budget, which led to three-fold growth in enrolments, establishment of 55 new universities, and expansion of PhD programmes with 5,000 doctoral research scholarships. The Commission began a major reform effort in producing the 'Medium Term Development Framework: 2005-10', which essentially focused on faculty development, increased access, quality improvement, and relevance of educational provision.

Over 2,000 people were sent on overseas fellowships towards undertaking PhDs and Master's degrees. The Higher Education Commission also instituted a system of ranking of universities—to reward excellence and investing in the strengthening of institutions that need improvement. Despite a general outcry against the rankings, universities now took data collection much more seriously (Salmi and Saroyan, 2007). Digital infrastructure was put in place, a digital library came into operation, some foreign faculty were hired, and more students were sent abroad for PhD programmes, albeit largely to second-order institutions. The number of universities doubled and then tripled again from the number that had already doubled. The number of PhD students registered at various universities exploded. Huge financial incentives were announced for publishing papers and for supervising PhD students. Academic salaries were made more lucrative, with significant incentives for performance, while a tenure-track system was introduced.

Consequently, after slow growth in the 1980s and 1990s, higher education enrolment in Pakistan grew very rapidly in the first decade of the twenty-first century—growing from some 275,000 candidates in 2002 to 800,000 in 2009. During the same period, the gross enrolment ratio (GER) more than doubled, from 2.2 per cent to 4.7 per cent. Currently, about 1 million students are enrolled in the universities in Pakistan, which corresponds to GER of 5 per cent. This is still relatively low, and is only one-third of the percentage of GER in India. But in addition, Allama Iqbal Open University and a Virtual University enrolled another 1 million students, including a large number of in-service teachers pursuing BEd degrees.

As in India, higher education expansion in Pakistan has been primarily through affiliated colleges. They increased exponentially—from

154 in 1990 to 1,202 in 2008. Also, as in India, colleges in Pakistan have very small enrolments, with fewer than 300 students on average per institution. Most colleges offer a two-year Bachelor's (pass) general programme, in arts, science, or commerce; and, unlike India, most colleges in Pakistan are government-run and government-aided (World Bank, 2011).

While the Pakistan government claimed great success for its reform initiatives, and defended top-down reform process as the only viable alternative after decades of institutional failure, not everyone concurred. A Pakistan scholarly authority, Professor Pervez Hoodbhoy of the Quaid-i-Azam University at Islamabad, has argued that, although public spending has increased significantly, the improvements are often cosmetic; and indeed that increased public spending has only aggravated some problems through failing academic standards (Hoodbhoy, 2009). In addition, Professor S. Zulfikar Gilani, Director of the Centre for Higher Education at Islamabad, has lamented the lack of overall governance transparency, and has criticised a university leadership that is hierarchical, uninspiring and too weak for any meaningful reform to be put in place (Gilani, 2006).

After unprecedented progress from 2002 to 2008 there have been continuous budget cuts for higher education during the subsequent years, with negative long-term consequences (Khan, 2011a). A move to abolish the Higher Education Commission was aborted after massive protests. The government wished to devolve this sector to the federating units; and consequently (in April 2011) the Constitution was amended by declaring education a provincial responsibility (Khan, 2011b). This was potentially crippling to the transformation process. These factors threaten to reverse the previous progress in higher education, to limit quality improvement, to reverse the attractiveness of university positions, to curtail enrolment increases, and generally to undermine the prospects for national development (Hayward, 2009).

Expansion of the Affiliating System

In both India and Pakistan (proportionately more in the former), a bulk of higher education enrolment is in affiliated colleges—where the university designs the syllabus, conducts exams, and gives degrees, while teaching is done in affiliated colleges that have no control over the academic content, and with minimal control over evaluation.

To some extent, the affiliating system provides quality control, but it also eliminates incentives and innovation at the college level. The continuing growth of the affiliated colleges has, in many ways, only exacerbated mass education problems. With their sub-optimal size and poor academic culture, the vast and growing network of affiliated colleges is often viewed as the 'weakest link' in the region's higher education sector (Singh, 2004).

The affiliating system, as noted, places responsibility for assessment and evaluation onto the university and may be behind the emphasis on easily tested (though complex) facts and simpler concepts, rather than the arguably more important assessment of complex concepts that can only be accessed through complex, customised mixes of group projects, class presentations, journal-writing, and the like, which require the instructor to interact with the students during the assessment process.

Private Sector Dominance

In Pakistan, the National Education Policy (1979) recognised the importance of higher education, including the need for private involvement; and it removed the ban on private institutions imposed in 1972. The national government now assumed financial responsibility for all universities, ensuring a centralised administration of the country's university system. Along with this step, all appointments of faculty and administrators were made by the national government, depriving universities of much of their autonomy.

The subcontinent once had a strong tradition of private philanthropy in higher education. However, with the abolition of private involvement in Pakistan, and nationalisation of private institutions in India, this tradition was largely extinguished. Responding to the rising demand for vocationally oriented education, the private involvement in higher education was revived in the 1980s—even though much of it may not have been driven by philanthropy.

Looked at comparatively, and beginning with the 1980s, there was a large expansion of private higher education both in India and Pakistan. This trend accelerated during the 1990s, and continues unabated today. Private higher education has gradually moved from the periphery to the centre. The private share in India exceeds a majority of other countries for which such data is available. As elsewhere in the world (except, perhaps, the United States of America), the private institutions are secular, demand-responsive, and vocationally and commercially oriented.

With the reversal of policy on private involvement in higher education in 1979, private universities began to be created in Pakistan, though slowly to begin with. In fact, Pakistan became the first country on the subcontinent to allow a private university, when Aga Khan University was established in 1983. Two years later, another private university, Lahore University of Management Sciences, was launched. But the next private universities came almost a decade later, after which the numbers rose rapidly. By 2000 there were 10 private universities in Pakistan, with numbers rising to 60 by 2010, and enrolling over 115,000 students.

The first few private, professional colleges (mostly for engineering education) in India arose in Karnataka, soon followed by Maharashtra, Andhra Pradesh, and Tamil Nadu in the early 1980s. Within a decade, several hundred private, professional colleges had arisen, all charging 'capitation fees'—a term often referring to the significant student fees charged, which are not shown in official accounts of the institution. The practice became closely associated with growth of the Indian private sector. In 1993, at the instance of the Supreme Court, a framework to regulate fees in such private institutions was put in place. This legitimised private higher education in India, yet it also opened the door to considerable litigation over the issue of regulation of admissions and fees in the private institutions. Such private institutions are deemed 'not-for-profit' entities, being usually established and operated under the provisions of charitable societies, or trusts laws, and lately even under section 25 of the Companies Act. These institutions meet almost all of their expenses from tuition fees, and are required to reinvest any surplus funds for the development of the institution itself. In reality, many private institutions are run as business enterprises, and some are owned by influential families, who siphon off certain funds. Interestingly, much of this private growth in India was through affiliation to the local state universities.

With a view to overcoming limitation of the affiliating system, and to foster innovation through private involvement in higher education, the national government proposed a central law for setting up private universities in India in 1995. But, for want of political consensus, this was abandoned. Other than the legislative route, where both the national and state government could set up universities, the national government had the power to confer university status on any institution it deemed to be appropriate, with authority to award degrees. While this power was used sparingly in the past, by the late 1990s the national government had begun to establish such new institutions (and existing private colleges) as 'universities', and did so quite liberally, an issue that became highly controversial over time. In 2012, there were now 80 such private universities. The state government has also begun to establish private universities through state legislatures, and as many 111 private universities have thus far been established. Overall, one-third of India's universities are now private.

In addition, 60 per cent of the colleges (and about 75 per cent of the diploma institutions) are private, and receive no financial support from the government. In terms of enrolment, 59 per cent of students are in private institutions, with merely 2.6 per cent in universities and colleges under the central government. The remaining 38.5 per cent are in the institutions under the state government. In professional education, the proportion of private institutions and enrolment is even higher, though there is significant private provision in general education across the country. Thus, private higher education is not only growing very rapidly in India, but the overall system itself is also moving towards a private dominance.

In contrast, within Pakistan, the private sector constitutes only about 17 per cent of total enrolments, and about one-third in terms of number of institutions; the private share is now on the rise.

It could be said, indeed, that in both the countries, private institutions are more agile and offer programmes in areas that are in high demand, while not requiring large investments. Both public and private provisions are now seen broadly to meet the growing demand for education, and there is less public versus private debate. Private provision is usually more expensive and of lesser quality. Average annual fees are three to four times the country's per capita income, and hence beyond the paying capacity of a large section of the population.

Private growth has had a consequential impact on private higher education in India as well. Many public universities have begun offering self-financing programmes, and derive substantial income from such operations. Distance education—where fees are relatively high—has grown fast too. Barring exceptions, fee levels have also increased in public higher education overall. Thus, the cost of higher education is continually shifting from government to households, resulting in privatisation of public institutions (Agarwal, 2009).

There have been serious concerns about equity, quality, and exploitative behaviour from private provision. Despite a multi-layered regulatory oversight, there are several loopholes, and the current voluntary accreditation in India has been ineffectual. As a result, perverse incentives dominate, with quality lagging, while a version of Gresham's Law often prevails—bad private providers driving out the good institutions.

Some of the private universities, however, pay higher salaries, and the very best offer high-quality libraries and research facilities. They tend to respond to the public's demand for modern, hands-on, practical training in business and technology majors. The schools are free to offer innovative curricula, unconstrained by bureaucratic demands to adhere to an outdated, set programme. They usually offer more appealing learning environments, free of political conflicts and physical decay. Both India and Pakistan have examples of such semi-elite private universities such as Birla Institute of Technology, Thapar University, and the recent Azim Premji University and Shiv Nadar University in India; and Lahore University of Management Sciences and the Aga Khan University in Pakistan.

Foreign presence is peripheral, and mainly an adjunct to the growing private sector. Independent campuses of foreign universities are rare, while partnerships are more common. Prestigious universities are cautious, and are content with merely setting up research centres to provide their home students with an exposure to the rapid changes in the region. Most partnerships are with second-tier foreign universities that often vie with each other to tap into the huge potential of the subcontinent.

The Relevance of English Language as the Medium of Instruction

Language for the medium of instruction in higher education has been an emotive issue both in India and in Pakistan.

In Pakistan, a policy was enacted from the 1980s gradually to replace English with Urdu. Despite this, higher education continues to be conducted mostly in English. Pakistan has a large non-Urdu-speaking population; for them, imposition of Urdu in universities has resulted in the systematic degradation of the learning environment, while also causing a decline of many of Pakistan's local, indigenous cultures (Coleman, 2010).

In India, post-independence developments and fundamental disagreements resulted in a hotchpotch of policies in respect of language of instruction across the country. In north India, the states stressed the use of Hindi, and the central government made some efforts to produce and translate textbooks into Hindi for use in undergraduate education, while

English continued to be used at higher levels. Most southern states continued to use English as the main language for higher education at all levels. Some permitted the use of regional languages; others used a combination of English and the regional language. In some special cases, specific universities preferred to retain instruction in English, despite the state policy. Thus, language policy and practice in higher education was, and remains, varied and contested throughout the country.

Overall, however, it is likely that the use of the English language has increased in Indian higher education with globalisation, especially in the more prestigious universities and colleges—notably in the highly selective institutions. Much of the private higher education sector functions in English as well. The research sector is entirely dominated by English, and most scholarly communication in journals (and on the Internet) takes place in English. The same is also by and large true of Pakistan. While the language debate has not entirely faded in India and Pakistan, English has emerged as the key, world language, and gives significant advantages to the countries in global higher education (Altbach, 2012).

Growing Campus Politicisation

Higher education in both the countries is infused with national and state politics. Political parties have student wings on the campuses. In addition, there are academic staff associations and unions of non-teaching employees. As a result, there is sometimes a complete breakdown of discipline in the universities.

According to Professor Usman Ali Isani (former Chairman of the UGC in Pakistan and Vice-Chancellor of Quaid-i-Azam University, Islamabad), 'the purpose of unionisation of the campus is not professional development, but to work for accelerated promotion, better perks and degrees without work' (Isani and Virk, 2003).

An external analyst who has closely watched the developments in India (Professor Philip G. Altbach) has argued that the situation is becoming equally bad for India. University and college elections are frequently politicised, political intrigue and infighting infuse campus life and, in extreme cases, campus politics can turn violent, so disrupting normal academic processes (Altbach, 2012).

In sum, five key developments in the post-1980 era in the two countries are noteworthy.

- First is dramatic growth in enrolment in both countries, though it was less significant in Pakistan due to policy uncertainty.
- Second is the increasingly dominant private sector.
- Third is a continuation of poor academic organisation, with an expansion of the affiliating college system.
- Fourth is even greater adoption of English as a language of instruction in higher education in both the countries—despite continuing policy efforts to replace it by the local languages.
- Finally, there is a growing and worrying politicisation of the campuses.

Reflections on Some Critical Issues

Despite some clearly positive growth, both India and Pakistan still have among the lowest global participation rates in higher education for major countries. In addition, there are communities and regions that are underserved. With growing young populations, improving economies and rising aspirations, there is a huge potential for significant educational growth in both countries. For this to take place, public as well as private resources will have to be harnessed, and technology deployed effectively.

Against the backdrop of developments over the last hundred years, certain critical issues affecting higher education in the two countries have now been identified as vital for the future.

Funding and Private Provision

Rapid higher education expansion over the past two decades has not been accompanied by a corresponding increase in public funding for higher education in the two countries. Thus, the quality of public higher education has deteriorated, with declining per student spending in the face of rising costs, particularly regarding staff salaries. A bulk of the federal spending in both the countries is focused on the universities (in the case of India, on a small number of universities and institutions directly under the federal government). Many experts, such as Hoodbhoy (2008), believe that spending ever more money on universities can only result in tiny, incremental gains, because of the existence of various non-resource-related constraints. Colleges, meanwhile, are grossly underfunded and are the worst affected by this strategy. They urgently require adequate funding and support. Overall, the rapidly expanding systems of higher education in the two countries require much higher levels of funding, from both public and private sources.

Recent higher education growth has been fuelled by the tuition fee-based private provision, and even public institutions have resorted to expansion of self-financing provision. Thus, a significant cost has already shifted from the government to students and their families. With the raising of tuition fees, and introduction of a self-financing scheme in public universities since 1994, universities in Pakistan have gradually become self-reliant, and now raise more than half their revenue through tuition (Isani and Virk, 2003). Though it varies between provinces, this is also generally the case in India. An adequate student aid system needs to be put in place, in order to address serious implications for equity. Despite the fact that the official policy has been to replace English by Urdu as the medium of instruction at all levels, there have also been practical difficulties in implementing this policy.

Private institutions that have arisen in recent years, even though de jure not-for-profit, are reaping significant profits from these enterprises. Working under a framework of weak accreditation and poor-quality monitoring, they pose concerns about quality, and even exploitation, quite apart from serious equity issues. Thus, the two countries urgently need to address the regulation and accountability of their increasingly dominant private sectors.

Academic Organisation

Some higher education institutions in India and Pakistan were established when the United States had become a powerful centre of learning after the Second World War, and they still bear the imprint of the universities of the United States. But, to a large extent, current academic systems, core principles, administrative organisation, the professoriate, research arrangements, curriculum development, teaching methods, examination systems, and the fundamental ethos still broadly follow the British model—even, ironically, after the British have largely abandoned these approaches.

The most significant of these is probably the legacy of the 'affiliating system', which has prevented curricular innovation. This has resulted in fragmentation, leaving students with very little choice of courses. Cumbersome governing structures make curricular revision an extremely arduous task. Systems of supervision and inspection by the university are weak, and no college is disaffiliated for want of failing to meet standards. Affiliation has become a mere formality, and once affiliation is granted, it simply continues. The universities have no mechanisms for taking action for unacceptable performance.

The affiliating system once provided a semblance of quality control from 1857, when the subcontinent's first universities were established. It is vast and deep-rooted, and hence it is neither feasible nor desirable to dismantle it. However, part-decentralisation of the curriculum holds a great promise for reform. In the new model of academic autonomy, the core courses could be retained by the university, while the entire responsibility of the remainder could be devolved to the colleges. This would potentially create the desired innovation culture in the colleges. Clustering, and even merger of colleges that are very small, would also have to accompany this strategy. In addition, universities that affiliate a very large number of colleges (such as Osmania—901, Pune—811, Nagpur—800, Rajasthan—735, Mumbai—711 in India; and Punjab in Pakistan—340) could be organised into two or more universities, in order to improve overall academic effectiveness.

Technology is just starting to change the way in which students are educated. It can improve learning and increase personalisation, while lowering costs. The affiliating system is optimally organised as a 'hub and spoke' arrangement to unlock the potential of technology, by ensuring that the lectures from the best teachers are available to hundreds of thousands of students through synchronous video-streaming. Facilitated by on-location trained instructors to enable interaction, this method has potential to bring about a significant improvement in teaching and learning process across the affiliated colleges. The structure also provides opportunities for large-scale use of massive online courses. Thus, a South Asian model of organising higher education is eminently possible.

There are, however, continuing concerns about the quality and relevance of the curriculum. It is often outdated and inflexible, and is not responsive to the changing trends in scholarship, taste and demands of an evolving society. General education is disjointed from vocational education, and currently happens in separate sets of institutions. It is necessary to bring general education, and skill-based or professional education, into a single fold for greater curricular diversity and two-way mobility of students, scholars, and academics.

Academic Culture

Due to continued politicisation, an academic culture that promotes meritocracy, honesty, and academic freedom is often absent in the two countries. Without an effective incentive structure, it becomes difficult to ensure that the faculty perform at an appropriate level. In order to enthuse and motivate college teachers, their involvement in curriculum formation, determining appropriate pedagogy and having an input into examination matters, is essential. This is also needed to promote innovation and experimentation at the college level.

Academics acquire full-time appointments early on in their careers, and have a predetermined career path, leaving them with little motivation and no incentives to improve. Thus, despite reasonable salaries of the academics in the two countries—on average much higher than those in, say, China—academic research performance is poor, and teaching standards are slipping. Nor has the tenure-track system started in Pakistan been very successful.

There are a large number of academic vacancies and, despite thousands of applicants for each position, selection committees often find it difficult to secure suitable appointees. There is very little mobility of academics from one institution to another. Hiring practices are highly centralised and suffer from inbreeding and nepotism. There is a real shortage of qualified faculty, with only 30 per cent of university teachers, and merely 2 per cent of college teachers, having a PhD degree. Faculty attrition is worryingly high.

Academics are not positive about the evaluation processes of faculty, based on academic performance indicators that were introduced after a recent pay revision in India. They feel that it is excessively focused on research, and not suited to broad teaching responsibilities. Not many universities conduct student evaluation of teaching; and even when it is done, it has few consequences.

Improving academic culture, based on professional ethos, merit and competition, is critical to higher education reforms in the two countries. This would require repositioning of the academic profession, to attract the best qualified professionals to work in the universities.

Governance and Diversity

In India, higher education governance is, moreover, too centralised and burdensome, while protecting vested interests and academic oligarchies.

There is no demand for accountability from the system; and, until the recent private growth, it faced no competitive pressures either. In the provinces, there is much political interference, even in purely academic matters. At the national level, several pieces of legislation that aim to provide a new regulatory framework for higher education are held up in the Parliament of India. Faced with an uncertain future, the existing regulatory bodies are demotivated and perhaps on the verge of collapse.

Pakistan has not been consistent in its policy on higher education with respect to private provision. The country also has to govern its state system better and to address the problem of coordination, duplication, and complex bureaucratic requirements. Large sections under state government control require special attention. Growing divergence and tensions between the central and state systems of higher education require more skilful handling.

The condition of research, both within and outside the institution of higher education in the two countries, is disappointing. Part of the problem is that the research institutes and laboratories have been developed outside the university system. Thus, reconnecting teaching with research, by bringing the large research laboratory system within the fold of the university system, is necessary towards creating a vibrant research system in the two countries. At the same time, it must be recognised that all institutions of higher education need not engage in both teaching and research. This is both unfeasible and unaffordable. A mass access higher education system necessarily comprises diverse types of institutions to meet a variety of needs in the economy and society, and it should provide a range of alternate pathways to success. While India and Pakistan must have some world-class research universities, it must also have a large number of sophisticated teaching institutions, and a very large number of institutions that impart vocational or generic skills. By being left somewhat to themselves, all institutions of higher education tend to drift towards a research orientation. For this reason, government at the central and state levels must assure, through policy and funding, that different types of institutions focus on their defined missions. Creating a quality and diverse system of higher education is both important and vital for national development.

As is evident from above, the challenges of higher education in the two countries are not merely about access and equity, where significant progress has been made in the recent years, but rather about colonial legacy, poor academic culture and faulty assumptions. These are not amenable to easy and routine solutions. Change in higher education cannot be brought about through top-down policy, but only by engaging diverse stakeholders in the massive rearrangement of provision for higher education, as well as public and private resources. Legacy issues require reconsideration in the context of new developments. Fundamental and systemic reforms will take time, and will demand significant (and sustained) efforts to bring about the necessary changes in mindsets, behaviours, and the overall culture of higher education. Only in this way can the two countries realise their full and extraordinary potential through aspirations for economic and technological advancement.

Summary and Conclusions

Despite their common origin and similar academic and affiliating structure, higher education in the two countries has now acquired distinct national identities. On the one hand, India has consistently accorded priority to higher education, and has increasingly used both the state and the private provision and funding for the purpose. In Pakistan, on the other hand, there have been a series of policy reversals on the involvement of the private sector and the state governments. Consequently, the higher education systems in the two countries are now at different levels of development in terms of their reach and quality.

Higher education in the two nations faces many and different challenges. These are not only about capacity constraints alone, but also related to serious quality concerns, and structural and governance issues. The curricula are overly theoretical and the teaching methods are inappropriate. As a result, graduate skills do not match labour market requirements. There is inadequate research capacity. Physical facilities and student support services are poor. Not least due to the sheer size of the two countries, the magnitude of the challenges is huge. In moving forward, the two countries would have to harness the potential of new technology, to ensure significant cost savings and high-quality learning, while providing access to growing numbers.

Both India and Pakistan are expected to have private sector–led growth of their higher education in future. The biggest challenge arising is to put in place financing and regulatory arrangements that remove binding constraints for harmonious growth of both the public and private sectors. In doing so, there is scope to benefit from each other's experience, and build upon their complementarities. Unfortunately, despite

India's dominant presence in the region, its influence in shaping the higher education sector in the region is marginal. For example, in recent years, the South Asia University (an international university established by the eight member states of the South Asian Association for Regional Cooperation) has been established in Delhi. This is the first right step towards building a co-operative structure, but it is unlikely to have any significant impact on addressing systemic and structural problems unless accompanied with deeper engagement at different levels.

By adopting the right strategies, the two countries could potentially move towards developing internationally competitive systems of higher education. This is critical for the future in meeting the aspirations of the large and youthful population of these two major nations in the new century ahead.

Bibliography

Agarwal, P. (2009) *Indian Higher Education: Envisioning the Future*. New Delhi: SAGE Publications.

——— (2012) India: Structural Roadblocks to Academic Reform. In *Confronting Challenges to the Liberal Arts Curriculum: Perspectives of Developing and Transitional Countries*, ed. P. McGill Peterson. New York: Routledge.

Altbach, P.G. (1971) Higher Education in India. In *Higher Education in Nine Countries*, ed. B.B. Burn. New York: McGraw Hill Book Company.

——— (2012) Afterword: India's Higher Education Challenges. In *A Half Century of Indian Higher Education: Essays by Philip G. Altbach*, ed. P. Agarwal. New Delhi: SAGE Publications.

Beteille, A. (2010) *Universities at the Crossroads*. New Delhi: Oxford University Press.

Coffman, J. (1997) Private higher education in Pakistan: The need for order. *International Higher Education*, 9, Fall.

Coleman, H. (2010) *Teaching and Learning in Pakistan: The Role of Language in Education*. British Council.

Gilani, S.Z. (2006) Problems of leadership and reform in Pakistan. *International Higher Education*, 42, Winter.

——— (2012) Pakistan: Liberal Education in Context, Policy, and Practice. In *Confronting Challenges to the Liberal Arts Curriculum: Perspectives of Developing and Transitional Countries*, ed. P. McGill Peterson. New York: Routledge.

Guha, R. (2010) *Makers of Modern India*. New Delhi: Penguin/Viking.

Hayward, F.M. (2009) Higher education transformation in Pakistan: Political and economic instability. *International Higher Education*, 54, Winter.

Hoodbhoy, P. (2008) Pakistan's universities—Problems and solutions. *Dawn*, 2 and 9 January.

——— (2009) How greed ruins academia. *International Higher Education*, 56, Summer.

Isani, U.A and Virk, M.L. (2003) *Higher Education in Pakistan: Historical and Futurity Perspective*. Islamabad: National Book Foundation.

Jayaram, N. (2006) National Perspectives: India. In *International Handbook of Higher Education*, eds. J.J.F. Forest and P.G. Altbach. Dordrecht: Springer.

Khan, A.A. (2011a) Pakistan: Universities budget slashed again. *University World News*, 177, 26 June.

——— (2011b) Pakistan: Central role for universities in new policy. *University World News*, 191, 30 September.

Kolhatkar, M.R. (2012) *Survey of Higher Education (1947–2007)*. New Delhi: Concept Publishing.

Perkin, H. (2006) History of Universities. In *International Handbook of Higher Education*, eds J.J.F. Forest and P.G. Altbach. Dordrecht: Springer, 186–87.

Salmi, J. and Saroyan, A. (2007) League tables as policy instruments. *International Higher Education*, 47, Spring.

Singh, A. (2004) *The Challenge of Education*. Hyderabad: ICFAI University Press.

Subbarao, E.C. (2008) *An Eye for Excellence: Fifty Innovative Years of IIT Kanpur*. New Delhi: HarperCollins.

World Bank (2011) *Affiliated Colleges in South Asia: Is Quality Expansion Possible?* South Asia Human Development Sector, World Bank, Report No. 47.

12

'Dominion' Legacies: The Australian Experience

Julia Horne and Geoffrey Sherington

By the Great War of 1914, Australia had six public university foundations: one in the metropolitan capital of each state, each publicly funded by state governments as institutions for local civic development. In 2012, there were 39 universities, almost all of them public in foundation, but now with diverse funding streams: they receive Commonwealth of Australia grants—both 'base' and 'competitive'—as well as an increasing range of private funds. Their operational missions have also been radically expanded to include goals of national endeavour and international enterprise in the education of both Australians and foreign nationals, as well as in research and 'innovation', plus the furthering of knowledge itself. Higher education has, moreover, been broadened, along with state control.

This chapter examines the transformative historical development of Australian universities over the course of the twentieth century and into the twenty-first.

Missions and Purposes of the 'Australian University'

The public purposes of Australia's universities were first formed in the nineteenth century as part of the transplantation of British settlers, values and culture of Empire (Sherington and Horne, 2010). When the first two Australian universities were established in the mid-nineteenth century, they cemented three central beliefs about the nature of public institutions:

- that public universities should not be beholden to any particular set of religious beliefs
- that access was to be based on academic merit alone (rather than on pedigree), reinforced through public examinations and enabled through a generous system of scholarships and bursaries
- that universities were part of a rising pride in colonial and national public enterprise, where support came not only from the state, but also from public-spirited citizens.

Such principles came out of debates about university reform in Britain and North America, which emerged in the 1830s and continued into the 1860s. Both the University of Sydney (1850) and the University of Melbourne (1853) were some of the very first universities to be established on these combined principles (Horne and Sherington, 2010; Selleck, 2003). By the time the Universities' Bureau of the British Empire (later the Association of Commonwealth Universities) was established in 1913, these beliefs had become the norm for most universities in the British Empire; and the challenge had now become how to extend and apply these principles equitably, and how to accommodate changing social patterns and expectations.

During the first half of the twentieth century, these foundational beliefs were consolidated into a common pattern of the 'Australian university'. During this period, much effort was expended to ensure broader social access to universities. Australia's universities were designed to produce a meritocratic elite, many of whom would themselves become future university teachers, creating cross-generational attachments to academic ideals. And if teaching was often local in purpose, research was increasingly imperial in focus and influence, creating networks among the academic elite of the Empire.

After the Second World War, university research was constructed more through international networks, which went beyond the older attachments to Britain and Empire. Diversity within the emerging system of higher education in Australia emerged with the foundation of new universities and colleges.

By the beginnings of the twenty-first century, Australia was moving towards an era of mass higher education in a globalised world, involving both Australian-born and international students. These changes challenged some of the earlier foundations of universities as public institutions, but also consolidated global links of research and academic performance.

The Meritocratic Ideal and Widening Social Access

From their founding in the mid- to late nineteenth century, the first Australian universities played an important part in extending an 'educational franchise' of wider social access to not only the established middle classes but also to others, including women and those who were the first of their family to attend university. As such, universities were crucial to establishing Australia as a meritocratic society within a broader national imagining of egalitarianism.

By 1912, the meritocratic ideal in Australian universities was about to be expanded, with the growth and reform of public education systems in the wake of Federation. In the second half of the nineteenth century, academic merit, demonstrated through the public exams conducted by universities, had begun to underpin most public institutions. Yet the strong belief in Australia's egalitarianism meant a constant questioning of merit as an equitable means of selection. Academic merit on the basis of examination continued to be the sole means of admission to university, yet university leaders realised from the beginning the problems of social access. To remove class or religion as barriers to university helped, but inequities arose if a child's socio-economic circumstances prevented access to the sort of schooling that equipped a student to pass the matriculation examination. All Australian universities at this time devised various strategies to improve social access with varying success. The beginning of the twentieth century saw increased interest in tackling this problem, and a desire to expand successful schemes and to undertake new commitments.

In 1911 the University of Queensland admitted its first students, followed a year later by the University of Western Australia. Both universities were established in states that together were more than half the size of Australia, but with less than a quarter of the population. Some queried whether universities could deliver the sort of practical instruction and scientific knowledge necessary to develop the increasingly prosperous primary industries. But since the economies of both were buoyant (a consequence of the 1890s gold rush in Western Australia and Queensland's strong growth in primary production), state governments began to listen to 'imaginative laymen' and women who were putting their minds to creating a local university (Alexander, 1963: 6).

University extension programmes had recently been established in both states, which helped the move towards a public university. Extension lectures drew on the expertise of university professors in Adelaide, Sydney, Melbourne, and England, attracting up to 1,500 people on occasion in Perth and several hundred in Brisbane. Rural outreach was also to be part of the programme, with plans to reach all corners of these enormous states—though in practice, lectures were only well attended in a few large regional centres. As the universities of Sydney, Melbourne and Adelaide had discovered, there was no easy solution to the problem of how to support state-wide access to the offerings of a city-based university.

The significance of the university extension movement to the establishment of these two universities was to show university expertise contributing broadly to the intellectual and cultural well-being of society, by engaging the interest of adults who had never contemplated university study. The programmes in both Western Australia and Queensland were, on the whole, successful and helped to establish a small community of interested people who agitated government to establish a university in each respective state. In Queensland, a university congress was held in 1906 to bring together a variety of groups, including trade unions and professional associations, to debate the type of university best suited to Queensland, and to draft a bill to that end. And in Western Australia, in 1909 the government appointed a Royal Commission to enquire into a university for Western Australia (Alexander, 1963: 20; Thomis, 1985: 10–14).

Through these discussions and debates it was agreed that the Oxbridge model was unsuitable for settler states like Queensland and Western Australia, where the population was more dispersed and rural. John Winthrop Hackett, a newspaper proprietor and parliamentarian who became the first chancellor of the University of Western Australia (and its first major benefactor), chaired the Western Australian Royal Commission. He commented pointedly:

> I believe that the influence of Oxford, Cambridge, and Dublin has been largely mischievous as far as the new countries of the empire are concerned. Those Universities devote themselves in a paramount measure to

the study of the dead languages or to the pursuit of what is called the higher mathematics.

(Alexander, 1963: 20)

Research into university models was undertaken with the aim of determining what worked, why and their suitability for local Australian conditions. There was particular interest in the implementation by German universities of a modern curriculum that placed emphasis on applying knowledge to everyday needs. And there was great admiration for American state and land grant universities as models of widened social access. In the end, though, both Queensland and Western Australia adopted a general liberal education curriculum along with professional training including the disciplines of agriculture and engineering.

While these new foundations shared an educational and curriculum heritage with Australian universities founded in the nineteenth century, the idea of the 'people's university' was also pursued, especially by the Labor Party, which in both states promoted the concept of a modern university. Indeed, both universities became an important focus of the efforts of the labour movement in Australia to ensure wider educational opportunities and social access.

On the question of social access—how to give access to a socially diverse range of students—each state took a slightly different approach. Free university education, one of the attractions of mid-western American universities, was seriously considered, but only adopted by the University of Western Australia. However, the high cost of state government support meant that until 1960, when the university introduced tuition fees, the university often revisited its decision, because fees were one of the few ways in which Australian universities could raise revenue. For many years, desperate for funds, the university got around the problem by adopting a surcharge for administrative purposes. Not technically tuition fees, their introduction did mean that the university was not really free (Alexander, 1963: 107–13, 346–49).

Queensland University decided against universal free education and, instead, followed the lead of other Australian universities, such as Sydney, by offering scholarships and bursaries, which provided free education and, in many cases, also a living allowance. For Queensland, the question of social access turned on the issue of matriculation. Serious consideration was given to having schools determine who went to university, thus removing the need for a school to teach to a particular examination curriculum. The Labor Party, in particular, believed that this measure would guard against grammar schools being the only conduit to university, and would help to broaden access throughout Queensland.

But in the end, a matriculation examination was adopted as the means of admission in order to ensure, supporters argued, the academic reputation of the new university. Some also argued to broaden the exam, so that languages, in particular Latin and Greek, were not compulsory matriculation subjects, but this attempt also failed (though the principle was adopted by the University of Western Australia at its foundation) (*Calendar*, 1914; Thomis, 1985: 37–43). As in the older universities, academic merit as determined by a liberal education in the classics became the norm, and questions of social access were addressed by other solutions.

Elsewhere in Australia, universities were also seeking reforms to social access. Most were strongly influenced by this new mood for universal education, yet continued to retain academic merit as the prime determiner of who was to be admitted to university. The older universities had long been concerned about how to engage a broader public. Most had university extension courses in place, which helped to consolidate the public importance of universities to their communities, especially in country regions. While some university students matriculated through university extension programmes, the prime purpose of these programmes was to reach a public interested in general intellectual engagement.

To extend educational franchise to a broader cross section of the public, the universities also offered evening lectures to matriculated students who might not otherwise be able to afford university. Under this option they could undertake university study and still be self-supporting. In the first half of the twentieth century, evening students were a sizeable minority, indicating the success of a programme that increased social access at least from the metropolis. At Sydney, evening students averaged 20 per cent of the total enrolment, with anecdotal evidence that many evening students were the first members of their families to attend university (Turney et al., 1991: 644). At Melbourne, it was noted that the university was beginning to be used by people 'who had not previously found it accessible' (Selleck, 2003: 498–99).

Matriculation requirements were also debated, especially whether Latin should be compulsory. Some argued—as had occurred in Queensland and Western Australia—that this worked against increasing access to universities. But in the first decades of the twentieth century, few professors were prepared to relinquish Latin as necessary to a proper education, arguing its superior value as preparation for university study, both in mental training and in the human cultural values transmitted through the study of the ancient world. Not until the Second World War, when it became clear that a sizeable number of high school students no longer studied Latin, did universities begin to drop it as a compulsory matriculation subject, with Sydney doing so in 1941, Queensland in 1943, and Melbourne in 1950 (Barcan, 1993: 38, 41).

Though no university except for Western Australia adopted free tuition, the older universities did examine how to extend university education more broadly. The University of Sydney was motivated by a determined head of the Department of Public Instruction, Peter Board, a Sydney graduate, who had been inspired by his inspection tour of American state schools and universities and the idea of the 'people's university'. His report had greatly influenced Western Australia's adoption of free tuition (Crane and Walker, 1957: 145–62). For Sydney, the solution came from the state government in 1912, which vastly increased expenditure on university education by offering an extra 200 university scholarships to cover all university fees and, additionally, instituted another scholarship system for teacher training that covered university fees and provided a living allowance indexed according to whether students lived in rural regions.

The primary aim of the 1912 scheme was teacher training. To accept a teachers' scholarship required a commitment (or 'bond', as it became known) to teach for a set number of years. Based on the notion that academically able students came from all social ranks, the scheme—with promising career prospects—was particularly attractive to those from modest backgrounds, especially the children of lower-paid white-collar or skilled blue-collar workers. It drew students from country and metropolitan high schools and low-fee Catholic schools (Sherington, 1995: 96–100). In Victoria, in the first decade of the twentieth century, the state education system underwent significant transformation and expansion, which created not only a demand for teachers (and teacher training) but also many more state schools to educate students to matriculation. Between 1904 and 1912, arts enrolments at Melbourne increased threefold largely as a consequence (Selleck, 2003: 498).

These new schemes were in addition to scholarship and bursary schemes that Australian universities had offered since their foundation, but now succeeded in extending free education to significantly more students. At Sydney, in 1901 only about a tenth of the total student enrolment received assistance, though this was more than Melbourne, where it has been estimated that only one in 45 students received scholarships (Selleck, 2003: 498–99). But by 1920, more than 42 per cent of Sydney University's total enrolment received free university education, significantly more in the faculties of Arts and Science, where teachers' college scholarship students were largely concentrated. By 1930, at least 46 per cent of all Sydney University students did not pay fees, and another 22 per cent attended evening lectures.

This new educational franchise also extended to women. In 1874 the founders of Adelaide University had legislated that women would be admitted to degrees on the same basis as men—including to degrees and classes generally perceived as male domains. But the Colonial Office refused to grant royal assent until 1881. Nonetheless, when the university opened in 1876, women were encouraged to attend university classes, and the university's support for women's matriculation helped to kindle the growth of girls' secondary schools in South Australia (Mackinnon, 1986: 22–26). Women were admitted on the same basis as men to the University of Sydney in 1881, and to Melbourne in the same year (though with restrictions that were removed by the twentieth century).

Expanded state education systems and increased numbers of scholarships brought more women into university. In 1911, some 21.9 per cent of students at Australian universities were women, increasing to 29.3 per cent in 1921, figures bolstered by larger enrolments of women at Adelaide University (Booth and Hiau, 2011: 257). At Melbourne, by the 1920s women were about 20 per cent of the enrolment, increasing from almost nothing in 1900 (Selleck, 2003: 588–89). At Sydney, the number of female undergraduates went from 13 per cent in 1910 to over 20 per cent in 1920, but in the faculties of Arts, Science, and Architecture, after the increase of the number of scholarships in 1912, women undergraduates were almost 50 per cent of total enrolments, a figure that remained relatively steady until the Second World War (Horne and Sherington, 2012: 19; Turney et al., 1991: 643).

It was clear that public examinations were instrumental in increasing educational opportunities for women, who took the opportunity to come to university in order to increase their career options (Dawson, 1965: 22, 25). There is also evidence that from the twentieth century the social backgrounds of university women varied considerably, and that university education was not just sought after by the wealthy middle classes. The 'ideology of femininity' was changing to include higher education and the pursuit of a profession, though the growing conservatism of the ideology of motherhood in the 1930s meant that having won the right to university education on the basis of merit, this increasing number of women students would face the realities of their gender upon graduation (Mackinnon, 1986: 202).

In his transatlantic study of merit and worth, the historian of education Sheldon Rothblatt argues that over the course of the twentieth century, liberal democracies have been faced with what he calls 'education's abiding moral dilemma'. In the twentieth century, merit became the marker of a student's capability, replacing the previous emphasis on worth, which based entry on moral character generally associated with the outlooks and perspectives of the upper classes. But with increasing demands for higher education, merit determined by examinations has its own limitations in selecting students who will thrive at university (Rothblatt, 2007: 49–62).

In institutional terms, merit had its strong supporters. Australian universities had small student populations until the Second World War (after which the intake doubled), educating only a small academic meritocracy, who gained entry through end-of-school examinations that the universities also controlled. Most students came from either elite corporate schools or church schools, or from the public high schools which also selected their students by academic tests and examinations. And from this small meritocracy came a small group of research students and later academic staff, some of whose careers would be shaped by the networks of research within the Empire that had been created since the late nineteenth century (Pietsch, 2009).

Post-war Expansion

When the Australian colonies federated in 1901—to create the Commonwealth of Australia—universities remained the responsibility of the newly created states. During the First World War, the new Commonwealth government approached universities to recruit people with relevant expertise, including medical undergraduates in the senior years of their course. Immediately after the war, the universities developed a scheme supported by the Commonwealth government to offer, on a modest scale, university education to returned soldiers. These new channels of communication meant that from time to time universities received small Commonwealth grants for fledgling projects.

But it was not until the last part of the Second World War, when war moved to the Pacific and Australia was directly under threat from Japan, that the Commonwealth government approached universities to assist with national issues, not simply the supply of troops. In 1943, the Commonwealth government established the Universities Commission 'to advise the Government on questions of man power in so far as they relate to the training of University students' (University of Sydney Archives, 1944–48). The commission initially funded places in universities for 'the vital necessity of a continuing flow of properly trained graduates' that would contribute to the war effort and the development of the nation. Then after the war, in order to deal with huge numbers—the tens of thousands of returned servicemen and women re-entering civilian lives—the Commonwealth government and universities devised a scheme that offered university education to returned soldiers.

The Commonwealth Reconstruction Training Scheme (CRTS) was developed towards the end of the war, initially to assist returned soldiers whose studies had been interrupted by war service and those who had matriculated before enlistment. But very soon, the programme became far more ambitious; it extended the possibility of assistance to all who had served for at least six months, regardless of whether they had ever passed university matriculation examinations. Universities scrutinised the admissions process and only awarded 'war matriculation status' to those who met certain criteria, including judgements made by the military about their suitability for professional or vocational training (Connell et al., 1995: 32–35; Gallagher, 2003).

The scheme ultimately brought into universities many thousands who may not otherwise have crossed the threshold. In terms of numbers, in 1948 the Australian government funded 10,182 university degree students under the CRTS, as well as 1,694 who held Commonwealth Scholarships (see below), of which almost half were at the University of Sydney. This was in addition to the free places that state governments and universities provided. At Sydney in 1948 about 60 per cent of students were not paying fees, many of whom were also receiving additional assistance. Half of these were CRTS students (Commonwealth Bureau, 1951: 240).

The CRTS experiment revealed how principles of academic merit could be adapted to assess a student's potential through means other than the matriculation examination. The CRTS was dismantled in the early 1950s, and passing the matriculation examination again became the only way of entering university. The unshakeable belief was that the fairest way of identifying academic merit was by examination. Not until the 1970s did Australian universities begin to question the examination as the only true way to determine who should undertake university study. Then, universities began to introduce 'special admissions' to recognise that academic merit did not always identify talent, especially when a student's schooling was disrupted because of social disadvantage or prejudice. This change finally, and very slowly, began to address the inequities of merit-based entry for certain social groups, including Australian Aborigines (Horne and Sherington, 2012: 82–90).

In the early post-war years, the ideal of merit was reinforced through new national scholarships, which also recognised issues of social access. In 1951, following national scholarships for science students during the Second World War, the Commonwealth government introduced an Australian Commonwealth Scholarship Scheme, which opened the universities to thousands more school-leavers (Horne and Sherington, 2012: 77–79). In 1953 alone, almost 8,000 students had Commonwealth Scholarships in addition to the various university and state government schemes already in place. The Commonwealth Scholarship Scheme partially embodied the principle of social inclusion, to ensure that 'able students would not be prevented from considering University courses because of their financial position' (Commonwealth Bureau, 1955: 410). The scholarships were two-pronged: those who won them on the basis of academic merit would have their fees paid; but, in addition, a scaled allowance was available on the basis of a means test, the final amount determined by a family's financial means and whether students lived in, or had to move to, Sydney in order to attend their course. The impact of the schemes was colossal. In 1973, on the eve of the introduction of the abolition of university tuition fees, almost 70 per cent of University of Sydney students were already receiving free tuition (Horne and Sherington, 2012: 79).

Eventually the major post-war changes extending access came from expanding the system in various ways. By 1950 there were eight universities and two university colleges. The Australian National University (ANU) was established in 1946, the seventh university in Australia, but the first to be established by the Commonwealth government convinced of how university research and expertise would contribute to post-war national development (Foster and Varghese, 1996: 1–48). ANU was, primarily, a research institution (with postgraduate research students). Its establishment did not directly contribute to the goals of widening social participation in universities, but it did build upon the ideal of academic merit to consolidate research, developing postgraduate degrees and centres of international excellence in medicine, the sciences, social sciences, and humanities. It thus created avenues for international connections in research that went beyond the older networks of Empire.

Regional and Rural Expansion

Other ways to extend access had been identified even before the Second World War. In Australia, the idea of affiliated university colleges, where colleges instructed students as part of a degree programme administered by a governing university, had been rejected in the mid-nineteenth century in favour of the Scottish model of a university having responsibility for both teaching and examination. This left only a few residential colleges attached to the metropolitan universities supposedly catering for students from the country, but in reality often enrolling only those who could afford the accommodation fees. By the 1930s, the idea of the 'college' was being revisited and adapted, as a way of bringing established universities to where they were needed in 'regional' Australia.

Canberra University College (1930) was set up in the Australian Capital Territory with the aim of servicing the educational needs of the new national capital, delivering courses devised by the University of Melbourne that could eventually lead to a University of Melbourne degree (Foster and Varghese, 1996: 8). Soon, the college established the School of Diplomatic Studies, which was seen to serve the needs of a nation beginning to seek an independent foreign policy.

The New England University College (1938), while borrowing from the Canberra model, was established by the University of Sydney for different reasons. The original push was from the local state parliamentary member of a largely pastoral district over 500 km from Sydney, who wanted an appropriate institution to serve the higher educational needs of northern New South Wales. Unable to commit its own scarce funding, the university required support from government and local philanthropists for such an ambitious project. The opportunity to create a college in regional New South Wales helped to focus the attention of Sydney's professors, who faced the continuing dilemma of how a state university located in a city could truly serve the needs of the people of New South Wales. Correspondence courses were not especially favoured by professors, who believed in the 'lecture' as a dependable form of pedagogy

(Turney et al., 1991: 615–19). But an affiliated college, the academic programme of which could be tightly controlled by the university's professors, might provide exciting opportunities for university extension and widening social access. The ultimate aim was that the university college, under such guidance, would eventually become an independent university: in 1954 the University of New England was formally established.

It was a model that came to be favoured by the New South Wales government—though not, interestingly, by other states. In 1951, Newcastle University College was established north of Sydney, and in 1962 Wollongong University College was established south of Sydney. Both colleges were governed by a new post-war university, the New South Wales University of Technology (later renamed the University of New South Wales). This new university was established in 1949 by a Labor Government to address the national demands for training and knowledge in science and technology. It also hoped to extend educational franchise to working men and women (though the engineering and technology focus of its academic programme meant mainly men). Evening classes were an important characteristic of the degree programme, which also came to be supported by industry scholarships, both of which helped to offset the cost of a university education. The university's supervision of courses in the highly industrialised regions of Newcastle and Wollongong (and also at the old School of Mines in Broken Hill in far-western New South Wales) meant that by the 1960s, the state of New South Wales had finally achieved a reasonable bricks and mortar reach into country regions—in the north, the south, and the west—following Tasmania, a significantly smaller state, which was the only other state to have done so (O'Farrell, 1999: 16–18, 47, 64, 78).

Turning Point: The 'Murray Report' (1957)

In 1957, the Australian Prime Minister, Robert Menzies, presented to parliament the *Report of the Committee on Australian Universities*. The 'Murray Report', as it was affectionately called, was named after the chair of the committee, Sir Keith Murray, the English chairman of the UK University Grants Committee, who was invited by the Commonwealth government to report on the state of Australian universities.

The Murray Committee established a few basic principles, which drew upon both nineteenth-century foundations of Empire as well as expectations of the mid-twentieth century: universities must educate enough graduates to expand post-war endeavours, must have liberal education as the basis of a university degree, must be the crucible for national research and, more generally, must develop and protect the national intellect. To do this, universities needed money, both large injections of capital funds as well as sustained funding, so that they could plan for the future. The immediate challenge was to accommodate the children of the post-war baby boom, which the Committee anticipated would produce a 120 per cent growth in students in the 1960s.

Menzies presented a plan of action that largely followed the recommendations of the Murray Report. Emergency funding was given to universities to address immediate shortfalls in equipment, buildings, facilities, and staff, and the states were encouraged to establish new universities (Marginson, 2000: 7–9; Tompkins, 1958: 361–64; Williams, 1977: 122, 126–28).

The Murray Report laid the foundations for expansion under national guidance and funding. Up until 1974, when the Commonwealth government took over full responsibility for funding higher education, there were nine new universities in Australia, eight of which were completely new institutions and one, the University of Newcastle, which had evolved from its status as a university college. Two new university colleges were also established, one in New South Wales and the other in Queensland.

Most of the new universities were located in the expanding suburbs of each of the state capitals (except Hobart)—with Melbourne gaining Monash University (1958) and La Trobe University (1964); Sydney gaining Macquarie University (1964); Adelaide, Flinders University (1966); Brisbane, Griffith University (1971); and Perth, Murdoch University (1973). But Deakin University (1974) was located in Geelong, a large regional centre of Victoria; Wollongong University College (1962) was in the coalmining port of Wollongong in New South Wales; University College of Central Queensland (1969), initially established as the Queensland Institute of Technology (Capricornia) in 1967, was in northern Queensland; and James Cook University of North Queensland (1970) in Queensland's far north. Rural outreach in the form of local universities was gaining a firmer foothold.

Older universities were upgraded with new buildings. The University of Tasmania received substantial building funds and moved to an entirely new campus with purpose-built buildings (Davis, 1990: 160–66).

Sydney University bought up most of a neighbouring working-class suburb, which it then tore down to construct new buildings for expanded courses in engineering. In little more than a decade, the architecture of universities was transformed from a combination of Gothic, Arts and Crafts, and Mediterranean styles, to the Modernist and Brutalist styles of a brave new world (Connell et al., 1995: 61–64; Thomis, 1985: 263–69). These new and expanded universities accommodated a huge increase in students, from about 20,000 in 1953 to over 133,000 in 1973.

These changes continued to help broaden social access to universities. A 1959–60 study on the occupations of fathers of full-time male university entrants indicated that the majority of university students were from working-class (26 per cent) or lower-middle-class backgrounds (29 per cent), though sons of professionals were still the largest minority (33 per cent). Unfortunately, the study did not include the backgrounds of part-time or external students, even though they were a significant proportion of the total student population and were enrolled under schemes designed to extend educational franchise to a broader population. But broadening social access is not the same as introducing mass education. The same study found that participation rates of all similarly aged males with working-class backgrounds were significantly lower than those from other backgrounds—though, again, these were calculated using only figures for full-time students (Karmel, 1965: 70–71).

In 1974, the new Labor Commonwealth Government abolished fees for all university students and introduced an assistance scheme awarded on need as part of a policy to provide greater participation by Australians to universities, especially from the working classes. But its real effect was to increase the overall number of women. Whereas in 1973, about a third of university students were women, in 1987, for the first time in Australia, women slightly outnumbered men (Commonwealth Bureau, 1974: 664; Commonwealth Bureau, 1992: 318).

Complementing the introduction of free tertiary education, the Labor Commonwealth Government brought in the Tertiary Education Assistance Scheme (TEAS), providing a universal but means-tested support to students, so replacing the Commonwealth Scholarship scheme awarded on the basis of merit. But free education and TEAS did little to change the social profile of Australian students, even though the proportion of students on TEAS support increased with more students living away from home (Irving et al., 1995: 137–38).

The Dawkins Revolution of 1988–90: Origins and Impact

Australian universities have had a long history of extending educational franchise across boundaries, and for generations have admitted a significant proportion of students whose parents or grandparents did not go to university. They have also grown significantly in size—from over 30,000 students in the late 1940s to more than 420,000 in 1988. Yet the proportion of young Australians going to university remained comparably low, with only 15.5 per cent of all 19-year-olds enrolled at university in 1985.

This situation quickly changed when, in 1989–90, colleges of advanced education (CAEs), which had been created mainly during the 1960s and 1970s, joined the university system, either as new faculties in existing universities or combined with other CAEs to form new universities. This was part of the Australian government's strategy to create a unified system of mass higher education, with over 14 new universities being created in the late 1980s and early 1990s, led by the creative minister of the day, the Hon John Dawkins.

In some respects, 1989–90 can be seen as the time when Australian universities began a new era in imagining themselves as institutions of mass education. Even so, participation rates have not reached the levels traditionally associated with mass education, only jumping from 15.5 per cent of all 19-year-olds in 1985 to 25.8 per cent in 1997—and that largely because a number of existing institutions were recreated as universities (Everingham, 1999: 41). Consolidation of higher education did not lead necessarily to expanded opportunities. If anything, the educational franchise was more extended during the 1960s to mid-1970s, when public expenditure on all education jumped from 2.1 per cent of GDP to 5.8 per cent, while enrolments in higher education increased six-fold (Williams, 1996: 139).

Soon the educational franchise was turned more into an educational commodity. In 1989, a Labor Commonwealth Government established the Higher Education Contributions Scheme (HECS), which essentially introduced university fees for all students, although under a type of co-payment system that had governments subsidise the greater proportion. Under this system, overseas students were charged full fees, and began to become a market of their own, which Australian universities still compete for among themselves and internationally.

The reforms were seen as necessary to fund a planned increase in the size of universities. But they also challenged well-established principles. Australian universities had long worked out ways to subsidise the cost of fees and living expenses for a good proportion of students. But HECS required all students to pay fees, though under an otherwise generous scheme of what amounted to interest-free loans to cover the smaller proportion of the actual cost of university fees. Universities could provide scholarships, and many do, but unlike in the past, they are available to only a tiny proportion of the total student population. The idea of a 'free education' upon which many universities were founded—where a reasonable proportion of the student enrolment received assistance to cover fees and living expenses, or where no one paid fees (as was the case at the University of Western Australia, and from 1974, at all Australian universities)—had finally ended.

Contemporary Developments

More recent policy changes have directed the sector towards new objectives.

From 1996, a Commonwealth Liberal Government changed HECS to allow universities to charge full upfront fees to Australian students. Again, this challenged first principles, as from the foundation of Australia's first university, student fees had been subsidised, and full fees (to cover the actual costs of educating a student) had not been charged—not even to private overseas students who began to come to Australia in large numbers from the 1950s (Megarrity, 2007: 88–105).

But it also challenged another foundation principle, that of meritocracy itself, because students who had missed out on HECS-funded places could now pay full fees and enter a course at five marks lower than the advertised entry score. There was much debate in universities around the nation about this disruption to long-held beliefs in the principles of free education and merit-based entry, but eventually financial necessity prevailed and many public universities began to allow a certain proportion of students into their courses who were prepared to pay full fees.

In 2005, the government granted universities the capacity to set fees for all HECS-funded places at up to 25 per cent above the HECS charge, a move designed to cover the shortfalls in public funding as the university sector grew. After more debate, many public universities began to charge the full 25 per cent. In less than a generation, Australian governments of both persuasions had changed fundamental principles of the provision of university education to Australians.

Since 2007, Labor Commonwealth governments have reversed the decision to enable universities to charge full fees to Australian students, and so what many saw as an inequitable provision that allowed the wealthy to enter courses with a lower mark has now increased the burden on universities to make up this shortfall with full-fee-paying international students.

Political focus is now on social inclusion, with funding incentives for universities that meet certain quotas. The 2008 'Bradley Review' strongly advocated a major shift towards social inclusion—by lifting the cap on enrolments, while linking funding directly to increasing student loads. In many ways, this reform will be the biggest challenge yet to the principle of meritocracy, as Australian universities finally adapt to their future as institutions of mass education, and attempt to balance access with quality.

From Local to Global

Almost all universities in Australia were established to serve local needs, initially those of the colonies and states that founded them and then, in the twentieth century, more were established to fulfil political commitments to support the regions. A notable feature of Australian universities until the 1990s was that students largely went to local universities. Even now, Australians are more likely to attend their local university than travel interstate, though increasingly many also look to undergraduate courses nationally and internationally.

Over the past two decades, the local has been subjected to the global. A growing emphasis on global profiles has been associated with recruitment of international students as well as a search for ways to demonstrate the global significance of academic activities, particularly in the area of research performance. This has helped to reshape the purpose of Australia's universities—from earlier ideas of secular and nation-building foundations towards images of corporate enterprises with both public and private aims. In the process, the older ideal of merit has been partly supplanted by notions of 'rank'.

The ranking of students emerged in the late 1970s and 1980s alongside moves towards mass higher education and the need to find new ways of admission, while retaining central examinations as a test of merit. The answer was to replace older forms of matriculation with a process of ranking each student's performance with that of their peers at state annual school-leaving exams, while also inserting a weighting towards subjects taken, with mathematics being given a preference for apparent difficulty.

This domestic form of ranking has now been supplemented by global ranking of university research performance. In some ways, research ranking has also arisen from the slow emergence of mass higher education. As the first national research institution, the ANU in the post-war period created the basis for individual research scholars to establish their reputations, particularly in their academic fields in Britain and North America but also in Europe and elsewhere. The ANU was free to create an institution devoted to bringing international research to Australian shores. Its founders saw this as an opportunity to bring back from foreign shores Australian scholars with international reputations, initially looking to the nuclear scientist Mark Oliphant, who accepted the invitation to lead one of the research schools, and the Nobel Prize winner Howard Florey and historian W.K. Hancock who, after significant early interest, did not. (Hancock was later to return in the 1950s.) Then began the process of searching for academic staff who had proved themselves as international researchers (Foster and Varghese, 1996: 20–27, 51–59).

The ANU was a model that other universities soon hoped to emulate. Some saw research as a demonstration of both academic merit and national service. In 1944, the English-born Eric Ashby, Botanist at the University of Sydney, called universities the 'trustees of Australian intellectual life' even those that were so run down as to barely accommodate staff and students (Forsyth, 2010: 45). Before the Second World War, the state-based universities had only fledgling research programmes, the paucity of which had been repeatedly noted since the 1920s by various American observers sent out by American philanthropic organisations, such as the Carnegie Corporation of New York and the Rockefeller Foundation. Both organisations funded research at Australian universities—the Rockefeller Foundation's funding of anthropology in the 1920s and 1930s helped to establish anthropology as a discipline in Australian universities and created a whole generation of researchers of Aboriginal culture and society—partly out of despair that a strong, liberal-democratic, and English-speaking Pacific nation had no national research agenda

(Conant, 2010; Horne and Sherington, 2012: 222). Yet the fact that the ANU in the late 1940s could attract such high-calibre Australian researchers indicated that Australian universities had for several generations prepared graduates to a standard that made them desirable postgraduates in renowned research laboratories and schools of humanities and social sciences.

Australian graduates who won research scholarships generally took advantage of British Empire networks, went to England (usually Cambridge or Oxford), and then on to other universities within the Empire, creating what has been termed a 'commonwealth of learning' (Pietsch, 2009). From the 1930s, Rockefeller fellowships assisted this exodus, though added American research institutions as a destination for postgraduates. In other words, though Australian universities were bound to serve local civic needs, they were also part of an international scholarly community, shaped largely, though not exclusively, by the contours of empire.

Australia's universities were thus part of international—if not global—research networks, well before the national government intervened. The Second World War provided the example of research as national enterprise, but earlier views still lingered. As late as 1957, the Murray Committee recognised research as an increasingly important aim of universities, but suggested that university research arose from individual, rather than institutional, effort (Forsyth, 2010). But from the 1960s, as the Commonwealth government became the major source of university funding, universities were transformed into sites of significant national research. The creation of the 'Unified National System' of universities and former CAEs in 1989 indirectly reinforced the moves towards research ranking. The older universities soon formed an association along with the ANU to become a 'Group of Eight', emphasising that they were 'research intensive' enterprises, which shared similar aims with other prominent international institutions. The creation of international tables of research performance was thus welcomed as a way to demonstrate that at least some of Australia's universities could achieve global recognition.

New global influences are also seen in the changing purpose of educating international students. From the 1950s, Australia had extended an educational franchise to emerging democracies of the British Commonwealth through such agreements as the Colombo Plan. Many Australian universities developed a new relationship with South and South-East Asia, educating the future civic and government leaders of the region, including academics and researchers. As new nations emerged from the tatters of colonialism in the 1950s and 1960s, Australia opened its universities to students from this wider region, not only through Colombo Plan scholarships but also Australian government schemes that encouraged private overseas students to study in Australia under the same matriculation conditions as Australians, including access to subsidised tuition fees and scholarships. Such arrangements were designed to foster international co-operation in the region. Now international students form an important part of a global market that sustains Australian universities. And rankings based on research became a way to position Australia's universities in this market and reassure students and their families about the quality of Australian higher education.

Perspectives

Research rankings and the emergence of a global market of students have thus helped to transform ideas of the Australian university as both a national and international institution. Even governments now seek to encourage choice rather than merit as the foundation of higher education. In April 2012 the Australian government announced the launch of a new website known as 'My University' (complementing an earlier site known as 'My School'). All of Australia's universities (along with more than 140 other higher education providers) were now ranked according to such attributes as graduate employment, student–staff ratios, attrition (or failure) rates of students, and proportion of international students. Even so, some future students still have more trust in social media as a way of choosing the best university (*Sydney Morning Herald*, 4 April 2012).

Those attached to the foundation principles of secularism, merit, and nation-building often see such values as intrinsic, if not permanent, features of the idea of the Australian university. However, notions of the market and institutional ranking, first in research and now in other areas, suggest a less permanent, more flexible university world. The twenty-first-century Australian higher education sector constitutes an Australian achievement in modernisation within a globalised environment.

Debate continues, however, around aspects of this national 'achievement'. For example, the recent 'Baird Report' (2010) has highlighted the dependence of Australian universities on fee-paying overseas students:

governments have progressively substituted government funding with such student fees. More broadly, Australian students themselves point to the relatively high cost of student contributions to their education. The research-intensive universities have, moreover, energetically lobbied through their 'Group of Eight' for a more differentiated funding formula that matches resources to mission. In addition, access has grown significantly, and in a commendable way. But government funding has not followed the increased student loads; staff–student ratios have worsened; and issues of quality outcomes are being raised. Finally, many educationalists, academic union leaders, and public policy advocates have come to express concern for academic autonomy in what has become an ever more government-regulated 'industry'.

Australia has created a relatively successful mass higher educational sector to meet global challenges. It has also done so in a policy and funding environment that remains controversial. The future of its public universities is now both positive and yet contested.

Bibliography

Alexander, F. (1963) *Campus at Crawley: A Narrative and Critical Appreciation of the First Fifty Years of the University of Western Australia*. Nedlands, WA: F.W. Cheshire for the University of Western Australia Press.

Barcan, A. (1993) Latin and Greek in Australian schools. *History of Education Review* 22(1): 32–46.

Booth, A. and Hiau, J.K. (2011) A long-run view of the university gender gap in Australia. *Australian Economic History Review* 51(3): 254–76.

Calendar of the University of Western Australia for the Year 1915 (1914). Perth: University of Western Australia.

Commonwealth Bureau of Census and Statistics (1951, 1955, 1974, 1992) *Official Year Book of the Commonwealth of Australia*. Canberra: Commonwealth Bureau of Census and Statistics.

Conant, J. (2010) Confidential report to the Carnegie Corporation on the university situation in Australia in the Year 1951. *History of Education Review* 39(1): 6–20.

Connell, W., Sherington, G., Fletcher, B., Turner, C., and Bygott, U. (1995) *Australia's First: A History of the University of Sydney 1940–1990*. Sydney: The University of Sydney in association with Hale and Iremonger.

Crane, A.R. and Walker, W.G. (1957) *Peter Board: His Contribution to the Development of Education in New South Wales*. Melbourne: Australian Council of Education.

Davis, R. (1990) *Open to Talent: The Centenary History of the University of Tasmania 1890–1990*. Hobart: The University of Tasmania.

Dawson, M. (1965) *Graduate and Married: A Report on a Survey of One Thousand and Seventy Married Women Graduates of the University of Sydney*. Sydney: Department of Adult Education, University of Sydney.

Everingham, P. (1999) *Education Participation Rates in Australia—1997*. Canberra: Department of Education, Training and Youth Affairs.

Forsyth, H. (2010) Academic work in Australian universities in the 1940s–1950s. *History of Education Review* 39(1): 42–47.

Foster, S.G. and Varghese, M. (1996) *The Making of the Australian University*. St Leonards, NSW: Allen & Unwin.

Gallagher, H. (2003) *We Got a Fair Go: A History of the Commonwealth Reconstruction Training Scheme 1945–52*. Kew, Victoria.

Horne, J. and Sherington, G. (2010) Extending the educational franchise: The social contract of Australia's public universities, 1850–1890. *Paedagogica Historica* 46(1–2): 207–27.

——— (2012) *Sydney: The Making of a Public University*. Melbourne: The Miegunyah Press.

Irving, T., Maunders, D., and Sherington, G. (1995) *Youth in Australia: Policy, Administration and Politics*. Melbourne: Macmillan.

Karmel, P.H. (1965) Supply and Demand—Comment. In *Higher Education in Australia*, ed. E.L. Wheelwright. Melbourne, Canberra and Sydney: F.W. Cheshire for the Federation of Australian University Staff Associations, 66–74.

Mackinnon, A. (1986) *The New Women: Adelaide's Early Women Graduates*. Netley, SAL: Wakefield Press.

Marginson, S. (2000) *Remaking the University, Monash*. Sydney: Allen & Unwin.

Megarrity, L. (2007) Regional goodwill, sensibly priced: Commonwealth policies towards Colombo Plan scholars and overseas students, 1945–72. *Australian Historical Studies* 38(129): 88–105.

O'Farrell, P. (1999) *UNSW: A Portrait*. Sydney: UNSW Press.

Pietsch, T. (2009) *'A Commonwealth of Learning'? Academic Networks and the British World 1890–1940*. Oxford: DPhil.

Rothblatt, S. (2007) *Education's Abiding Moral Dilemma: Merit and Worth in the Cross-Atlantic Democracies, 1800–2006*. Oxford: Symposium Books.

Selleck, R.J.W. (2003) *The Shop: The University of Melbourne 1856–1939*. Melbourne: Melbourne University Press.

Sherington, G. (1995) Student Life, 1918–1945. In *Sydney Teachers' College: A History 1906–1981*, eds Graham Boardman, Arthur Barnes, Beverley Fletcher, Brian Fletcher, Geoffrey Sherington, and Cliff Turney. Sydney: Hale and Iremonger.

Sherington, G. and Horne, J. (2010) Empire, state and public purpose in the founding of universities and colleges in the antipodes. *History of Education Review* 39(2): 36–51.

Thomis, M. (1985) *A Place of Light and Learning: The University of Queensland's First Seventy-five Years*. St Lucia: University of Queensland Press.

Tompkins, P. (1958) Australian higher education and the Murray report. *The Journal of Higher Education* 29(7): 361–68.

Turney, C., Bygott, U., and Chippendale, P. (1991) *Australia's First: A History of the University of Sydney*. Sydney: University of Sydney in association with Hale and Iremonger.

University of Sydney Archives (1944–48) *Conference with Registrars: Memorandum on Reconstruction Training—Session B, in Universities Commission—Reconstruction Training Scheme*, G12/43/15b.

Williams, B. (1977) Universities and the Universities Commission. In *The Commonwealth and Education 1964–1976: Political Initiatives and Development*, eds I.K.F. Birch and D. Smart. Richmond, Vic.: Drummond.

——— (1996) Some predicted and unpredicted changes in higher education. *Journal of Higher Education Policy and Management* 18(2): 139–48.

13

Small States: Higher Education in the English-speaking Caribbean

E. Nigel Harris

The Caribbean: A Geopolitical Overview

When the ACU was established in 1913, no university existed in the English-speaking Caribbean and only a tiny number of local persons had access to tertiary education, albeit, as we shall discuss below, universities had existed in the Spanish-speaking Caribbean since the sixteenth century. One cannot appreciate a discourse on education in the Caribbean without an understanding of its unique geography, history, cultural diversity, and social and economic construct.

The Caribbean Basin, in which 'sits' the Caribbean Sea, contains hundreds of islands, with land masses varying from the large islands, such as Cuba and Hispaniola, to isolated rocks and sandbars. It is bounded in the north by the islands of the Bahamas (just South of Florida), Cuba, Hispaniola (divided between the nations of Haiti and the Dominican Republic), Jamaica, Puerto Rico, and smaller islands such as St Kitts, the Virgin Islands, and Antigua. On the eastern boundary of the Caribbean Basin are a chain of smaller islands, often termed the Windward Islands, which include Guadeloupe, Martinique, Barbados, and Trinidad and Tobago. The southern boundary is made up of the north coast of South America and Central America (which includes the English-speaking country of Belize); and, finally, the north-west portion of the Basin is made up of states of the southern United States, which include Texas, Alabama, and Florida.

The total population of island nations in the English-speaking Caribbean is 5.5 million—compared to that of Cuba at 11.3 million, the Dominican Republic at 9.9 million, and Haiti at 9.7 million, while Puerto Rico is smaller at 3.7 million. Jamaica's population of 2.7 million accounts for about half of the English-speaking Caribbean and, except for Trinidad and Tobago, other island nations have populations under 500,000 (some under 100,000). Given these small numbers, one can understand efforts to link the nations together—economically, politically, educationally, and even in sports. Hence the existence of the Caribbean Community (CARICOM), modelled after the European Union, the (regional) University of the West Indies (UWI), and the (regional) West Indies cricket team.

Many of Caribbean islands were once populated by the indigenous peoples of the Americas, but with the arrival of Christopher Columbus in 1492 and subsequent European settlers, the indigenous population quickly disappeared, either being 'put to the sword', succumbing to disease or expiring because of overwork on the plantations established by the European settlers. Needing cheap labour to plant large plantations of sugar, cotton, and other crops that fetched untold riches in European markets, the owners turned to Africa, where millions of people were captured and transported across the Atlantic Ocean to be sold into slavery. With the abolition of slavery in 1832 (this occurred later in the Spanish Caribbean and North America), indentured labourers were imported primarily from India, but also from China and Portugal, to replace the Africans—the latter moving off the plantations to set up small townships and villages in their various island homes. The populations of the Caribbean Islands are hence made up of African, East Indian, Chinese, European, and small numbers of the indigenous people, the majority of these being mixtures of some or all of the above peoples.

From the seventeenth century through to the nineteenth century, the yield of riches from sugar, other cash crops, and mining was so considerable that European powers battled constantly for control of one or other Caribbean island—for example, the island of Saint Lucia changed hands between the French and British more than 20 times.

Today, based on the colonial power that eventually dominated one or other island, the language, culture, and architecture of each may be Spanish (Cuba, Dominican Republic, Puerto Rico); French (Haiti,

Martinique, Guadeloupe, St Martin); Dutch (Aruba, Curaçao, St Maarten); or English (Jamaica, Barbados, Trinidad and Tobago, and many more in the Eastern Caribbean).

There are various types of government. Most of the islands boast stable, independent democracies, but Puerto Rico is a 'commonwealth of the USA'; Martinique and Guadeloupe are 'Departments of France'; and tiny islands such as Anguilla, Cayman, Montserrat, and the British Virgin Islands are British dependencies. (The latter group have elected governments, albeit with a British governor, and are responsible for their finances, the UK being responsible for their foreign affairs.)

Universities in the Caribbean

The establishment of universities in the Spanish-speaking Caribbean preceded that of universities in North America and many in Europe by many years.

The first university in Santo Domingo was established in 1538, less than 50 years after Columbus' arrival. A listing of dates of the establishment of other universities in the 'New World' is provided in Table 13.1. The early Spanish settlers and Puritans in North America placed much emphasis on education, their motivation being preservation of religion and learning for their descendants, whom they expected to live in the 'New World'. Except for Codrington College in Barbados, no university was established in the English-speaking Caribbean until 1948 (nearly

Table 13.1:
Dates of Establishment of Some Universities in the 'New World'

Country/University	*Date established*
Santo Domingo	1538
Mexico	1551
Columbia	1580
Harvard	1636
Yale	1701
Cuba	1788
Haiti	1830s
Puerto Rico	1903
The University of the West Indies (Jamaica)	1948

400 years after the university in Santo Domingo), perhaps because the plantations were owned by absentee landlords, and the smaller numbers of English families that did live in the islands preferred to send their children to what universities existed in the UK. Prior to the twentieth century, the question of a university education for the enslaved population and their descendants was not significantly mooted anywhere except in Haiti, where the black population had won their freedom from the French in 1804, after 13 years of war (1791–1804).

It is noteworthy that the first university in Santo Domingo was established within 50 years of Columbus landing in Hispaniola (1492), and Harvard was established within 16 years of the Pilgrims landing in North America in 1620; but the UWI was established about two centuries after the arrival of English settlers.

It should be borne in mind that universities in North America and Latin America were established for European settlers, and persons 'of colour' were probably not admitted until the late eighteenth or early nineteenth century. The subsequent discussion in this chapter will concentrate primarily on university education in the English-speaking Caribbean.

The University of the West Indies

While there are now a variety of universities operating in the Caribbean, the first and still dominant player is the UWI.

Today, the UWI has major campuses in three island nations—Jamaica, Trinidad and Tobago, and Barbados—and smaller sites in 13 other countries: Anguilla, Antigua, the Bahamas, Belize (in Central America), British Virgin Islands, Cayman, Dominica, Grenada, Montserrat, Saint Lucia, St Kitts, St Vincent, and the Grenadines, and the Turks and Caicos.

The total student population of the UWI (as at 2012) is 47,000 (having increased from 22,000 a decade ago):

- St Augustine Campus, located in Trinidad and Tobago, with 18,000 students
- Mona Campus in Jamaica with 16,000
- Cave Hill campus in Barbados with 8,000
- the Open Campus, providing online and face-to-face learning for students in all 16 countries, with about 5,000

There are 32,000 applications to the whole system annually (increasing from 16,000 a decade ago) and about half of the applicants are admitted. Each of the three residential campuses has Faculties of Medicine, Law, Humanities and Education, Pure and Applied Sciences, and Social Sciences; at St Augustine, there are Faculties of Engineering and Agriculture; and each of the three major campuses has a major business school. Together, these campuses provide hundreds of undergraduate and postgraduate programmes.

The UWI has unquestionably been the major contributor to the growth of the middle and upper-middle classes in the English-speaking Caribbean in the second half of the twentieth century. Since its establishment in 1948, the university has produced 17 prime ministers, seven of whom are current heads of government, countless cabinet ministers and parliamentarians, and the majority of professionals (physicians, lawyers, engineers, teachers, nurses) in nearly all of its 16 contributing countries. Placing a heavy emphasis on research relevant to the Caribbean from its very beginning, the University has contributed a wealth of scholarship towards an understanding of the history, culture, social and economic circumstances, health, topography and biodiversity of the island nations, and of the marine life in the Caribbean Sea.

That a regional institution, encompassing and funded by so many nations, has survived more than 60 years is itself remarkable. The story of its beginnings may account for its success. The University had its origins in 1942, when Oliver Stanley, British Colonial Secretary, anticipated that in the post-war years to follow, colonies of the British Empire would become self-governing, and would need educated leaders and managers drawn from the local population. He established a special commission, chaired by High Court Judge Sir Cyril Asquith (named the 'Asquith Commission'): 'to consider the principles which should guide the promotion of higher education, learning and research and the development of universities in the colonies' (Sherlock and Nettleford, 1990).

A sub-committee of the Asquith Commission was established, to report on the need for a university in the colonies of the West Indies, and this was led by Sir James Irvine, Vice-Chancellor of the University of St Andrews. The commission, comprising prominent West Indians and English educators, held broad consultations with all sectors of the island nations, including (then) British Guiana (now Guyana), and found that there was an overwhelming desire for a university. Up to that time, few persons of colour had access to tertiary education; opportunities were often limited to 'one island scholar' annually, who went to one of the prominent universities in the United Kingdom. A few families of colour who had the means sent their children to universities in the USA. A small number of students also took external degrees from the University of London.

The Irvine Commission recommended that there be a 'single' university in the West Indies, that it be established as a university college in its formative years, and that, after a short period of apprenticeship, it should obtain its own Charter. In 1948, with Thomas Taylor (later, Sir Thomas Taylor), an English chemist, as its first Principal, and a small number of largely British staff, the University College of the West Indies (attached to London University) was established, with 33 students enrolled in the Faculty of Medicine (Sherlock and Nettleford, 1990).

Of historical importance is the fact that the Mona Campus in Jamaica, where the UWI was founded, was once a plantation where ancestors of some of the first and subsequent students toiled as enslaved workers. Similarly, the St Augustine Campus in Trinidad and Tobago was also established (in 1960) on land that was once a sugar cane plantation (Brereton, 2011). The campus at Mona grew quickly after its founding, with the establishment of Faculties in Arts, Sciences, and Education.

From the very beginning, research was emphasised, with the establishment of:

- the Institute of Social and Economic Research in 1948 (now the Sir Arthur Lewis Institute of Social and Economic Studies [SALISES])
- the Tropical Metabolism Research Unit (TMRU) in 1954
- the *Caribbean Quarterly* journal in 1951, which published a variety of scholarly works largely written by the fledgling university community

Today, in addition to SALISES and the TMRU, there are dozens of other centres and institutes, all with creditable records of scholarship, primarily relevant to the Caribbean and developing world.

The original idea of a university in a single country came to an end in 1962, with the establishment of Faculties of Agriculture and Engineering in Trinidad and Tobago. The new Faculty of Agriculture was founded out of the Imperial College of Tropical Agriculture, which had been established in 1920, and which by 1962 had become one of the leading centres of research in tropical agriculture, as well as in training agricultural administrators and specialists for the British Colonial system

(Brereton, 2011). In 1964, the Barbados government established a UWI Campus at Cave Hill.

The foundation of new campuses in the early 1960s coincided with the independence and nationhood of: Trinidad and Tobago (1962); Barbados (1966); and Jamaica (1962). Over the succeeding two decades, other islands gained their independence, though some with tiny populations (British Virgin Islands, Cayman, Montserrat, and Anguilla) remain British dependencies. The colonies of the West Indies attempted a Federation in 1959, but this was short-lived and ended in 1962.

After independence was achieved, West Indians recognised that there was still a need to establish some form of union, because of their small size and population. Their commonality of history, culture, and government were also important factors in favour of collaboration. Thus, in 1965, they established a Caribbean Free Trade Association and, in 1972, this was transformed into a CARICOM common market. It is this enduring wish for some form of co-operation that has undoubtedly contributed to a commitment to preserve the regional university, a regional examination system for high school students and a regional (West Indies) cricket team.

The UWI has not remained a monolithic system. For the first few decades of its existence, the University was governed centrally from Jamaica by a Vice-Chancellor, who was also the Principal of the Mona Campus. However, the more influential countries—Jamaica, Barbados, and Trinidad and Tobago—wanted more control over their own campuses. Thus, in 1984, the governance of the University was significantly changed, so that each of the three campuses got their own campus councils, academic boards, and appointment committees (for promotion up to senior lecturer), with budgets for the campus largely determined by the country where that campus was located.

The whole system was still ultimately governed by a University Council, and there was a central Senate and an Appointments and Promotions Committee (for promotion to professor—promotions to senior lecturer were devolved to the campuses). The 12 contributing countries without campuses were governed out of the Vice Chancellery, and in a subsequent restructuring in 1994, these were assembled into the Board for Non-Campus Countries and Distance Education, under a Pro-Vice-Chancellor. In 2008, the latter entity was grouped with the UWI Distance Education Centre to form a fourth 'virtual campus', named the Open Campus.

UWI: A Unique Regional Structure

Today, the UWI can best be described as a federal system, with the central administration (the Vice Chancellery) overseeing the University's strategic planning, policy formation, quality assurance of undergraduate and graduate programmes, finances and fundraising (shared with the campuses), and appointments at the professorial level.

The three residential campuses, led by Principals (who are also Pro-Vice-Chancellors), are responsible for management of their own campuses. Each campus has its own Council, Finance and General Purposes Committee, Academic Board and Appointments Committee, Faculties of Humanities and Arts, Social Sciences, Pure and Applied Sciences, Medicine and Law (since 2012). Only the Faculties of Engineering and Agriculture are confined to one campus, St Augustine (Trinidad and Tobago). The budgets of each of the campuses are largely provided by the government where the campus resides, and the Principals control expenditures and fashion revenue-generating enterprises for that campus. The downside of this arrangement is that the 'well-being' of each campus often reflects the health of the finances of its local government.

There are three cross-campus meetings each year, with delegated powers from Council, chaired by the Vice-Chancellor and attended by:

- all Deans (the Committee of Deans)
- Quality Assurance Committees (undergraduate and postgraduate separately)
- Appointments Committee
- Finance and General Purposes Committee

Ongoing operational management is overseen by an Executive Management Team, which meets monthly and comprises:

- the Vice-Chancellor
- Principals and Deputy Principals
- the Pro-Vice-Chancellors for Research, Undergraduate Studies, Graduate Studies, and Planning and Development
- the University Registrar
- the Chief Financial Officer
- a representative of the Committee of Deans
- other senior leaders

National Universities and Community Colleges

During the past two decades, peoples and governments of the English-speaking Caribbean, like those in many other parts of the world, demanded more access to university education. Some CARICOM governments at the beginning of the third millennium announced that they wanted 30 per cent of their working population to have postsecondary degrees by 2015. The UWI responded by a huge expansion of enrolment, so that between 2002 and 2012 enrolment increased from 22,000 to 47,000.

But this was not sufficient to meet the growing demand both by private citizens and governments. The UWI did not wish to liberalise its matriculation requirements beyond certain defined limits. Hence, in the past two decades, there has been a gradual increase in the number of national universities (Roberts, Long, and Estwick, 2007).

The University of Guyana is the oldest, founded in 1963 when Guyana opted out of the UWI system, and has about 5,000 students. Approximately 60 undergraduate and postgraduate degree programmes are offered in the arts, natural sciences, social sciences, education, agriculture and forestry, and health sciences.

The University of Technology, in Jamaica, traces its origins to 1958, when it began as a College of Arts, Sciences and Technology, modelled in many ways after polytechnic institutions in the United Kingdom. In 1995, the institution was awarded formal university status, becoming the University of Technology, Jamaica. This university has expanded to nearly 12,000 students, offering programmes in natural and applied sciences (with a sizeable engineering and computer information programme), business and hospitality management, applied health and nursing, education, humanities, and social sciences. Where Jamaican students travelled in the past to Trinidad and Tobago to do their engineering programmes at the UWI School of Engineering, the majority now do so at the University of Technology in their own country.

Other public universities include the University of Belize (founded in 2000), the University of Trinidad and Tobago (founded in 2004), and the University College of the Cayman Islands (founded in 2004).

There are a few private universities, owned and run by local entities, including the Northern Caribbean University (Jamaica) and the Southern Caribbean University (Trinidad and Tobago), both closely affiliated with the Seventh Day Adventist Church, which has very large congregations in these two island nations. The University College of the Caribbean, established in 2004, is a private institution located in Jamaica.

There are a sizeable number of community colleges in the Caribbean (Roberts, Long, and Estwick, 2007). In Jamaica in particular, there are more than 40 such institutions, many of which are specialty colleges offering certificate, diploma, associate and even degree programmes in areas such as visual and performing arts (Edna Manley College), agriculture (G.C. Foster College), the Caribbean Maritime Institute, and several teachers' colleges. The most notable teachers' college is Mico College, which was established in 1836. It is the oldest teacher education and training institution in the Western Hemisphere, and has recently achieved university status.

There are similarly large numbers of community colleges in Trinidad and Tobago, Barbados, the Bahamas, and Belize, which have relatively large populations (by Commonwealth Caribbean standards). Each of the smaller Eastern Caribbean islands has at least one community college, many established in the early post-independence years of the 1960s and 1970s, and together they offer opportunities for postsecondary education that would not otherwise be possible.

'Off-shore Medical Schools'

Unfortunately, universities in the Caribbean that are often most visible to the outside world are the 'off-shore universities'. The vast majority are medical schools, but there are a handful of veterinary and nursing schools, all run as private entrepreneurial ventures that are heavily marketed globally. In recent times, a Google search for the 'University of the West Indies', or any other West Indian based institution, results in a 'pop-up' advertising St George's University—the oldest of the off-shore institutions.

These institutions cater to students seeking professional degrees, in particular medicine, veterinary sciences, and nursing. The preponderance of students come from countries where competition for similar places is stiff (only one in four applicants to medical schools in the USA is admitted, and in the UK it is reputedly one in nine). Some students who cannot get into professional schools at home opt to go overseas (and pay high fees to the off-shore schools), because the potential rewards on graduation are significant.

There are now over 30 off-shore medical schools operating in the English-speaking Caribbean, the most prominent and first established being St George's University (established in 1976 in Grenada) and Ross University (established in 1978 in Dominica).

Compared to medical schools in the USA, the country from which most students are attracted, St George's and Ross have huge classes with huge numbers (500 to 1,000) admitted annually and curricula that reportedly are heavily biased towards preparing students for the United States Medical Licensing Examination (USMLE), which is their 'passport' to entry into residency training programs in the USA. The demand for medical residents ('junior doctors' in practical postgraduate hospital training) in the USA exceeds the supply of graduates from USA-based medical schools, hence graduates of off-shore schools with decent USMLE scores have a good chance of securing residency positions. Many off-shore school graduates do residencies in rural and inner-city hospitals that are less attractive to USA-based medical school graduates.

The off-shore medical schools usually admit students who have completed their Bachelor's degree. The first two years of basic medical education are conducted at the location in the Caribbean, and the final two years of clinical training at hospitals in the USA (particularly in New York and California).

While some graduates of these institutions are undoubtedly very able, there is considerable debate in the USA about the quality of some graduates (Parolini and Platek, 2010; Hundley, 2010). None of these schools are accredited by the medical accrediting body in the USA—the Liaison Committee on Medical Education (LCME)—but St George's and Ross are recognised by the California and New York State Medical Boards, enabling graduates of those schools to do clinical rotations and residency training in those states (Parolini and Platek, 2010; Hundley, 2010).

In 2004, the Caribbean established the Caribbean Accreditation Authority in Medicine and the Health Professions (CAAM-HP), primarily because the General Medical Council (GMC) in the UK, which accredited the UWI medical programme, stopped accrediting overseas medical schools. Loss of access to accreditation forced CARICOM to establish an accreditation body of its own.

The CAAM-HP developed accreditation standards based on the LCME and the GMC; and it is now recognised by the GMC in the UK. It is seeking recognition by the Education Commission for Foreign Medical Graduates in the USA. To date, medical programmes at the UWI, the University of Guyana, St George's University, Ross University, Saint

James School of Medicine (Anguilla), the UWI School of Veterinary Medicine, and the UWI School of Dentistry are the only accredited programmes. The UWI programme is alone in receiving accreditation for the full six years. Regrettably, many of the off-shore institutions are operating without any form of accreditation, raising serious questions about competencies of some of their graduates (Parolini and Platek, 2010; Hundley, 2010).

Whatever the questions about off-shore medical schools, their host governments in West Indian island nations view them as good sources of revenue. While the profits derived from operating these institutions are primarily repatriated to the home countries of the investors, the island nations derive financial benefits from hundreds of resident students, visiting parents and friends, and international academic staff living and spending where they are located. Revenues generated from these off-shore educational enterprises can make up a sizeable percentage of total GDP in countries where the local population is small and business opportunities are limited. The term 'educational tourism' is an apt description for these ventures. The challenge is that some officials in these tiny island states may sometimes be tempted to sacrifice quality and credibility for economic gain.

International Universities in the Caribbean

There are a number of universities based in the USA and the UK that are delivering undergraduate and postgraduate programmes in the Caribbean, utilising online, face-to-face, and blended teaching modalities. A few have established campuses in small Eastern Caribbean islands.

Programmes offered are usually high-demand ones—business administration, management studies, and computer and information studies. Some (but not all) of these entities are extensions of reputable institutions in the North, though there is the question as to whether programmes offered externally are of the same quality as that of the 'home institution'. It should be borne in mind, too, that the University of London has offered external degree programmes to students resident in the Caribbean for many decades—indeed, prior to the establishment of the UWI, this was the primary avenue by which West Indian students could access higher education.

Of more concern are a number of questionable for-profit institutions, which may or may not be based in North America or Europe, and which provide education of uncertain quality. These institutions may have a charter, may be registered and may even, in a few instances, be 'accredited' locally, but there are still questions about quality, based on some of the concerns discussed above.

Caribbean Nationals Educated Internationally

A substantial number of Caribbean students are educated in North America or Europe. Leading universities in the USA and Canada actively recruit talented Caribbean students. In addition, parents in the upper and upper-middle classes have traditionally sent their children 'abroad' to universities outside the region. Presently, there are more students from Belize, the Bahamas, and some Eastern Caribbean island nations studying in North America or the UK than in the Caribbean itself.

Also of note is that many students who receive first degrees in Caribbean schools elect to do their postgraduate studies at universities in North America, the UK, Europe, or elsewhere. This has been particularly true of those who become academics in tertiary institutions in the Caribbean, as evidenced by the sizeable number teaching at the UWI and other national universities with postgraduate degrees obtained outside the region.

One facet of tertiary education in the English-speaking Caribbean is the sizeable number of their students who are being educated in Cuba, particularly in medicine, nursing, and engineering. The Cuban government has provided these opportunities free of charge, or at low cost. Given that many students in the English-speaking Caribbean do not have the means (or sometimes the grades) to get access to the limited number of places at the UWI in their professional fields, some governments have opted to send many of their students to Cuba. Today, increasing numbers of the physicians practising in the Eastern Caribbean are Cuba-educated. There are legitimate concerns about the quality of these graduates, who may go straight into practice—unlike their Cuban counterparts, who are required to do additional years of postgraduate training before going into practice.

Challenges to Tertiary Education in the Caribbean

As summarised above, there is much to celebrate with respect to the achievements of Caribbean education in the past half-century.

The UWI, and other national universities, have graduated several thousand graduates (the UWI alone has 120,000 alumni), who have played key leadership roles and contributed to the growth of every sector of their countries. One such graduate, Derek Walcott, is a Nobel Prize Laureate (for literature); and a former UWI Vice-Chancellor, Sir Arthur Lewis, was awarded the Nobel Prize for economics (incidentally, both are from the tiny island of Saint Lucia, population only about 160,000). Approximately 60 UWI graduates have won Rhodes Scholarships. Over its six-decade history, the UWI has produced stellar scholars in many fields, whose researches have gained significant international recognition, as have some of its institutes and centres—for example, the Sir Arthur Lewis Institute for Social and Economic Studies, the TMRU (Forrester, Picou, and Walker, 2007), the Sickle Cell Unit, and the Institute for Gender Studies.

These undoubted accomplishments do not detract from the challenges that universities in the region face. Many are under-staffed and under-resourced, a situation made worse by the expansion of enrolment in the last decade and the global economic crisis beginning in 2008. Except for the UWI, many national universities and community colleges have a dearth of faculty members with terminal (PhD) degrees and, at a few, the majority of instructors have just first (Bachelor's) degrees. Except at the UWI, few universities and community colleges have sizeable numbers of academic staff who have attained the rank of full professor—at the UWI, attainment of such a rank includes rigorous assessment by external assessors with expertise in the field in which the professorship is being sought.

Library resources and infrastructure to conduct cutting-edge basic research in the sciences are limited. The UWI library system is the best resourced and best managed; but, even in this case, the sort of access to journals available to large USA and UK institutions is difficult. Infrastructure for cutting-edge basic scientific research is also limited to a few specific areas. Absence of regional or national funding agencies to support scientific research (with the exception of Trinidad and Tobago) limits opportunities to garner resources for advanced research. Some academics have found 'creative ways' to access necessary funding support, and a few very enterprising ones collaborate with international laboratories to do first-rate work.

One of the long-standing challenges in this region has been the considerable emigration of graduates from Caribbean schools to North America and Europe. World Bank figures claim that up to 80 per cent of university graduates from some island nations and Guyana emigrate to North America or Europe; but these figures are open to question, as the USA and the UK are limiting immigration, and more students may well be opting to stay at home.

It must, however, be acknowledged that there is a significant 'brain drain', with a relatively high number of graduates leaving the region to seek job opportunities elsewhere. So long as West Indian economies are not sufficiently robust to absorb these graduates, emigration to more prosperous countries will remain a reality. A recent internal study by the UWI showed that 20–30 per cent of graduates with humanities and science degrees are finding it difficult to secure jobs within six months of graduation.

Adequate financing for tertiary education is also a significant problem. Economies of the English-speaking Caribbean are dependent on tourism, mining, and agriculture, and the economic woes of countries in the Organisation for Economic Co-operation and Development, after the global economic collapse in 2008, has negatively impacted on all of the Caribbean—with the exception of Trinidad and Tobago, whose economy is largely 'fuelled' by petroleum and natural gas production. Even in better times, economic growth had been modest and indebtedness high in many island nations. These economic conditions have had a negative effect on tertiary education institutions, some of which are entirely supported by their governments (Barbados, Trinidad and Tobago). Where students pay fees, these have been modest, making up only a fraction of the economic cost of their education (UWI charges students 20 per cent [approximately US$2,500] of total economic costs for education). Despite the relatively low fees, and the existence of a Student Loan Bureau, the student default rate on payment of fees is high, further challenging revenue streams of universities. To add to these challenges, some governments are significantly in arrears with respect to payments to the universities. It is noteworthy that, despite the apparent inability of many students to meet their tuition/fee requirements, overseas private institutions operating in the Caribbean appear to be doing sufficiently well to profitably sustain their operations.

Finally, there is a concern about competition—both between local institutions and with their international counterparts. With the liberalisation of higher education services by the World Trade Organization, the Caribbean has been inundated with major international universities coming to its shores, posing a huge competitive challenge for local students in subjects that might prove 'profitable' for local universities. The offshore medical schools largely cater to students from outside the region, albeit that St George's has introduced humanities, social sciences, and other programmes that attract Eastern Caribbean students, particularly from Grenada, where that institution is located.

Competition need not be all negative. For the UWI and national universities, considerable efforts are being made to improve student services and quality of teaching to better attract and satisfy student needs and that of local governments.

Summary: The Value of Universities in the Caribbean

The contribution of indigenous tertiary education institutions to the Caribbean has been considerable in the latter half of the twentieth century. They have helped to create a sizeable middle and upper-middle class, which now makes up the majority of leaders, managers, and the educated workforce, contributing to the growth and stability of these societies after achievement of independence from Britain.

Thanks to research and knowledge development in many fields, contributions to improvement in health, social, and economic conditions—and a better understanding of the history, culture, and environment of these island nations—have proven invaluable. The development of countries is ultimately dependent on knowledge about themselves, and to the degree that universities enable this, their societies benefit.

Finally, it is increasingly the case that leading novelists, poets, politicians, and other prominent Caribbean people are providing gifts of their original works and collected papers to the UWI. It is often forgotten that indigenous universities can serve as cultural repositories of their nation's history and patrimony. It is noteworthy that the people of the English-speaking Caribbean are becoming secure enough in the durability of their universities that they are ready to gift their works to the care of these institutions for the enduring benefit of their communities.

Bibliography

Brereton, B. (2011) *From Imperial College to University of the West Indies: A History of the St. Augustine Campus, Trinidad and Tobago.* Ian Randle Publishers.

Forrester, T., Picou, D., and Walker, S. (2007) *The University of the West Indies, Jamaica 1956–2006: The House That John Built.* Jamaica: Ian Randle Publishers.

Hundley, K. (2010) Investigators want to know if the quality of off-shore medical schools justifies the cost. *Tampa Bay Times*, 1 January 2010.

Parolini, A. and Platek, C. (2010) Offshore medical schools in the Caribbean. *World Education News and Reviews* 23(5).

Roberts, V., Long, J., and Estwick, S. (2007) *Caribbean Tertiary Education Development (1996–2006).* The University of the West Indies, Tertiary Level Institutions Unit Publishers.

Sherlock, P. and Nettleford, R. (1990) *The University of the West Indies: A Caribbean Response to the Challenge of Change.* London: Macmillan Publishers Ltd.

PART IV

Prospect: University Futures

Prelude

If the past remains 'a foreign country', as a common idiom among historians runs, so the future is an even more unknown landscape. However, we study the past to understand our present; and also, if we are honest, to grasp the likely futures that await us.

'Looking beyond the horizon' is therefore not just an intellectual game: it involves serious reflections on current trends across society and the world of knowledge. In the case of higher education it is indeed an important consideration for long-term planning of a strategic kind. Not to think ahead is to ignore the 'intelligences' that we can build up about the 'foreign country' that is the future. Universities pride themselves on being learning institutions. One representation of that capacity should be to self-awareness—an understanding of both the institution and the fast-changing environment in which it exists.

Part IV considers that debate around three of the many core issues that are impacting on universities in the twenty-first century.

Universities and Postmodernity

How is the major drive to develop knowledge economies through focused research policies within the university systems changing the very nature of university missions and of institutional cultures? A world authority on science policies considers (in Chapter 14) the potentially fissiparous impact of science centres within institutions. At a basic level, questions have increasingly been raised about how the research-only faculty challenges the teaching–research nexus on which many great universities have been built over the last century. But the chapter raises a larger question regarding the resultant corporate and collegial character of the university: have we indeed now entered the era of transformed institutional form—the 'postmodern university'?

Looking over the Horizon

The purposes of the university appear to have come to us from the past relatively unchanged: notions of tradition and collegial cultures are often evoked in rituals of apparent continuity. In fact, universities have changed markedly over time, with certain periods being especially formative—not least in the era of industrialisation and the growth of the professions. But these processes have undergone a notable acceleration over the last few decades. The history of the ACU Network members testifies to a veritable 'reinvention' of the notion of 'the University'—towards not only wider social functions but also a considerable variety of institutional forms. For some critics, this brave new world of engagement and widening access has stripped the notion of 'university' of meaning: there is only 'higher education' of a protean and uneven kind. Others again have recognised the pluralism as a new era of institutional existence, akin to the impact of industrialisation. The question then becomes one of defining missions and of purposeful differentiation within a plural set of options. Of course, it is not quite a free environment of choice, and Chapter 15, by a former Oxford vice-chancellor, addresses three absolutely fundamental questions: What are the pressures today on universities and higher education in general? What are the consequences of working within that changing environment? What, then, are the implications for charting the future of universities in the medium- and long-term scenarios? There are no easy answers; but the chapter offers sage reflections on the need for 'principled and firm leadership', combined with academic support among those 'who do not cling to every form of the past for fear of the future'.

The Values of Universities

In Chapter 16, the final chapter of the book, we have a strong and bold meditation on the essential question raised by the original proposition of

Newman's famed 'Idea of the University'. Writing against the backdrop of industrialisation in the middle of the nineteenth century, Newman was concerned not merely to address the new utility of knowledge in an increasingly utilitarian age, but also to defend the values on which he saw a university education resting. 'Values' have become somewhat unfashionable in institutional analysis; and yet it is increasingly agreed that a key aspect of the discourse over the role of universities relates to their core mission goals and the culture of the organisation. In that context it is increasingly unreal to discuss the nature of universities without evolving the values that inform 'institutional character'. Major university leaders and analysts have begun to turn the debate towards the question 'What are the values behind a university?' The Secretary General of the ACU concludes: 'here is possibly the greatest challenge for members of this oldest of all global networks in higher education'.

Bibliography

'Beyond the Horizon'

Douglass, J.A., Judson King, C., and Feller, I. (eds) (2009) *Globalization's Muse: Universities and Higher Education Systems in a Changing World*. Berkeley, California: Berkeley Public Policy Press.

Duderstadt, J.J. (2000) *A University for the 21st Century*. Ann Arbor: University of Michigan Press.

Gallagher, S. (2013) MOOCS means more time for different kinds of learning. Higher Education Supplement, *Australian*, 20 March 2013, 32.

Kerr, C. (2001) *The Uses of the University*, 5th ed. Harvard: Harvard University Press.

King, R. (2004) *Universities into the 21st Century*. London: Palgrave.

Marginson, S. (ed.) (2007) *Prospects of Higher Education: Globalization, Market Competition, Public Goods and the Future of the University*. Rotterdam/Taipei: Sense Publishers.

Maskell, D. and Robinson, I. (2001) *The New Idea of a University*. London: Academic Imprint.

Rhodes, F.H.T. (2001) *The Creation of the Future. The Role of the American University*. Ithaca and London: Cornell University Press.

Trow, A. and Nyborn, T. (eds) (1991) *University and Society*. London: Jessica Kingsley Publishers.

Vincent-Lancrin, S. (2009) An OECD Scan of Public and Private Higher Education. In *Globalization's Muse: Universities and Higher Education Systems in a Changing World*, eds J.A. Douglass, C. Judson King, and I. Feller, Chapter 1. Berkeley, California: Berkeley Public Policy Press.

Knowledge Economies and Research Strategies

Gibbons, M. (2001) Engagement as a Core Value in a Mode 2 Society. In *As Time Goes by: From the Industrial Revolutions to the Information Revolution*, eds C. Freeman and F. Louca. Oxford and New York: Oxford University Press.
Gibbons, M., Limoges, C., Nowotny, H., Schwartzman, S., Scott, P., and Trow, M. (1994) *The New Production of Knowledge: The Dynamics of Science and Research in Contemporary*. London: SAGE Publications.
King, R. (2004) *Universities into the 21st Century*. London: Palgrave.
Mokyr, J. (2002) *The Gifts of Athena: Historical Origins of the Knowledge Economy*. Princeton, NJ: Princeton University Press.
Sommer, J.W. (1995) *The Academy in Crisis: The Political Economy of Higher Education*. New Brunswick and London: Transaction Publishers.

Why Universities?

Boulton, G. and Lucas, C. (2008) *What Are Universities For?* Paris: League of European Research Universities.
Coady, Tony (2000) *Why Universities Matter: A Conversation about Values, Means and Directions*. Sydney: Allen and Unwin.
Collini, S. (2012) *What Are Universities For?* London: Penguin Press.
Davis, G. (2010) *The Republic of Learning*. The Boyer Lecture Series, 2010. Sydney: ABC Books.
Kenny, A. and Kenny, R. (2007) *Can Oxford Be Improved? A View from the Dreaming Spires and the Satanic Mills*. Oxford: imprint-academic.com
Pelikan, J. (1992) *The Idea of a University: A Re-examination*. New Haven, Conn.: Yale.
Ryan, A. (1999) *Liberal Anxieties and Liberal Education: What Education Is Really for and Why It Matters*. London: Profile Books.
Thomas, K. (2010) What are universities for? *The Times Literary Supplement*, London, 7 May.
Wolf, A. (2002) *Does Education Matter? Myths about Education and Economic Growth*. London: Penguin Books.

14

The Rise of Postmodern Universities: The Power of Innovation

Michael Gibbons

For many years now, national science policies have been focused on drawing government-owned research laboratories and universities into the innovation process. There have been a variety of policies attempting to do this but, as interesting as they may be, they are secondary in importance compared to the changes that these policies have induced in the heart of the university; that is, in the practice of research itself.

It is the aim of this essay to try to describe how the drive for innovation is modifying research practice in contemporary universities—changes profound enough to be called 'a regime change'.

Science and Innovation

National science policies have been focused on supporting technological innovation for the simple reason that it is mainly through innovation that firms develop the new products and processes that position them in the marketplace from which profits arise and economic growth is generated. Moreover, unremitting technological innovation is now regarded as a key factor in the ability of national firms to maintain leading positions in the global economy.

It is for these reasons that, over the last 50 years, science policy research itself has been focused on the nature of technological innovation; what promotes it and what inhibits it. Research into the innovation process has ballooned across most of the major economies, as scientists, technologists, organisational theorists, and industrial managers, and a new breed of science policy analysts, have tried to identify its major drivers. This research has discovered innovation to be a very complex process, involving many interacting variables, but one factor is recurrent: the crucial role played by knowledge of various kinds. Throughout, a crucial question has been: 'How much of this knowledge derives from prior pure science?'

Despite the generally acknowledged importance of knowledge in the innovation process, close links between science (specifically the curiosity-oriented research of the universities) and innovation have proved difficult to establish empirically. Indeed, there has been much research to suggest that as far as the sources of innovation go, it is technological knowledge rather than scientific knowledge that has been primary (Freeman and Soete, 1990).

Nonetheless, despite the efforts of economists and science policy researchers to elucidate the complexity of the innovation process, a linear model persists, in which discoveries in science drives to innovation. Typical of the genre is Cole's 2007 treatment of the role of science in innovation in the rise of American universities. This work focuses mainly on research universities and medical schools, 'those institutions which do the most to foster the innovations that raise the standard of living and enhance the quality of our lives' (Cole, 2007). The section of the book labelled 'Discoveries That Alter Our Lives' is 150 pages long and provides brief histories of innovations in science and medicine that, Cole argues, have originated in universities. These discoveries include gene splicing, recombinant DNA, Hepatitis B vaccine and stem cells, human capital theory and traffic jam reductions.

However, Harvard economist Claudia Goldin has pointed out that while

> no one can for a moment doubt the special role universities play in innovations that arise from research in pure science and an interest in solving problems ... [an] inventory like the one Cole provides here tells us as much about why some universities are 'great' as a list of names of accomplished

> people in a large family shows us why their family is 'great' relative to others.

Moreover, Goldin argues, the list on its own does nothing to illuminate whether universities did the research alone or what kinds of incentives were used to enhance researcher productivity, and leaves unclear 'who contributed what to a particular innovation' (Goldin, 2010).

These qualifications and methodological weaknesses are noted here not because they are unique, but rather because they are not substantially different from those that have been made by historians, economists, and others who have studied the innovation process since the 1960s. It seems that, despite the acknowledged complexity of the role played by knowledge in the innovation, the linear model is still operative in the minds of many academics and government policymakers.

In sum, the current consensus among economists and policy analysts is that while science does contribute to the generation of innovation and economic growth, it does so indirectly and perhaps only in the long term. The dominant knowledge source for innovation seems to be technological knowledge and the integration of that knowledge into what Dosi has labelled 'stable technological paradigms' (Dosi, 1982). It is the *differential* development of these paradigms by individual firms themselves that forms the basis for competition between them. If science makes any contribution, it is made before, rather than after, a stable paradigm has emerged.

It should come as no surprise, then, that governments, while supporting scientific activities in the universities in general, would also try, through various stratagems, to encourage universities to broaden the portfolio of research they undertake and, where appropriate, to engage more closely with industry in the search for stable technological paradigms. There is, however, another aspect of the linear model, which is germane to the argument being developed herein.

The Peer Review System

Whatever the view about the substantive contribution of science to innovation, there has never been much disagreement within the scientific establishment about who should determine the topics for research and who should undertake the investigations. Indeed, at a very early stage of government involvement with science, a view was articulated that the direction of scientific research was a matter for scientists. In other words, the best science would emerge if the scientists themselves were left to pursue what they regarded as the important questions and how they should be addressed.

Though the scientific community has grown substantially and articulated into myriad specialisations, the funding of science—particularly that performed in the universities—has continued to invoke the principle that scientists themselves are the best equipped to decide upon research priorities. Across the world, this principle has been embodied in funding structures of national research councils and remains a key determinant of what research is funded and who shall perform it.

Still, it is not the case that different approaches were never proposed. For example, one provocative alternative was put forward early on in the history of science policy, not by government officials or industrialists but by a respected American nuclear scientist. Alvin Weinberg advocated that all projects proposed for funding should be ranked according to five criteria: two internal criteria and three external ones. The internal criteria were: 'Is field ripe for exploitation?' and 'Are the scientists in the field really competent?'. The external criteria were evaluations of the scientific, technological, and social merit of a particular project or line of research (Weinberg, 1963). Weinberg argued that while the internal criteria might be settled by practitioners in a given field, the external ones required broader experience of science, technology and industry.

It is relevant for what follows to note that Weinberg's aim was to open up internal decision-making within science, by suggesting that the system of peer review could be improved if representatives not only of the field being judged, but also of neighbouring fields were represented on assessment panels. At that time, Weinberg's external criteria were not generally adopted by the funding institutions, in part because it was found to be too difficult to rank the different criteria, but also because, as some argued, they did not take sufficiently into account the possibility of radical breakthroughs where basic information as to impact would be lacking. In brief, any interference with the internal procedures of science would be likely to lead to inferior science.

Nonetheless, the role of peer review committees in funding science has gradually changed. Peer review now constitutes only one in a hierarchy of decision-making levels through which all funding recommendations by peer review committees have to pass before funding can awarded. Thus, while peer review judgements internal to each specialism continue to be made by the relevant specialists, others operating higher levels of the decision-making tree now apply something not very different from Weinberg's external criteria, which ranks the scientific, technological, and social merit of proposals in relation to current government priorities.

Locating Science in the Universities

It was during the period after the Second World War that curiosity-oriented research was taken up by the universities, transforming them into the major players in the forward march of science that they are today. Crucially, it was at this time that, through the persuasive efforts of Vannevar Bush and others, governments decided to back universities as the prime sites of the research that would lead to technological innovation (Bush, 1945).

Thus it was that the science of the universities became a responsibility of national governments, advised by high-level science advisory boards. Across the Commonwealth, research was funded through a research council system, which made extensive use of peer review in making decisions about who did what in science. In this process, universities were radically reorganised, taking the form of departmentally based units that carried out research as well as providing undergraduate teaching and postgraduate training. It is too easily forgotten that during this period, not only in the Commonwealth but globally, universities changed from being schools devoted to teaching the liberal arts to research institutions organised to advance knowledge through the disciplinary structure of science.

Peer review and its committee structure, based in research councils which fund research in universities, is now a formidable system. To date, it has been a stable one, and it still shapes the content of the majority of the research carried out in universities. The endgame, it is now clear, has been the establishment, pretty well globally, of what could be called the 'Regime of Basic Science' (Rip, 2012).

The Customer-Contractor Principle

Despite the lack of robust empirical verification, the linear model of innovation has remained a central idea in the provision of funding for science in the universities. In terms of this model, the widely held belief that more science implies more innovation remained unchanged and, to a large extent, unchallenged. Indeed, governments across the world continued to launch new universities, in no small part because of the anticipated economic benefits that science-based innovation would generate.

And so it was until the reigns of Prime Minister Margaret Thatcher in the UK and President Ronald Reagan in the USA, when the New Economics (influenced by the work of F. Hayek and M. Kalecki in Europe and by Milton Friedman at the University of Chicago in the USA) brought a distinct market orientation into the centre policymaking (Edgerton and Hughes, 1989).

As far as science policy in the UK was concerned, the event that launched the change was the publication of the Rothschild Report in 1971. It articulated what became widely known as the 'customer–contractor principle'. Put simply: customers indicate what they want; the contractors do it; and the customers pay. Under this rubric, the customer—government in this case—would set its priorities. It was the job of the particular government departments to determine what research would support these priorities and to contract with the appropriate research establishments to get it done. As the New Economics permeated policy thinking in major economies, the basic idea behind the customer–contractor principle was taken up in many Commonwealth countries, notably in Australia, Canada, New Zealand, and South Africa, as well as in the United Kingdom.

While it is true that the customer–contractor principle was aimed initially at government research establishments, it was not long before it was extended to the national research council systems and, through them, approached the heart of the peer review process. Despite the imperative to tie research to national objectives, governments continued to accept that it was primarily from the research of the universities, perhaps more than that of its research establishments, that the innovation process would best be stimulated. As a result, the total amounts available for university research did not decline, but an element was now aimed at promoting research in specific priority areas.

In sum, while government-funded research councils and similar institutions in other jurisdictions continued to support university science, the Weinberg criteria adumbrated above were subtly introduced, not only by broadening the experience and skill base of those evaluating specific prospective proposals in priority areas, but also by passing peer review judgements through a hierarchy of filters operating at different levels.

The end product was a 'funding package' that supported both university science and research in government priority areas.

The Entrepreneurial University

From the 1980s, governments also encouraged universities to become more entrepreneurial.

First, the management of intellectual property (now a requirement in virtually all research grants) became a responsibility of university central management: new technology transfer services were established or older ones refurbished, and patenting activity was encouraged, as was the development of science parks, business schools, and incubator units to develop potentially profitable technologies.

Second, universities themselves introduced new types of senior positions to manage an increasing number of complex, often multi-partner, projects and to ensure that all of the goals set out in research proposals, including the commercialisation of results, were met on time and within budget. Latent in all of these changes was something that was to change universities profoundly—the coming of dedicated 'research centres'.

Research Centres

Following the introduction of the customer–contractor principle, policies aimed at promoting selectivity and concentration in university research were put in place. These were research-oriented initiatives intended to give a boost to academic research in areas that had been identified as having industrial relevance. In addition, governments supported these policies, by offering university staff research fellowships and 'research only' professorial fellowships. In retrospect, these initiatives were viewed by some as the initial steps in the gradual separation of teaching and research in universities.

Over time, these departmentally based, informally organised areas of research concentration gradually evolved into the relatively independent multi-partner configurations that now populate university campuses. Research centres are funded not only by government but also by industry, charitable foundations, and, particularly in the USA, by wealthy individuals. They do not operate within the disciplinary structure of science, but independently, alongside it.

As multi-party organisations, research agendas have to reflect the interests of those partners. It is in these later manifestations that research centres now press most acutely on the ethos of knowledge production in universities, and will perhaps begin to challenge the assumption that universities have become ivory towers that have lost interest in doing science that is of interest to their communities. It is precisely these communities—whether industrially oriented or organisations focused on social issues—that play a major role in constructing the research agenda of many research centres.

From their inception, research centres always attracted some (often senior) academics to leadership positions, often on a part-time basis. However, for the most part, centres were staffed by researchers employed by universities on a contract basis. Centre staff worked, often for years, without tenure, indeed with a reducing prospect of it. So large did this cadre of researchers become that universities were forced to review their hiring policies. For example, at the outset of this policy, a researcher employed in a research centre on a contract for, say, five to seven years, might expect to get tenure in the usual way. However, as the number of centres began to grow, it soon became clear that, if tenure was eventually granted to all contract staff under the normal conditions of peer review, the long-term salary burden would be unsustainable. Often, no tenure was granted but, in some cases, researchers were still required to leave their jobs after a fixed period, simply to avoid the legal tenure implications of repeatedly renewing contracts.

Despite this uncertainty, the numbers of staff employed in research centres on a contract basis has grown, as the centres evolved from single to multiple-party funding. Indeed, recent research has shown that there are more researchers on contract than there are researchers with tenure (Boden et al., 2004).

Research centres are the harbingers of a distinctive type of university. That is, not the traditional one, in which research is carried out primarily within the discipline-based departmental structures alongside undergraduate and postgraduate teaching as well as other academic administrative functions; but instead one comprising both traditional faculties as well as time-limited 'units', whose sole function is to carry out research oriented by the aims and objectives of its funders and whose interests extend from basic science, to medical research, to technological development and community-based initiatives.

It is unquestionably the case that universities have, for a long time, acted as homes for research centres of various kinds. The difference here is that the research centre has become a 'preferred mode' not only for research councils but for industry, foundations, and private charities. It is a mode that is unlikely to be abandoned because, ironically, as research councils have long recognised, accommodating government priorities through research centre funding has provided a way for them to protect the funding base for curiosity-oriented research.

However, for universities, there was a sting in the tail involved in supporting the development of research centres. Aspiring universities had to demonstrate that funding from industry and other relevant organisations in the wider community had also been obtained. In addition, the universities themselves also had to provide some support for research centres, whether in cash or in kind. Many universities accepted this approach as a way of demonstrating that they were in some measure pursuing research in line with government priorities. Whatever, the intent of government policy, both industry and organisations in the wider community seldom commit funds without having some influence on the research agenda. Quite the reverse: multiple sources of funding bring in their train the imperative to develop a research agenda that meets a range of objectives well beyond that of advancing the frontiers of any particular science. In this, inputs from the 'Regime of Basic Science' (Rip, 2012) may constitute one among many.

The endgame of these developments amounts to nothing less than the inauguration of a 'Regime of Strategic Science'. This regime exists in tension with the already established Regime of Basic Science, because it inaugurates an alternative mode of practising science, what might be called 'research in the context of application' (Gibbons et al., 1994). It is an alternative to which many academics have responded positively. It cannot leave the universities unchanged.

A Postmodern University?

A major feature of postmodernism has been its loss of faith in the ideas of the Enlightenment. Thus, it is argued by many postmodernists that people in general have become disillusioned with the idea of progress and are sceptical that science and rational thought can make the world a better place. Consequently, postmodernism relies on concrete experience over abstract principles, always aware that the outcome of one's own experience will necessarily be fallible and relative, rather than certain and universal. One manifestation of this is the emergence of critical analyses of the possible negative effects of scientific and technological 'progress', such as pollution, and damage to the environment and human populations therein.

One consequence of changes such as these has been that definitions of status and authority have become elastic. Thus, along with other social institutions, science, too, is becoming a more porous system, is broadening the range of those deemed fit to participate in research, and revising the criteria of research excellence. These developments, so the argument runs, have also made their way into the university and are reflected in the practice of science itself, opening up the research process to a wider range of participants, of which research centres are but one example. Changes in the modes of delivering undergraduate education, as argued by Daniel in this volume (see Chapter 5), are another.

These differences between modernity and postmodernity invite the possibility of an isomorphism: the Regime of Basic Science is to the modern university as the Regime of Strategic Science is to the postmodern university.

Characteristics of a Postmodern University

What, then, might be the principal characteristics of a postmodern university? Several characteristics are already evident, albeit in embryonic form.

- The research is located in the university but in a variety of forms. It is funded, in part, by government through the normal channels, but also increasingly in other 'configurations' involving, in different ways, partnership funding with industry, charitable foundations, wealthy alumni, and the universities themselves.
- These configurations form loci that can operate in a quasi-independent manner, each one linked to the university by a particular set of 'arrangements', which themselves may alter over its lifetime.
- Some tenured university staff may be recruited to these centres, perhaps on a part-time basis, while other researchers are employed

full-time but on time-limited contracts. Together, they devote themselves to full-time research.

- Centres also provide a range of opportunities for contract staff to work towards Master's and PhD degrees in a wider range of contexts than are available within the traditional disciplinary structure.
- These features, together with the emergence on (or near) university campuses of business parks, independent research institutes, and small start-up companies associated with universities in a variety of ways, have all contributed to making the 'campus' a more complex entity to manage.

In the language of contemporary postmodernism, established academic boundaries have been transgressed and the status of traditional academic elites modified.

For example, for many years now academics have been able to concentrate on research, because some of the teaching burden was borne by graduate students. On balance, this was regarded as a good thing, particularly for those postgraduates who sought to join the academic community. The development of research centres acknowledges that many postgraduates will not be able to find employment in traditional academic departments. As university staff take up secondments in research centres, they will expose any graduate students they bring with them to more complex research environments. These offer postgraduates not only forms of training beyond those that would routinely be available within the traditional university departments, but also a wider range of job opportunities when their training is completed.

However, research centres are not an unalloyed blessing for tenured staff in traditional academic departments. While it is true that conventional academics must square their research activities with the demands of undergraduate teaching and administration, those academic staff who opt for life in a research centre must be prepared to develop their research careers in the context of the centre's aims and objectives, while continuing to make contributions to the scientific literature. It follows that achieving research excellence in the Regime of Strategic Science may not be for everyone. Research centres will certainly not provide a hospitable environment for those who simply want to advance their careers by hoping to carry on doing what they have always done. Contemporary research centre initiatives have moved a long way from the 'research only' professorial fellowships which, some have argued, have often gutted mainline academic departments.

To say the least, there are institutional tensions implicit in these developments. For example, it is not difficult to anticipate that, should this trend continue—and given the prestige that research enjoys—for those who are able to function effectively in research centres a pecking order may soon be established within some universities. This will give greater recognition to those who are able to function full-time in the more open and complex environments of research centres compared to those who, because of the nature of academic life and their own abilities, cannot.

Further, some have argued that the development of research centres will lead to the unravelling of the teaching–research nexus that has for so long been regarded as a distinctive characteristic of university education. That may be so but, equally, being trained in the more open environment of a research centre will, in Jacques Menand's memorable phrase, 'transform the ways in which knowledge producers are produced'—a change which, he argued, was essential if the universities were ever to deliver the multidisciplinary training that they have for so long promised (Menand, 2010).

Short-term Gain but Long-term Pain?

Apart from offending traditional academic amour-propre, there are also some aspects of these developments with which presidents and vice-chancellors, in particular, are already familiar. Indeed, it has frequently been remarked that, for institutional leaders, quasi-independent research centres are a 'short-term gain but a long-term pain'.

The gain may seem obvious: more research income and greater prestige. However, there is not infrequently some pain to be endured.

- To acquire a research centre, it can be the case that the university itself is the applicant. As such, it is expected to cover the costs of any refurbishment, find offices for staff and provide administrative support services of various kinds. This is usually a small inconvenience, given levels of funding that these centres can attract over many years.
- Further pain may be experienced because research centres are funded for a finite period, after which funding will cease unless alternative sources can be found.
- In addition, whether on tenured or short-term contracts, all staff are university employees, and closing a centre can lead to expensive

severance arrangements, which may not have been covered by the initial funding arrangements.

- Finally, capital investments that may have gone into creating new labs and other facilities may not be re-deployable without refurbishment and further cost. Fear of offending sponsors who have supported research over many years can put pressure on vice-chancellors to 'adopt' the centre and ensure its long-term viability, putting strain on university finances. For the university, seeming not to have valued prior investments by others in research centres can be both an embarrassment and a burden in the longer term.

Still, not many universities have turned down the money and prestige that often comes from having research centres on their campuses. What has gone largely unremarked is that research centres are contributing to the creation of universities that house a wide range of activities, administrative arrangements, and staff contracts. As has already been indicated, the outcome is a blurring of lines of authority, status, salary arrangements, and working conditions. These are generally recognised as the characteristics of a postmodern society, and research centres are the vehicles that bring these very characteristics into the heart of the university.

The current, 'postmodern' situation facing universities with research ambitions has been described succinctly by one former vice-chancellor in a recent review of global higher education developments:

> [I]n the context of mass higher education and of a pervasive knowledge economy, it no longer makes sense to regard the generation of knowledge as a restricted activity. Instead, it has become a reflexive rather than a linear process, with multiple actors rather than primary producers. Fundamental discoveries can be made in near-market, or socially embedded, environments just as would-be applied research can be undertaken in academic environments.
>
> (Scott, 2010)

More Open, Porous, and Flexible Universities

In sum, a Regime of Strategic Science is being established alongside the Regime of Basic Science. It is making universities more open, porous, flexible organisations than many would have thought either possible or desirable in the Regime of Basic Science. The new regime exists in tension with what, in the Regime of Basic Science, was regarded as the fundamental ethos of universities: the pursuit of independent, free inquiry.

Yet research has become a capital-intensive activity. It is expensive and is becoming increasingly so. The need for research funding is imperative and recurrent, and the search for it is drawing universities into a different kind of world. It is perhaps not wrong, then, to suggest that the evolution of the Regime of Strategic Science is a harbinger of the postmodern university.

The Power of Innovation

In postmodern universities, the traditional boundaries of universities will be more open, and links between the academy, the economy, and society more generally will diversify and become more complex. In this way, universities become active players in systems of open innovation of the type being championed by Chesbrough and his colleagues at the University of California, Berkeley (Chesbrough et al., 2006). In this, innovation policies have moved decisively beyond the simple linear model that dominated policy thinking since the 1960s. Now, it seems, successful innovators not only need to take stock of what knowledge they possess, but also to seek out what knowledge they need.

Of course, universities—and to some extent firms—are knowledge producers. However, as regards the innovation process, each has tended to see itself as primary, possessing plenty of knowledge to transfer beyond its borders but otherwise self-sufficient. Accordingly, they have been less interested in identifying and making use of inward flows of knowledge produced by others. Yet, as Chesbrough argues, efficiency in the innovation process depends upon inward as well as outward flows of knowledge and an acknowledgement that relevant knowledge may be found in a variety of places. In the postmodern university, research centres, because of their growing engagement with government, industry, and the institutions of wider society, can be crucial vehicles for identifying and appropriating the inward flows of knowledge that are now regarded as essential to sustain open innovation.

In the environment of open innovation, two things should be noted. First, innovation now depends critically not only on technology and markets but also on the social milieu with which the innovation must be in synch if expectations are to be achieved—be they profits for a firm, or increased standard of living and social well-being more generally. Second, this implies that in addition to conventional knowledge producers, the users or potential beneficiaries of research may also hold relevant knowledge, and so need to be involved in the innovation process from the outset. For example, no firm can afford to launch new processes or products that might compromise health and safety guidelines or global environmental considerations, nor can medical researchers fail to involve patients' knowledge in developing their research protocols. In the search for stable technological paradigms, inputs to innovation must, initially at least, move forward on a very broad front. That is why research centres have become key actors in the drama of innovation. They are better placed to recruit expertise, albeit on a temporary basis, from the wide range of sources that are now regarded as central to successful innovation, particularly in its early stages.

It is also perhaps now clear why earlier research into the process of industrial innovation (described above) failed to identify much evidence of the priority of science in innovation. As Dosi's research has shown (Dosi, 1982), firms search not so much for a particular piece of knowledge as for a stable technological paradigm. Much collaborative research goes into finding this paradigm but, once it is found, collaboration may be attenuated, as companies embrace the new paradigm and invest their own resources to develop it in specific ways that will allow them to compete with other firms that are working within broadly the same paradigm. At this point, technology, rather than science, is carrying the dominant paradigm forward into commercialisation, and earlier contributions from basic science may simply be lost.

The point of noting this theoretical development within the field of innovation studies is to call attention to the fact that university-based research centres are key entities, not only in the search for scientific discoveries but also for stable technological paradigms—a role that was certainly more difficult to play, given the organisation of universities, in the Regime of Basic Science.

However, innovation cuts two ways: it produces new knowledge to be sure, but it also changes the organisational frameworks within which knowledge is produced. Collectively, these constitute the Regime of Strategic Science. Through the medium of research centres, this regime is being embraced by many universities. The point is that it cannot leave them unchanged.

Universities as Knowledge Validators

In the Regime of Basic Science, research is legitimated by the peer review process itself. In the Regime of Strategic Science, the universities must manage a more variegated knowledge production process that can be left neither to peer review nor to a research centre's management committee. To guarantee the legitimacy of the work of their research centres, universities need to adopt a more 'hands on' approach to their management, not only because much of the work is being carried out near the boundaries of established disciplines where peer review itself may not be reliable, but also because the knowledge produced may have legal, medical or social implications that need to be taken into account throughout the knowledge production process.

In addition, the ethos that has become established in the Regime of Basic Science has led to the social perception that the universities can be trusted to preserve open and independent inquiry. As has already been noted, Weinberg recognised the implications of this, and so developed three external criteria for evaluating the worth of a proposed research activity. However, he continued to rely on government to manage the broadening of the peer review system to include users and beneficiaries of the proposed research.

In the Regime of Strategic Science this responsibility falls squarely on the universities themselves. The implication is that universities *as institutions* need to become active participants in the work of their research centres, making university values integral to the research undertaken. Indeed, in the Regime of Strategic Science, universities may be ranked according to their ability to manage the quality and maintain the integrity of the research carried out in their centres. Effective ethical management is but one implication of carrying out research in the context of application.

Laboratories for Community

It is a tough call for presidents and vice-chancellors to manage a range of research centres, which they may only partially own or be able to control, as well as the traditional departments. Within the Regime of Strategic Science, this is becoming a principal task for university management and it is pressing upon leadership at the highest level.

In this respect, the distinguished scholar Randolph Bourne argued many years ago that 'the issues of the modern university are not those of private property but of public welfare,' and that 'irresponsible control by a board of amateur notables is no longer adequate for the effective scientific and technological *laboratories for the community* that universities are becoming' (Cole, 2007: 352).

As argued here, establishing laboratories for community is fast becoming a primary function of universities, and research centres are their mode of knowledge production. To be sure, Bourne grasped the ethos-changing nature of the research centres as the homes of laboratories for the community.

What, then, are the implications of this for members of the university—its councils, presidents, and vice-chancellors, deans and professors and, perhaps most importantly of all, its students? These are matters that urgently need to be addressed, if these 'laboratories' are to flourish in universities and not elsewhere. To establish new research centres, to support their development, and to finesse the closure of older ones and, above all, to ensure the integrity of the research carried out within their institutions, constitutes a principal challenge—if not *the* principal challenge—for postmodern universities in the Regime of Strategic Science. Such is the power of innovation.

Conclusion

As if to further strengthen their commitment to innovation, many countries have replaced their former 'science and technology' systems with 'science, technology and innovation' ones (Halliwell and Smith, 2012). In the latter, some funding, albeit still at a relatively low levels, flows to research centres; that is, to groups of researchers who are demonstrably able to couple their agendas to social, economic, and political priorities. Many are being set up in universities.

Research centres constitute a distinct source of funding for universities. However, because they have predefined goals and a finite lifetime, research centres can require different modes of recruitment, organisation, and management, which must co-exist with those of the prevailing disciplinary structure. Over time, this can be expected to alter the internal structure of universities, creating a set of changes which may be indicative of the diffusion of the Regime of Strategic Science into postmodern universities. Universities cannot embrace national innovation agendas and its modes of knowledge production and expect to remain exactly as they are.

For universities, it has been more than a century-long road of transformations from Newman's classic liberal arts curriculum (Newman, 1852) to Kerr's 'multiversity' modern higher education institution (Kerr, 2001). But we are far from its end. Perhaps Richard Bourne was not wrong when, having grasped the magnitude of the task ahead, he insisted that universities need to be 'thoroughly re-imagined' if they are to meet their responsibilities of becoming laboratories for community. The potency of research centres may well provide just the catalyst to ignite that process.

Bibliography

Works Cited

Boden, R., Cox, D., Nedeva, M., and Barker, K. (2004) *Scrutinising Science: The Changing UK Government of Science*. Palgrave, Macmillan.

Bush, V. (1945) *Science the Endless Frontier*. Washington, DC: Office of Scientific Research and Development.

Chesbrough, H.W., Vanhaverbeke, W., and West, J. (2006) *Open Innovation: Researching a New Paradigm*. Oxford: Oxford University Press.

Cole, J.R. (2007) *The Great American University: Its Rise to Preeminence, its Indispensable National Role, Why It Must Be Protected*. New York: Public Affairs.

Dosi, G. (1982) Technological paradigms and technological trajectories. *Research Policy* 11: 147–62.

Edgerton, D. and Hughes, K. (1989) The poverty of science: A critical analysis of scientific and industrial policy under Mrs Thatcher. *Public Administration* 67, Winter: 419–33.

Freeman, C. and Soete, L. (eds.) (1990) *New Explorations in the Economics of Technological Change*. London and New York: Pinter Publishers.

Gibbons, M., Limoges, C., Nowotny, H., Schwartzman, S., Scott, P., and Trow, M. (1994) *The New Production of Knowledge: The Dynamics of Science and Research in Contemporary Societies*, 9–10. London: SAGE Publications.

Goldin, C. (2010) Tales out of school. Sunday Book Review, *New York Times*, 7 February, 26.

Halliwell, J. and Smith, W. (2011) Paradox and potential: Trends in science policy and practice in Canada and New Zealand. *Prometheus* 29(4): 373–91.

Kerr, C. (2001) *The Uses of the University*, 5th ed. Harvard: Harvard University Press.

Menand, J. (2010) *The Marketplace of Ideas: Reform and Resistance in the American University*. London: Norton.

Newman, J.H. (1852) *The Idea of a University*, 1948 ed. Harlan Davidson.

Rip, A. (forthcoming 2012) Recent changes in scientific institutions. Paper presented at Noors Slott, Stockholm, 16–18 October 2009, *Prometheus*.

Scott, P. (2010) Higher education: An overview. *International Encyclopaedia of Education* 4: 217–28.

Weinberg, A.M. (1963) 'Criteria for scientific choice', *Minerva* 1: 59–71.

Further Reading

History of Innovation, the Economy, and Public Policy

Barry, N.P. (1979) *Hayek's Social and Economic Philosophy*. London: Macmillan.

Carter, C.F. and Williams, B.R. (1957) *Industry and Technical Progress*. Oxford University Press.

Caves, R.E. (1968) *Britain's Economic Prospects*. London: Allen and Unwin.

Cozzens, S.E. (forthcoming 2012) End of Empire: External and internal transitions in U.S. policies for science, technology, and innovation. *Prometheus*.

Freeman, C. and Louca, F. (2001) *As Time Goes by: From the Industrial Revolution to the Information Revolution*. Oxford and New York: Oxford University Press.

Hayek, F.A. (1978) Competition as a Discovery Procedure. In *New Studies in Philosophy, Politics, Economics and the History of Ideas*. London: Routledge.

Illinois Institute of Technology (1968) *Technology in Retrospect and Critical Events in Science* (TRACES). Prepared for the National Science Foundation, Vol. 1.

Langrish, J., Gibbons, M., Evans, W.G., and Jevons, F.R. (1972) *Wealth from Knowledge: A Study of Innovation in Industry*. London: Macmillan.

Metcalfe, J.S. (1998) *Evolutionary Economics and Creative Destruction*. London: Routledge.

Nelson, R.R. and Winter, S.G. (1982) *An Evolutionary Theory of Economic Change*. Cambridge, Mass.: The Belknap Press of Harvard University Press.

Utterback, J.M. (1998) *Mastering the Dynamics of Innovation*. Boston: Harvard Business School Press.

von Tunzelmann, G.N. (1995) *Technology and Industrial Progress: The Foundations of Economic Growth*. Brookfield, VT: Edward Elgar.

Society and Higher Education

Brennan, J., Huber, M., and Shah, T. (1999) *What Kind of University? International Perspectives on Knowledge, Participation and Governance*. Buckingham: Open University Press.

Clark, B.R. (1998) *Creating Entrepreneurial Universities: Organisational Pathways of Transformation*. Oxford: International Association of Universities Press, Pergamon.

Cloete, N. and Muller, J. (1998) South African Higher Education: What Comes after Post-colonialism? *The European Review*, June.

Hughes, A. (forthcoming 2012) Innovation policy, university-industry links, open innovation and the new production of knowledge, *Prometheus*.

King, R. (2004) *Universities into the 21st Century*. London: Palgrave.

Mokyr, J. (2002) *The Gifts of Athena: Historical Origins of the Knowledge Economy*. Princeton, New Jersey: Princeton University Press.

Nowotny, H., Scott, P., and Gibbons, M. (2001) *Re-thinking Science: Knowledge and the Public in an Age of Uncertainty*. London: Polity Press.

Scott, P. (1990) *Knowledge and Nation*. Edinburgh: Edinburgh University Press.

Trow, A. and Nybom, T. (eds) (1991) *University and Society*. London: Jessica Kingsley Publishers.

Useful Websites

National Innovation Policies

Australia: http://www.universitiesaustralia.edu.au; http://www.innovation.gov.au/innovation

Canada: http://www.nce-rce.gc.ca/_docs/8pager-eng.pdf

Hong Kong (with specific reference to strategic research initiatives): http://www.ugc.edu.hk/eng/ugc/publication/press/2011/pr13072011.htm

India: http://www.knowledgecommission.gov.in

New Zealand: http://www.morst.govt.nz

South Africa: http://www.dst.gov.za

United Kingdom: http://bis.gov.uk/policies/innovation/

Universities' National Innovation Systems

Australia: www.go8.edu.au/university-staff/go8-policy-_and_-analysis/2011/role-of-universities-in-the-national-innovation-system

Europe: http://ec.europa.eu/research/

India: http://www.ugc.ac.in

University Governance

http://siteresources.worldbank.org/EDUCATION/Resources/278200-1099079877269/547664-1099079956815/Global_Trends_University_Governance_webversion.pdf

United Kingdom: http:/www.lfhe.ac.uk/governance

Universities and Global Economic Growth

http://www.worldbank.org/research/

Innovation and higher education in South-East Asia: http://go.worldbank.org/H82ZZ5EZM0

The Changing Academic Profession

Australia: www.lhmartininstitute.edu.au/research-and-publications/research/20-the-changing-academic-profession

United Kingdom: www.vitae.ac.uk/policy-practice/237421/Resources.html

15

Looking Forward: Reflections for Universities in the Twenty-first Century

Colin Lucas

Universities worldwide are engaged in a process of rapid change. It is difficult to see Commonwealth universities as a discrete category in this respect. On the one hand, the Commonwealth contains such a diversity of social forms, economic conditions, and national ambitions that it mirrors in effect the diversity of experience worldwide. On the other, its universities are inescapably enmeshed in relationships that transmit major shifts in focus and innovation originating outside the Commonwealth. This chapter aspires to an analysis that holds true—if not in all respects—both in the Commonwealth and elsewhere. Admittedly, however, its arguments are principally drawn from the currently predominant forms of university and university system.

The future of universities is a huge subject. Old certainties in our assumptions about organisation and function seem liable to subversion at this time. The implications of our changing environments offer scope for multiple potential changes and developments, often mutually contradictory and often imagined only by inference. A comprehensive discussion is not possible in this brief essay. In any case, a historian (such as I am) knows better than anyone that, as financial advisers warn, the past is no guide to the future. This chapter is, therefore, very selective as well as frequently speculative. It falls into three areas.

- What are the pressures on universities and higher education?
- What are their consequences?
- What are the implications?

First of all, however, let us remind ourselves of the adaptability of universities, which is sometimes obscured by the impatience of outside observers and the nostalgias of some academics. The Euro-American model (as we may call it now, despite its regional variations and differing historic inspirations) has shown itself to be resilient and flexible over its history, despite moments of torpor, and has spread worldwide. Both in its earlier, solely European form and in the later, nineteenth- and twentieth-century reciprocating transatlantic version, we see universities evolving in terms of curriculum, origins and destinations of their students, definitions of knowledge and intellectual project, and changing relationship with civil society and public power. Over the last 150 years, their adaptability has been remarkable. For example, one has only to think, especially but not only in North America, of the multiplication of disciplines and their re-combinations, of the growth of professional education and credentialing, and of the variety of postsecondary provision. Equally, as examples of exceptionally successful transformation since the late 1940s, we can point to the massification of higher education and the simultaneous rise of the research enterprise in research-intensive universities.

We may, therefore, remain reasonably confident about the general capacity of universities to adapt to the pressures of contemporary circumstances and to absorb change. Nonetheless, great anxieties can (and do) exist about the character and extent of that change. Certainly, in general, universities do not appear at this time (and especially not collectively) to define the nature of change nor to implement a broadly strategic approach to the future of universities. Rather, they tend to react to the opportunities of the moment, while managing policy priorities and incitements from outside as well as competitive initiatives wrought from motives often alien to their own core values. In part, the reason for this lies in the fact that the pace of contemporary change is well outside the historic experience of universities. That sits ill with the academy's instinct to establish first principles and to construct forms that endure rather than temporary ones capable of further adjustment to ongoing changing contexts. In part also, however, the reason lies in the fact that the forces at work for the last 10 to 20 years are so fundamentally revolutionary in university terms that they bring into question the core business of universities and their function.

What are the pressures on universities now? Their origins are so interconnected and mutually informing that it can be difficult to ascribe particular consequences to particular causes. Moreover, the effect of contemporary pressures is quite often simply to accelerate pre-existing trends, albeit taking them in some unexpected directions. Thus, what some people now see as the triumph of the sciences and the crisis of the humanities cannot be understood without reference to a long development since 1940 at least. There is an obvious tendency for our present environment to play upon the natural dynamic of university systems. However, whatever the complexity of contemporary pressures, the current context is largely defined by the digital revolution, globalisation, and the actions of governments.

The digital revolution is in the process of transforming how knowledge is constituted, how it is disseminated, how it is accessed, and above all, who has access to it. It is transforming the way in which wider communities of knowledge are constructed. It is transforming the means of discovering, compiling, comparing, processing, and storing information. It is multiplying the possibilities for teaching. Indeed, it may presage transformations in the definitions of knowledge itself and of who authenticates it. In this last respect, an outcome of the digital revolution may be to bring into question the very functions and purpose of the university; at all events, universities are likely to emerge considerably modified in shape, behaviour, and expectations. The digital revolution allows universities and their academics to extend and innovate prodigiously in what they do, but simultaneously threatens their settled patterns and their coherence. This is both the most pervasive of the pressures on universities and also the one whose long-term outcomes are the most difficult to predict.

Much the same dual quality of transformative opportunity and threat can be seen in globalisation. On the one hand, the rapid growth of the global knowledge economy and of global accessibility to learning promotes new and more extensive networks of collaboration between academics and universities, as well as intensified flows of students, researchers, and professors. On the other hand, just as in the geography of economic power and financial success, globalisation is accompanied by notable redistribution and rebalancing, so too it promotes a new geography of university power and success, new sites of innovation, new patterns of competition and collaboration. At one level, we can see this as simply another example of a natural dynamic at work, albeit accelerated, in which success goes to those most adept at seizing opportunity and understanding potential advantage (although inherited resources and appropriate external funding are certainly a help). They are not necessarily those at the top of a currently perceived hierarchy of excellence; but then, the history of universities records the decline or disappearance of numbers of institutions.

At the same time, there is a deeper possibility of subversion here. One symptom of the vitality of the Euro-American university model has been its spread to much of the globe during the last two centuries. Yet, this has been an effect either of imperial/colonial control or of the needs of international mercantile/financial systems or of imitation of the most successful and prosperous nations or else simply a by-product of missionary zeal. This success has itself been a significant element in accrediting a Western claim that its methods of constituting, verifying, and disseminating knowledge are normative, as are its universalist value systems, thus obscuring or dismissing alternatives. Even if one believes that the rationalism underpinning the procedures of the sciences in universities is unchallengeable, it would be unwise to consider that other assumptions and values that we see as central to our systems are self-evidently beyond erosion in the longer run.

The third major pressure identified here is the action of governments. This is a confusing area, since the play of influences on or within different governments (and, indeed, different political systems) has produced dissimilar behaviour over the last 10 or 15 years—for example, in the allocation of public funds to universities. Furthermore, it is not clear whether the economic turmoil of the last decade in the developed countries will have had a lasting or a temporary impact. Nonetheless, some clear trends exist. In systems where the state is the principal funder of universities, there is an important sense in which public policy is the most direct transmitter of the transformative pressures of our time. It does so either by seeking responses to perceived global challenges through universities or else by inciting universities directly or indirectly to seek opportunities elsewhere in the changing national and international environment. This phenomenon is capable of distorting the character of universities' action as we advance in the early twenty-first century.

The most obvious trends in this area are these: public policy linking universities and the global economy; the effect of social policy on higher education; and the use of public funding. Once again, it is difficult to separate these into discrete categories. However, we may use them as an entry point to a more specific discussion of how pressures to transform are playing out in our universities in practice—now and in a potential future.

Justification by economic relevance began to creep into Western universities' discourse on themselves during the 1980s—less so perhaps in the USA, where the perceived relationship between higher education and citizenship remained strong. This coincided with the waning of the Cold War, which, in Europe and North America at least, had been providing a sense of relevance for the wide spectrum of universities' activities. In the mid-1990s, however, many Western governments became increasingly aware of the threats posed to national prosperity and competitiveness by the shifts in the world economy encapsulated in the term 'globalisation', most especially the formidable growth of China's economic power along with that of India and Brazil and the re-emergence of Russia. More explicitly in some countries than in others, governments enrolled universities as prime actors in their strategies. This was natural enough since, whether individual academics have welcomed that or not, one function of universities has always been to respond to the needs of their societies.

More specifically, governments identified two features. First, success in the new knowledge economy required that higher skills be spread among wider sections of the population, in which universities had a necessary part. In this, governments were doubtless right. Second, public policy in this domain was rooted in the belief that the new economy was shaped by (if not the product of) the digital revolution. The technology of communication provided instant, universal dissemination of information. The digital world both made innovation the true heart of competition and provided the means for a rich diversity of innovations. From here, it was an easy step to the conclusion that this was essentially a matter of scientific discovery, its translation into applicable technologies and its transfer to entrepreneurs. Universities have, therefore, been assigned a prime role in promoting economic prosperity, which is a renewed version of the Cold War vocation of Western universities to promote and defend a better society than that of the rival ideological camp. This last 'easy step' contains some serious flaws, to which we will return below.

At all events, at the turn of the millennium, governments and their advisers (in the UK and Australia, for instance) were making frankly overblown statements about universities as dynamos of growth in the innovation process and as huge generators of wealth creation. It is not simply a matter of the UK and Australia. The European Union, for example, has been preoccupied by the lack of Europe's international competitive success, which it ascribes in large measure to a limp record of innovation. Throughout the first decade of the twenty-first century, it too has sought remedies through European universities and through its framework programmes for research. Individual European countries have taken similar paths—for example, the *Exzellenzinitiative* in Germany, the reform of the Centre National de la Recherche Scientifique in France, and so on.

This emphasis on the social value of science has had some influence on thinking about undergraduate study. At this point, however, let us look at its profound impact on research and the culture of universities. There is no doubt that, from China to most points west, public funding of research has turned predominantly to science and technology. Although a kind of machismo of research income size has developed recently, it is a bit silly to brag about or lament the disparity with the arts: science and technology are high cost, often very high cost. Nonetheless, there is a real contraction of the funding of arts and humanities. This has been occurring in a context of public discourse (as above) that suggests, sometimes perhaps unconsciously, the irrelevance of these domains of academic activity to the urgent needs of contemporary society. There is, in consequence, a growing change in the culture of universities—with significant potential consequences. This is a large subject, to which we will return later.

Most governments continue to make substantial investments in science and technology, although direct investment by industry is much more patchy. However, the size of investment required has had consequences, accentuated by the fiscal effects of the economic crisis. Outside the emergent economies led by China, there are issues about infrastructure funding, which may or may not have long-term effects. More significantly, governments and their agencies for indirect funding are increasingly focusing finance on selected research domains, defined both as critical nationally and as the most likely to generate economically beneficial innovation. It would be somewhat unfair to say that this is 'official' science, defined and imposed from outside. Academics collaborate in the process: they populate the agencies that identify and roll out programmes; they ensure that the programmes do address large and crucial issues; and they do the assessments. Nonetheless, there is no doubt that in most of the Euro-American system, public funding for research is being seriously constricted.

There are significant implications here. This is not just an expression of the current economic conditions, but rather the symptom of a transition. It represents a new phase in the rise of research as one of the great defining activities of universities in the second half of the twentieth century. Even for rapidly enriching societies with substantial investments in higher education, university research on the broad scale is too expensive, if not somehow funded selectively. The sense that universities need to be assigned a more closely defined role in their necessary function as society-serving institutions has been matched by a belief that they must be held to providing value for taxpayers' money (and private universities encounter their own version of that). Symptomatic of the thrust of value for money through outcome-evaluation has been the rise of 'league tables', the flaws in their assumptions shaping yet further the distortions that we have been examining. Even one of the directorates of the European Commission has been trying to develop a league table that is better able to assert continental European universities alongside Anglo-Saxon ones.

There are demonstrable risks to a university that does not 'get it right' in this situation where research success and reputation are mutually sustaining. Institutions are very conscious of this, and seek more and more aggressively to hire research leaders, whole teams and postgraduate students into profile-building areas. Naturally, there is nothing new about the movement of academics. However, leaving aside the forced migration of refugee academics in the last century, those who remember the rather decorous drift across the Atlantic (even so, dubbed the 'brain drain') can see a palpable difference of degree. Moreover, the patterns are different now, especially in terms of a great multiplication of destinations (one can foresee that movement into Chinese universities will cease to be predominantly by returning Chinese academics). In Finland, for instance, those universities that have abandoned rules limiting some appointments to local candidates have found 80 per cent of their applicants to be from abroad. There is here potential for the erosion of coherence within individual universities and within national university systems. The internal architecture and disciplinary balance of individual universities could be destabilised, with consequences as yet hard to see. As for those universities that have insufficient research and reputation success, they will face serious decisions about function and income. This, in turn, could put strain on the coherence of university systems through pressures of fragmentation.

Furthermore, it is credible to predict that the continuing high cost of research will produce a situation where considerations of efficiency combine with patterns of excellence to confine public research funding to a small number of 'preferred suppliers', so to speak. The tendency has already been visible in outline in those countries with periodic general assessments of research performance: the outcomes separate a small group of institutions from the rest (echoing usually the distribution of competitive grants). This does not necessarily preclude the appearance of 'preferred suppliers' situated in other, less generally successful institutions. However, isolated units do have a way of migrating to larger clusters.

If the escalating cost of high-level research in the sciences points towards concentration, it is also the case that both the cost and the progressively fluid frontiers of research disciplines suggest that, increasingly, the capacity for the most ambitious and potentially innovative research cannot be contained within one university. This is true as much of the humanities and social sciences as it is of science. The digital revolution will continue to enable more complex research questions and richer collaborations. Clearly, inside universities collaborations bridging conventional disciplinary borders are likely to grow, adding whole new dimensions to the internal economy and dynamic of individual institutions. One cannot, at present, predict the extent to which this will eventually reshape individual universities. More importantly, this situation is already accelerating the growth of international collaborations in research, bringing together multiple sites of complementary skills, equipment, and resource investment. That, in turn, points towards the probable emergence of a complex pattern of collaborations—both ad hoc and longer term, both institutional and individual and group—which will modify considerably the configuration of universities and university systems with which we are currently familiar. This theme is developed further below.

The discussion so far has concentrated on research that may seem limited in application to only parts of the university world. However, it is a convenient place to begin, because the growth of university research has been one of the most striking developments of the second half of the twentieth century upon which contemporary change is impacting. There is now an unbreakable relationship between research performance and public reputation for institutions. This has central importance for matters ranging from the recruitment of high-quality academic staff and students through to simple issues of funding income. Certainly, in many places, universities with less substantial research records bear witness to this situation in their expressed ambitions and the strategies articulated in their mission statements. If one were to read only such documents, one would be tempted to believe that the major direction of travel was towards convergence of model and activity.

A further reason to lead here with themes relating to research is the changing culture of academics, visible before but accelerated by contemporary pressures. Just as research underpins the reputation of institutions, so also do academics increasingly validate themselves by the quality of their research, acknowledged by peer review. Beyond the inherent satisfaction of personal interest in research, high performance brings esteem to the academic and, through the mechanisms discussed above, career opportunity and financial reward. For numbers of them, that increasingly appears to compromise their availability for, and commitment to, other aspects of university activity. There is here a potentially damaging challenge to what one may call the 'ecology of the university enterprise'—that is to say, the conditions under which a university seeks to accomplish coherently its multiple functions.

Indeed, some of the same stresses that we have discussed earlier are visible elsewhere in the work of universities, most obviously (but not only) in education. As in the area of the earlier discussion, some of the immediate challenge comes through public policy, more openly so in some countries than in others. Most governments have understood that national success in the high value-added knowledge economy requires a much larger proportion of the population to be educated to a higher level, often with an emphasis on scientific and technological subjects. At the same time, considerations of social fairness in access to higher education have coloured public policy in this area. This is perfectly logical in terms of economic transformation, although in some places there has been confusion about the priority of objectives and sometimes a tension between excellence and inclusiveness that neither governments nor universities have been good at resolving. In general, the direction of travel is towards continued growth in the size of institutions.

However, alongside these objectives, it has also become increasingly apparent that the cost of sustaining a larger student population is certainly more than the taxpayer is willing to pay—and probably more than it is sensible for it to pay. The fiscal problems of the early twenty-first century have focused this dilemma, but are not its simple cause. Few countries outside the fast-developing economies have managed to maintain the position of a generally well-funded university teaching and learning sector. More broadly, public funding has been reduced—either by outright reduction or by reduction in real terms, associated in some systems with the concentration of allocation on subjects and initiatives deemed consonant with national objectives. By and large, the basic instinct is to transfer the cost away from the public purse. Most usually, this has been to hand the problem to universities, leaving them to respond by a broad and doubtless growing set of measures—ranging, for example, from worsening student–staff ratios, cutbacks in selected disciplines, and budget controls through to diversifying sources of income through fundraising, intellectual property, and types of fee income.

The more general issue of transferring part of the cost to students (on the basis of some sense of an individual benefit from higher education) is matter for high-octane political controversy, especially where no fees (or only insignificant ones) had previously been levied. At the end of the first decade of the new century, there is no clear pattern—taking Europe for instance, England continues to press forward on student fees, Germany is retreating from fees, and France maintains its minimal fee. Nonetheless, it is difficult to avoid thinking that, in the medium term, the part-privatisation of higher education will come, whether through the transfer of some cost to students or through the commercialisation of some core activities or through the growth of wholly private institutions in some potentially lucrative areas of directly employable skills.

Insecurity of funding will not cease to press upon all but a handful of institutions. Even those currently experiencing the investments of fast-growing economies will come to it. How individual universities manage that insecurity will be the great differentiator. A good part of this will involve being alert to new opportunities in this time of transformation.

The most obvious of these opportunities is trans-border education. Once again, this is not a new phenomenon (both the USA and the UK have long been magnets for non-local students), but there has been a qualitative change amounting to a transformation. As far as the trans-border movement of students is concerned, the change is in part simply the accelerating volume of demand, in particular from Asia. In part also, the change is in the great multiplication of destinations to which students go, compared with the later twentieth century. There is now a global market for students and, as a consequence, global competition. The increasing investment in recruitment and the development of multiple models of trans-border activity are unlikely to diminish, nor, indeed, is the number of institutions involved. Trans-border education is not simply the movement of students, but involves more generally the offshore delivery of teaching and learning through franchising, distance learning, the embedding of units in other institutions, formal networks of sharing between two or more universities, and the creation of campuses abroad. These models will certainly continue to evolve.

Of course, these developments are both a symptom of globalisation and a contributor to its further development. New digital technology sustains and enhances the capacity to deliver trans-border education, and we can expect more innovation here. Where we are dealing with the full-time, residential experience, the mingling of students of different nationalities and cultural backgrounds is no doubt beneficial well beyond academic experience. It should prove effective in preparing better mutual understanding and relations in a fast-paced, interconnected world. Furthermore, the quality of learning outcomes for all is certainly improved by the participation of high-achieving and ambitious overseas students. The benefit that such incoming students bring to universities is betrayed by the increasing degree to which institutions are willing to offer financial incentives to attract them. In particular, foreign postgraduates have already become indispensable to research-intensive universities. At this level, they have become an integral part of the research-ranking-reputation-funding structure that we discussed earlier. More generally, involvement in this and other forms of trans-border education gives a university a profile of internationality that contributes to its standing. At root, though, the stimulus to universities here is financial. Directly and indirectly, international students bring income. Governments have seen this benefit too. For a number of them, higher education has become a commodity, an article of trade. In this vein, a number of places (particularly those with relatively small populations, for instance Singapore, Hong Kong, and in the Gulf) have launched policies to make them 'education hubs'. That points towards further changes in the patterns of global education.

Even if precise outcomes are unpredictable, there are clear implications here. International students (especially those from Asia) tend to concentrate in a number of areas: in particular, sciences and areas around medicine, business, economics. They tend to be skill-seekers, interested in career-enhancing courses. Although this is by no means exclusively the case, it is where the balance lies. The cultural assumptions and the focus of subject matter in the humanities and the parts of social sciences closer to them make these areas difficult, if not unattractive, for students from outside those regions already deeply imprinted by Europe and North America. Indeed, that point highlights the more general, serious dilemma facing the teaching of humanities: do they prepare students for life in the transforming global world by teaching them about the cultural inheritance of the world they have grown up in, or by trying to make some sense of the cultural complexity of the world they are going into (a situation exacerbated in North America by the loss of homogeneity in cultural origins among college students)? At all events, the clustering of international students around particular disciplinary areas constitutes a distorting pressure inside universities that some may find hard to manage.

The model of bringing international students into full-time residential courses is not necessarily stable. It is sustained for the moment by the urgent desire of populations without sufficient access to adequate higher education at home to seek it abroad (together with added personal prestige). It is a desire driven by a need to take advantage of the opportunities offered by a still fluid globalisation for those who can equip themselves with requisite skills. For the time being, this demand seems vigorous and capable of extension to new geographical areas where secondary education either is at a reasonable level of quality and accessibility or becomes so. Nonetheless, in the short term, this demand can be very volatile, as the sudden drop in recruitment in Australia recently demonstrated. Such volatility is likely to be emphasised by the further emergence of competing poles of attraction, particularly in countries with higher investment in universities.

In the longer term, other transformations can be foreseen, though perhaps too distant for active concern at present. It seems likely that as universities in student-exporting countries rise strongly in quality and range of provision, and as the cachet of a foreign education wanes (especially in Asia), the type of demand will change markedly. Opportunities at home may well remove the justification of expense and disruption in foreign study. Demand may well turn to more specialised courses; postgraduates may travel to learn a particular technique or in the context of major collaborative projects; joint degrees shared between institutions could become much more the norm; the international reputation of a university and of individual professors would be the decisive issue in determining the flow of students. Universities that have created campuses abroad or entered into deep collaborations internationally with one or more universities will have been wise, for this will ring-fence for them a supply of students and will generate opportunities for recruitment of academic staff and research collaborations. Similarly, development of distance learning through new applications of digital technology will provide powerful extension to universities since, whatever its limitations, its cost to students is infinitely less than study abroad. All this implies a significant change in the focus and character of universities, whether in their financial models or in the future of the full-time residential degree.

Other pressures and opportunities for change raise a number of similar considerations in more domestic or national environments. At root, the distinction between research-intensive and teaching-intensive universities is likely to become more explicit than it is at present, though that presents challenges to the former, where teaching income is indispensable to the research economy. How this will be reflected in the organisation of the higher education system of any country is unclear. The opportunities for different types of emphasis for individual universities will continue to multiply. One example is the potential power (and the relative financial security) of a strong local focus. Let us leave aside the model offered by New York in its attempt to commission a city-focused great specialist and research-based institution, as this is more a reflection of the local economic impact around Palo Alto (California) or Cambridge (Massachusetts). The perspective here has more to do with the capacity of a teaching-intensive university to respond to the skill requirements of its locality or region, to direct a significant part of its action towards civic engagement, and to shape its student recruitment on the basis of social need.

Of course, in many ways this is not an innovation at all. Such institutions exist in many countries, sometimes classed as universities but more often not, sometimes organised as systems and sometimes not. The perspective here concerns the potential for an effective retreat of some universities from a national dimension and the gathering of such functions within a local university context. There would be consequent changes in some curricular matter and in relationships with local interests; one would also expect to see some fusions (or indeed disappearances) of institutions.

Pressure for increased localisation could also come from student demand. Earlier in this chapter, we argued that although the contemporary economic crisis has increased financial pressure on students, the general trend is likely to continue to be to transfer costs away from the public purse. One consequence may be to direct more enrolment to the nearest local university. However, in many countries, study at a local university is already the established pattern for the large majority of students. The more likely effect seems to be frequent interruptions of study and repeated returns to it. This would amplify another phenomenon, frequently cited by commentators who argue that rapid changes wrought by a knowledge economy—itself in a continuing state of self-renewal—will require people to re-skill themselves periodically. Whether, when and in what form the transforming knowledge economy will stabilise is probably unpredictable. However, a pattern of repeated visits to higher education is likely to be a continuing strong theme. This does, of course, furnish a role for local teaching universities. At the same time, it has other implications. The organisation of teaching and learning will be challenged; curricula will be increasingly demand-led and defined by practical applications; and the campus functions of a university will be brought into question.

However, the most transformative force is the digital revolution. It is very far from complete and its effects are still to be elaborated. Truly, in this domain we see through a glass darkly. Since the core business of universities is the creation and transmission of knowledge, the digital effect pervades the whole of what they do. We have already alluded to the impact of the digital revolution on research and scholarly communication. The transformations in teaching and learning, already visible in outline, may have larger implications. It is clear that teaching and learning in universities must adapt to the modes and habits of learning that students have acquired before coming. There is no sense in ascribing some inherent educational virtue to processes of formal instruction and personal performance upon which university systems have long relied. Universities have to understand the ways in which students acquire information and behave collectively through digital media. Open-source publishing will affect undergraduate learning as much as it will influence research; and group learning will find its model increasingly in social networking media. Learning how to find sources and to search them will be replaced by learning how to discriminate among the mass of instantly available sources and how to use search engines in order to identify credible sources. In the balance of the elements that make up the craft of teaching, the instruction mode will recede in favour of mentoring and guidance. Thus, even within the system with which we are familiar, teaching and learning will change profoundly (as it has already begun to do) and the classroom is destined to lose its defining role in the relationship between teacher and student.

The digital revolution also contains much more serious challenges to standard university practices and systems. Digital learning has very broad applications—from being part of the delivery of learning within traditional campus structures through to the remote delivery of whole degree programmes. To date, online degree systems have acted more as a supplement rather than a challenge to traditional universities, reaching a different population in terms of age, education, and social background. The overheads are high and there are inflexibilities in purely online student support. Nonetheless, the rapid progress of digital tools is helping to overcome these. The changes in much longer-established distance-learning operations are a pointer (see, for example, the development of the Open University in the UK).

It is debatable whether online education will simply continue to extend the reach of higher education by bringing it to new markets locally, regionally, worldwide, or whether it will offer a credible alternative to traditional degrees as they are now or will become. Certainly, it will make it easier for private for-profit universities to appear (including ones set up by commercial enterprises in a related area), usually specialising in career-enhancing areas such as business, law, and economics—on the model of the small private universities set up in parts of Latin America in a more classic form in the 1980s and 1990s. Certainly, too, the search for income may well drive numbers of existing universities to enter this domain, thus modifying their character and priorities. Indeed, online education is driven by market demand. It tends, therefore, to be organised around the potential student numbers for a course and the kind of career-enhancement skills that are appropriate to them. At all events, there are many possible versions of the place of digital learning, ranging from the wholly online university (such as the University of Phoenix) through a kind of hybrid university to a digital enhancement of teaching and learning in a more traditional institution.

The recent appearance of Massive Open Online Courses (MOOCs) suggests other directions. MOOCs place course material online and furnish the ability to follow that course free of charge. There are two models. One has been initiated by some leading American universities. It offers no more than the course (though, in fact, support mechanisms exist in the form of online communities crowd-sourced through forms of social media). Carnegie Mellon University puts it in lapidary form: 'no instructors, no credits, no charge'. The other model is provided by two for-profit companies (Coursera and Udacity), set up by professors from such universities, though Coursera seeks to be an international network of university providers, whereas Udacity does not. These enterprises do offer some forms of instruction and Udacity, at least, does provide a certificate of completion, which could eventually be seen as a credential.

MOOCs are the direct expression of the digital revolution. Some commentators have excitedly seen in them a major threat to established university forms. This is unlikely in the short-to-medium term. For one thing, it is extremely difficult to generate income through this model. The model itself is very unstable. Nonetheless, there are interesting features. Some of the originators have explicitly seen this as a vehicle for subverting existing university structures and systems, in what they see as a democratisation of higher education through mass participation. There is, therefore, a potential for challenge here. Moreover, a new feature is the appearance of institutions with high international reputations as major players, whereas they had previously held back. This is doubtless one reason for the very high numbers beginning to follow some of these courses. Thus, the research-reputation-success nexus operates in this domain too. Moreover, these numbers show the potential for the development of a mass digital learning audience. Finally, what are currently on offer are single courses, principally in science and technology. A whole degree course is presumably possible, but that would involve some major challenges. What is outlined here is a system where individuals take discrete courses, either to help them understand some issue or mechanism or else to provide them with the enhancement of a particular skill. That is not so different from existing forms of online learning, other than in the numbers of participants. It is possible, though, to see here the hint of a future where in some cases the possession of the skill or understanding might be more important than the credential to prove it.

Equally interesting is what universities involved in MOOCs have chosen not to do. It would be cynical to argue simply that the lack of a competent revenue-taking mechanism has limited them to providing only the course material. In fact, it shows that whereas in earlier times access to the materials of knowledge was precious and had to be guarded, the digital revolution has reversed that. It is the guiding, mentoring, teaching, and personal training in interpreting and resolving complexity that is precious. That is still optimally done in the physical company of academics and other students. Its outcome has to be evaluated, before being recognised by a university's degree. Access to these things requires payment. Above all, these universities are not offering access to unprocessed or unstructured information but instead to courses, that is to say to organised knowledge and structured exposition. In other words, these universities are protecting the crucial role of universities to define useful knowledge as distinct from the assertion of the validity of any interpretation constructed out of a random trawl of digitally accessible sources.

Notwithstanding, whether it is in the potential of MOOCs or in the more general implications of evolving modes of delivery, there is a challenge over time to the current dominant model of full-time, residential universities. That model is bound to evolve and change; such universities are bound to diversify their business and how they conduct it; they are bound to have to co-habit with different types of institutions and forms of higher education. Indeed, they may well, over time, cease to appear self-evidently the norm or superior.

We may perhaps understand these issues a little more clearly if we look at libraries. The digital revolution imposes change on them. In the pre-digital age, the most efficient way to preserve and access knowledge was to gather in one place as much of its hard-copy record as possible for people to come to study. Now, on the contrary, the most efficient way to access knowledge is to distribute it electronically to the individual. There is a parallel here to the kind of issues that hang over the full-time campus university. Libraries are digitising their rarest materials; Google has been digitising much of the commonest parts of libraries' collections (though the future of copyright publication remains uncertain in this context); digital publishing (whether open-source or commercial) can easily by-pass libraries. Once again, this demonstrates that access to information and the record of structured knowledge is no longer the preciously guarded task in which libraries excelled.

A need for research on paper-based sources will remain; yet, in order to keep their place, libraries will have to rely on other skills that they have. On the one hand, their function is likely to evolve towards, first, a role of mentoring and guiding readers in the use of material; and, second, providing a kind of switchboard to link readers to multiple types of digital record and depository, thus becoming, so to speak, essential tailor-made search engines in an environment of ever-expanding digital production. On the other hand, the very nature of digital production offers matter to two traditional library skills. First, much digital material is ephemeral and, indeed, often seen by relatively few people. Librarians are by training the best people to seek out material and decide what should be kept and what can be allowed to disappear. Second, the pace of change in the digital media is so great that operating systems, software and so on come and go, leaving predecessors increasingly unreadable while the physical disks degrade. Libraries' traditional vocation of conservation will be essential, if we are not to lose access completely. The digital record is as vulnerable to neglect and decay as the written and printed record has been to malice, fire, water, and war.

Whether the future of university libraries, in particular, will be as stand-alone institutions, or whether they will be absorbed into the teaching structure or integrated into information systems, is unclear. Probably, different models will appear. However, by analogy they do offer lessons to the currently dominant form of the full-time, comprehensive campus university—libraries will have to transform, by modifying the focus of what they do and by renewing traditional skills and functions to modified circumstances.

Where does all this leave us, in thinking through the complex uncertainties of the future? The selection of present trends may be arbitrary; the identification of potential outcomes is often speculative; above all, one cannot calculate influences as yet invisible. Nonetheless, if one were to draw a sliding scale from little change on the left to dissolution on the right, one would say that the left end represented complacent folly and the right end is imaginable only by the deepest pessimist. Quite where on the scale we shall rest, and when, is unpredictable in detail. Over time, each university will make its own strategic choices, some sound and some not. We began this chapter by saying that universities are resilient and adaptable: no doubt, but that adaptability will be seriously tested in the coming century.

There are perhaps two messages to take away here. The first is that one can foresee a progressive fragmentation of the current university landscape as institutions reformulate parts or the whole of themselves. Public policies designed to enrol a university system behind strengthening the national economy may ironically end up by hastening a fragmentation of the national system. In numbers of countries, as we suggested above, we see individual universities seeking their future in international networks and relationships. As noted, these networks serve different purposes, but the fact is that such universities are increasingly looking outside their own country, outside their national network; they are factoring international considerations into their thinking and modifying the composition of their student and staff populations. The possibility of the intensified localisation of some universities may echo the increased delocalisation of others. Furthermore, the likely multiplication of types and versions of a university has the potential eventually to isolate institutions in separate individual or group identities. Finally, we might see, ultimately, a submerged fragmentation inside institutions, as the pursuit of income and self-worth reduces the commitment to—or even the sense of—a common project. Quite how far such centrifugal forces would go is unclear. However, the potential for loss of coherence is clear.

A second message derives from the potential loss of coherence. We must beware that universities do not lose a sense of their essential functions. The American Philosophical Society was set up in 1743 in order to promote 'useful knowledge'—a good motto for universities, too. But who defines what 'useful' is? President Obama praised the Far East nations' progress in technology and science education, saying: 'They are spending less time on teaching things that don't matter, and more time on teaching things that do.' So, what are the things that matter? There is a deep flaw in the perception of contemporary governments that useful knowledge is that which contributes to economic prosperity, especially through the outcomes of scientific discovery. Leave aside the notion that economic prosperity can, in fact, be produced in this way. Leave aside the question of whether the right research themes have been chosen to the exclusion of others. Leave aside the fact that close government requirements, procedures for selecting grantees, and mechanisms of accountability put a premium on 'safe' science (that is, more likely to produce a positive outcome for the money spent) and narrow the opportunities for more 'risky', creative, unknown areas of science. The central point is that this is not how research and discovery work (whether in science or in the arts).

The core function of universities is to create knowledge and to transmit it, together with knowledge inherited from predecessors that each generation subjects to renewed tests of verification. All universities subscribe to this common project, even if they do not all engage fully in all parts of it. It is universities that define what knowledge is—on the basis of rules of evidence and critical reasoning, which have themselves been elaborated over time by the same means. Others may find forms of utility in application, but that cannot be without the prior supply of this knowledge. The great danger of loss of coherence is the erosion of this function and the distortion of values.

The current preoccupation with the short term, with immediate knowledge and its application, is simply to fasten on the by-product of a much less precise process. The creation of new knowledge—and one cannot distinguish here between sciences and arts—depends upon a culture and individual attitudes that value curiosity, scepticism, serendipity, creativity, and genius. The nature of research is that its outcome is basically unpredictable. If one knew what one was going to find, who would set out to find it? It is the freedom to speculate, to go look, to imagine, to notice details, to indulge in wonder that produces the future. Destroy that, and we impoverish the future. Universities deal in big questions, whatever the discipline involved. The vitality of universities lies in the constant recognition of the instability of meaning and knowledge, the constant questioning, the unremitting search for new understanding across the full spectrum of disciplines. Indeed, even though science appears to deal in cumulative certainties, scientists themselves acknowledge that, beyond a quite advanced level of competence in observable interactions, their 'truths' are not that much more stable than those with which humanists deal. The chain of emergent complexity pulls scientists forward, but challenges often what have hitherto been taken as fundamental truths.

Of course, there are obvious differences between the sciences and the humanities. Sciences are concerned with penetrating the mysteries of the natural and physical world of which we are part, and they base themselves on the premise of the universality of physical phenomena; humanities are about human beings, about another sort of complexity characterised by difference. Scientific enquiry addresses how physical matter (including the human body) works and why it is the way it is. The humanities address what it means to be human: the stories, the ideas, the words that help us to make sense of our lives and the world we live in, of how we have created it and been created by it. They give voice to feeling and artistic shape to experience, exploring issues of morality and value. Work in the humanities (and indeed in the social sciences) is concerned with issues that are essential to the stability, good order, creativity, and inspiration in society. They gather the thinking, learning, and explanation of what binds and separates human beings. They seek to understand and make accessible that extraordinary intensity and complexity of beauty by which human beings specify themselves in the merging of thought, emotion, and expression. They provide understanding of why and how we express differently our common characteristics of being, as well as how we differ as individuals, groups, and cultures.

Differences in objects and procedures of study should not disguise that all academics, whether in research or teaching, are essentially engaged in the same process of constituting knowledge, the same process of discovery—whether by uncovering the previously unknown or by refining what we think we know by reinterpretation, the same process of understanding what previously we did not understand. All domains are complementary, all are mutually sustaining within the general purpose of universities. Indeed, in broad terms, all are capable of bringing practical improvement in the human condition—controlling, benefiting from, and repairing the physical environment; nurturing the human body; improving social justice and market conditions; and meeting the urgent need for understanding and mediation generated by the rapid growth of global immediacy and of the contact of once distant populations.

This mutually sustaining quality of university action is equally visible in its other function of transmitting knowledge. Among different forms of transmission, let us examine just teaching and learning. Of course, at one level, universities serve to provide skills and preparation through which individuals will access better-quality and better-paid work. But there is more to it, and once again all academics participate in that purpose, irrespective of discipline. Generation by generation, universities serve to make students think. They do so, by feeding and training their instinct to understand and seek meaning. In this process, students are taught to question interpretations that are given to them, to reduce the chaos of information to the order of analytical argument. They are taught to seek out what is relevant to the resolution of a problem; they learn progressively to identify problems for themselves and to resolve them by rational argument supported by evidence and tests; and they learn not to be dismayed by complexity, but to be capable and daring in unravelling it. They learn to seek the true meaning of things: to distinguish between the true and the merely seemingly true, to verify for themselves what is stable in that very unstable compound that is presented as knowledge. These are deeply personal goods, but they are also public goods. They are the qualities that every society needs in its citizens. In particular, this is essential in cultures which believe that fair and open societies, which can resolve legitimate competition between individuals and harmonise legitimate differences, are only maintained by participatory democracy. It is universities that produce these citizens, or at least enough of them to leaven and lead society generation by generation.

The contemporary observer must remain anxious about the ability of universities to protect these essential functions of the definition and transmission of knowledge through the predictable and unpredictable transformations of the advancing century. Of course, we can respect specialist institutions held within a system; but all must subscribe to the same purpose of knowledge. Universities alone are the bulwark against systems of pseudo-knowledge based on unverified sources and fantasies of meaning. The last century demonstrated clearly enough not only the panic, hatred, and devastation that derived from such ignorance, but also how universities could be intimidated and suborned in their function. Yet, ultimately, universities alone can protect their own importance. No one much from outside is going to help, for there is much to covet in universities. It requires intelligent, principled, and firm leadership, supported by academics who understand the issue but who do not cling to every form of the past for fear of the future.

16

Mission Impossible? The Challenge of 'Institutional Character' for Twenty-first Century Universities

John Wood

> There are three main global trends emerging today that will shape the world in 2030: the empowerment of individuals, which contributes to a sense of belonging to a single human community; greater stress on sustainable development against a backdrop of greater resource scarcity and persistent poverty, compounded by the consequences of climate change; and the emergence of a more polycentric world characterised by a shift of power away from states and growing governance gaps as the mechanisms for inter-state relations fail to respond adequately to global public demands.
>
> (ESPAS Report, 2012)

'The future is not what it used to be' is a well-worn cultural cliché. But that has never been more apposite than today, when the very future of society and the planet is at stake. The need for universities to train flexibly thinking people, and to look for equitable solutions to the challenges before the world, is immediate and essential.

Probably the most dramatic change to affect universities during the past hundred years has been in the speed and volume of global communications. In 1913, the founding year of the ACU, heads of universities would spend up to several weeks on ocean liners in travelling to London to exchange ideas and take part in discussions with fellow vice-chancellors of the British Empire, while enjoying several social events, before taking the long sea voyage home. When, in 2012, the ACU's executive heads conference was held in Kingston, Jamaica, at the University of the West Indies (and looking to the new century ahead), only two days later several of the same executive heads were already to be found at a major educational conference in Doha, Qatar. Those discussions continued issues from Kingston, before leaders headed to the next higher education forum. While on these international duties, they had no doubt sent hundreds of text messages, emails, and tweets and had made many mobile telephone calls over the few days away from their home campus.

It used to be said that 'a week is a long time in politics', but now it can be said that 'one day is a long time in universities'. Although it has to be acknowledged that not all areas of the world have the same high-speed access—and this may actually be a blessing in disguise—that is also unlikely to persist for long. The pressure on senior university managers is now increasingly intense for many reasons, and this is manifesting itself in the length of time that heads of universities remain in post. The Canadian experience suggests that the average tenure in office of a university president is now approximately one-fourth of the time compared with a few decades ago.

In addition to the pressures of immediacy, most universities are under pressure—both politically and socially—to expand significantly, either in terms of student numbers, or by increasing their so-called 'relevance' in areas such as research and innovation, or by making a greater 'social impact' through community and industry engagement.

Increasingly, output metrics are cited to show the superiority of one university over another. The 2012 ACU conference in Kingston rightly highlighted just how ridiculous it is to have a single league table number to demonstrate institutional quality. Just as we do not measure a human life by digits alone, so too with the complexity of a human institution such as a university. A numerical measure means that all aspects of character are lost to the observer, all nuances of inflection removed. This lack of appreciation of diversity, especially among state policymakers, has led to some perverse outcomes for universities. ACU members (of which there are over 500 across the globe) are very familiar with this burdensome issue in defending institutional diversity and fitness-of-purpose in their diverse missions.

The 'Character' of a University

The trenchant and memorable words of the late General Norman Schwarzkopf resonate in this context: 'Almost every leadership failure that has occurred in the last fifty years has not been a failure in competence but a failure in character.'

While it may seem unusual to talk about the 'character of a university', this is perhaps the very issue behind John Henry Newman's famous formulation in *The Idea of a University* (Newman, 1852). Newman too was writing against social trends in an industrialising age, which were unsympathetic to his notion of what a university should be, and what values it should uphold in its educational mission. In the language of today's social sciences, the issue could be encapsulated around institutional form, structure, and character.

Universities naturally look for those characteristics which not only show them in their best light in performance rankings, but those which most faithfully represent their organisational mission. These can, of course, look different to different audiences.

- At one extreme, this could be the funders (whether public, private, or individuals), who look at the outcomes in terms of graduate numbers, added value, employability, and the general impact on the economy.
- At another extreme, there is the need to attract students into areas of study where employability is important; but probably not as high as other key educational factors, such as the total student experience, the courses, and delivery methods on offer and, increasingly in some parts of the Commonwealth, the cost to the student, or the possibility of finding a part-time paid job during their studies.
- A third contingent concerns the staff at all levels—those who service the university infrastructure (technical, administrative, and academic), all of whom are investing their talents in the success of the university.

The increase in dispersed campuses, virtual universities and the mobility of students (including those studying split-site courses) further makes the idea of 'a university character' difficult to assess, let alone define. The harsh reality is an increasing pressure to be able to demonstrate to all apparent stakeholders, who have access to global information tables regarding other institutions. Thus, it is difficult to compare without full and rounded knowledge of the specific mission and character of a specific university.

Avoiding 'Brain Drain'—Recruiting and Retaining Excellent Staff

Another common cry, in this apparently bewildering matrix of pressures, is the problem of recruiting and retaining talented staff committed to both excellence and the institution. Attracting such staff is starting to look like the buying and selling of football players, and it is inevitably a complex problem involving whole families and, sometimes, complete research groups (where 'golden hellos' are not uncommon).

This puts extreme pressure on universities that cannot operate in this arena on financial or quality-of-life grounds. Certain wealthier countries, such as Canada, Australia, and South Africa, have adopted variants on the 'National research chairs' idea, whereby finance is made available to appoint and foster the concept of research training, by making new appointments that are then 'ring-fenced' from many aspects of teaching and administration which conventional academics are required to perform in those institutions. A major objective of these schemes is to attract talent from outside the country. Other international institutions—such as the World Bank, large charitable foundations, national governments, and the European Commission—have numerous fellowship and scholarship schemes and other modes of fiscal support to grow research capacity in universities within emerging countries. Another method of support is via 'partnering' of universities, but this has mainly been at the individual or departmental level, rather than at the institutional mode. A key question is increasingly: how effective are such schemes? And do they create sufficient critical mass to change the culture of an institution?

There are great opportunities here for the ACU, as a co-operative association, to use conventional and new social media to facilitate networking between individuals and groups. However, this is hardly the whole answer to the problem of increasing the number of highly talented academics within a diverse range of universities.

A recent editorial in *Nature* reinforces the scale of the challenge concerning this critical issue of the mobility of academic scientists between countries:

> Of the world's most highly cited scientists from 1981 to 2003, one in eight were born in developing countries, but 80% of those had since moved to developed countries (mostly the United States), according to a 2010 study by Bruce Weinberg at Ohio State University in Columbus… Proportionally, however, Switzerland, Canada and Australia all housed more foreign researchers than the United States, with Switzerland having the highest foreign share, at 57%. India had the lowest proportion of foreign scientists, followed by Italy and Japan, but also the largest diaspora, with 40% of its home-born researchers working overseas.
>
> Career-stage affects scientists' mobility. Chiara Franzoni, who studies science and innovation at Milan Polytechnic in Italy, has done an unpublished analysis of the GlobSci data and shows that a nation's 'postdocs' are much more likely to be foreigners than its professors. In the United States, for example, 61% of postdocs were brought up overseas—but only 35% of assistant, associate or full professors. Nature found similar patterns when it surveyed readers about their attitudes toward migration, and their own personal histories. Those who had just obtained their PhDs were much more likely to be living outside their country of origin than were more senior scientists; and they were also more open to an international movement, presumably because their career paths were not settled, and they were less likely to be tied down by relationships and families. The proportion of respondents who said they were 'not interested' in international relocation rose from a mere 10% in those who gained their doctorates within the past two years, to 40% in those who had done their PhD at least 16 years previously.
>
> One take-away from a policy perspective is that 'if you are trying to bring people back who have studied overseas, then you should target the young because they are more likely to move', according to Patrick Gaule, an economist who studies science and innovation at Charles University in Prague. He has tracked the movements of almost 2,000 senior-level foreign chemists affiliated with US universities between 1993 and 2007. Only 9% will return home by the end of their professional career, he estimates, and those that do are seven times more likely to return between the ages of 35 and 45 than after 50. For policy-makers eager to attract foreign scientists—or stem a loss of domestic talent—most want to know is accordingly: 'what then entices scientists across borders?' Gaule's analysis reviews the impact of quality of life, long term job opportunities, national and institutional bureaucratic systems and other indirect issues related to the prevailing culture.
>
> (Van Noorden, 2012)

The area of 'early career opportunities and support' is becoming a key theme for the ACU actively to pursue, both in the analysis of the issues and in providing practical support.

It is interesting to note, for example, that more and more institutions are following a long-established practice of the Oxford and Cambridge colleges in appointing young scholars (directly after completing a PhD in most cases) as junior research fellows, and who will then have complete freedom to follow a line of research (in all disciplines), assuming that the appropriate facilities are available in that institution. This compares with, for example, the South African SARChi scheme, where postdoctoral fellows are considered 'students'. Although this is done for tax reasons, it does say much about the prevailing research culture nationally, and in the universities, which suggests a hierarchical rather than collegial model.

Appointing such young researchers for a fixed period of time is high risk, since some may fail; and yet the record shows that the rewards are well worth the risk in nurturing talent as part of the supply chain for future, top-level university appointments. It is not just a question of making such appointments without regard to the overall prevailing culture across the whole university.

The ability to meet and discuss ideas at an equal level with top academics, including Nobel Prize winners (in a social or collegial context), is equally essential in fostering new ideas. The great Francis Crick's favourite question to science researchers was: 'And what new discovery have you made today?' The famed humanities scholar WK Hancock had a similar intellectual challenge when meeting young researchers: 'And what is the question at the heart of your researches?'

Academic Work Profiles

The nature of an academic fellowship (as defined as a group of academics from different disciplines respecting each other's point of view in debate) is under considerable threat today, even if it did exist in the past, since the importance given to individual performance and ratings is still considered to be a key criterion for promotion.

- Are the modern criteria for promotion then conducive to creating a vibrant intellectual environment in the future?
- Will there be a rise in what Jamil Salmi calls the 'i-professor' (Altbach and Salmi, 2011)?

- Will the rise in so-called 'Science 2.0' force universities to sharpen their criteria for promotion yet further?

The definition of 'Science 2.0' is still loose, but a recent reference article (Wikipedia, 2012) reasonably summarises the difference between the conventional way of doing academic research with what is emerging as the new mode and conceptualisation (see Table 16.1)

Table 16.1:
The Emerging Model of Science 2.0

Current model of research	*Emerging model of Science 2.0*
Research done privately; then submitted to journals; then peer-reviewed by gatekeepers in major journals; published	Research data shared during discovery stages; ideas shared; scientists collaborate; then findings are disseminated online
Scientific literature behind paywalls online	Scientific discoveries free online
Credit established by name attached to journal article	How is credit established for contributors?
Data is private until publication	Data is shared before publication
Papers generally protected by copyright	Many different licenses possible: copyright, public domain, Creative Commons 3.0, etc.
Reviewers paid by journals via subscriptions, fees	Who will pay the reviewers? How will they be paid?
Journal article summaries available online after publication	Share methods, data, findings via blogs, social networking sites wikis, computer sites wikis, computer networks, Internet, video journals

Source: Wikipedia, 2012.

This is a rapidly developing area and issue, which is then linked to other initiatives such as 'open access data' as now being pursued globally by the Research Data Alliance (http://rd-alliance.org; see also European Commission, forthcoming). Initially launched as a joint activity between the USA, the European Union and Australia, other countries are now indicating their willingness to join the alliance, towards aiding interoperability, common standards for data sharing, authentication, and attribution rights across countries and across disciplines. Other initiatives include:

- the growth in organisations such as the Public Library of Science (PLoS, arXiv), which is extensively used by the physics community

- the huge rise in 'Citizen Cyberscience' and 'crowd sourcing' (for example, www.zooniverse.org)

The use of the word 'science' in this context is deceptive; a better word would be 'scholarship' or '*Wissenschaft*', which both seek to break down discipline barriers. At the 2012 'Citizen Cyberscience Summit' (16–18 February 2012, in London: www.citizencyberscience.net/summit12), for example, a project on global warming also involved several thousand participants around the world in a huge social history study, while another project on de-forestation in Africa also involved another very large group. Likewise, mathematicians are posting problems on the Internet to which anyone can offer contributions towards the solution. Effectively, this approach 'democratises' scholarship and research, and universities will have to develop strategies for this new situation.

Again, a Wikipedia article (see Table 16.2) reasonably summarises the advantages and disadvantages of Science 2.0.

Table 16.2:
The Advantages and Disadvantages of Science 2.0

Benefits of Science 2.0	*Drawbacks of Science 2.0*
more productive	difficulty getting credit for discoveries
more collaborative	difficulty getting paid
more collegial working environment	how is credit established for contributors?
freer, less expensive	risk others will copy preliminary work to get credit, patents, money
faster development	how will reviewers and editors get paid?
wider access	it is not clear how Science 2.0 will work
diverse applications: homeland security, medical care, environment, etc.	needs infrastructure
easier	
lets other scientists see results instantly and comment	

Source: Wikipedia, 2012.

'The Fourth Paradigm': Data and Global Collaborations

Scholars are also now beginning to speak of 'The Fourth Paradigm', in which it is argued that '[i]ncreasingly, scientific breakthroughs will be powered by advanced computing capabilities that help researchers manipulate and explore massive datasets' (Hey et al., 2009).

The speed at which any given scientific discipline advances will depend on how well its researchers collaborate with one another (and with technologists) in areas of e-science such as databases, workflow management, visualisation, and cloud computing technologies.

An Organisation for Economic Co-operation and Development (OECD) Global Science Forum report (OECD, 2012) highlighted the impact that global social sciences data sharing will have on issues such as health and well-being. Increasingly, global collaborations in humanities research are forming (for example, Common Language Resources and Technology Infrastructure [CLARIN]: www.clarin.eu/external/index.php?page=about-clarin), often using the expertise of organisations and people from physics and engineering backgrounds. An example is that of Lifewatch (www.lifewatch.eu), which is an international biodiversity research infrastructure combining several sources from space surveying to established collections in natural history museums and also allowing field observers with cameras on their mobile phone to contribute evidence. All the information from whatever sources is sent to CERN in Geneva—the home of European particle physics—for data analysis.

With such possibilities there also comes a warning. In a significant report from the European Commission entitled *Riding the Wave*, which is concerned with how large scientific data sets are handled in an open and transparent way, the following critique is made:

> Data-intensive science operates at a distance and in a distributed way, often among people who have never met, never spoken, and, sometimes, never communicated directly in any form whatsoever. They must share their results, opinions and data as if they were in the same room. But in truth, they have no real way of knowing for sure if, on the other end of the line, they will find a man or machine, collaborator or competitor, reliable partner or con-artist, careful archivist or data slob. And those problems concern merely the scientific community; what about when we add a wider population? How will we judge the reliability and authenticity of data that moves from a personal archive into a common scientific repository?
>
> (European Commission, 2009)

It is for this reason that the ACU itself is co-operating with the Consortia Advancing Standards in Research Administration Information (CASRAI). The aim of CASRAI is to support individuals and members in joining ORCID (Open Researcher and Contributor Identification; www.orcid.org), and other similar initiatives, which are involved in the authentication of publications, CVs, etc., so allowing some confidence to be restored to the fluid environment where some CVs, publication lists, and even qualifications are falsified. Publishers are noting that, despite computers to check content, plagiarism is still rife, especially among those whose academic reputation and salary are measured mainly by the numbers of papers published.

Not only is this just the territory of scholarly research; increasingly, the power of social networking and open access to information is also becoming a strong teaching tool. Interactive group work both inside a lecture theatre with the lecturer (now acting more like a conductor posing problems and bringing ideas to a conclusion or with clusters of students sharing ideas outside of a lecture theatre) and by using a common interactive screen has been shown to increase student understanding significantly. This will put considerable strains on any academic staff who are not at the forefront of the latest scholarly knowledge in their own discipline, as indeed will the increasing use of online teaching content from prestige universities around the world.

Training of staff to operate outside their comfort zone will seriously affect institutions that remain hierarchical in this environment. New ways of assessing students in this environment, such as their ability to contribute to the collective learning experience, will need to be explored further—as Jonathan Adams writes in *Nature*:

> A fundamental shift is taking place in the geography of science. Networks of research collaboration are expanding in every region of the globe. The established science superpowers of the United States and Europe have dominated the research world since 1945. Yet this Atlantic axis is unlikely to be the main focus of research by 2045, or perhaps even by 2020. New regional networks are reinforcing the competence and capacity of emerging research economies, and changing the global balance of research activity. This may well reveal different ways of approaching challenges, and solutions that are different to those of Western institutions. If the science superpowers are to avoid being left behind, they will need to step out of their comfort zones to keep up with the dynamism of the new players in this shifting landscape.
>
> (Adams, 2012)

The same trenchant article also contains a major warning for the Commonwealth about being complacent by assuming that, as an association, it will be a natural vehicle for collaboration:

> These clusters indicate that proximity is just one of several factors in networks. Nigeria, for example, collaborates not with its neighbors in West Africa but with co-linguists in East Africa. This mirrors a global tendency to use paths of least resistance to partnership, rather than routes that might provide other strategic gains. Such language links have historically benefited the United Kingdom through alliances with Commonwealth countries that speak English and have adopted similar research structures. The United Kingdom cannot rely on this to continue. This growth of regional collaboration has many implications. It amplifies the development of emergent research economies. Researchers in Asia, for example, do not need recognition from European and US authors if their research is being cited and used by partners within the region. In the short term, students will recognize attractive opportunities closer to home, with fewer alienating cultural challenges than many European campuses have offered.
>
> (Adams, 2012)

A still greater global challenge exists, which demands that universities across the world collaborate not only with each other but with all parts of society. This is best summed up in the excellent introduction to the first report of the European Research Area Board of the European Commission, published in 2009:

> Our world is changing. We face mounting challenges: of global warming, scarce water, energy shortages and healthcare, to name a few. Their solution will require new ideas, discoveries, talents and innovations—the fruits of research. To achieve them, we must start by changing the way we do research. We must reorganize, to create a truly open European Research Area marked by free movement of people and ideas. We must rethink the way science interacts with politics and society, so our governance is based on best-available evidence. We must rewrite the social contract between the researcher and society, so that freedom of thought is balanced by responsibility for action. We must open our markets, our companies and our knowledge institutions so they work together more productively. Above all, we must create an environment in which the best ideas thrive, the brightest people prosper, and our excellence is rewarded—while at the same time improving the cohesion of our society. These are big demands, and imply fundamental change in the way we think, work and research—indeed, change as great as any in our history. We call this change a 'new Renaissance', deliberately invoking the memory of a comparable revolution in thought, society and science.
>
> (European Research Area Board, 2009)

Although this specifically refers to Europe, the message is actually global. So what is this 'new Renaissance?' Again the report is quite clear:

> A paradigm shift in how we think, live and interact together, as well as a paradigm shift in what the role and place of science should be. A new, holistic way of thinking is required as technological answers alone are not the end-solution to a given problem. Science and research have to look at the systemic effect of any action rather than merely the localized gain. We need to develop better tools to predict trends, to supply evidence for decisions. We need to train a broadly educated citizenry, better able to participate in public debate on the benefits and risks of research and technology.
>
> (European Research Area Board, 2009)

It is a lesson well made; and it should be well heeded.

Plainly, many economies in the world are increasingly looking to universities to work together in looking for holistic solutions to the challenges before society—from food security to the provision of drinkable water. Just as governments look to maximise social impact through joined-up policies, so too they look to efficiencies in higher education.

In a major study, *The Road to Academic Excellence: The Making of World-class Research Universities*, Altbach and Salmi examined how several countries are now approaching the issue via a number of seminal institutional case studies, many of whom are members of the ACU (Altbach and Salmi, 2011). Again, the 'lessons' are clear. From both the political and academic point of view, the new paradigm shift, in what is needed and what is emerging, has not been grasped.

Perhaps a grander challenge for the ACU is, then, to raise the level of strategic thinking among members—although it is acknowledged that most executive heads' time is focused on immediate needs, with little time for long-term strategic planning.

Some universities are, however, seeing the need to form global partnerships, for example, the World University Network. Yet funding of international projects is difficult where several countries are involved with different schemes and cycles for support. It is proposed by the European Commission that there should be a regular 'Global Summit' that addresses these problems, and ongoing discussions are now taking place between the G8+5 members on how this might be done.

Campus and Community 'Engagement'

Despite all these high-level challenges, there remains the question of locality: what role does a physical university in one place have to offer in the future? Indeed, where is the very notion of a past campus inheritance in this mobile world, where the virtual is king?

David Eastwood, Vice-Chancellor of Birmingham University, believes that the concept of 'place' in the 'global' context is even more necessary today than it has ever been. He asserts forcefully:

> Place matters; and however universal knowledge might be or become, however borderless the world of ideas might be, a university has had and still has a profound and defining physicality and normative location.
>
> (Eastwood, 2012)

His thesis speaks to the whole learning experience, the need for physical social interactions, and the vital need for individual universities to remain distinctive, rather than to work to outdo each other on similar terms.

Here is something that politicians and bureaucrats find difficult to grasp, often seeing universities as glorified colleges for mass learning, and not as an educational experience that develops the mind and character of the person involved, both student and teacher (as Newman indeed argued long ago).

Preserving the 'uniqueness' of each university in a global environment will be an ever-increasing challenge of the future. In addition to the actual university infrastructure (both human and physical), much of the experience of 'place' is with the wider civic community where the university is located. There is a big difference between a university that is devolved across multiple campuses in an urban environment and a university with a rural campus. Likewise, there is a considerable difference between universities that expect most students to live away from home and those that are inhabited by students whose families live locally.

Increasingly, and despite being labelled ivory towers, universities are becoming closely engaged with local civic society; the walls have come down from around the campuses.

The ACU has a strong record of involvement with the issue of civic engagement through policy discussions and regional meetings—out of which came its pioneer study, *The Idea of Engagement: Universities in*

Society, edited from within the organisation by Svava Bjarnason and Patrick Coldstream (2003).

The ACU is accordingly a natural partner and supporter of the current Talloires Network, whose vision statement contains a commitment to just such 'engagement':

> We believe that higher education institutions do not exist in isolation from society, nor from the communities in which they are located. The Talloires Network envisions universities around the world as a vibrant and dynamic force in their societies, incorporating civic engagement and community service into their research and teaching mission.
>
> (Talloires Network, 2013)

Some enlightened universities are now assessing the civic service of individuals in their promotion criteria, in order to strengthen local support for the institution as a whole. This is likely to become more prevalent in the future, as universities try to justify their existence.

The 'Negotiable University'

In a significant paper entitled *An Interactive Wisdom: Knowledge, Formation and Collegiality in the Negotiable University*, David Ford asked a critical question (of both Berlin and Cambridge Universities):

> Will this sort of institution, which attempts to integrate the six key elements in the interests of a long-term intellectual and social 'ecology', be able to survive, flourish and help shape the wider global intellectual and cultural environment in the twenty-first century?
>
> (Ford, 2007)

The 'six key elements' to which Ford is referring are worth noting:

- uniting teaching and research across a wide range of disciplines (i.e., not a mono-university)
- all-round educational formation to encourage wisdom that seeks the common good
- collegiality allowing debate and discussion between all members
- polity and control realising that it is accountable to many stakeholders

- contributions to society
- interdisciplinarity across all areas of a university, including the support and administrative staff

Ford also poses a seventh and even tougher challenge to be addressed: that of creative rethinking about the future role of universities, given that the pressures of the here and now do not allow space or energy for such a rethinking on the campus of today.

For there is indeed a reluctance in universities to actually ask the large question: what is really their future role?

Ford's practical suggestion is to form internal 'circles of wisdom, to interact at the highest level of intellectual debate within a campus, so allowing a university to reform itself'—not least by stating and re-stating what its mission really is. That may well be the difference between institutional survival and institutional achievement of the highest quality.

Conclusion

A personal reflection to close these comments.

Some years ago, when I was Dean of Engineering at Nottingham University, a small group of the youngest academics was set the task of formulating a model for the faculty, which would be in place when they finally became senior members and leaders of the faculty. Helped by a facilitator over 18 months, and using expert witnesses from stakeholders, including government and industry, they developed a strategic report, which was subsequently presented to the senior management of the university. This activity was undertaken against the wishes of almost all the senior members of the faculty, including the then pro-vice-chancellor. When so challenged, none of the latter apparently had a model in their minds of significant change for the future. Very fortunately for the university, the vice-chancellor at the time was not of that view, and indeed praised the young team, saying it was the first time he knew in what direction the faculty actually wanted to go over time. To ensure that the reform impetus was not lost, many of the 'Young Turks' were fast-tracked into professorial positions. Without doubt, such an exercise within an established university responding to the day-to-day pressures is threatening, but a university that only responds to external pressures has lost its soul and vision.

At the 2012 Kingston Conference of the ACU, the centenary lecture was delivered by Sir David King. In looking both back over the achievements of the universities within the Association and to their future challenges in the next century of development, he highlighted one macro issue as defining all others: 'What are the values behind a university?'

Here is possibly the greatest challenge for members of this oldest of all global networks in higher education. The dialogue within the ACU, and the papers in this centenary volume, point to institutional character and mission as being central to universities globally in this new era.

Bibliography

Adams, J. (2012) *Nature* 490, 335–56.

Altbach, P. and Salmi, J. (eds) (2011) *The Road to Academic Excellence: The Making of World-class Universities.* World Bank.

Bjarnason, S. and Coldstream, P. (2003) *The Idea of Engagement: Universities in Society*. London: ACU.

Citizen Cyberscience Second Summit, London, 16–18 February 2012: www.citizencyberscience.net/summit12 (downloaded on 3 January 2013).

Common Language Resources and Technology Infrastructure (CLARIN): http://clarin.eu

Eastwood, D. (2012) Global Tunes and National Melodies: Being Global and Sounding Local. In *The Globalisation of Higher Education*, eds C. Ennew and D. Greenaway. New York: Palgrave Macmillan, 34–39.

ESPAS Report (2012) *Citizens in an Interconnected and Polycentric World: Global Trends 2030.* European Strategy and Policy Analysis System (ESPAS).

European Commission (2009) *Riding the Wave: How Europe Can Gain from the Rising Tide of Scientific Data.* European Commission.

——— (forthcoming) *Open Infrastructures for Open Science: Framework for Action*. European Commission.

European Research Area Board (2009) *Preparing Europe for a New Renaissance: A Strategic View of the European Research Area: First Report of the European Research Area Board—2009.* European Commission.

Ford, D. (2007) An Interactive Wisdom: Knowledge, Formation and Collegiality in the Negotiable University. In *Christian Wisdom*, 304–49. Cambridge University Press.

Hey, T., Tansley, S., and Tolle, K. (eds) (2009) *The Fourth Paradigm*. Microsoft.

Lifewatch: www.lifewatch.eu (downloaded on 3 January 2013).

Newman, J.H. (1852) *The Idea of a University Defined and Illustrated.* London.

OECD (2012) *New Data for the Understanding of the Human Condition: International Perspectives*, Global Science Forum Report. Organisation for Economic Co-operation and Development.

ORCID: www.orcid.org (downloaded on 3 January 2013).

Research Data Alliance: http://rd-alliance.org (downloaded on 3 January 2013).

Talloires Network (2013) What Is the Talloires Network? Available online at http://talloiresnetwork.tufts.edu/what-is-the-talloires-network/ (downloaded on 2 January 2013).

Van Noorden, R. (2012) *Nature*, 490, 326–29.

Wikipedia (2012) Science 2.0. Available online at http://en.wikipedia.org/wiki/Science_2.0 (downloaded on 28 December 2012).

PART V

Appendices of Data

Appendix 2

Profiles of ACU Executive Officers (Secretary/Secretary General), 1913–

1913–29: Dr Alex Hill, OBE, JP
Secretary, Universities Bureau of the British Empire, 1913–29
Organising Secretary, Inaugural Congress of the Universities of the British Empire, 1911–12. Principal, University College, Southampton, 1912–19. Master of Downing College, 1888–1907, and Vice-Chancellor, University of Cambridge, 1897–99. Professor, Royal College of Surgeons, 1884–85. President of: Neurological Society; Teachers' Guild of Great Britain. Fellow, Royal College of Surgeons.
Personal: *b* 1856 England, *d* 1929. *Education:* University of Cambridge (MA); St Bartholomew's Hospital, London (MB, MD).

1929–30: Sir (Henry) Frank Heath, GBE (1927), KCB (1917), CB (1911)
Secretary, Universities Bureau of the British Empire, 1929–30, and Honorary Director, 1930–34
First Permanent Secretary, Department of Scientific and Industrial Research (UK), 1916–27. Director, Office of Special Inquiries and Reports, Board of Education (UK), 1903–16, and Principal Assistant Secretary, Universities Branch of the Board, 1910–16. Member, UK Treasury Advisory Committee on Grants to University Colleges, 1909–11. Education Correspondent to the Government of India, 1904–16. Joint Secretary, Royal Commission on University Education in London, 1909–13. Academic Registrar and Acting Treasurer, University of

Appendix 1

ACU Membership, 1931–2012

Membership growth (date refers to Annual Report year)—complete sequence (Figures ba

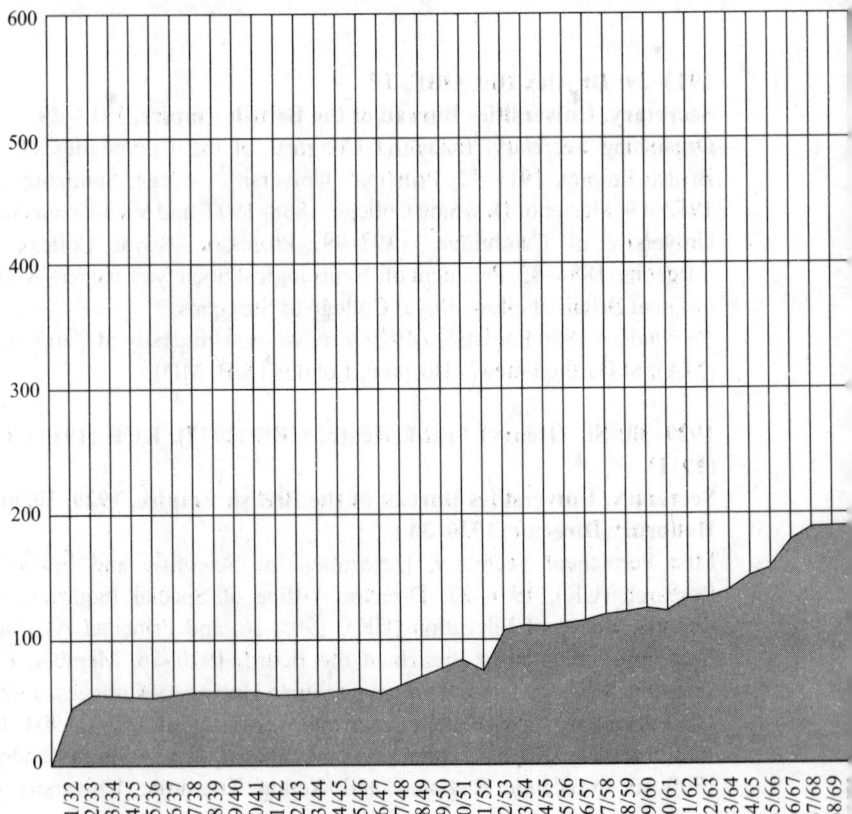

ed on published annual report or [more recently] financial statements every July)

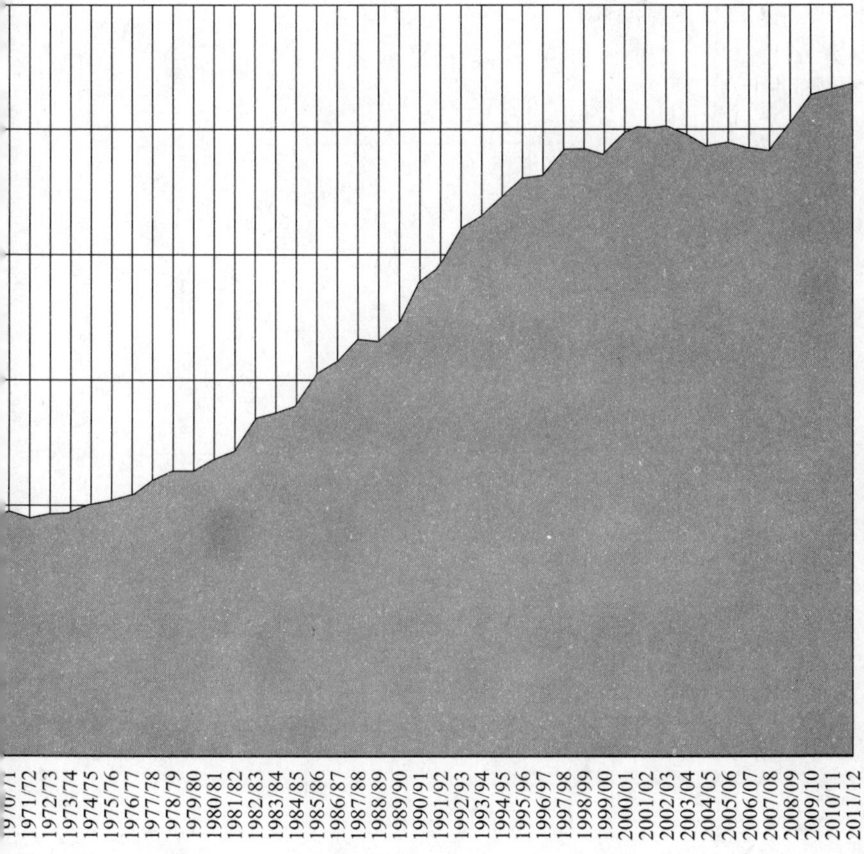

London, 1901–03. Lecturer and Professor of English, Bedford and King's Colleges, London, 1890–95.
Personal: b 1863 England, *d* 1946. *Education:* University College, London; Strasbourg.

1930–47: William Browne Brander, CIE (1927), CBE (1918)
Secretary, Universities Bureau of the British Empire, 1930–47

Indian Civil Service (ICS), 1904–30. ICS appointments held: Under-Secretary to Government of Burma; Registrar, Chief Court, Lower Burma; Deputy Commissioner; Excise Commissioner; Secretary to Government; Commissioner; Additional Secretary to Government; Chief Secretary to the Government of Burma. Chairman of the Development Trust, Rangoon.
Personal: b 1880 Scotland, *d* 1951. *Education:* University of Edinburgh; University of Oxford.

1947–70: John Frederick Foster, CMG (1964)
Secretary-General, Universities' Bureau of the British Empire (later Association of Universities of the British Commonwealth; Association of Commonwealth Universities), 1947–70

Registrar, University of Melbourne, 1937–47. Secretary, Australian Vice-Chancellors' Committee, 1936–47. Secretary, Committee of Vice-Chancellors and Principals of the United Kingdom, 1947–64. UK National Secretary, Council of Europe Committee on Higher Education and Research.
Personal: b 1903 Australia, *d* 1975. *Education:* University of Melbourne (LLB, LLM, MA). Honorary degrees: seven, including University of Melbourne (LLD).

1970–80: Sir Hugh Worrell Springer, GCMG, KCMG (1971), GCVO, KA, CBE (1961), OBE (1954)
Secretary General, Association of Commonwealth Universities, 1970–80

Member, House of Assembly (Barbados), General Secretary, Barbados Labour Party, and General Secretary, Barbados Workers' Union, 1940–47. Member, UK Commission on Higher Education in the Colonies, West Indies Committee, 1944. Registrar, University College of the West Indies, 1947–63. Director, Institute of Education, University of the West Indies, 1963–66. Director, Commonwealth Education Liaison

Unit, and Commonwealth Assistant Secretary General (Education), Commonwealth Secretariat, 1966–70. Governor General of Barbados, 1984–90 John Simon Guggenheim Fellow, Harvard University, 1961–62; Senior Visiting Fellow, All Souls College and Honorary Fellow, Hertford College, University of Oxford.
Personal: b 1913 Barbados, *d* 1994. *Education:* University of Oxford (MA). Honorary degrees: 15, including University of the West Indies.

1980–96: Anastasios (Chris) Christodoulou, CBE (1978)
Secretary-General, Association of Commonwealth Universities, 1980–96
District Officer, District Commissioner and Magistrate (HM Overseas Civil Service (Tanganyika Government)), 1956–62. Assistant Registrar, Deputy Secretary, Leeds University, 1963–68. (Foundation) Secretary, Open University, 1968–80. Member, Commonwealth Secretary General's Standing Committee on Student Mobility, 1981–91. Visiting Professor of Education, University of Surrey.
Personal: b 1932 Cyprus, *d* 2002. *Education:* University of Oxford (MA). Honorary degrees: including Open University (UK) (DUniv).

1996–2004: Professor Michael G. Gibbons, MBE (2002)
Secretary-General, Association of Commonwealth Universities, 1996–2004
Lecturer, Senior Lecturer, Professor (1976–94), Department of Science and Technology Policy, University of Manchester, 1967–92. Dean of Graduate School and Director, Science Policy Research Unit (SPRU), University of Sussex, 1992–96 (Honorary Professorial Fellow, SPRU, 1994–96 and 2004–07). Visiting Professor: Université de Montreal, 1976; University of California, Berkeley, 1992. Chairman of the Board, Quest University, Canada. Fellow, Royal Swedish Academy of Engineering Sciences. Specialist Advisor, Parliamentary Committee on Science and Technology (UK). Consultant to OECD and the National Centres of Excellence in Research, Canada. Golden Jubilee Medal, Canada, 2002.
Personal: born Canada 1939. *Education:* Concordia University (BSc); McGill University (BEng); Queen's University at Kingston (MSc); University of Manchester (PhD). Honorary degrees: University of Ghana (LLD); Concordia University (Canada); University of Surrey (UK). He has published widely in the field of science and technology policy.

2004–07: Dr John S. Rowett, OBE (2005)
Secretary-General, Association of Commonwealth Universities, 2004–07

Lecturer, History, University College Wales, Aberystwyth, 1978–80. Fellow and Tutor in Modern History (1980–99), and Professorial Fellow (1999–2004), Brasenose College, University of Oxford. Chief Executive, Rhodes Trust, and Warden, Rhodes House, 1999–2004. Founder Chief Executive, Mandela Rhodes Foundation, 1999–2004.
Personal: born UK 1949. *Education:* University of Oxford (MA, DPhil).

2007–10: Professor John R. Tarrant
Secretary-General, Association of Commonwealth Universities, 2007–10

Lecturer, University College Dublin, 1966–68. Lecturer, Senior Lecturer, Professor, Dean, School of Environmental Sciences, University of East Anglia, 1968–81. Pro-Vice-Chancellor (1981–88) and Deputy Vice-Chancellor (1989–95), University of East Anglia. Vice-Chancellor and Principal, University of Huddersfield, 1995–2006. Visiting Research Associate, International Food Policy Research Institute, Washington, DC, 1977–78. Visiting Scholar, Food Policy Research Institute, Stanford University, 1978.
Personal: born UK 1941. *Education:* University of Hull (BSc, PhD).

2010 to Date: Professor John V. Wood, CBE (2007)
Secretary-General, Association of Commonwealth Universities, since 2010

Goldsmith's Junior Research Fellow, Churchill College, University of Cambridge, 1974–78. Lecturer/Senior Lecturer, Open University (UK), 1978–89. Professor, Head of Department, Dean, University of Nottingham, 1989–2001. Chief Executive (on secondment), Council for the Central Laboratory of the Research Councils, 2001–07. Principal, Faculty of Engineering, Imperial College London, 2007. International Relations Advisor, Imperial College London, 2008–10. Chairman: European Strategy Forum for Research Infrastructure, 2005–08; European Research Area Board, 2008–12. Fellow: Institute of Materials, Minerals and Mining; Institute of Physics; Royal Academy of Engineering. Grunfeld Medal, 1986; Ivor Jenkins Award, Institute of Materials, 2000; William Johnson International Gold Medal, 2001; Officer's Cross of the Order of Merit, Germany, 2010.

Personal: born UK 1949. *Education:* University of Sheffield (BMet, DMet); University of Cambridge (PhD). Honorary degrees: including Technical University of Cluj-Napora (Romania) (DSc).

About the Editor and Contributors

The Editor

Deryck M. Schreuder is an international historian and Visiting Professor, Faculty of Education and Social Work, University of Sydney. He was a Rhodes Scholar to Oxford from Central Africa, and has worked in eight Commonwealth universities (in Africa, the UK, Canada, and Australia). He was Challis Professor of History at the University of Sydney, before becoming Vice-Chancellor of the University of Western Sydney, and later Vice-Chancellor of the University of Western Australia. He was President of the Australian Vice-Chancellors' Committee in 2002–04. He has published (with Stuart Ward) the 'Australia' volume in the *Oxford History of the British Empire Series* (2nd ed., 2010).

The Contributors

Pawan Agarwal is a Senior Adviser in the Planning Commission of India, involved in developing 'The 12th Plan for Higher Education'. He has previously served in major positions in the Department of Higher Education and the University Grants Commission. A Fulbright New Century Scholar at Harvard and Emory Universities, he has recently been a Visiting Scholar at the Centre for the Study of Higher Education, and the Australia India Institute, at the University of Melbourne. He has acted as a consultant to the World Bank, the Asian Development Bank, and the Inter-American Development Bank. He has published widely on higher education in India and South Asia, including *Indian Higher Education: Envisioning the Future* (SAGE, 2009), and has edited *A Half-Century of Indian Higher Education: Essays by Philip G. Altbach* (SAGE, 2012).

Svava Bjarnason is a Principal Education Specialist at the World Bank Group/International Finance Corporation (IFC), currently based in Dubai. Prior to joining the IFC in 2007, she was the founding Director of the Observatory on Borderless Higher Education, and held a dual post as Director of Research and Strategy at the ACU. She has published widely on changes in higher education, notably in benchmarking and community engagement.

Sir John Daniel was a vice-chancellor for 17 years (Laurentian University, Canada; Open University, UK) before appointments as UNESCO's Assistant Director General for Education and President of the Commonwealth of Learning. Knighted in 1994, he has received the ACU's Symons Medal and 31 honorary doctorates from universities in 17 countries.

Sir Graeme Davies is Emeritus Vice-Chancellor of the University of London, having been Vice-Chancellor from 2003 to 2010. He was previously Principal and Vice-Chancellor at the University of Glasgow (from 1995), and Vice-Chancellor at the University of Liverpool, before becoming Chief Executive of the Higher Education Funding Council for England, a post he held from 1986 to 1991. He is currently Chair of the Higher Education Policy Institute in the UK.

Dorothy Garland is Director, Professional Networks, and former Deputy Secretary-General at the ACU, which she joined in 1985. Working initially in academic recruitment, then on statutory meetings and major conferences, she also developed the Gender Equity Programme and initiated the ACU's work on HIV/AIDS. Her earlier career included 12 years of working for the Nigerian university system, initially as London representative for one university and teaching hospital, and subsequently as Principal Assistant Secretary, later Under-Secretary, at the National Universities Commission London Office.

Michael Gibbons, MBE, was Secretary-General of the ACU from 1996 to 2004. He was previously Dean of the Graduate School and Director, Science Policy Research Unit (SPRU), University of Sussex, 1992–96 and subsequently an Honorary Professorial Fellow; Chairman of the Board, of Quest University, Canada. He has been elected a Fellow, Royal Swedish Academy of Engineering Sciences and acted as Consultant to OECD, and the National Centres of Excellence in Research, Canada.

He was awarded a Canadian Golden Jubilee Medal in 2002; and holds Honorary degrees from the University of Ghana; Concordia University; and the University of Surrey (UK). He has published widely in the field of science and technology policy.

E. Nigel Harris assumed office as Vice-Chancellor of the University of the West Indies in 2004. He is also Chairman of the ACU Council in 2011–13. Professor Harris was Dean and Senior Vice President for Academic Affairs at Morehouse School of Medicine in Atlanta, USA, 1996–2004. Internationally known for his work as a rheumatologist, he has received many honours and awards, including the Centennial Award for contributions to medicine by the National Medical Association (USA) in 1995, the Martin Luther King International Award 2010, and the Caribbean Health Research Council Award 2011 for contributions to medical research.

Julia Horne is University Historian and Senior Research Fellow at the University of Sydney. She has written on the history of universities and the history of landscape and travel. She is the author of *The Pursuit of Wonder* (2005) and, most recently (with Geoffrey Sherington [see below]), *Sydney: The Making of a Public University* (2012).

Asha Kanwar became President and CEO of the Commonwealth of Learning (COL) in June 2012. She joined COL in 2003 as an education specialist for higher education, and became Vice President in 2006. Previously, she held a joint UNESCO/COL appointment at UNESCO-BREDA in Dakar, Senegal, and was Pro-Vice-Chancellor of the Indira Gandhi National Open University in India.

John Kirkland is Deputy Secretary General of the ACU. He is also Executive Secretary of the Commonwealth Scholarship Commission in the UK, and Executive Secretary of the Marshall Aid Commemoration Commission, both of which are administered by the ACU. Prior to joining the ACU, John was Secretary of the UK National Institute for Economic and Social Research (1994–99), and Director of the Research Services Bureau at Brunel University (1988–94).

Sir Colin Lucas is a historian who has mostly worked on the French Revolution. He has also been successively a Tutorial Fellow of Balliol College, Oxford; Dean of Social Sciences at the University of Chicago;

Master of Balliol; Vice-Chancellor of the University of Oxford; Fellow of All Souls College, Oxford; Warden of Rhodes House; and Chairman of the British Library.

Nicholas Mulhern has been the ACU Librarian since 1997 (having worked at the ACU since 1990). His role includes supporting and contributing to the ACU's projects and publications, including those of its various networks.

Michael Omolewa, Professor of the History of Education at the University of Ibadan, was former Ambassador of Nigeria to UNESCO and President of the 32nd session of the General Conference of UNESCO. He has served on the Executive Committee of the International Standing Conference of the History of Education, and has been both Deputy Chair of the Governing Board of the Commonwealth of Learning, and Chairman of the Committee of Deans of the Faculties of Education of Nigerian Universities.

Hilary Perraton is a historian who worked for many years in international education. He gained first-hand experience of the Commonwealth Scholarship and Fellowship Plan through spending 10 years in the Commonwealth Secretariat and seven years as a member, and later Deputy Chair, of the Commonwealth Scholarship Commission in the United Kingdom. To mark the 50th anniversary of the plan, he published its history in 2009 (*Learning Abroad*, Cambridge Scholars Publishing).

Tamson Pietsch is Lecturer in Imperial and Colonial History at Brunel University in London. Her research interests encompass the cultural and intellectual history of Britain and its Empire during the nineteenth and twentieth centuries. Her work focuses on the ways that imperial and transnational forces shaped the production of culture and ideas in this period. Tamson has published in the *Journal of Global History*, the *Journal of Historical Geography* and *History of Education*. Her first book, *Empire of Scholars: Universities, Networks and the British Academic World, 1850–1939*, will appear with Manchester University Press in 2013.

Geoffrey Sherington is an Emeritus Professor at the University of Sydney. For the past 40 years he has written extensively on the history of education, including schools and universities, as well as immigration. He has recently co-authored (with Julia Horne [see above]) a concise history of the University of Sydney (2012), and is currently preparing (also with Julia Horne) an account of the foundations of the state universities of Australia, 1851–1914.

Jasbir Singh obtained a PhD in 1974 from the University of Malaya in Kuala Lumpur. She has been Professor at the Faculty of Education, University of Malaya in Kuala Lumpur, and Chief Programme Officer (Higher Education Co-operation) at the Commonwealth Secretariat in London. Since 1998 she has been Consultant to the ACU's Gender Programme, for which she has prepared reports on the status of women in Commonwealth universities and has assisted in training workshops. She has formed an educational consulting company that undertakes projects locally in Kuala Lumpur and internationally.

Thomas H.B. Symons, CC, is the Founding President and Vanier Professor Emeritus of Trent University in Canada. He has chaired the Council of the ACU (1971–72) and was Honorary Treasurer (1974–88) as well as Chair of the Association's 75th Anniversary Appeal and Special Projects (1986–89). He later led a Commission on Commonwealth Studies (1995–96), and subsequently became Founding Chair of the Association for Commonwealth Studies. Professor Symons became a Companion of the Order of Canada in 1997. He is a recipient of the Queen Elizabeth II Diamond Jubilee Medal (2012) and of a Vatican Knighthood in the Order of Saint Sylvester.

Stamenka Uvalić-Trumbić was Secretary General of the Association of Universities of Former Yugoslavia, Programme Specialist at UNESCO's European Centre for Higher Education and Head of Higher Education at UNESCO Headquarters in Paris. She is currently an independent consultant, based in China.

Peter Williams is Honorary Secretary of the Commonwealth Consortium for Education. He previously served as: education planning adviser to Ministries of Education in Kenya and Ghana 1966–72; Lecturer, then Professor of Education in Developing Countries, at the University of London Institute of Education 1973–84; and Director of Education at the Commonwealth Secretariat 1984–94.

John V. Wood, CBE, is the current Secretary-General of the ACU. He took up his post in 2010. He was previously a Professor, Head of

Department, and Dean at the University of Nottingham, 1989–2001; Chief Executive (on secondment), Council for the Central Laboratory of the Research Councils, 2001–07; Principal, Faculty of Engineering, Imperial College London, from 2007; Chair of the European Strategy Forum for Research Infrastructure (2005–08); European Research Area Board (2008–12). He has been recognised with Fellowships of the Institute of Materials, Minerals and Mining; the Institute of Physics; and the Royal Academy of Engineering. He has received a Grunfeld Medal (1986); the Ivor Jenkins Award, Institute of Materials (2000); William Johnson International Gold Medal (2001); and Officer's Cross of the Order of Merit, Germany, 2010.

David Woodhouse is currently Commissioner for Development with the Commission for Academic Accreditation in the United Arab Emirates, and Immediate Past President of the International Network for Quality Assurance Agencies in Higher Education. After leading quality assurance agencies in Hong Kong and New Zealand, he was the founding Director of the Australian Universities Quality Agency (2001–11). He had previously been a professor and dean in mathematics, computer science, and education.

Index